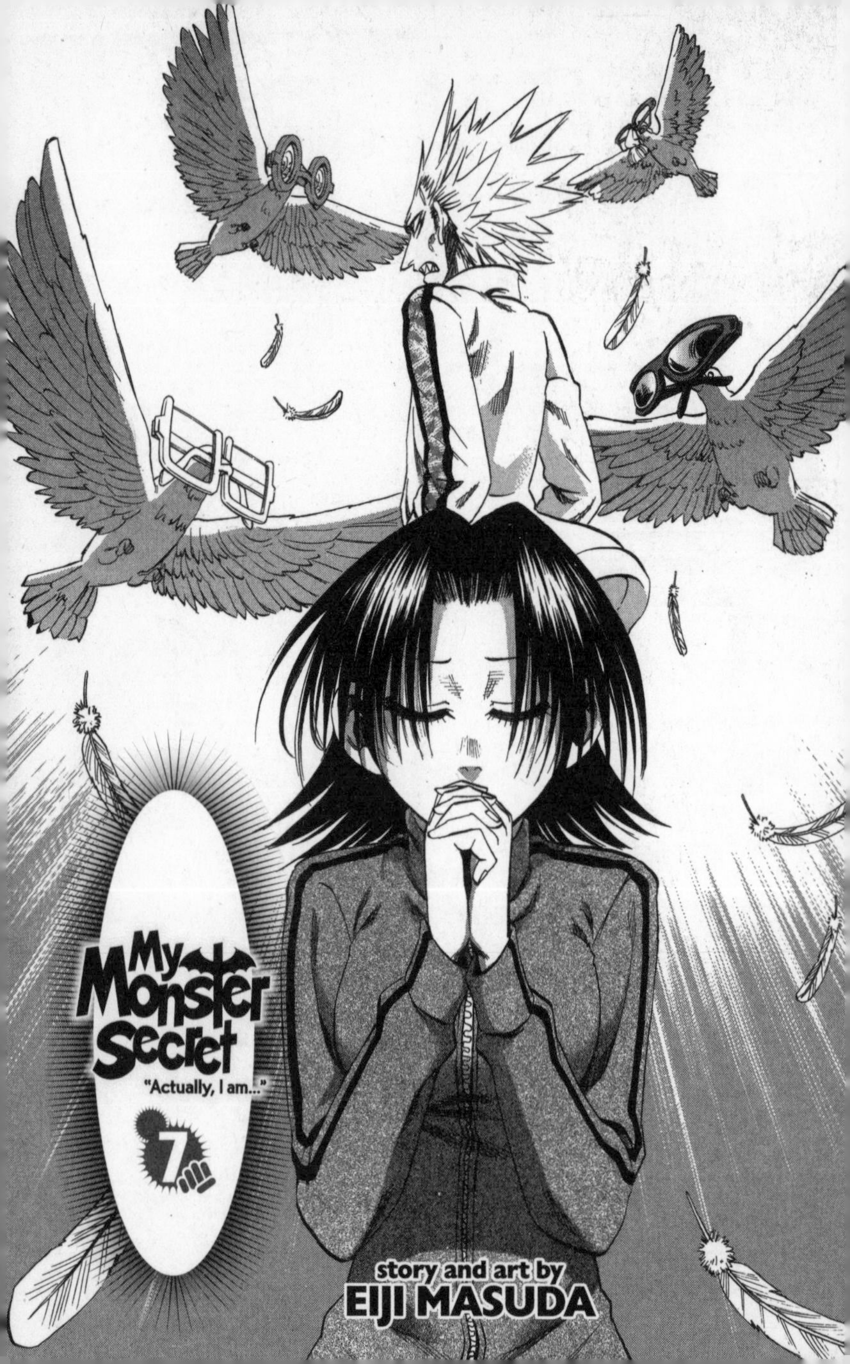
My Monster Secret
"Actually, I am..."
7
story and art by
EIJI MASUDA

My Monster Secret

"Actually, I am..."

Story & Character

After school one day, **Kuromine Asahi** opened the door to his classroom to confess his love to his crush **Shiragami Youko**... and discovered that she's actually a vampire! His goal was to tell Shiragami that he loved her, but he instead resolved to keep her secret--as a friend. It means they can continue to go to school together, but their problems are only beginning...

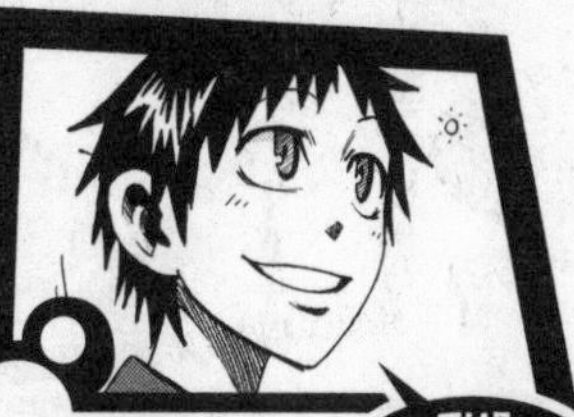

THE HOLEY SIEVE

KUROMINE ASAHI

The man with the worst poker face in the world, he's known as **The Sieve With A Hole In It**...because secrets slide right out of him. Has feelings for Shiragami-san.

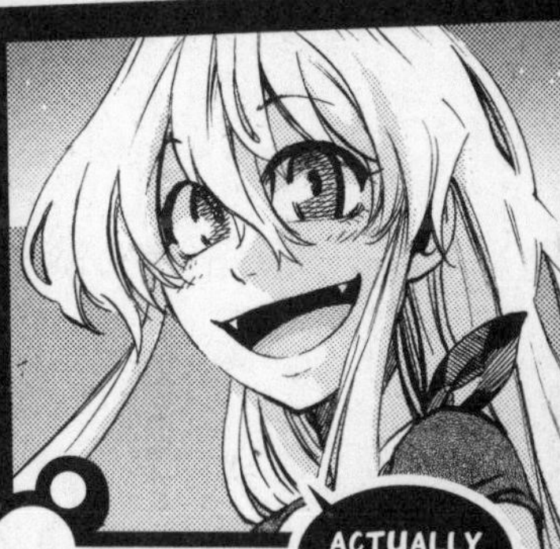

ACTUALLY A VAMPIRE

SHIRAGAMI YOUKO

She's attending a human high school under the condition that she'll ***stop going immediately*** if her true identity is discovered. She's managed to hide the fact that she's a vampire and is living a normal high school life, somehow!

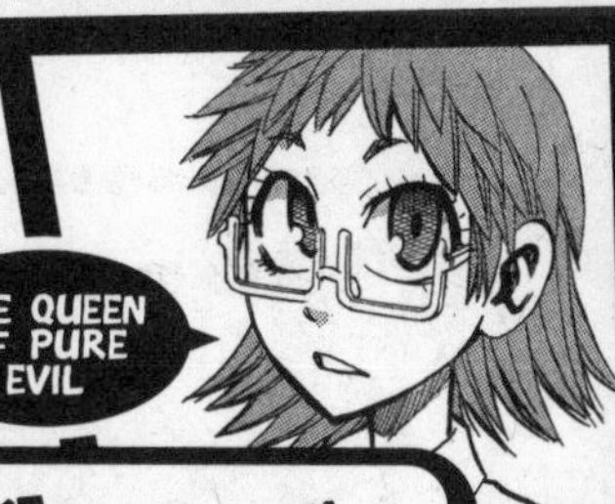

THE QUEEN OF PURE EVIL

AKEMI MIKAN

Editor-in-chief of the school newspaper and a childhood friend of Asahi's. Her favorite pair of glasses has become the **Goddess of Fortune, Fuku-chan.** In love with Asahi.

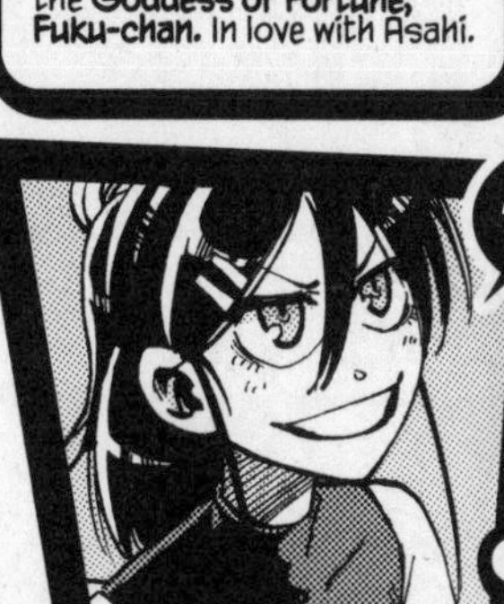

ACTUALLY AN ALIEN

AIZAWA NAGISA

Currently investigating Earth as a class representative, she once mercilessly tore Asahi to shreds before he could confess his love, but she now harbors an unrequited crush on him. Her true (tiny) form emerges from the screw-shaped cockpit on her head. Her brother **Aizawa Ryo** is also staying on Earth.

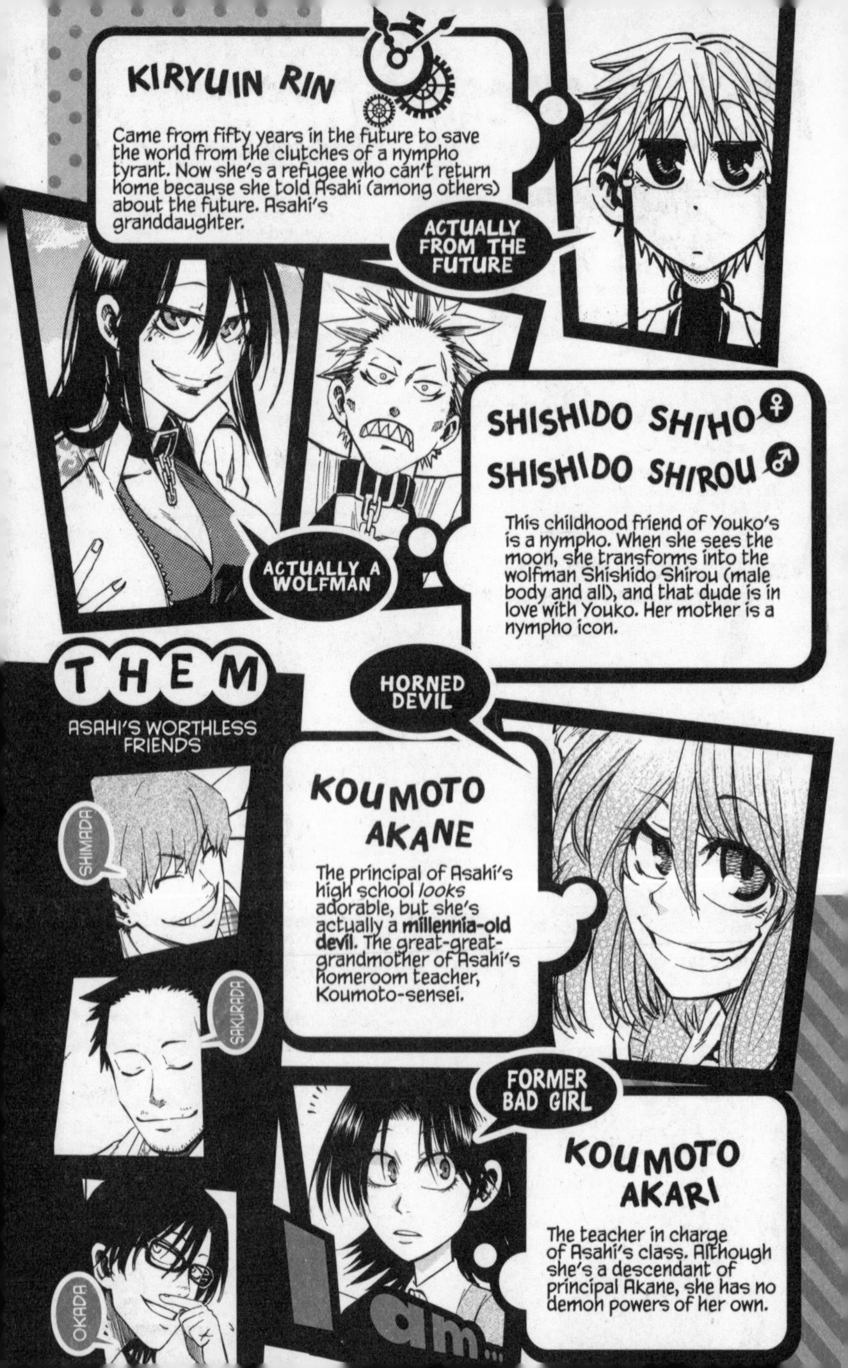
KIRYUIN RIN
Came from fifty years in the future to save the world from the clutches of a nympho tyrant. Now she's a refugee who can't return home because she told Asahi (among others) about the future. Asahi's granddaughter.
ACTUALLY FROM THE FUTURE
SHISHIDO SHIHO ♀
SHISHIDO SHIROU ♂
This childhood friend of Youko's is a nympho. When she sees the moon, she transforms into the wolfman Shishido Shirou (male body and all), and that dude is in love with Youko. Her mother is a nympho icon.
ACTUALLY A WOLFMAN
HORNED DEVIL
KOUMOTO AKANE
The principal of Asahi's high school *looks* adorable, but she's actually a **millennia-old devil.** The great-great-grandmother of Asahi's homeroom teacher, Koumoto-sensei.
THEM
ASAHI'S WORTHLESS FRIENDS
SHIMADA
SAKURADA
FORMER BAD GIRL
KOUMOTO AKARI
The teacher in charge of Asahi's class. Although she's a descendant of principal Akane, she has no demon powers of her own.
OKADA
I am...

SEVEN SEAS ENTERTAINMENT PRESENTS

My Monster Secret

"Actually, I am..."

story and art by **Eiji Masuda**

VOLUME 7

TRANSLATION
Alethea and Athena Nibley

ADAPTATION
Lianne Sentar

LETTERING AND RETOUCH
Annaliese Christman

LOGO DESIGN
Karis Page

COVER DESIGN
Nicky Lim

PROOFREADER
Shanti Whitesides

ASSISTANT EDITOR
Jenn Grunigen

PRODUCTION ASSISTANT
CK Russell

PRODUCTION MANAGER
Lissa Pattillo

EDITOR-IN-CHIEF
Adam Arnold

PUBLISHER
Jason DeAngelis

JITSUHA WATASHIHA Volume 7
© EIJI MASUDA 2014
Originally published in Japan in 2014 by Akita Publishing Co., Ltd.
English translation rights arranged with Akita Publishing Co., Ltd.
through TOHAN CORPORATION, Tokyo.

Seven Seas books may be purchased in bulk for promotional, educational, or
business use. Please contact your local bookseller or the Macmillan Corporate
and Premium Sales Department at 1-800-221-7945, extension 5442, or by
e-mail at MacmillanSpecialMarkets@macmillan.com.

Seven Seas and the Seven Seas logo are trademarks of
Seven Seas Entertainment, LLC. All rights reserved.

ISBN: 978-1-626925-03-8

Printed in Canada

First Printing: July 2017

10 9 8 7 6 5 4 3 2 1

FOLLOW US ONLINE: *www.gomanga.com*

READING DIRECTIONS

This book reads from *right to left*, Japanese style.
If this is your first time reading manga, you start
reading from the top right panel on each page and
take it from there. If you get lost, just follow the
numbered diagram here. It may seem backwards at
first, but you'll get the hang of it! Have fun!!

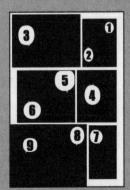

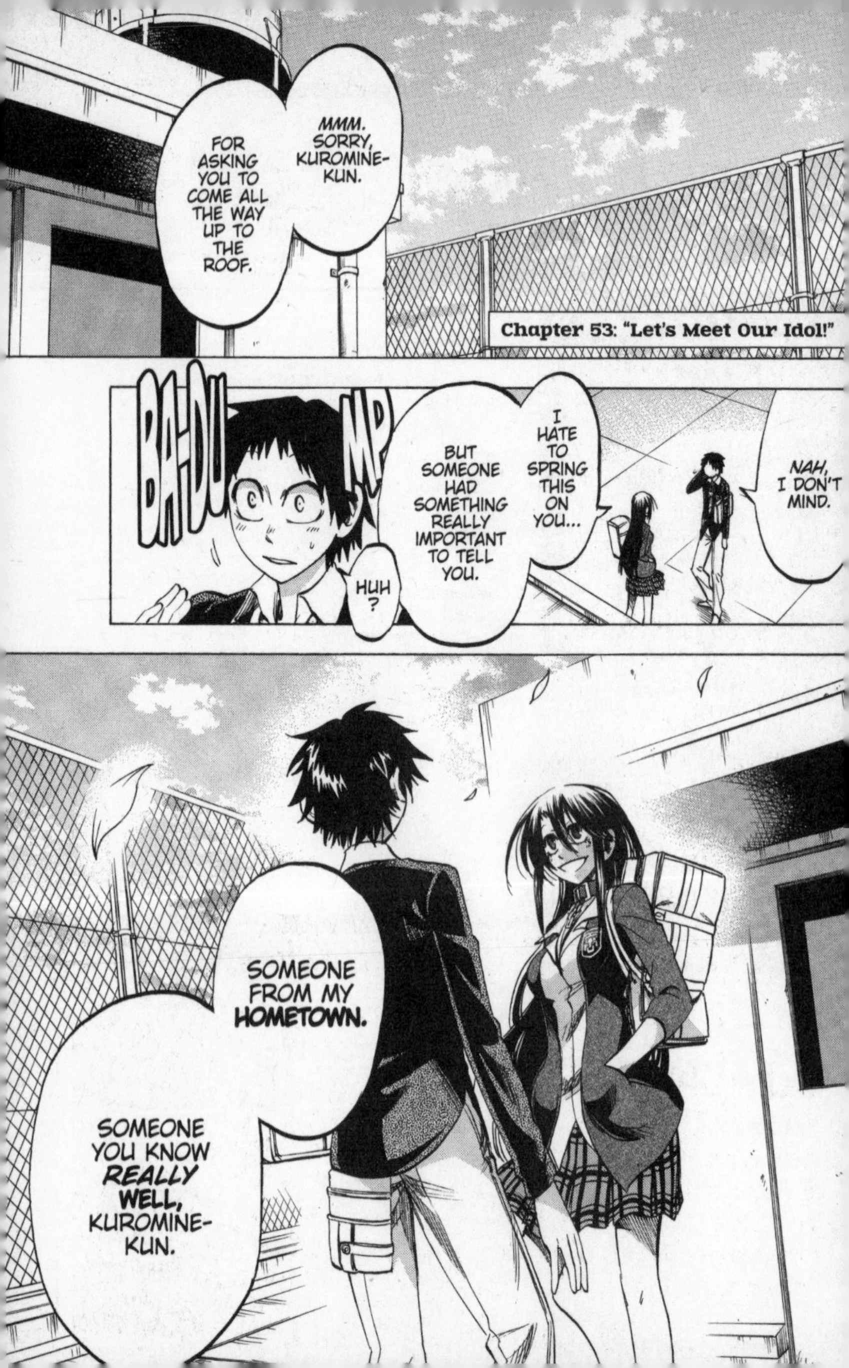
MMM. SORRY, KUROMINE-KUN.
FOR ASKING YOU TO COME ALL THE WAY UP TO THE ROOF.
Chapter 53: "Let's Meet Our Idol!"
NAH, I DON'T MIND.
I HATE TO SPRING THIS ON YOU...
BUT SOMEONE HAD SOMETHING REALLY IMPORTANT TO TELL YOU.
BA-DUMP
HUH?
SOMEONE FROM MY **HOMETOWN.**
SOMEONE YOU KNOW ***REALLY* WELL,** KUROMINE-KUN.

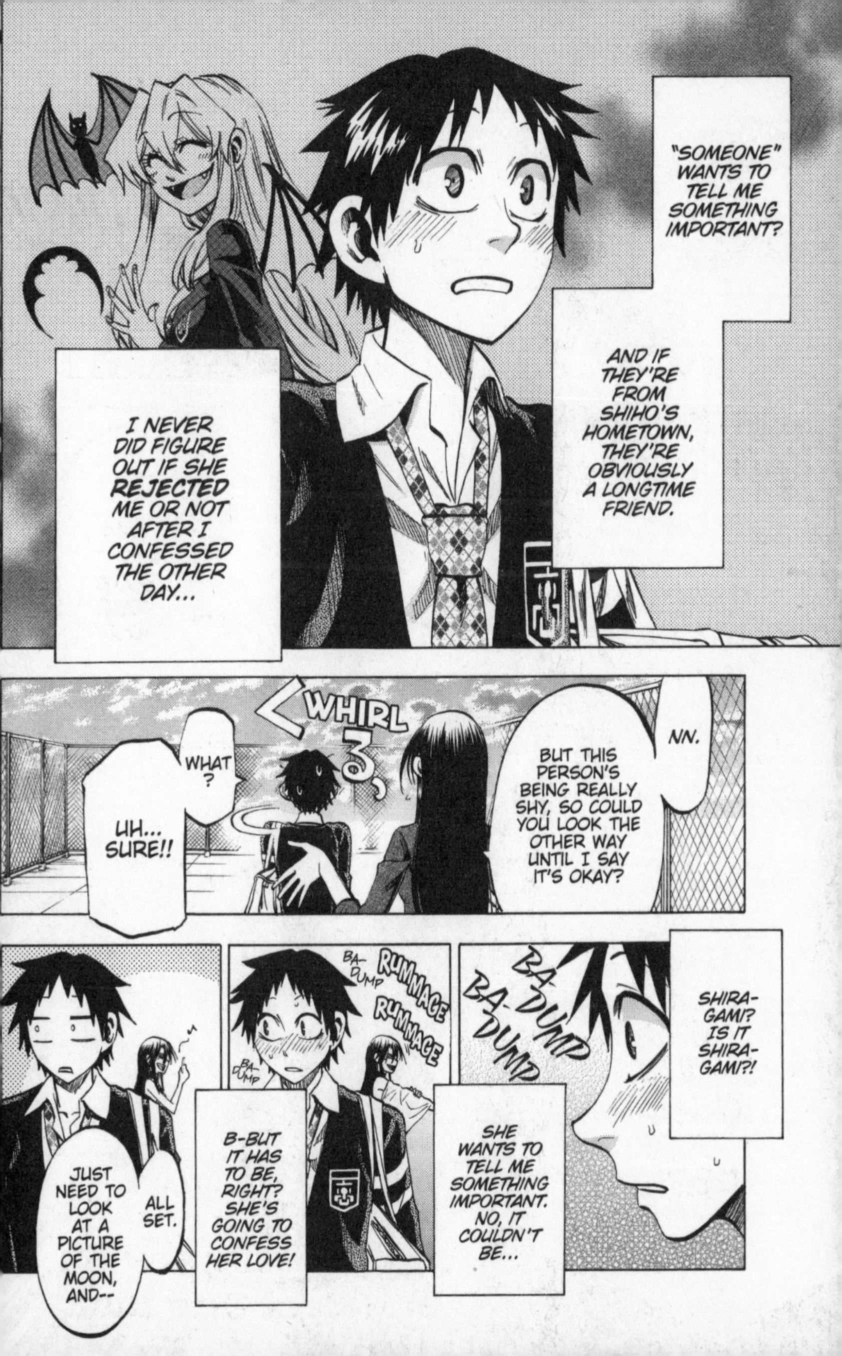
"SOMEONE" WANTS TO TELL ME SOMETHING IMPORTANT?
AND IF THEY'RE FROM SHIHO'S HOMETOWN, THEY'RE OBVIOUSLY A LONGTIME FRIEND.
I NEVER DID FIGURE OUT IF SHE **REJECTED** ME OR NOT AFTER I CONFESSED THE OTHER DAY...
NN.
BUT THIS PERSON'S BEING REALLY SHY, SO COULD YOU LOOK THE OTHER WAY UNTIL I SAY IT'S OKAY?
WHIRL
WHAT?
UH... SURE!!
SHIRA-GAMI? IS IT SHIRA-GAMI?!
BA-DUMP BA-DUMP
SHE WANTS TO TELL ME SOMETHING IMPORTANT. NO, IT COULDN'T BE...
RUMMAGE RUMMAGE
BA-DUMP
BA-DUMP
B-BUT IT HAS TO BE, RIGHT? SHE'S GOING TO CONFESS HER LOVE!
ALL SET.
JUST NEED TO LOOK AT A PICTURE OF THE MOON, AND--

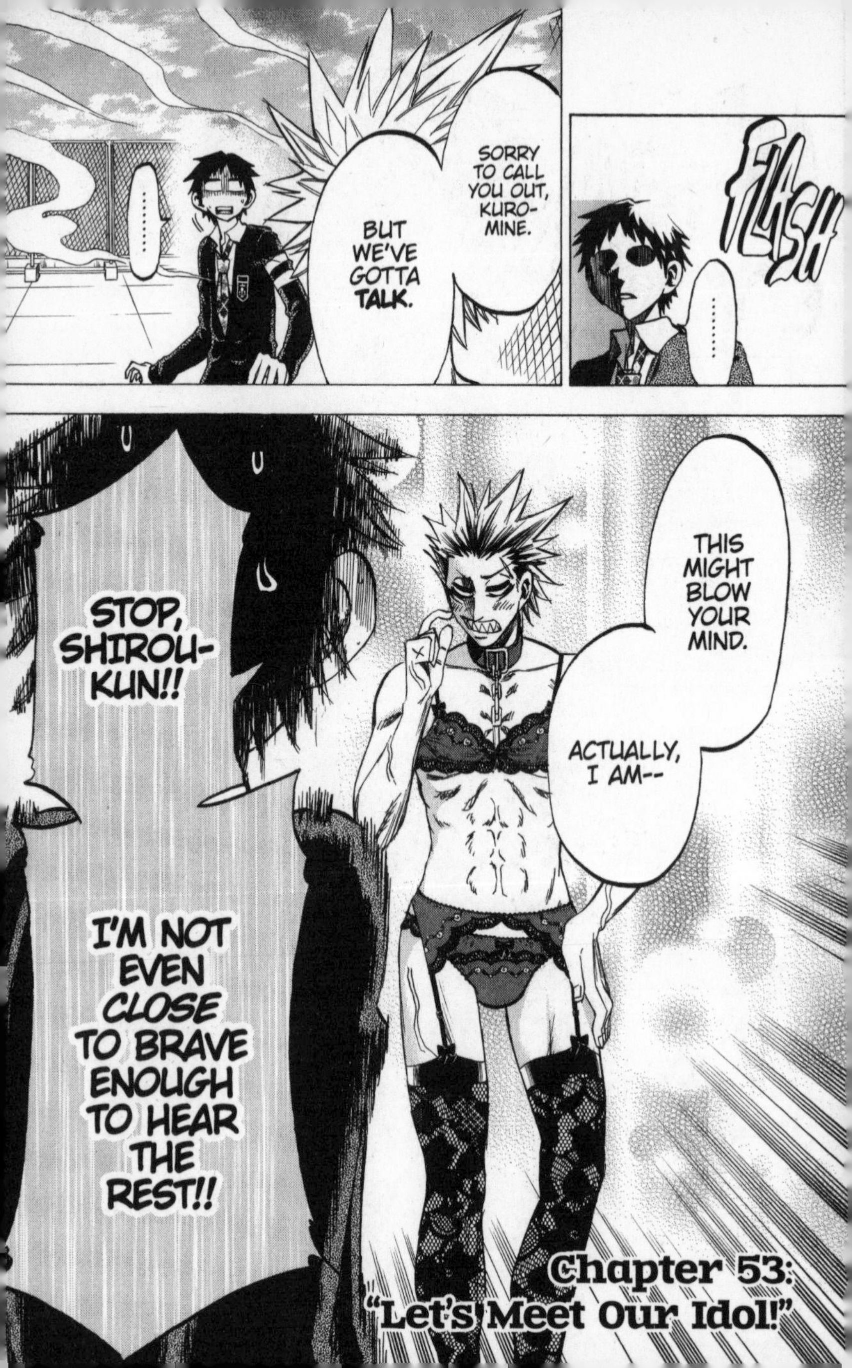
FLASH
......
SORRY TO CALL YOU OUT, KURO-MINE.
BUT WE'VE GOTTA TALK.
......
THIS MIGHT BLOW YOUR MIND.
ACTUALLY, I AM--
STOP, SHIROU-KUN!!
I'M NOT EVEN CLOSE TO BRAVE ENOUGH TO HEAR THE REST!!
Chapter 53: "Let's Meet Our Idol!"

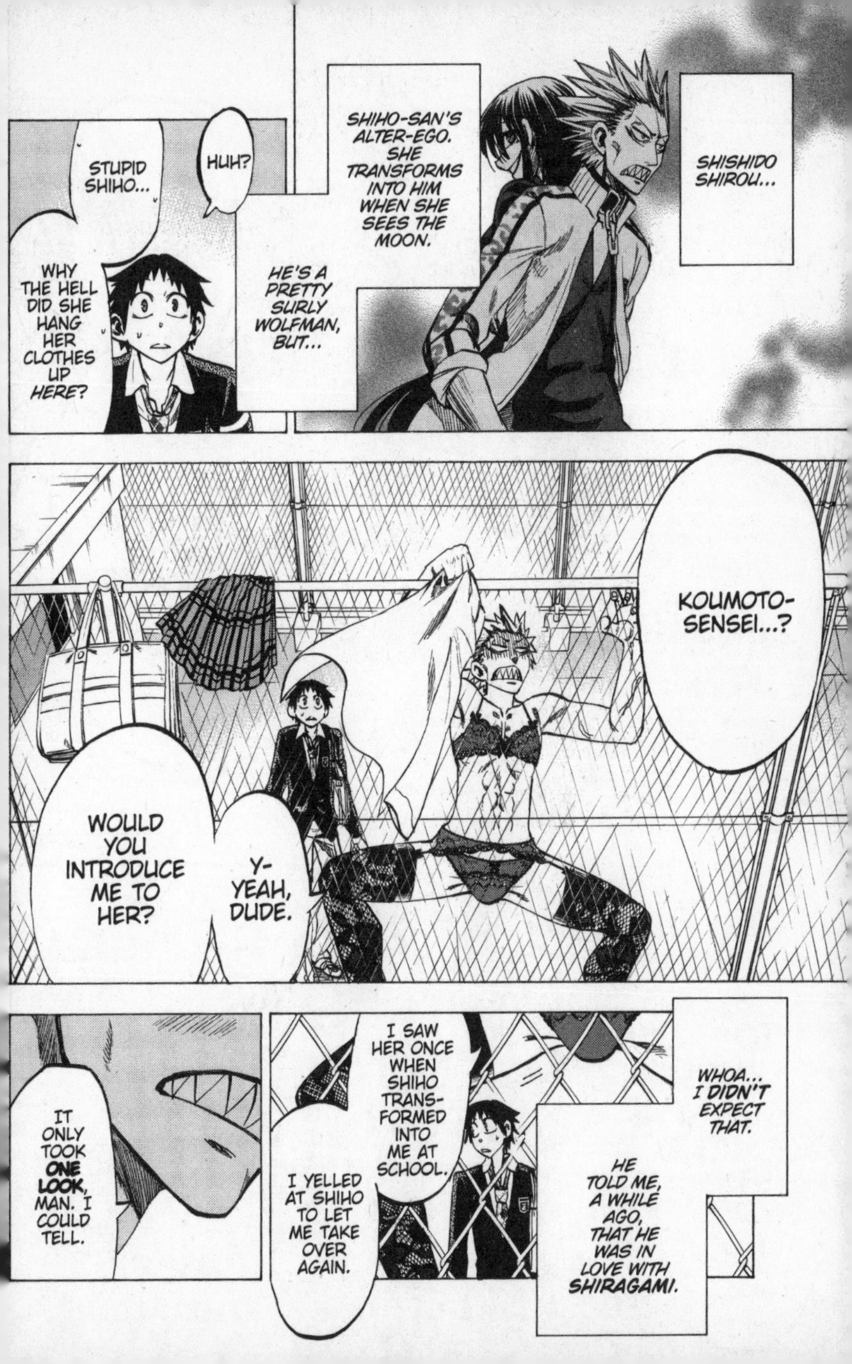
SHISHIDO SHIROU...
SHIHO-SAN'S ALTER-EGO. SHE TRANSFORMS INTO HIM WHEN SHE SEES THE MOON.
HE'S A PRETTY SURLY WOLFMAN, BUT...
HUH?
STUPID SHIHO...
WHY THE HELL DID SHE HANG HER CLOTHES UP HERE?
KOUMOTO-SENSEI...?
WOULD YOU INTRODUCE ME TO HER?
Y-YEAH, DUDE.
WHOA... I DIDN'T EXPECT THAT.
HE TOLD ME, A WHILE AGO, THAT HE WAS IN LOVE WITH SHIRAGAMI.
I SAW HER ONCE WHEN SHIHO TRANSFORMED INTO ME AT SCHOOL.
I YELLED AT SHIHO TO LET ME TAKE OVER AGAIN.
IT ONLY TOOK ONE LOOK, MAN. I COULD TELL.

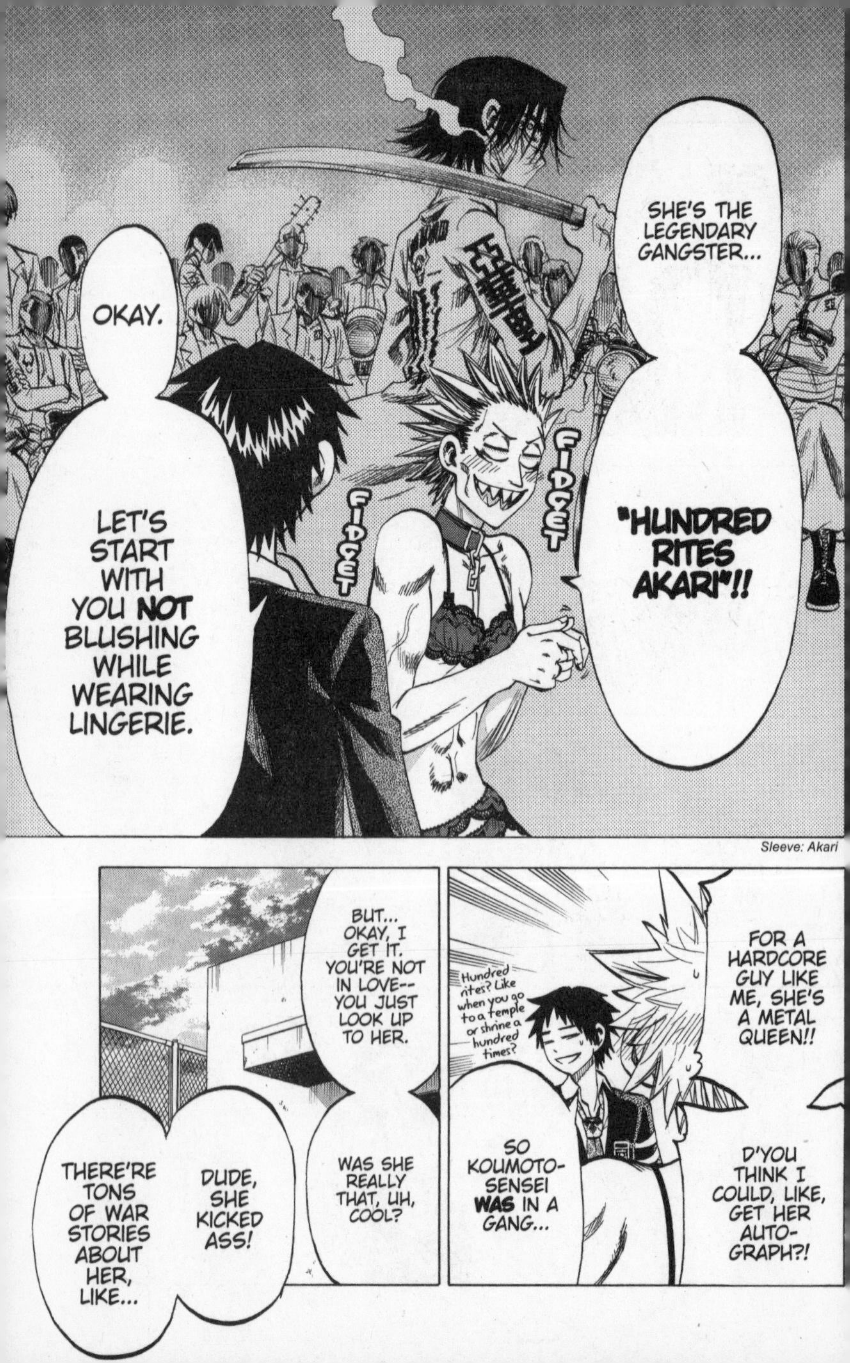
SHE'S THE LEGENDARY GANGSTER...
"HUNDRED RITES AKARI"!!
FIDGET
FIDGET
OKAY.
LET'S START WITH YOU **NOT** BLUSHING WHILE WEARING LINGERIE.
FOR A HARDCORE GUY LIKE ME, SHE'S A METAL QUEEN!!
Hundred rites? Like when you go to a temple or shrine a hundred times?
D'YOU THINK I COULD, LIKE, GET HER AUTO-GRAPH?!
SO KOUMOTO-SENSEI **WAS** IN A GANG...
BUT... OKAY, I GET IT. YOU'RE NOT IN LOVE-- YOU JUST LOOK UP TO HER.
WAS SHE REALLY THAT, UH, COOL?
DUDE, SHE KICKED ASS!
THERE'RE TONS OF WAR STORIES ABOUT HER, LIKE...

Sleeve: Akari

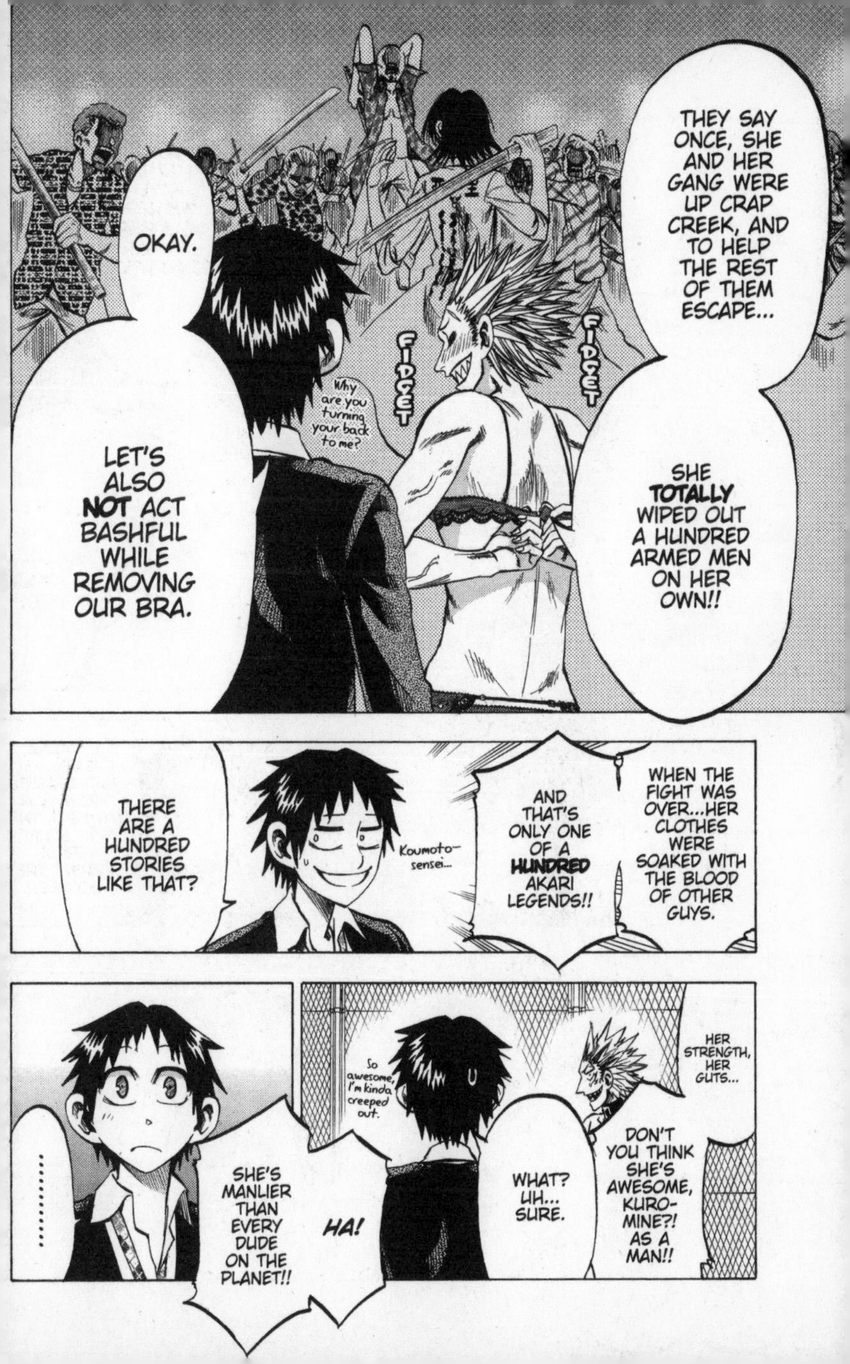
THEY SAY ONCE, SHE AND HER GANG WERE UP CRAP CREEK, AND TO HELP THE REST OF THEM ESCAPE...
SHE TOTALLY WIPED OUT A HUNDRED ARMED MEN ON HER OWN!!
FIDGET
FIDGET
Why are you turning your back to me?
OKAY.
LET'S ALSO NOT ACT BASHFUL WHILE REMOVING OUR BRA.
WHEN THE FIGHT WAS OVER...HER CLOTHES WERE SOAKED WITH THE BLOOD OF OTHER GUYS.
AND THAT'S ONLY ONE OF A HUNDRED AKARI LEGENDS!!
Koumoto-sensei...
THERE ARE A HUNDRED STORIES LIKE THAT?
HER STRENGTH, HER GUTS...
DON'T YOU THINK SHE'S AWESOME, KURO-MINE?! AS A MAN!!
WHAT? UH... SURE.
So awesome, I'm kinda creeped out.
HA!
SHE'S MANLIER THAN EVERY DUDE ON THE PLANET!!
....

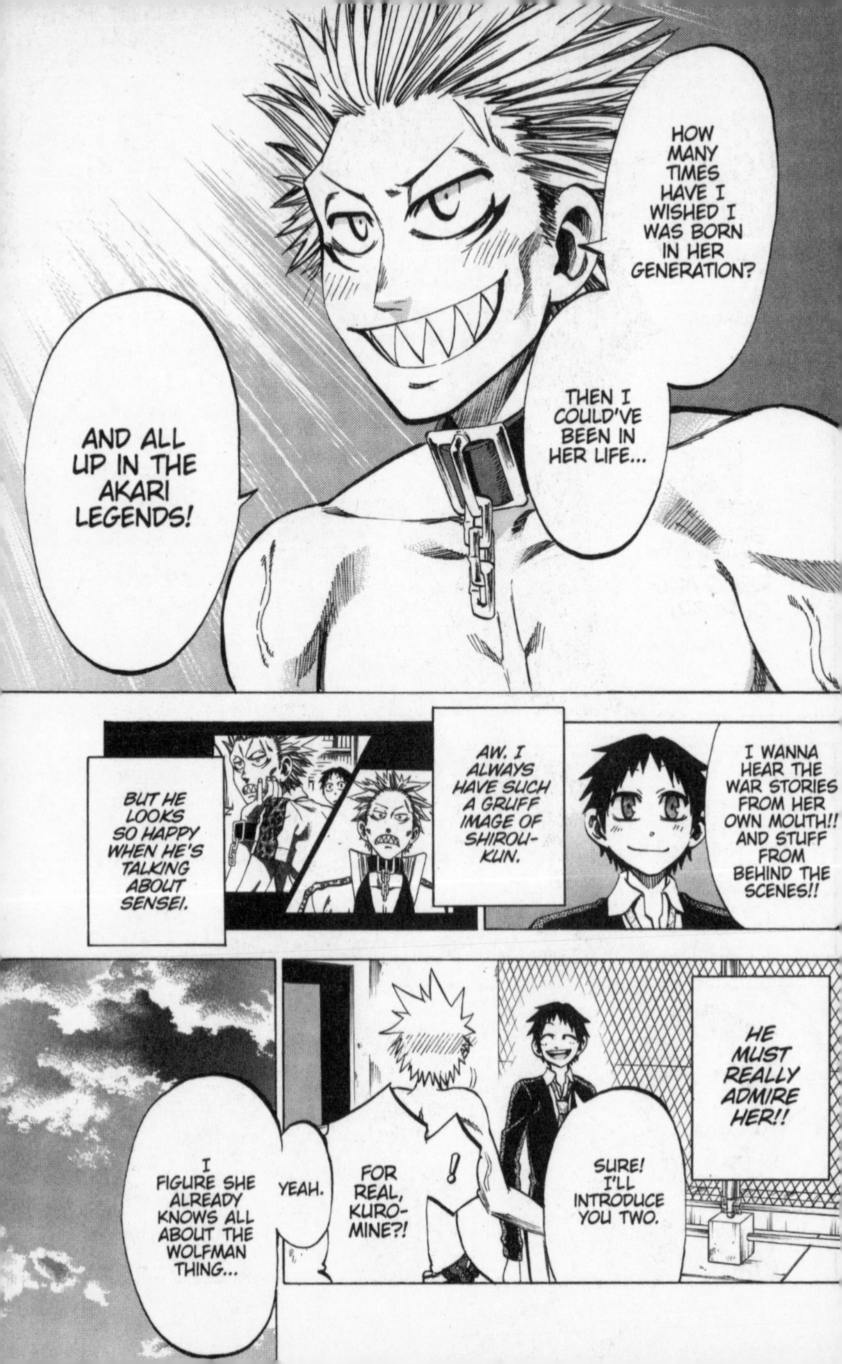
HOW MANY TIMES HAVE I WISHED I WAS BORN IN HER GENERATION?
THEN I COULD'VE BEEN IN HER LIFE...
AND ALL UP IN THE AKARI LEGENDS!
I WANNA HEAR THE WAR STORIES FROM HER OWN MOUTH!! AND STUFF FROM BEHIND THE SCENES!!
AW. I ALWAYS HAVE SUCH A GRUFF IMAGE OF SHIROU-KUN.
BUT HE LOOKS SO HAPPY WHEN HE'S TALKING ABOUT SENSEI.
HE MUST REALLY ADMIRE HER!!
SURE! I'LL INTRODUCE YOU TWO.
!
FOR REAL, KURO-MINE?!
YEAH.
I FIGURE SHE ALREADY KNOWS ALL ABOUT THE WOLFMAN THING...

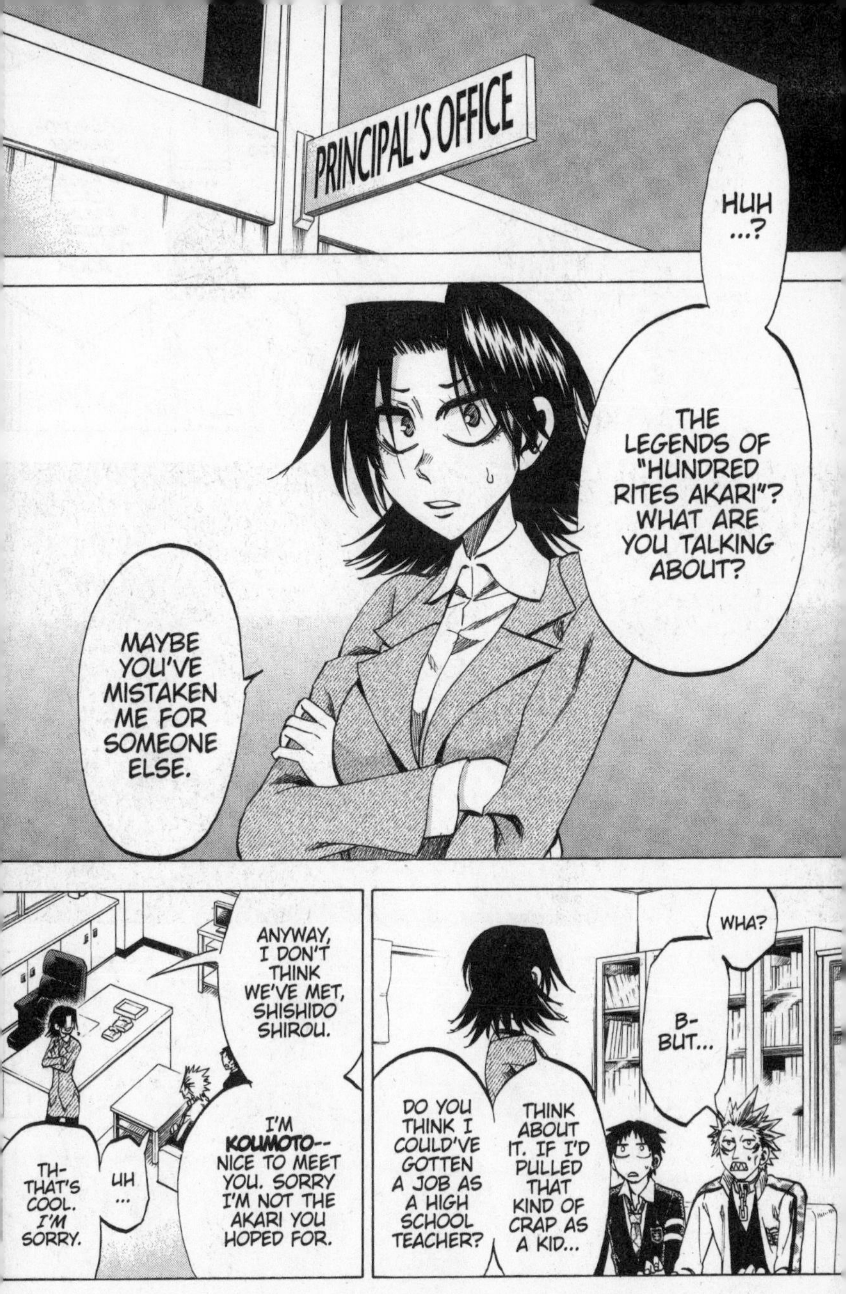
PRINCIPAL'S OFFICE
HUH ...?
THE LEGENDS OF "HUNDRED RITES AKARI"? WHAT ARE YOU TALKING ABOUT?
MAYBE YOU'VE MISTAKEN ME FOR SOMEONE ELSE.
WHA?
B-BUT...
THINK ABOUT IT. IF I'D PULLED THAT KIND OF CRAP AS A KID...
DO YOU THINK I COULD'VE GOTTEN A JOB AS A HIGH SCHOOL TEACHER?
ANYWAY, I DON'T THINK WE'VE MET, SHISHIDO SHIROU.
I'M **KOUMOTO**-- NICE TO MEET YOU. SORRY I'M NOT THE AKARI YOU HOPED FOR.
UH ...
TH-THAT'S COOL. I'M SORRY.

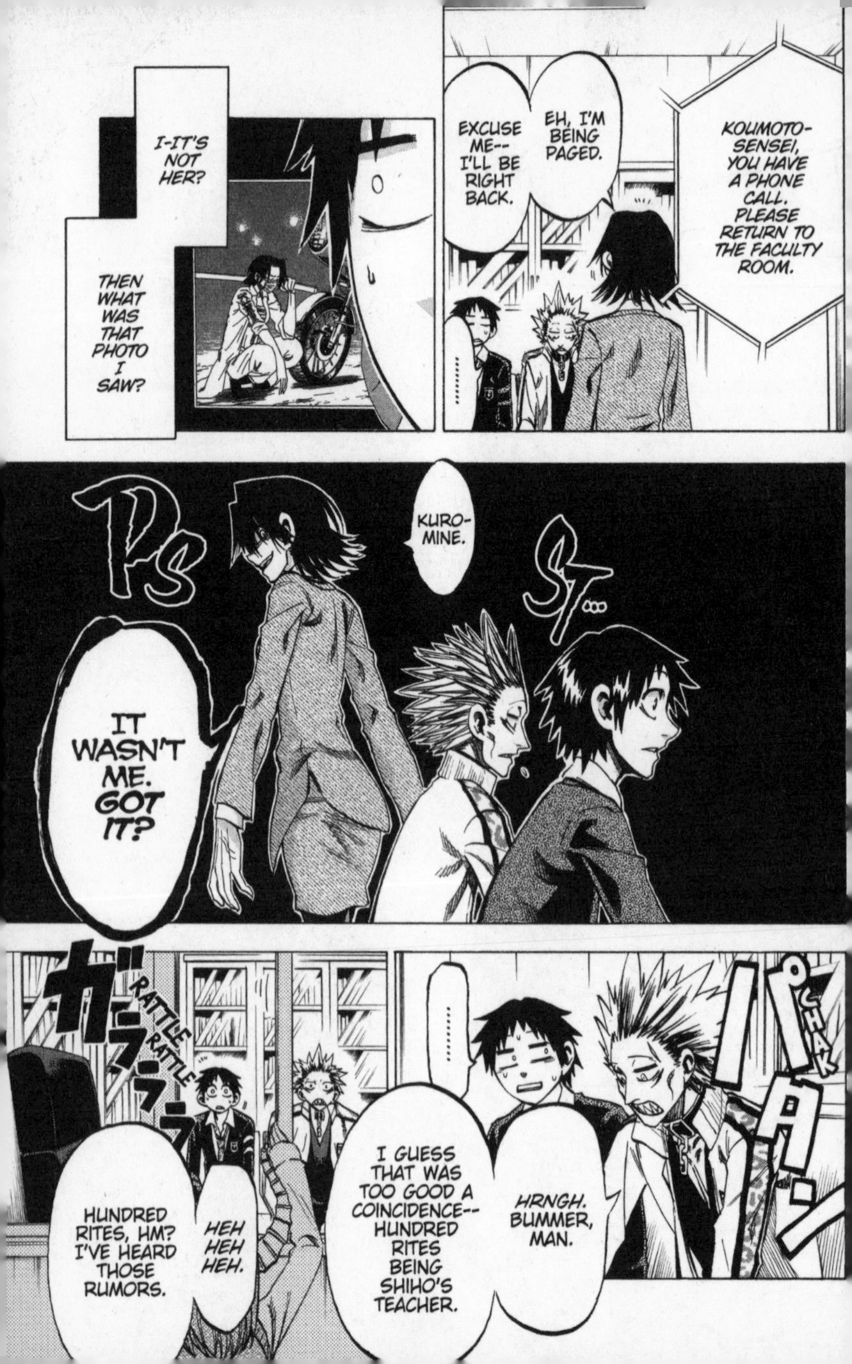
KOUMOTO-SENSEI, YOU HAVE A PHONE CALL. PLEASE RETURN TO THE FACULTY ROOM.
EH, I'M BEING PAGED.
EXCUSE ME-- I'LL BE RIGHT BACK.
......
I-IT'S NOT HER?
THEN WHAT WAS THAT PHOTO I SAW?
KURO-MINE.
PSST...
IT WASN'T ME. GOT IT?
パタン
PCHAK
HRNGH. BUMMER, MAN.
I GUESS THAT WAS TOO GOOD A COINCIDENCE-- HUNDRED RITES BEING SHIHO'S TEACHER.
......
ガラララ
RATTLE RATTLE
HEH HEH HEH.
HUNDRED RITES, HM? I'VE HEARD THOSE RUMORS.

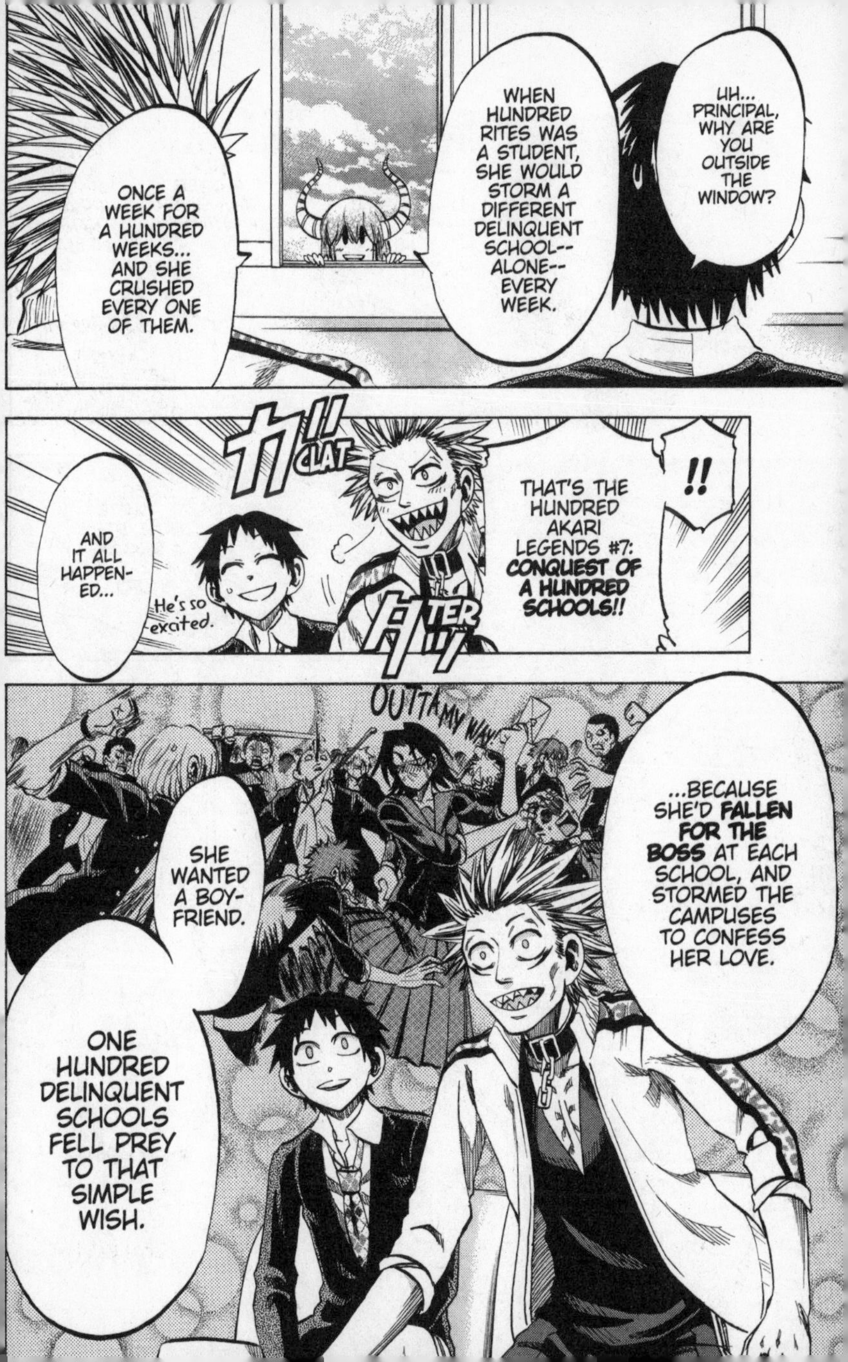
UH... PRINCIPAL, WHY ARE YOU OUTSIDE THE WINDOW?
WHEN HUNDRED RITES WAS A STUDENT, SHE WOULD STORM A DIFFERENT DELINQUENT SCHOOL-- ALONE-- EVERY WEEK.
ONCE A WEEK FOR A HUNDRED WEEKS... AND SHE CRUSHED EVERY ONE OF THEM.
!!
THAT'S THE HUNDRED AKARI LEGENDS #7: **CONQUEST OF A HUNDRED SCHOOLS!!**
CLAT
TER
AND IT ALL HAPPEN-ED...
He's so excited.
OUTTA MY WAY
...BECAUSE SHE'D **FALLEN FOR THE BOSS** AT EACH SCHOOL, AND STORMED THE CAMPUSES TO CONFESS HER LOVE.
SHE WANTED A BOY-FRIEND.
ONE HUNDRED DELINQUENT SCHOOLS FELL PREY TO THAT SIMPLE WISH.

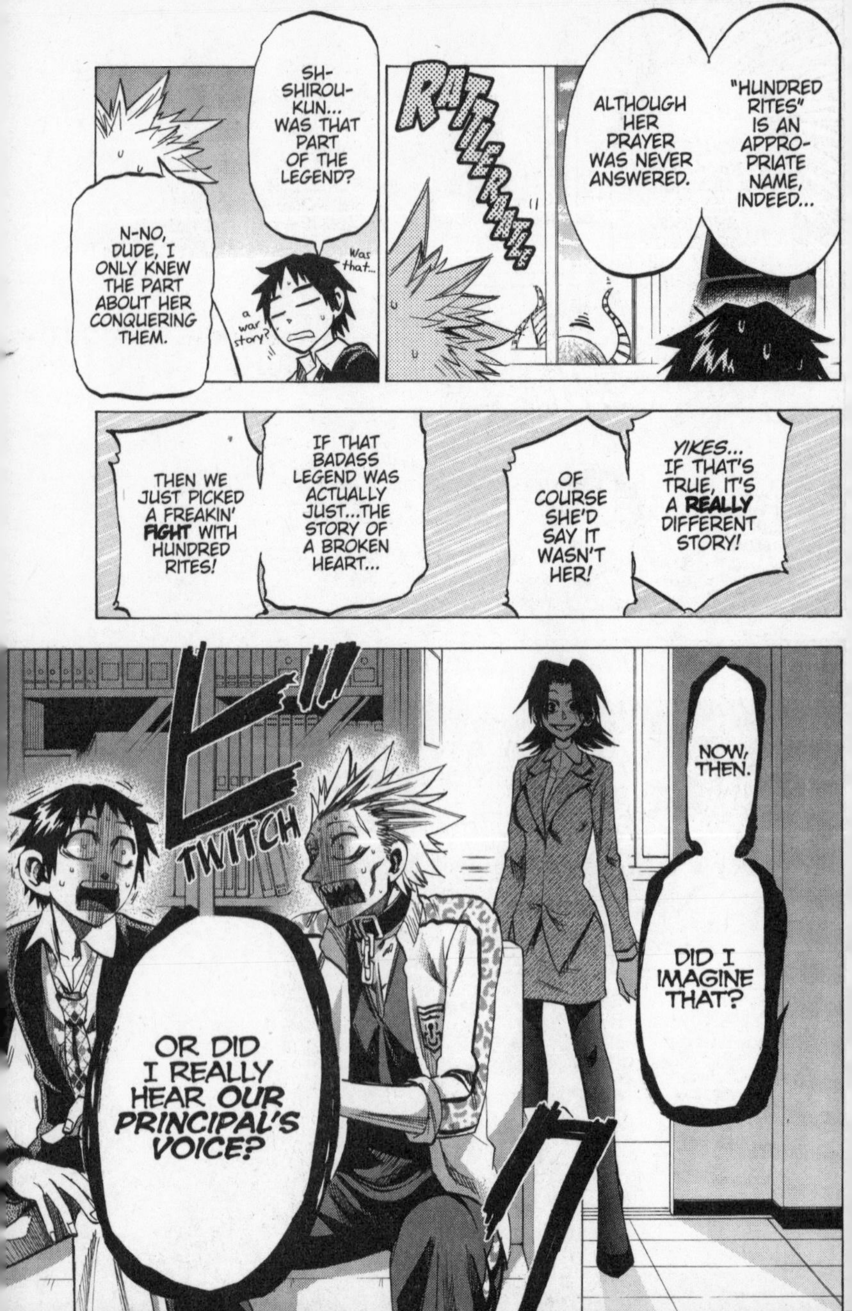
"HUNDRED RITES" IS AN APPROPRIATE NAME, INDEED...
ALTHOUGH HER PRAYER WAS NEVER ANSWERED.
RATTLE
SH-SHIROU-KUN... WAS THAT PART OF THE LEGEND?
Was that...
a war story?
N-NO, DUDE, I ONLY KNEW THE PART ABOUT HER CONQUERING THEM.
YIKES... IF THAT'S TRUE, IT'S A **REALLY** DIFFERENT STORY!
OF COURSE SHE'D SAY IT WASN'T HER!
IF THAT BADASS LEGEND WAS ACTUALLY JUST...THE STORY OF A BROKEN HEART...
THEN WE JUST PICKED A FREAKIN' **FIGHT** WITH HUNDRED RITES!
NOW, THEN.
DID I IMAGINE THAT?
TWITCH
OR DID I REALLY HEAR ***OUR PRINCIPAL'S VOICE?***

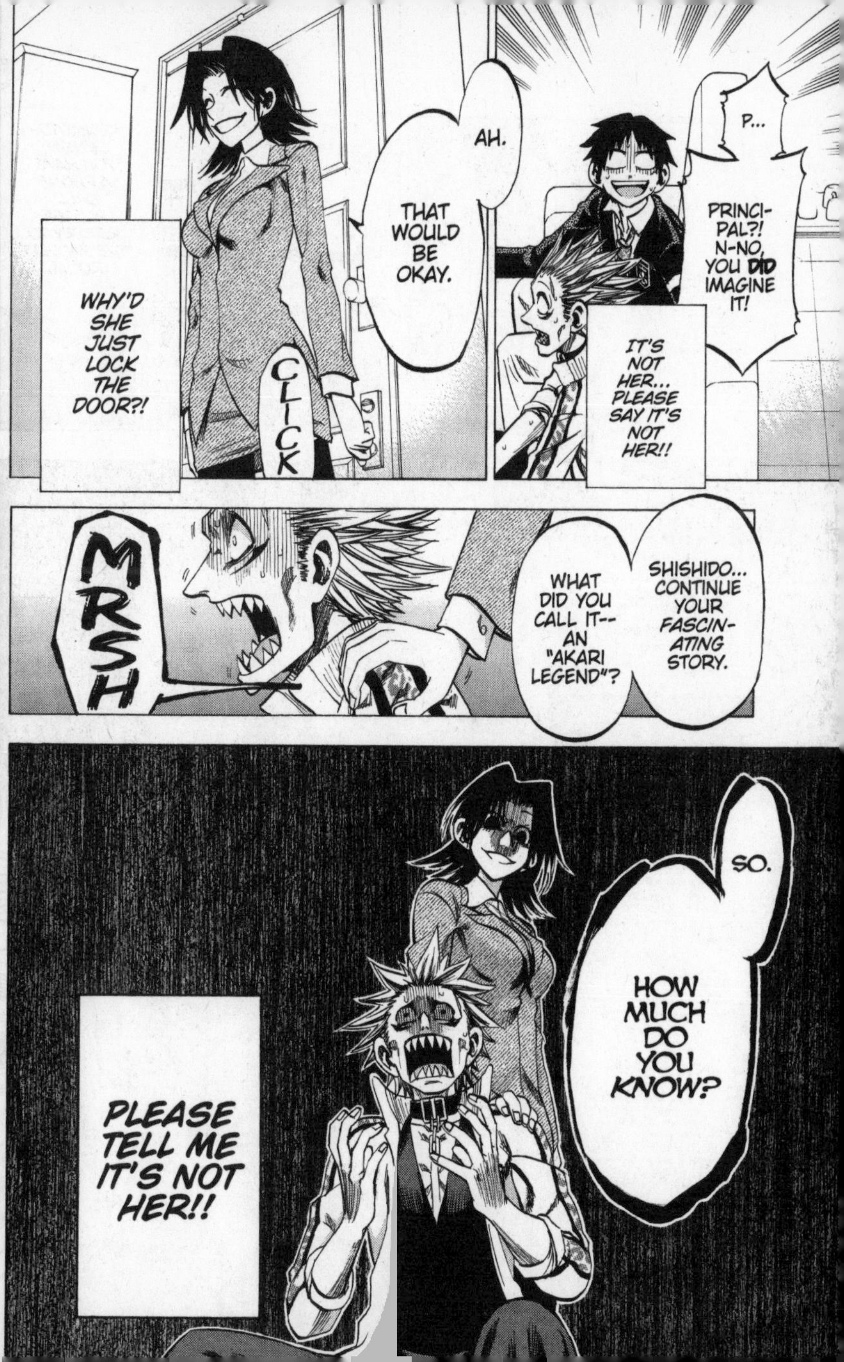
P...
PRINCIPAL?! N-NO, YOU **DID** IMAGINE IT!
IT'S NOT HER... PLEASE SAY IT'S NOT HER!!
AH.
THAT WOULD BE OKAY.
CLICK
WHY'D SHE JUST LOCK THE DOOR?!
SHISHIDO... CONTINUE YOUR FASCINATING STORY.
WHAT DID YOU CALL IT-- AN "AKARI LEGEND"?
MRSH
SO.
HOW MUCH DO YOU KNOW?
PLEASE TELL ME IT'S NOT HER!!

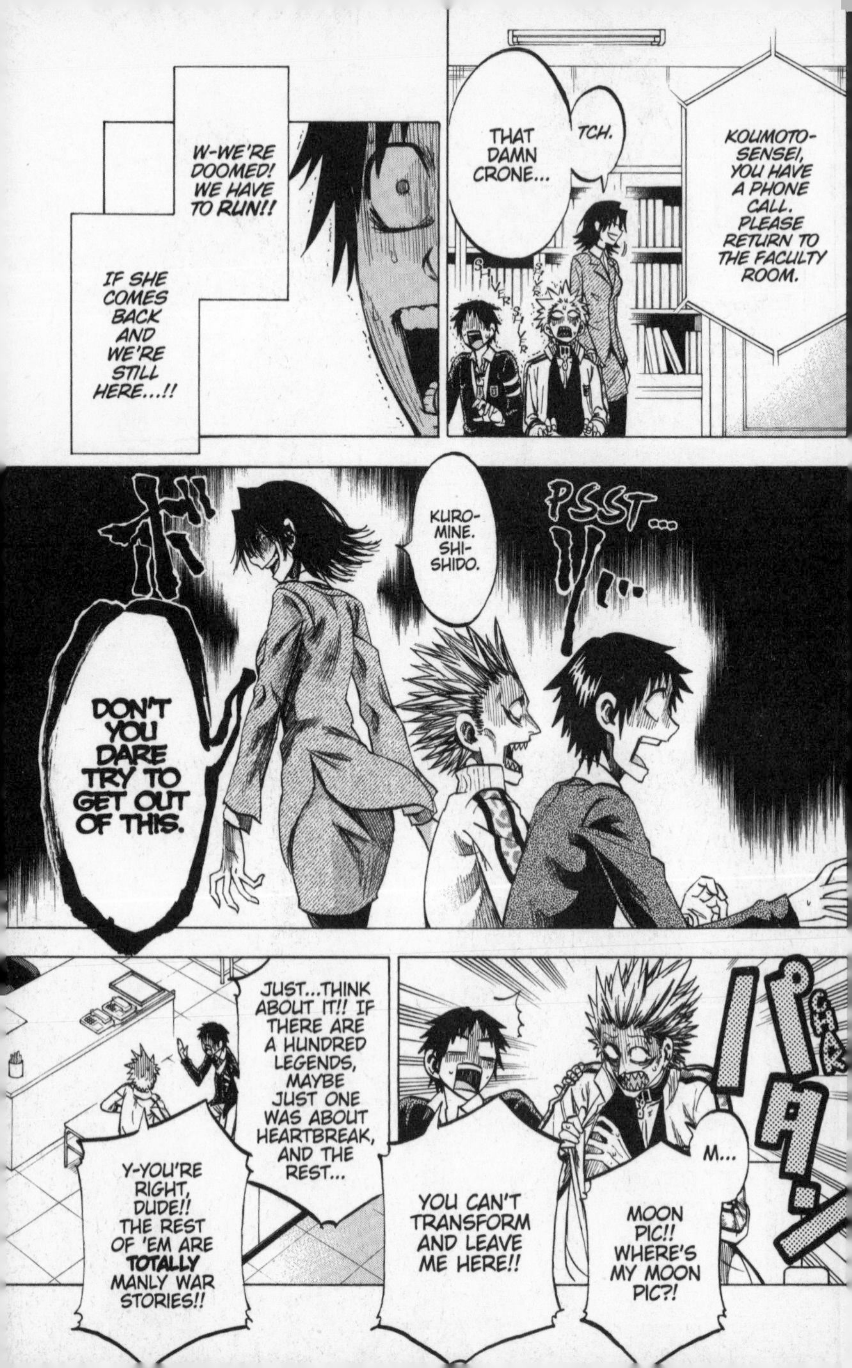
KOUMOTO-SENSEI, YOU HAVE A PHONE CALL. PLEASE RETURN TO THE FACULTY ROOM.
TCH.
THAT DAMN CRONE...
SHIVER SHIVER
SHIVER SHIVER
W-WE'RE DOOMED! WE HAVE TO RUN!!
IF SHE COMES BACK AND WE'RE STILL HERE...!!
PSST...
KURO-MINE. SHI-SHIDO.
DON'T YOU DARE TRY TO GET OUT OF THIS.
M...
MOON PIC!! WHERE'S MY MOON PIC?!
YOU CAN'T TRANSFORM AND LEAVE ME HERE!!
JUST...THINK ABOUT IT!! IF THERE ARE A HUNDRED LEGENDS, MAYBE JUST ONE WAS ABOUT HEARTBREAK, AND THE REST...
Y-YOU'RE RIGHT, DUDE!! THE REST OF 'EM ARE TOTALLY MANLY WAR STORIES!!

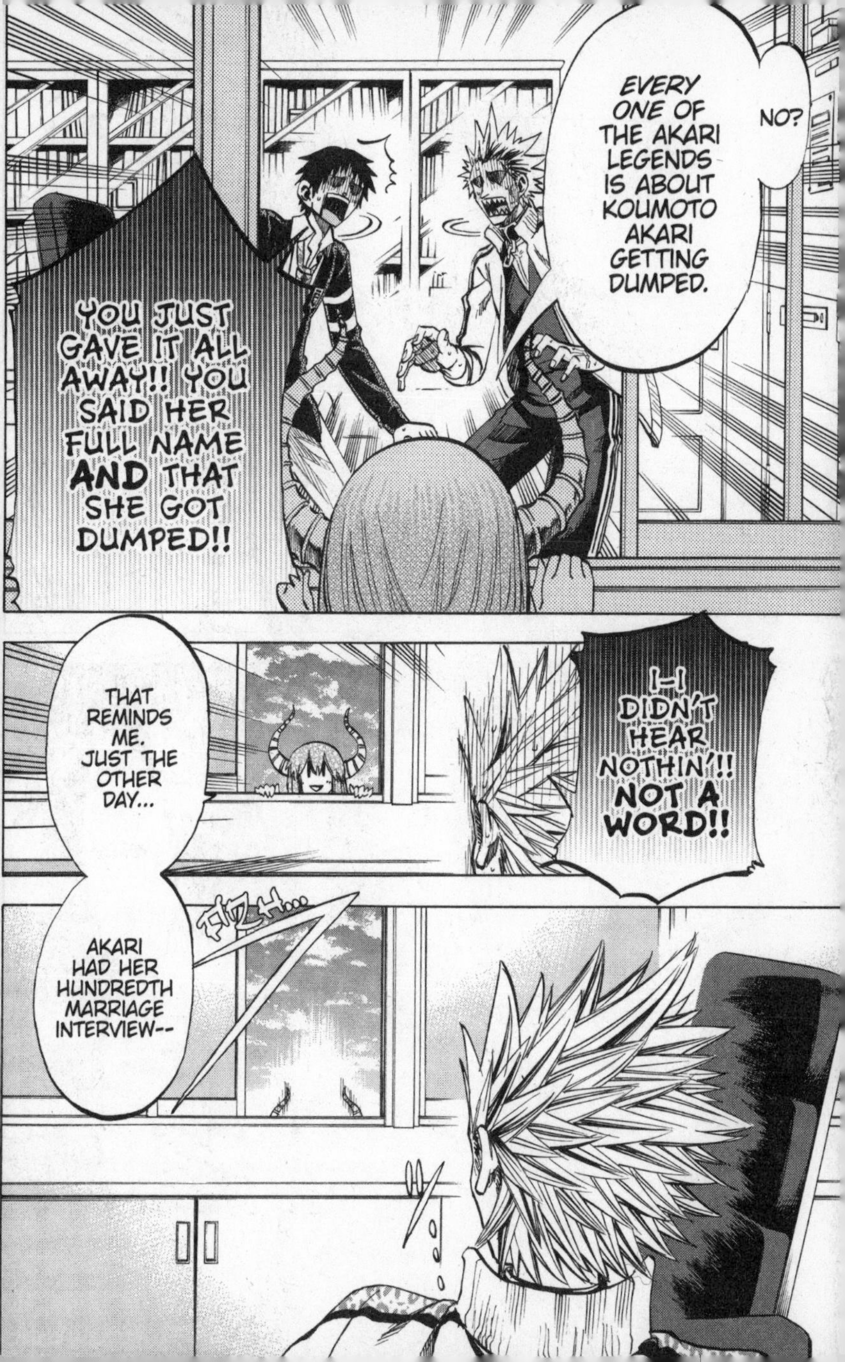
EVERY ONE OF THE AKARI LEGENDS IS ABOUT KOUMOTO AKARI GETTING DUMPED.
NO?
YOU JUST GAVE IT ALL AWAY!! YOU SAID HER FULL NAME AND THAT SHE GOT DUMPED!!
I-I DIDN'T HEAR NOTHIN'!! NOT A WORD!!
THAT REMINDS ME. JUST THE OTHER DAY...
AKARI HAD HER HUNDREDTH MARRIAGE INTERVIEW--

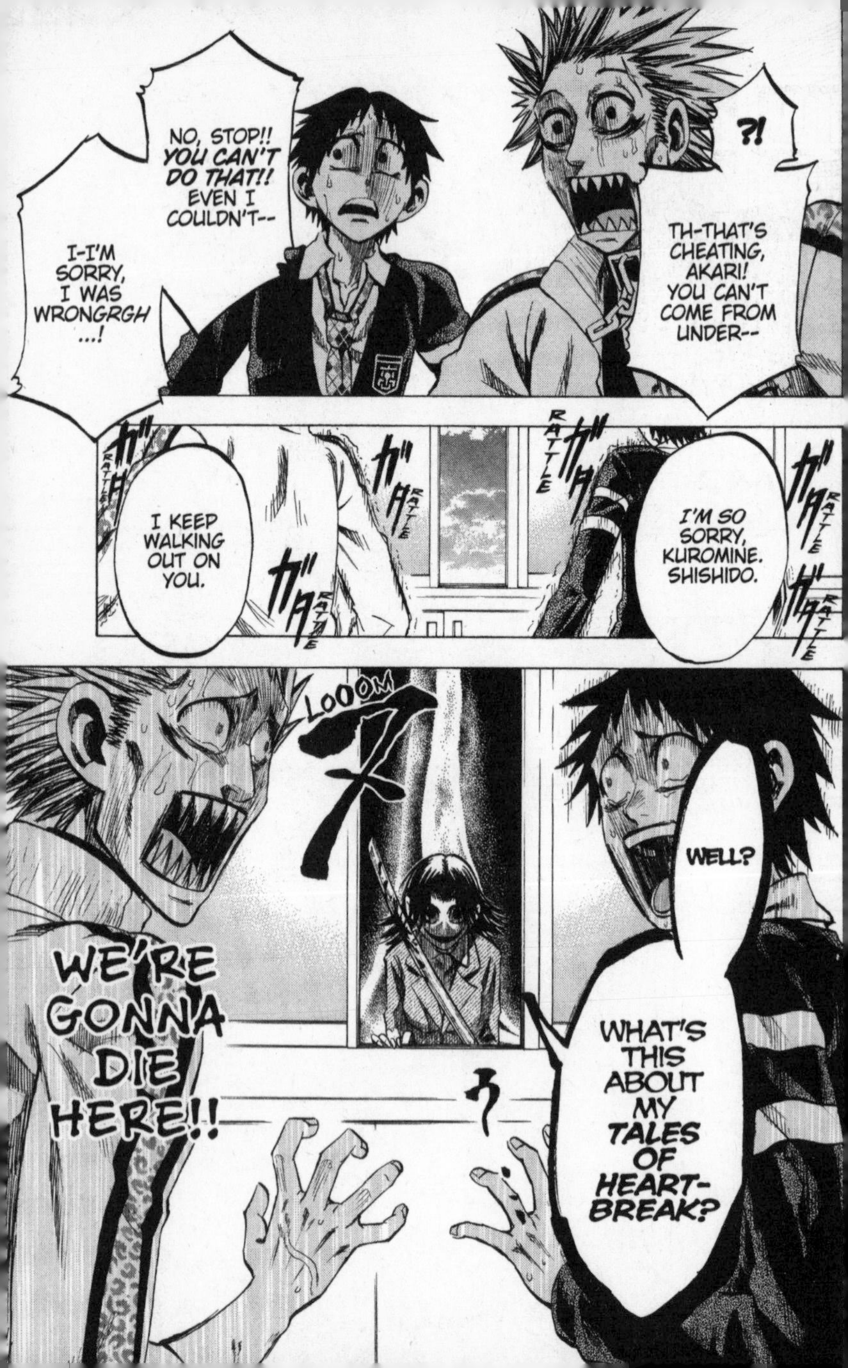
?!
TH-THAT'S CHEATING, AKARI! YOU CAN'T COME FROM UNDER--
NO, STOP!! YOU CAN'T DO THAT!! EVEN I COULDN'T--
I-I'M SORRY, I WAS WRONGRGH ...!
RATTLE
I'M SO SORRY, KUROMINE. SHISHIDO.
RATTLE
RATTLE
RATTLE
I KEEP WALKING OUT ON YOU.
RATTLE
LOOOM
WELL?
WHAT'S THIS ABOUT MY TALES OF HEART-BREAK?
WE'RE GONNA DIE HERE!!

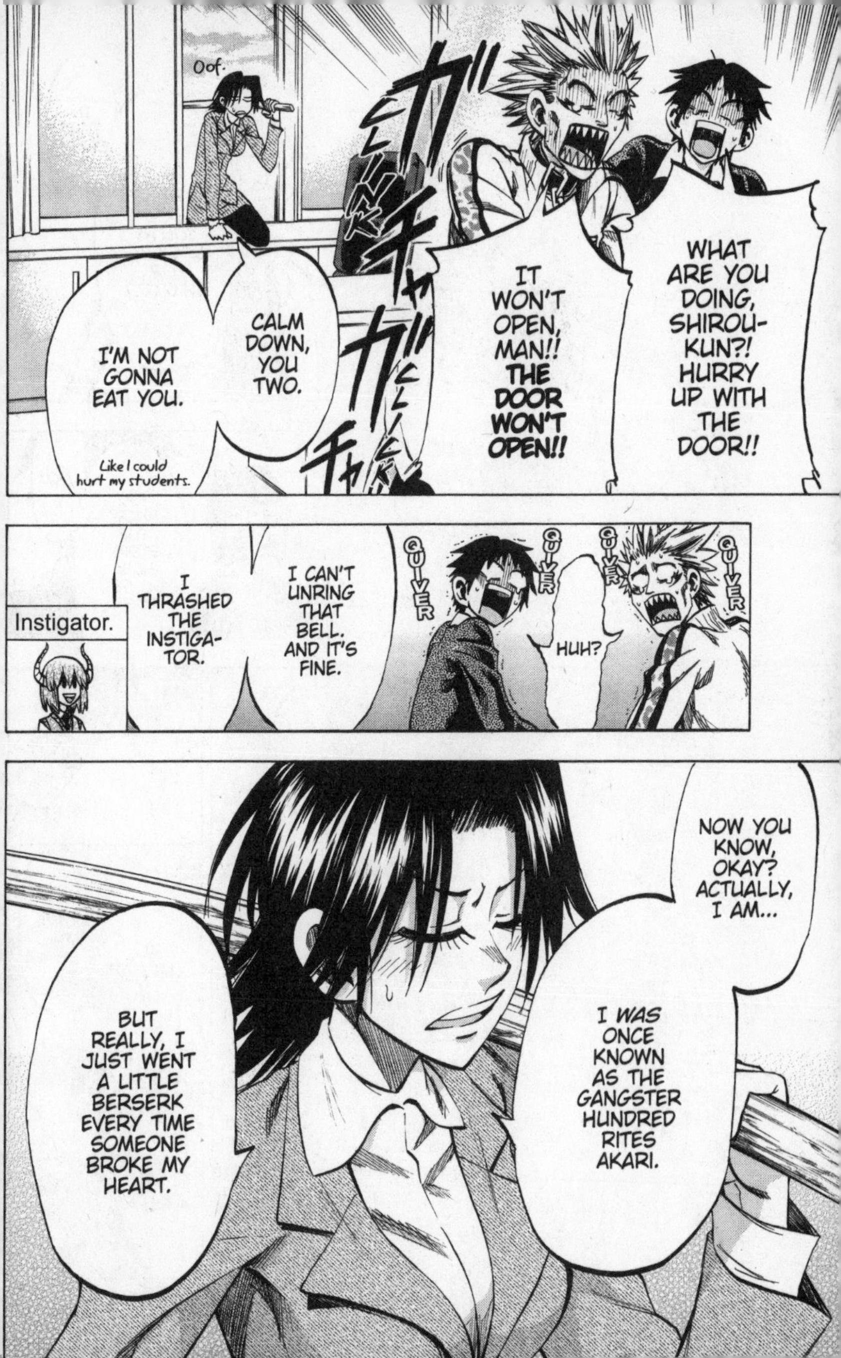
WHAT ARE YOU DOING, SHIROU-KUN?! HURRY UP WITH THE DOOR!!
IT WON'T OPEN, MAN!! **THE DOOR WON'T OPEN!!**
CLINK
Oof.
CALM DOWN, YOU TWO.
I'M NOT GONNA EAT YOU.
Like I could hurt my students.
QUIVER
QUIVER
HUH?
QUIVER
QUIVER
I CAN'T UNRING THAT BELL. AND IT'S FINE.
I THRASHED THE INSTIGATOR.
Instigator.
NOW YOU KNOW, OKAY? ACTUALLY, I AM...
I *WAS* ONCE KNOWN AS THE GANGSTER HUNDRED RITES AKARI.
BUT REALLY, I JUST WENT A LITTLE BERSERK EVERY TIME SOMEONE BROKE MY HEART.

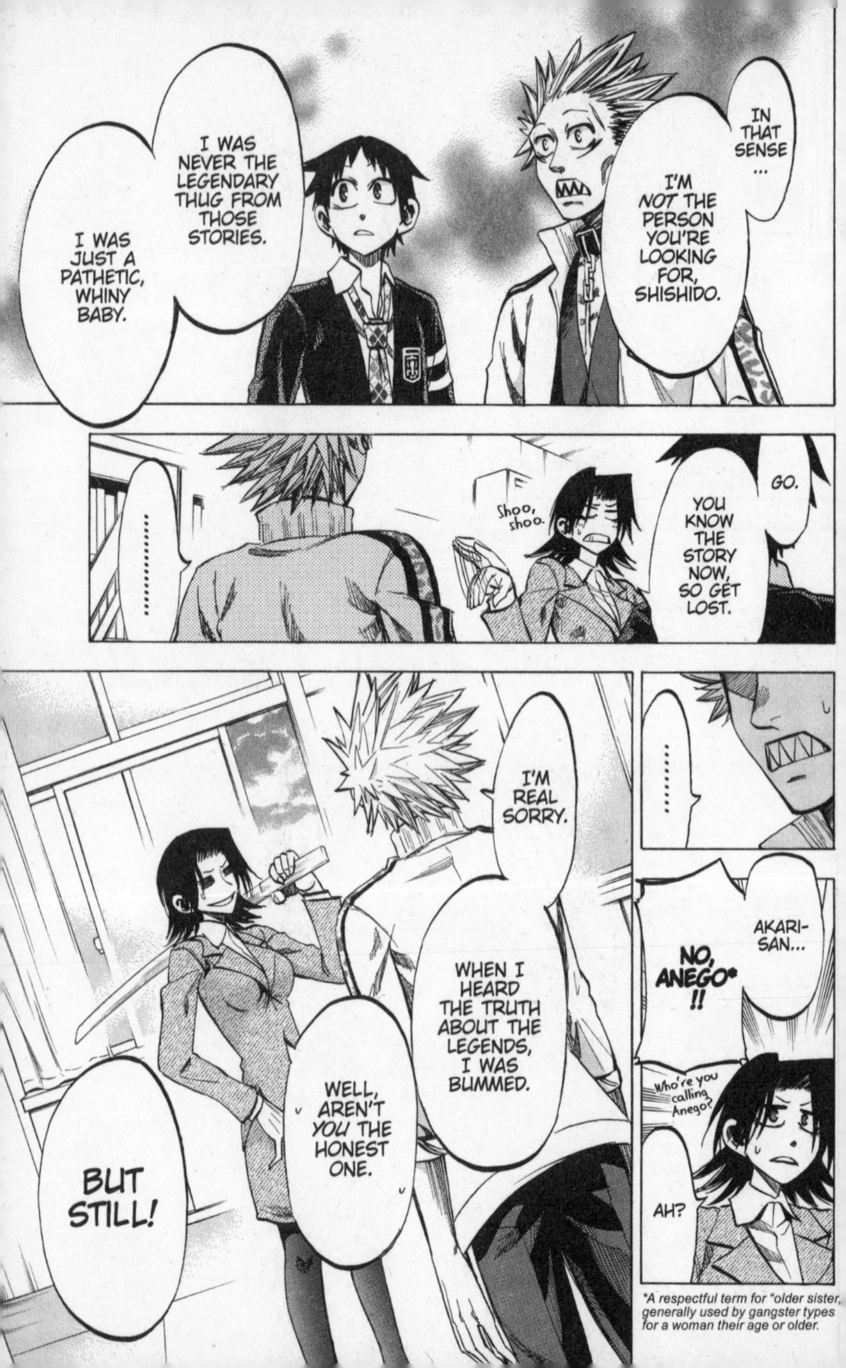
IN THAT SENSE...
I'M *NOT* THE PERSON YOU'RE LOOKING FOR, SHISHIDO.
I WAS NEVER THE LEGENDARY THUG FROM THOSE STORIES.
I WAS JUST A PATHETIC, WHINY BABY.
GO.
YOU KNOW THE STORY NOW, SO GET LOST.
Shoo, shoo.
....
....
AKARI-SAN...
NO, ANEGO*!!
Who're you calling Anego?
AH?
I'M REAL SORRY.
WHEN I HEARD THE TRUTH ABOUT THE LEGENDS, I WAS BUMMED.
WELL, AREN'T *YOU* THE HONEST ONE.
BUT STILL!

*A respectful term for "older sister, generally used by gangster types for a woman their age or older.

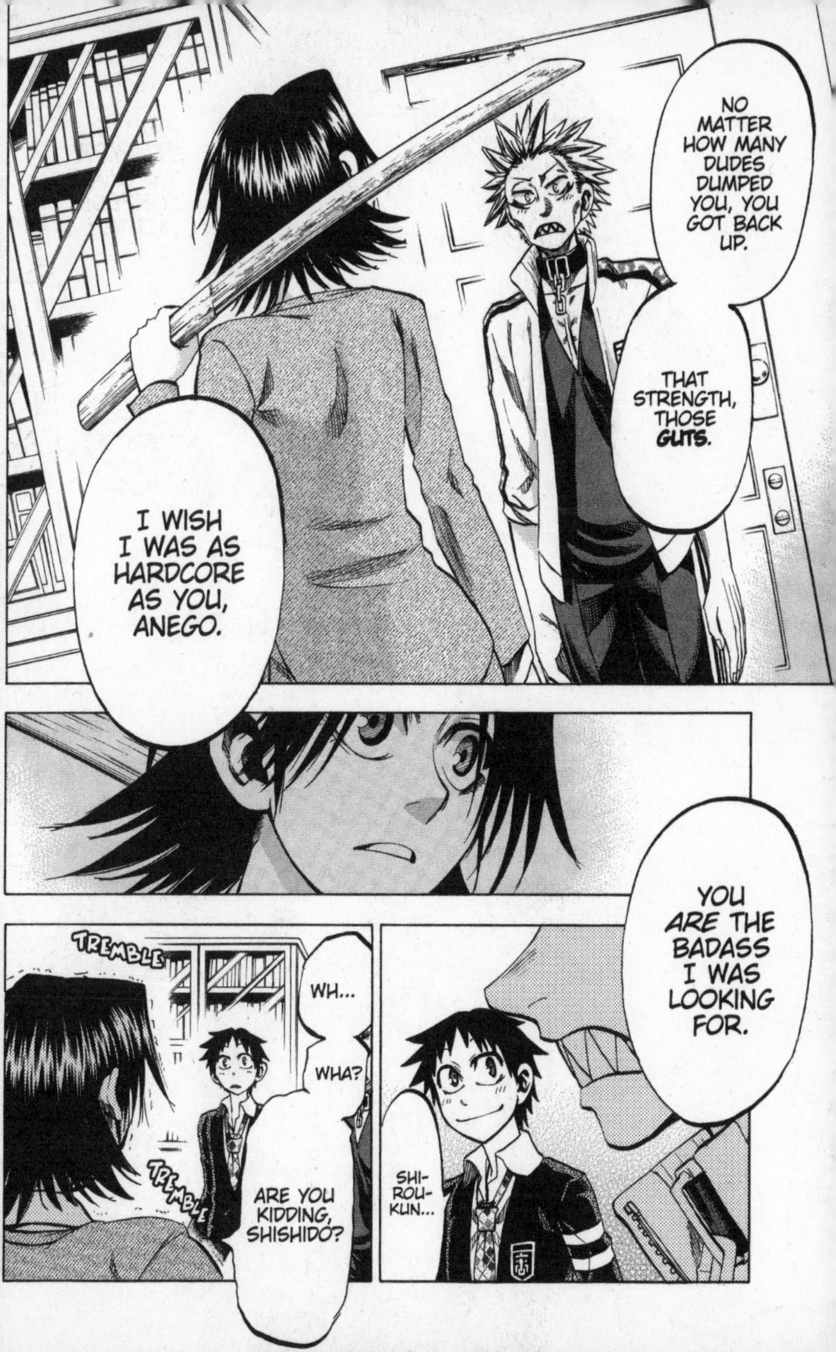
NO MATTER HOW MANY DUDES DUMPED YOU, YOU GOT BACK UP.
THAT STRENGTH, THOSE **GUTS**.
I WISH I WAS AS HARDCORE AS YOU, ANEGO.
YOU *ARE* THE BADASS I WAS LOOKING FOR.
SHIROU-KUN...
TREMBLE
WH...
WHA?
TREMBLE
ARE YOU KIDDING, SHISHIDO?

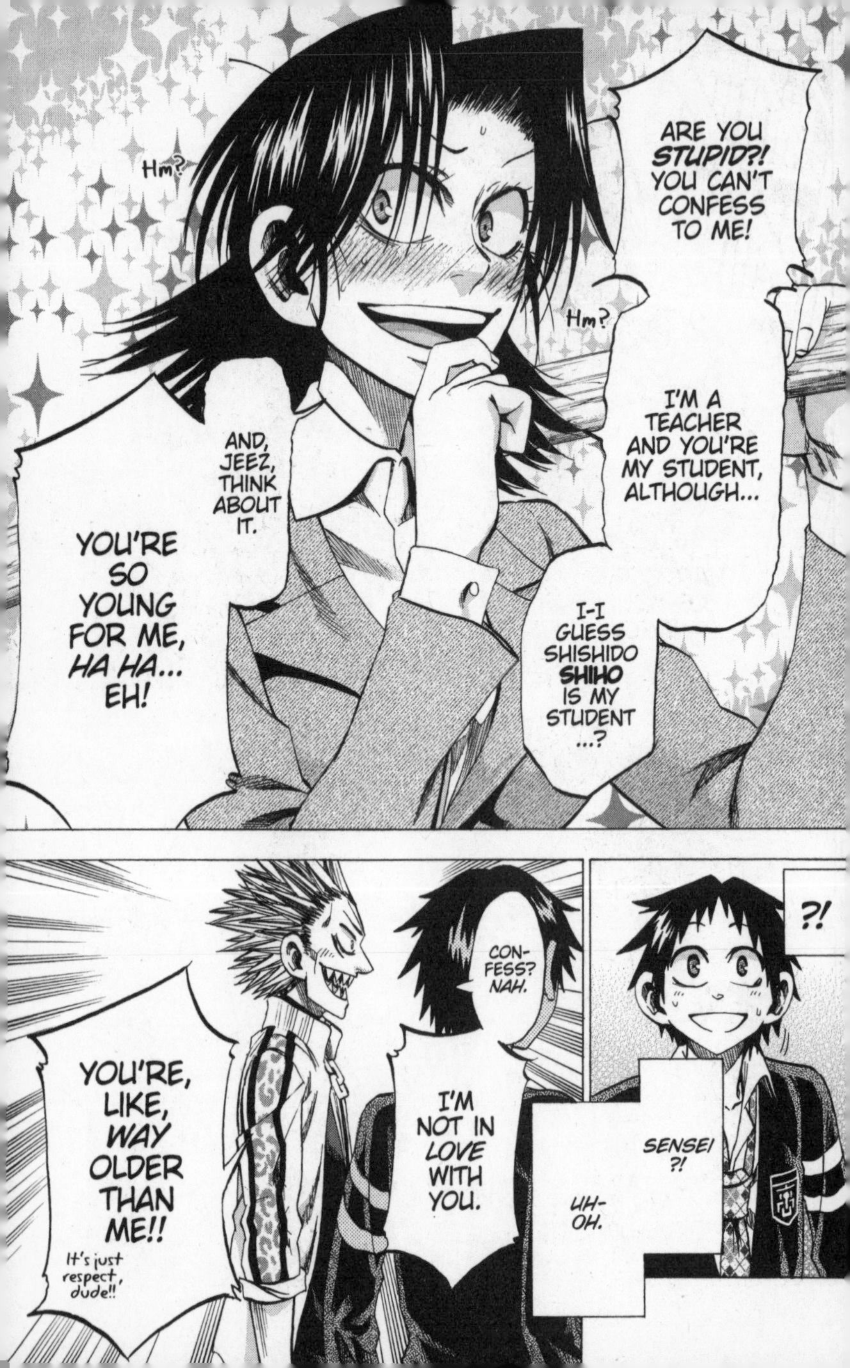
ARE YOU STUPID?! YOU CAN'T CONFESS TO ME!
Hm?
I'M A TEACHER AND YOU'RE MY STUDENT, ALTHOUGH...
I-I GUESS SHISHIDO SHIHO IS MY STUDENT ...?
Hm?
AND, JEEZ, THINK ABOUT IT.
YOU'RE SO YOUNG FOR ME, HA HA... EH!
?!
SENSEI ?!
UH-OH.
CON-FESS? NAH.
I'M NOT IN LOVE WITH YOU.
YOU'RE, LIKE, WAY OLDER THAN ME!!
It's just respect, dude!!

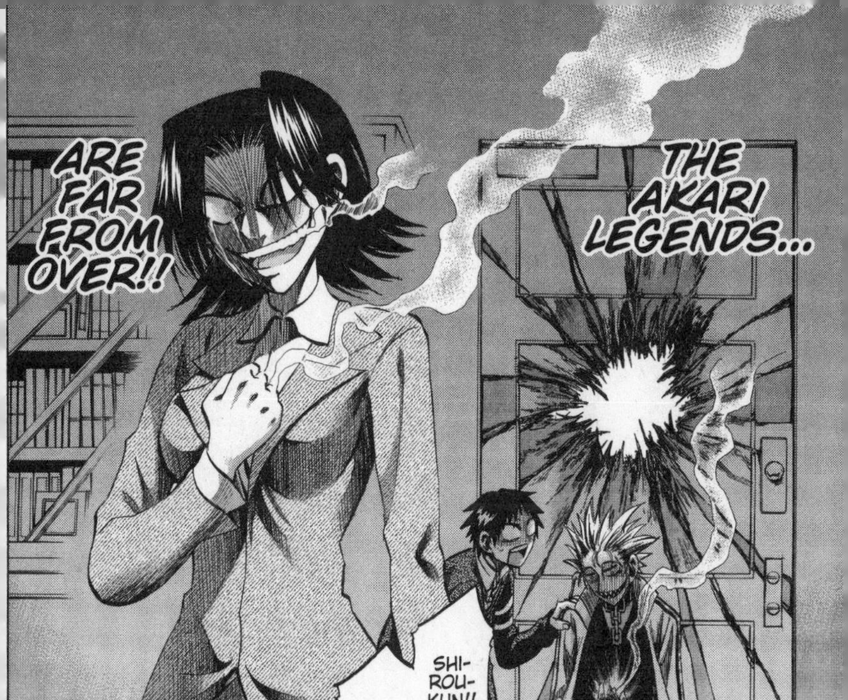
THE AKARI LEGENDS...
ARE FAR FROM OVER!!
SHIROU-KUN!!
STAY WITH ME!!

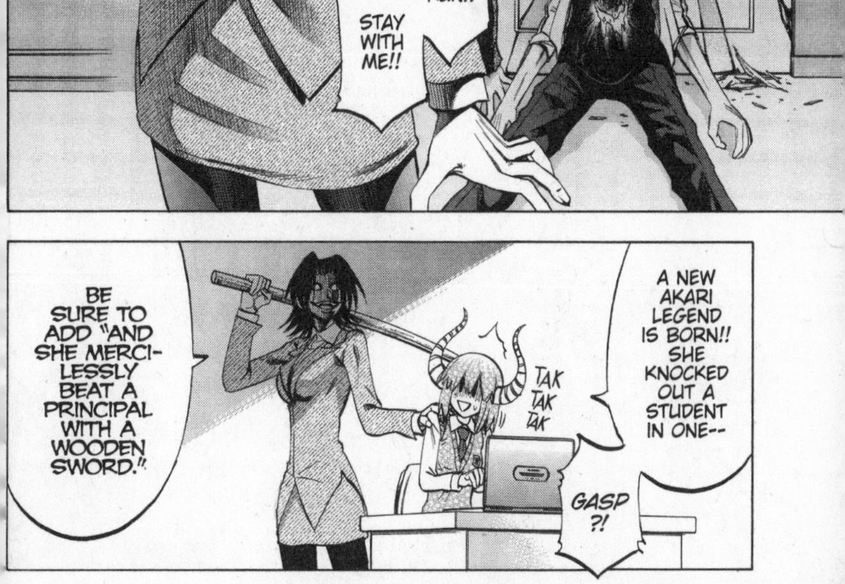
A NEW AKARI LEGEND IS BORN!! SHE KNOCKED OUT A STUDENT IN ONE--
GASP ?!
TAK TAK TAK
BE SURE TO ADD "AND SHE MERCILESSLY BEAT A PRINCIPAL WITH A WOODEN SWORD."

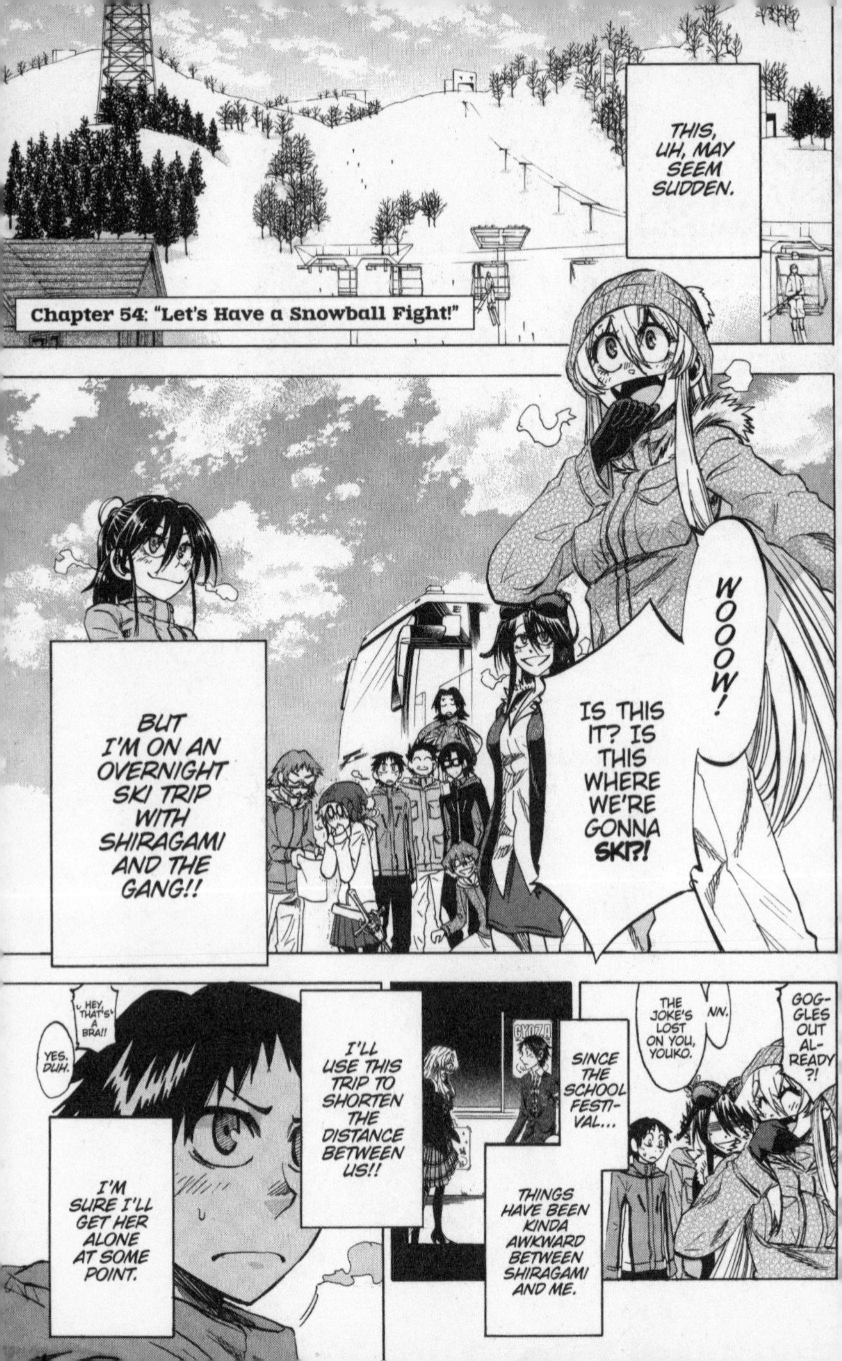
THIS, UH, MAY SEEM SUDDEN.
Chapter 54: "Let's Have a Snowball Fight!"
WOOOOW!
IS THIS IT? IS THIS WHERE WE'RE GONNA SKI?!
BUT I'M ON AN OVERNIGHT SKI TRIP WITH SHIRAGAMI AND THE GANG!!
GOG-GLES OUT AL-READY?!
NN.
THE JOKE'S LOST ON YOU, YOUKO.
SINCE THE SCHOOL FESTI-VAL...
THINGS HAVE BEEN KINDA AWKWARD BETWEEN SHIRAGAMI AND ME.
GYOZA
I'LL USE THIS TRIP TO SHORTEN THE DISTANCE BETWEEN US!!
HEY, THAT'S A BRA!!
YES. DUH.
I'M SURE I'LL GET HER ALONE AT SOME POINT.

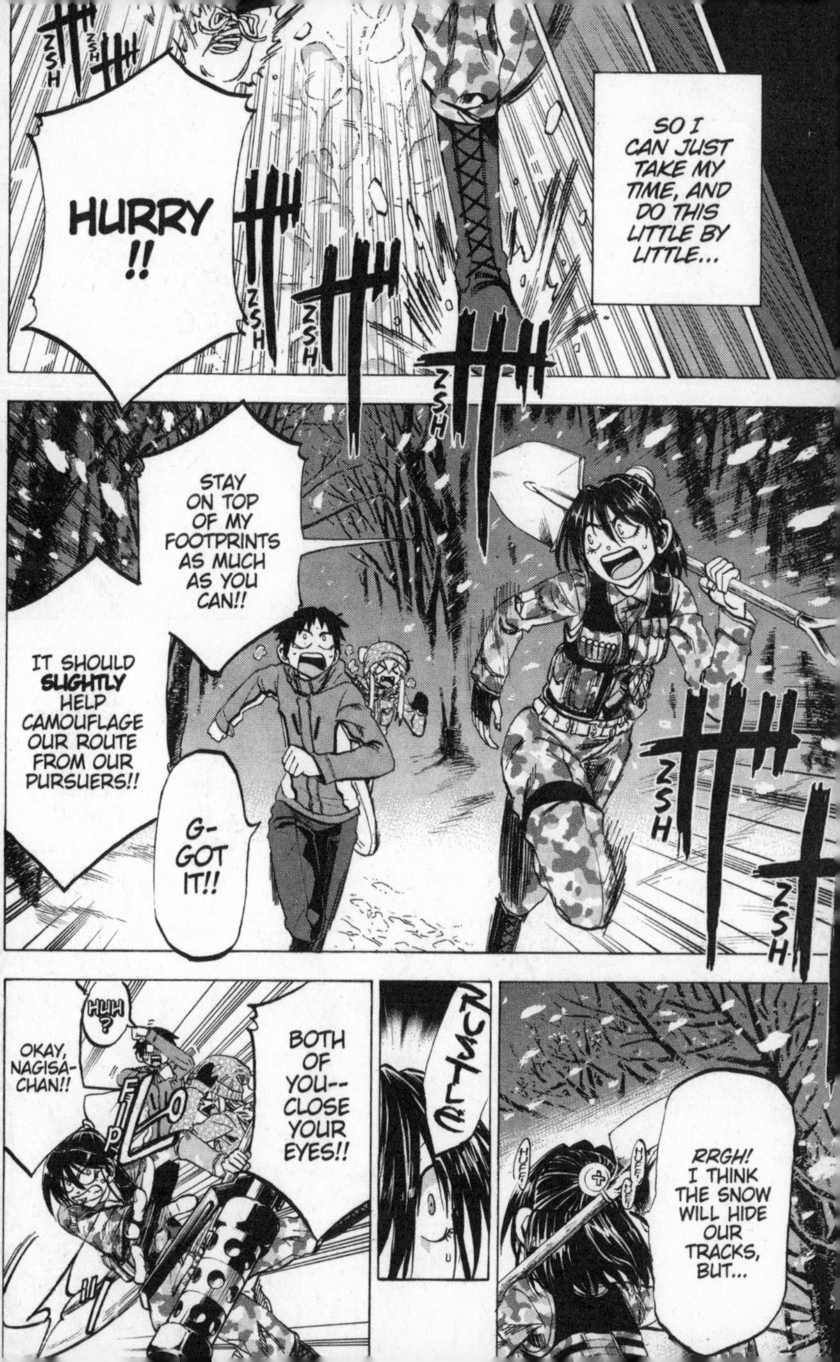

SO I CAN JUST TAKE MY TIME, AND DO THIS LITTLE BY LITTLE...
ZSH
ZSH
HURRY!!
ZSH
ZSH
ZSH
ZSH
STAY ON TOP OF MY FOOTPRINTS AS MUCH AS YOU CAN!!
IT SHOULD **SLIGHTLY** HELP CAMOUFLAGE OUR ROUTE FROM OUR PURSUERS!!
G-GOT IT!!
ZSH
ZSH
RRGH! I THINK THE SNOW WILL HIDE OUR TRACKS, BUT...
HUFF
HUFF
HUFF
RUSTLE
BOTH OF YOU--CLOSE YOUR EYES!!
HUH?
OKAY, NAGISA-CHAN!!
FLIP

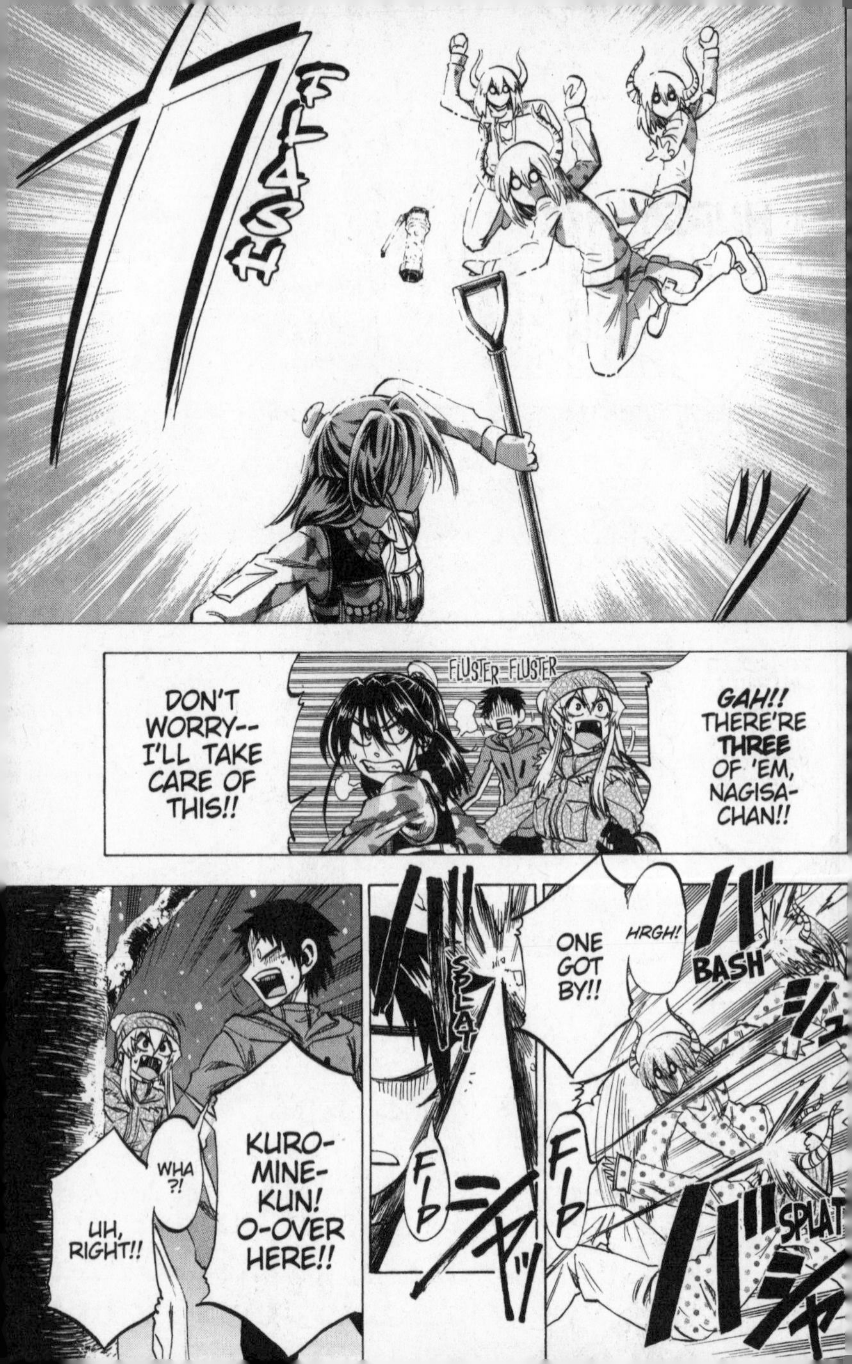
FLASH
GAH!! THERE'RE THREE OF 'EM, NAGISA-CHAN!!
FLUSTER FLUSTER
DON'T WORRY-- I'LL TAKE CARE OF THIS!!
BASH
HRGH!
ONE GOT BY!!
SPLAT
FLIP
SPLAT
FLIP
KURO-MINE-KUN! O-OVER HERE!!
WHA?!
UH, RIGHT!!

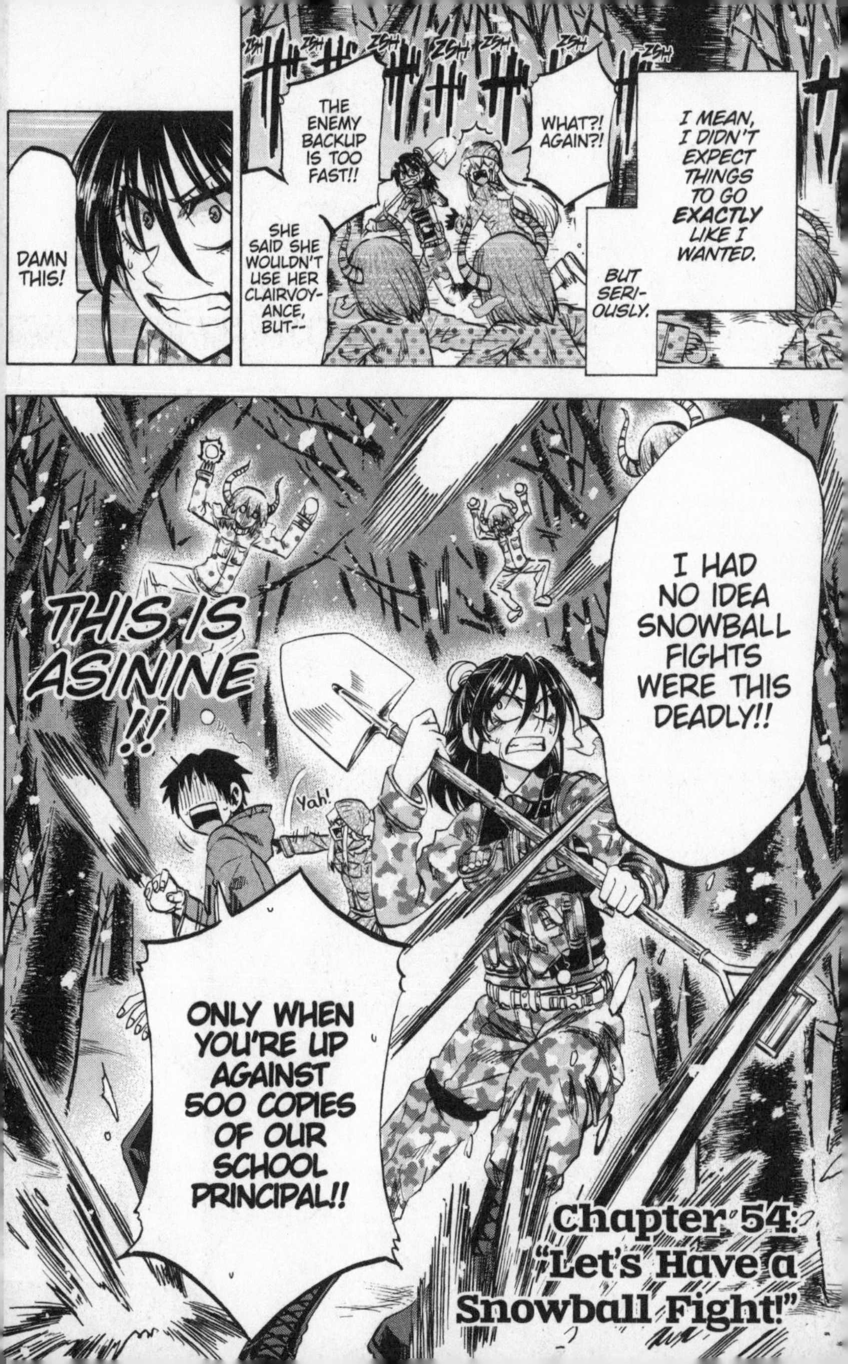
I MEAN, I DIDN'T EXPECT THINGS TO GO EXACTLY LIKE I WANTED.
BUT SERIOUSLY.
ZSH ZSH ZSH ZSH ZSH ZSH ZSH
WHAT?! AGAIN?!
THE ENEMY BACKUP IS TOO FAST!!
SHE SAID SHE WOULDN'T USE HER CLAIRVOYANCE, BUT--
DAMN THIS!
I HAD NO IDEA SNOWBALL FIGHTS WERE THIS DEADLY!!
THIS IS ASININE!!
Yah!
ONLY WHEN YOU'RE UP AGAINST 500 COPIES OF OUR SCHOOL PRINCIPAL!!
Chapter 54: "Let's Have a Snowball Fight!"

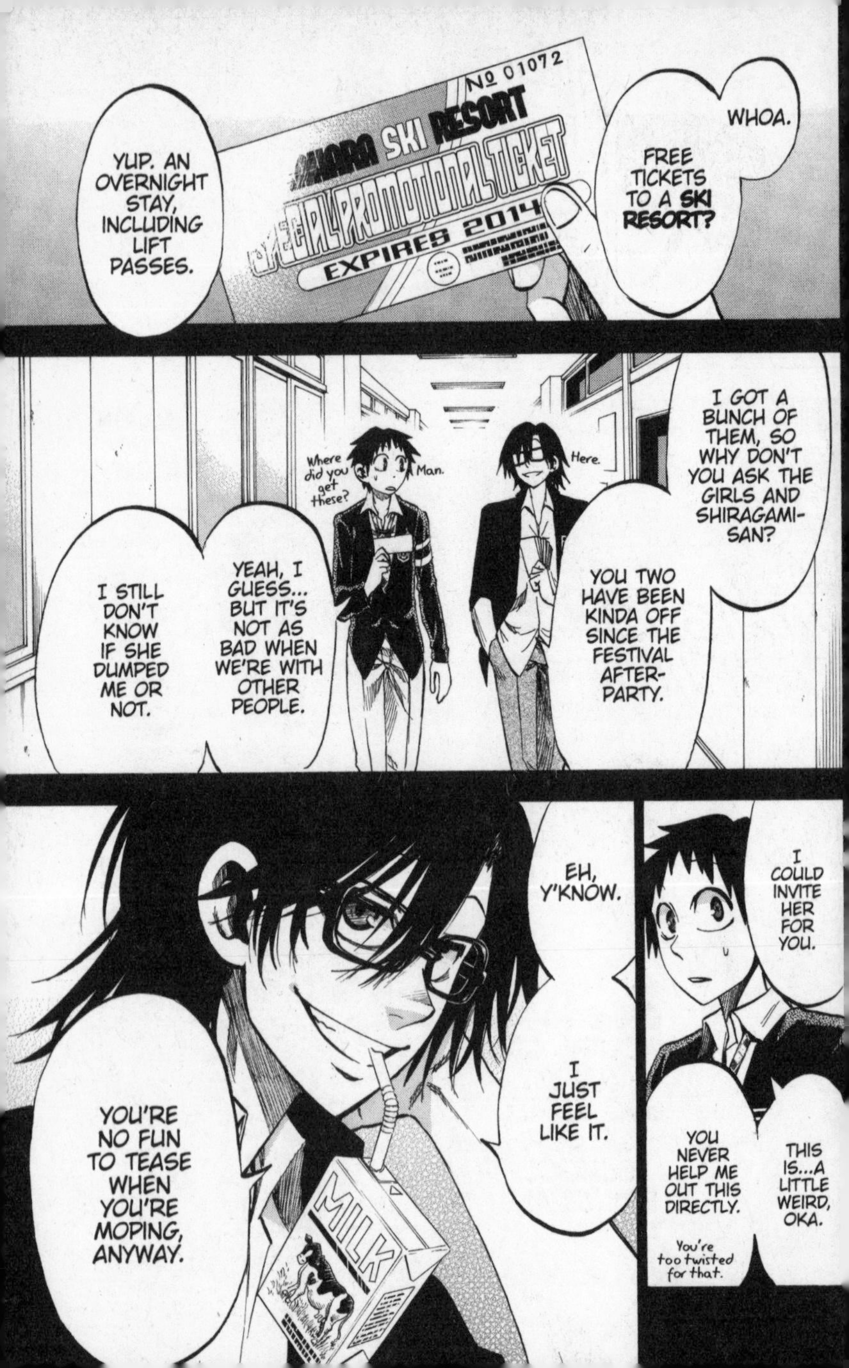
WHOA.
FREE TICKETS TO A SKI RESORT?
№ 01072
SKI RESORT
EXPIRES 2014
YUP. AN OVERNIGHT STAY, INCLUDING LIFT PASSES.
I GOT A BUNCH OF THEM, SO WHY DON'T YOU ASK THE GIRLS AND SHIRAGAMI-SAN?
Here.
YOU TWO HAVE BEEN KINDA OFF SINCE THE FESTIVAL AFTER-PARTY.
Man.
Where did you get these?
YEAH, I GUESS... BUT IT'S NOT AS BAD WHEN WE'RE WITH OTHER PEOPLE.
I STILL DON'T KNOW IF SHE DUMPED ME OR NOT.
I COULD INVITE HER FOR YOU.
THIS IS...A LITTLE WEIRD, OKA.
YOU NEVER HELP ME OUT THIS DIRECTLY.
You're too twisted for that.
EH, Y'KNOW.
I JUST FEEL LIKE IT.
YOU'RE NO FUN TO TEASE WHEN YOU'RE MOPING, ANYWAY.
MILK

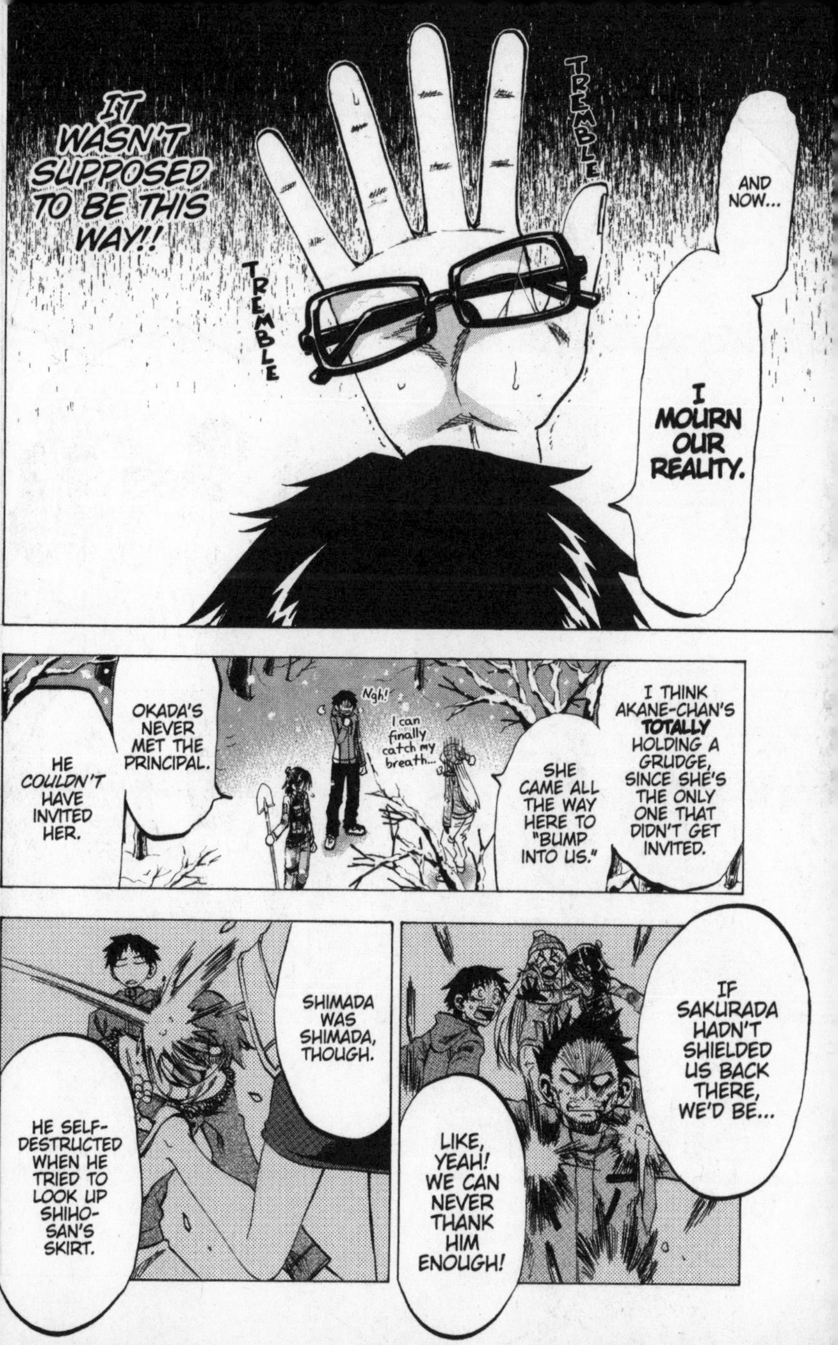
TREMBLE
AND NOW...
I MOURN OUR REALITY.
IT WASN'T SUPPOSED TO BE THIS WAY!!
TREMBLE
I THINK AKANE-CHAN'S **TOTALLY** HOLDING A GRUDGE, SINCE SHE'S THE ONLY ONE THAT DIDN'T GET INVITED.
SHE CAME ALL THE WAY HERE TO "BUMP INTO US."
Ngh!
I can finally catch my breath...
OKADA'S NEVER MET THE PRINCIPAL.
HE COULDN'T HAVE INVITED HER.
IF SAKURADA HADN'T SHIELDED US BACK THERE, WE'D BE...
LIKE, YEAH! WE CAN NEVER THANK HIM ENOUGH!
SHIMADA WAS SHIMADA, THOUGH.
HE SELF-DESTRUCTED WHEN HE TRIED TO LOOK UP SHIHO-SAN'S SKIRT.

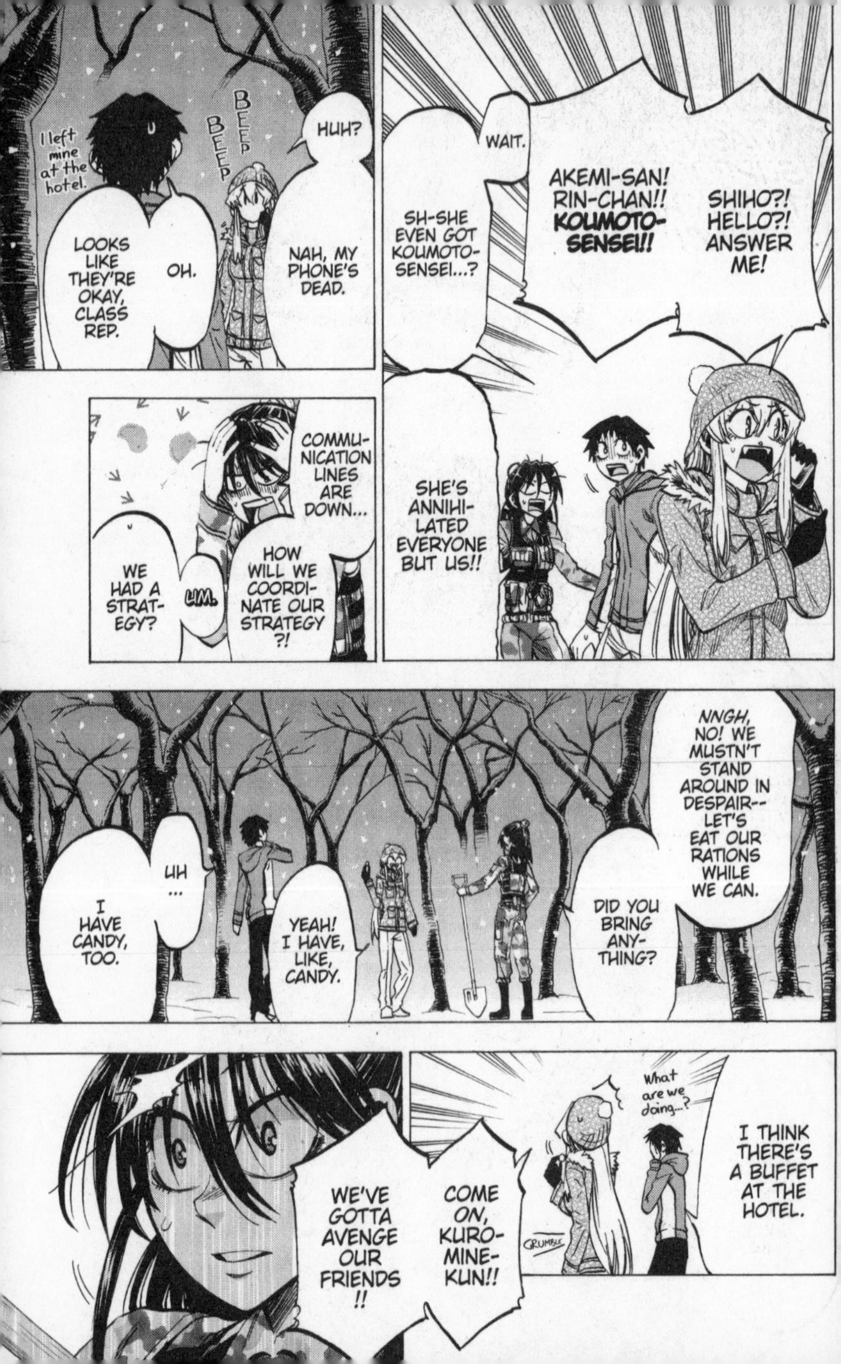
SHIHO?! HELLO?! ANSWER ME!
AKEMI-SAN! RIN-CHAN!! **KOUMOTO-SENSEI!!**
WAIT.
SH-SHE EVEN GOT KOUMOTO-SENSEI...?
SHE'S ANNIHILATED EVERYONE BUT US!!
HUH?
BEEP BEEP
NAH, MY PHONE'S DEAD.
I left mine at the hotel.
OH.
LOOKS LIKE THEY'RE OKAY, CLASS REP.
COMMUNICATION LINES ARE DOWN...
HOW WILL WE COORDINATE OUR STRATEGY?!
UM.
WE HAD A STRATEGY?
NNGH, NO! WE MUSTN'T STAND AROUND IN DESPAIR-- LET'S EAT OUR RATIONS WHILE WE CAN.
DID YOU BRING ANYTHING?
YEAH! I HAVE, LIKE, CANDY.
UH ...
I HAVE CANDY, TOO.
I THINK THERE'S A BUFFET AT THE HOTEL.
What are we doing...?
GRUMBLE
COME ON, KUROMINE-KUN!!
WE'VE GOTTA AVENGE OUR FRIENDS!!

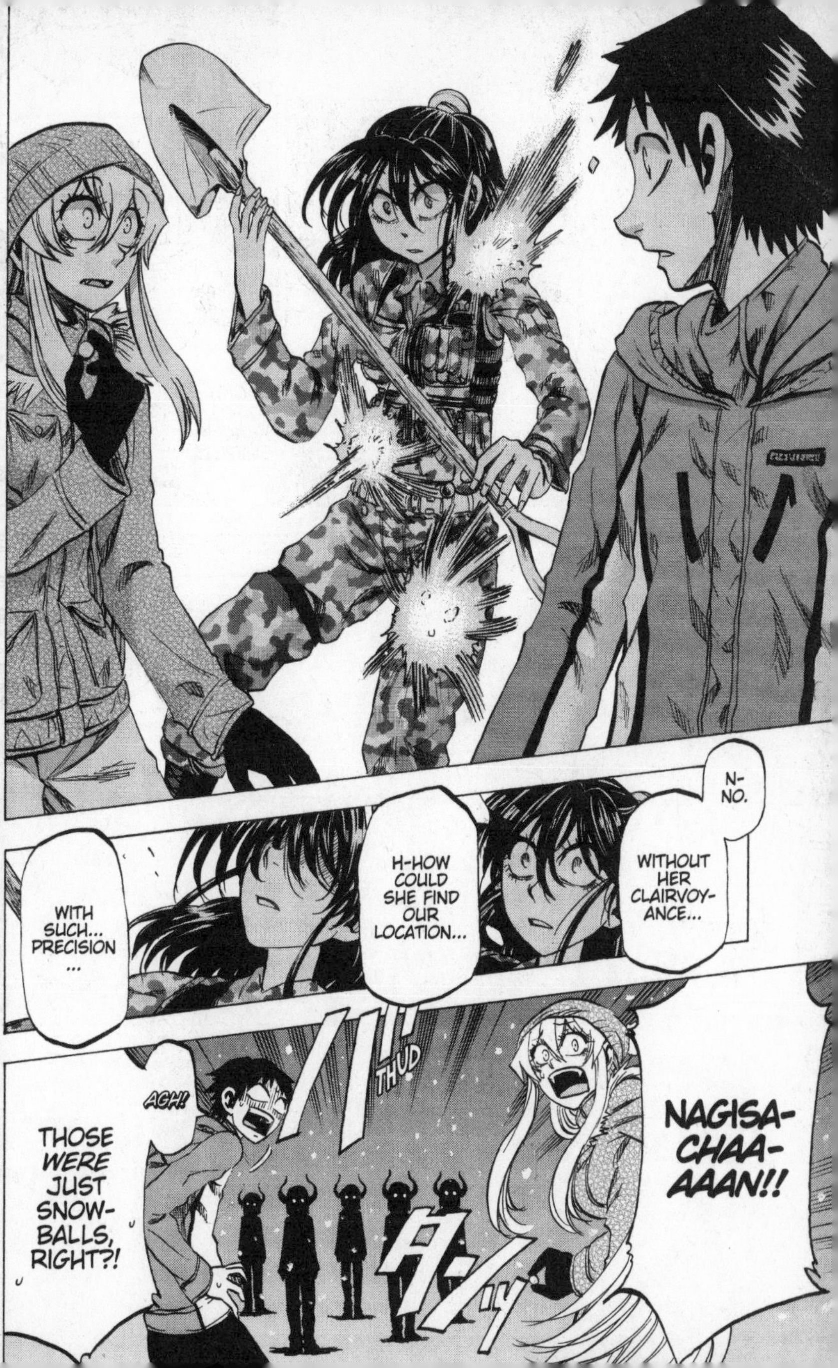
N- NO.
WITHOUT HER CLAIRVOY-ANCE...
H-HOW COULD SHE FIND OUR LOCATION...
WITH SUCH... PRECISION ...
NAGISA-CHAAA-AAAN!!
THUD
AGH!
THOSE WERE JUST SNOW-BALLS, RIGHT?!
タッ

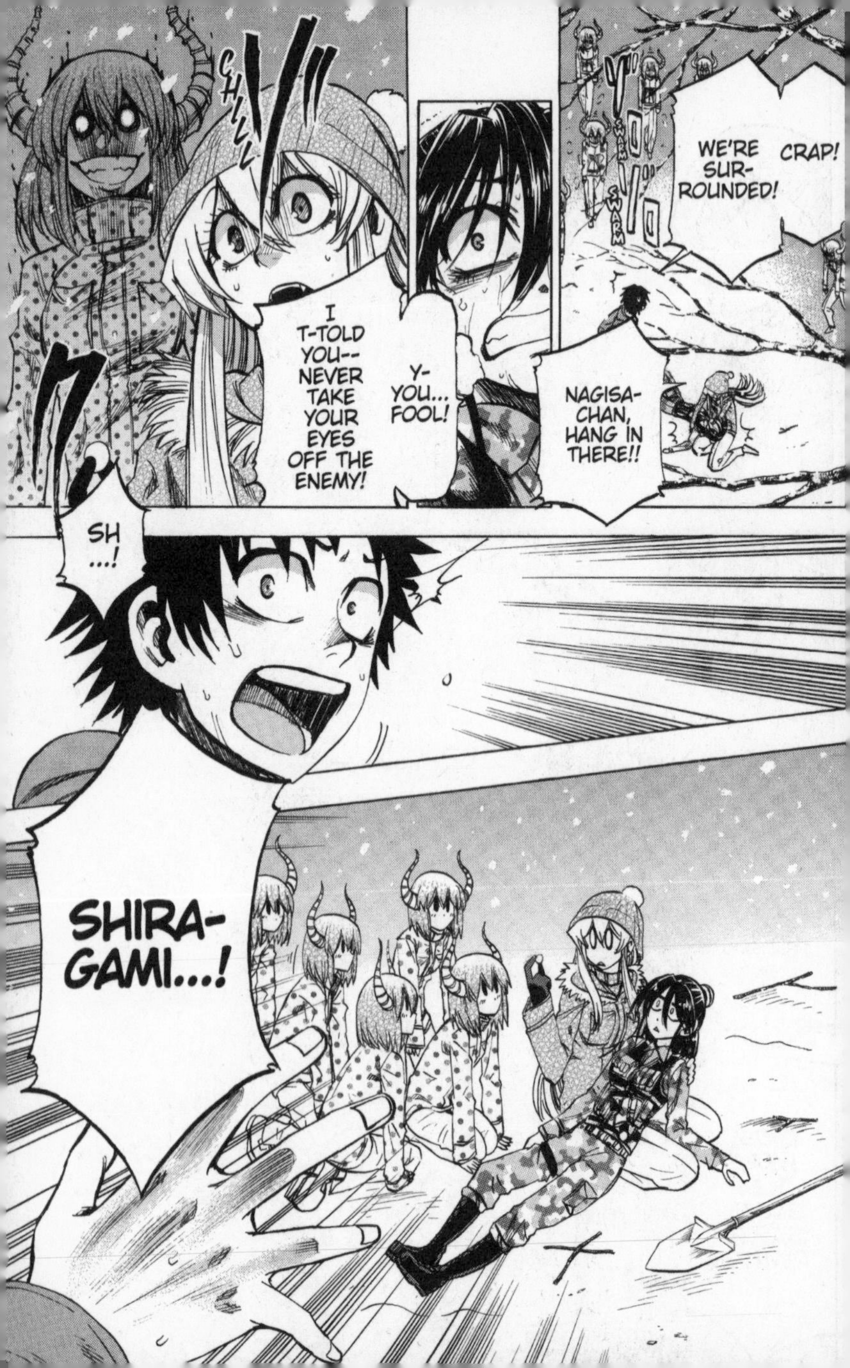
CRAP!
WE'RE SURROUNDED!
SWARM
SWARM
NAGISA-CHAN, HANG IN THERE!!
Y-YOU... FOOL!
CHILL
I T-TOLD YOU-- NEVER TAKE YOUR EYES OFF THE ENEMY!
SH...!
SHIRA-GAMI...!

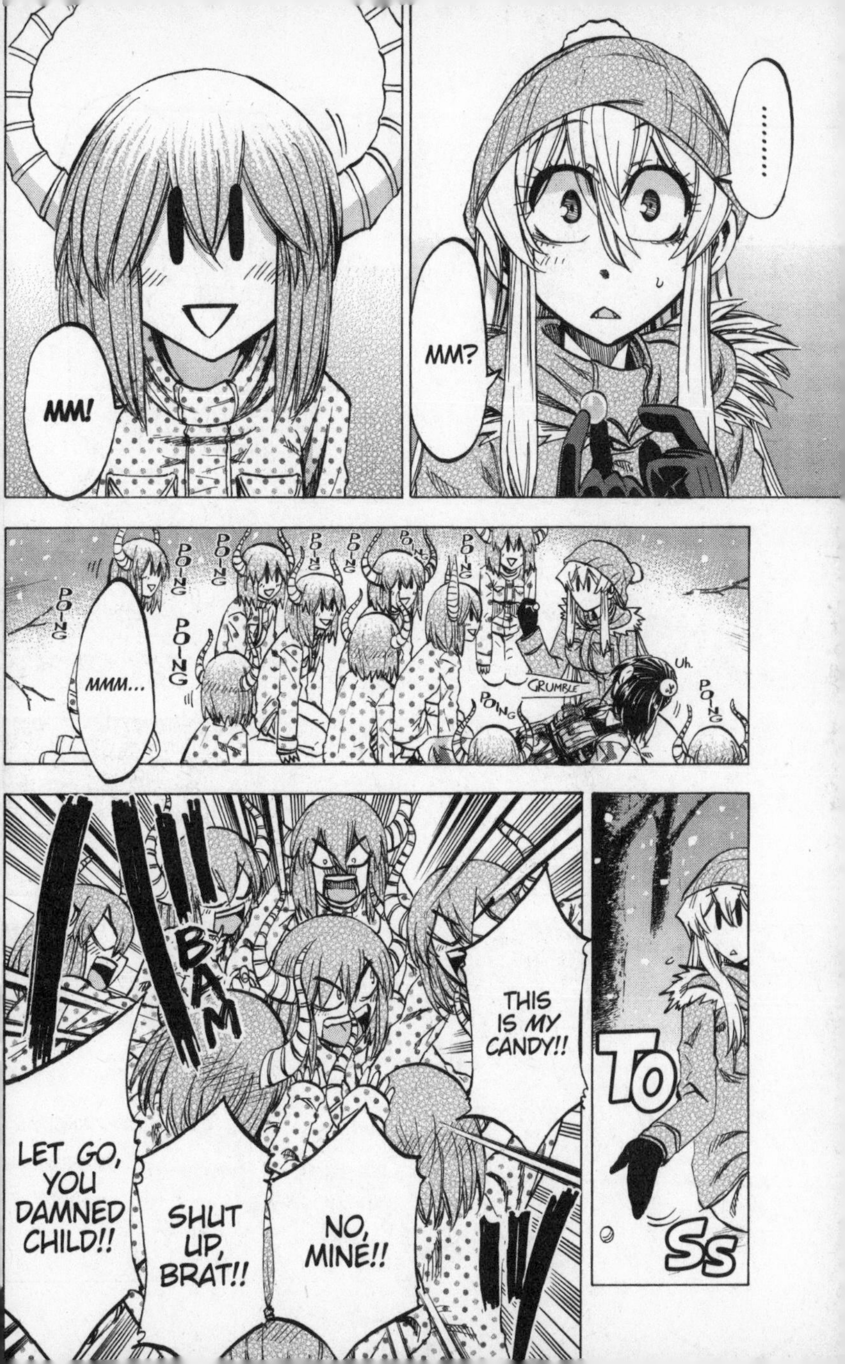
......
MM?
MM!
Uh.
POING
GRUMBLE
POING
POING
POING
POING
POING
POING
MMM...
POING
TO
Ss
THIS IS MY CANDY!!
BAM
NO, MINE!!
SHUT UP, BRAT!!
LET GO, YOU DAMNED CHILD!!

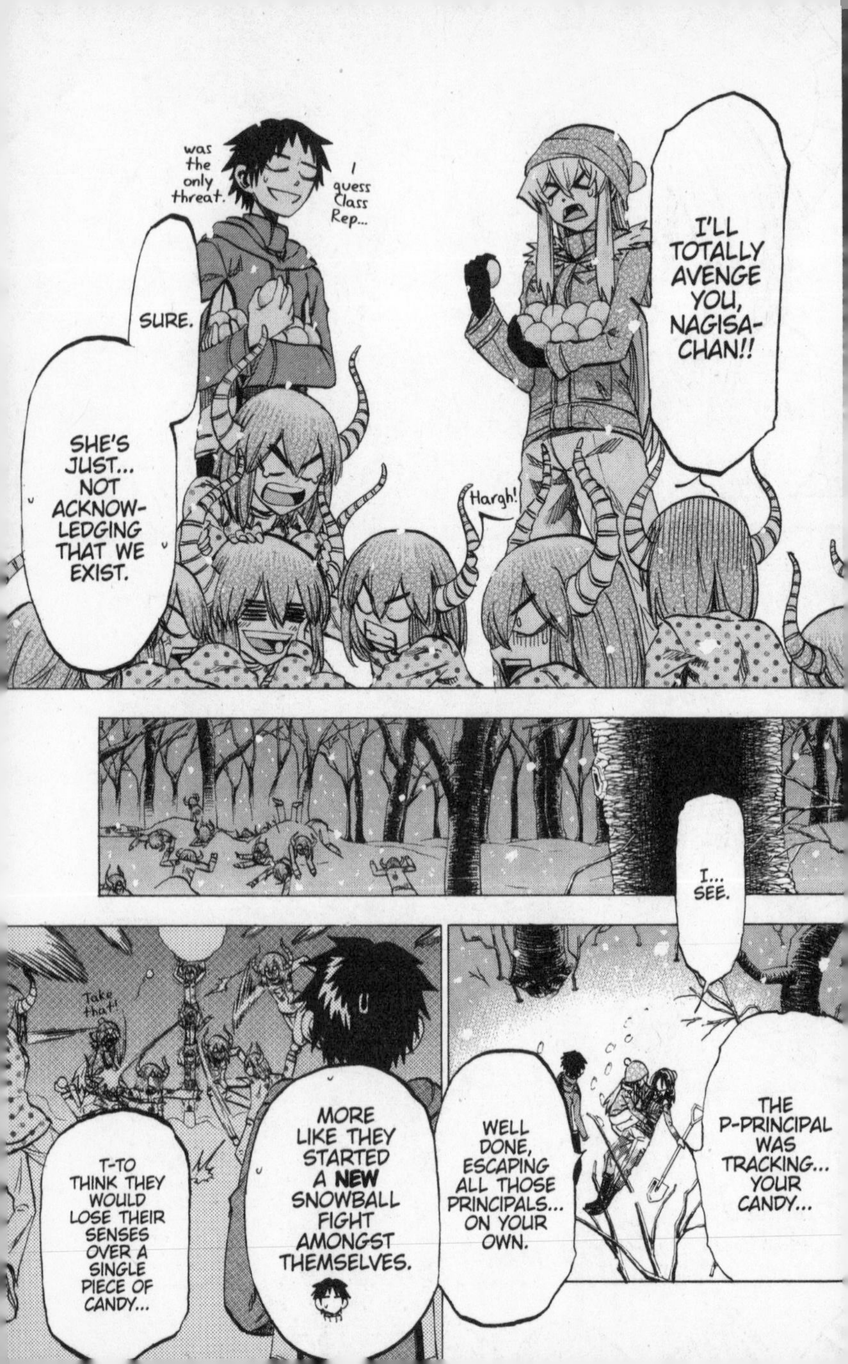
I'LL TOTALLY AVENGE YOU, NAGISA-CHAN!!
I guess Class Rep...
was the only threat.
SURE.
Hargh!
SHE'S JUST... NOT ACKNOW-LEDGING THAT WE EXIST.
I... SEE.
THE P-PRINCIPAL WAS TRACKING... YOUR CANDY...
WELL DONE, ESCAPING ALL THOSE PRINCIPALS... ON YOUR OWN.
MORE LIKE THEY STARTED A **NEW** SNOWBALL FIGHT AMONGST THEMSELVES.
Take that!
T-TO THINK THEY WOULD LOSE THEIR SENSES OVER A SINGLE PIECE OF CANDY...

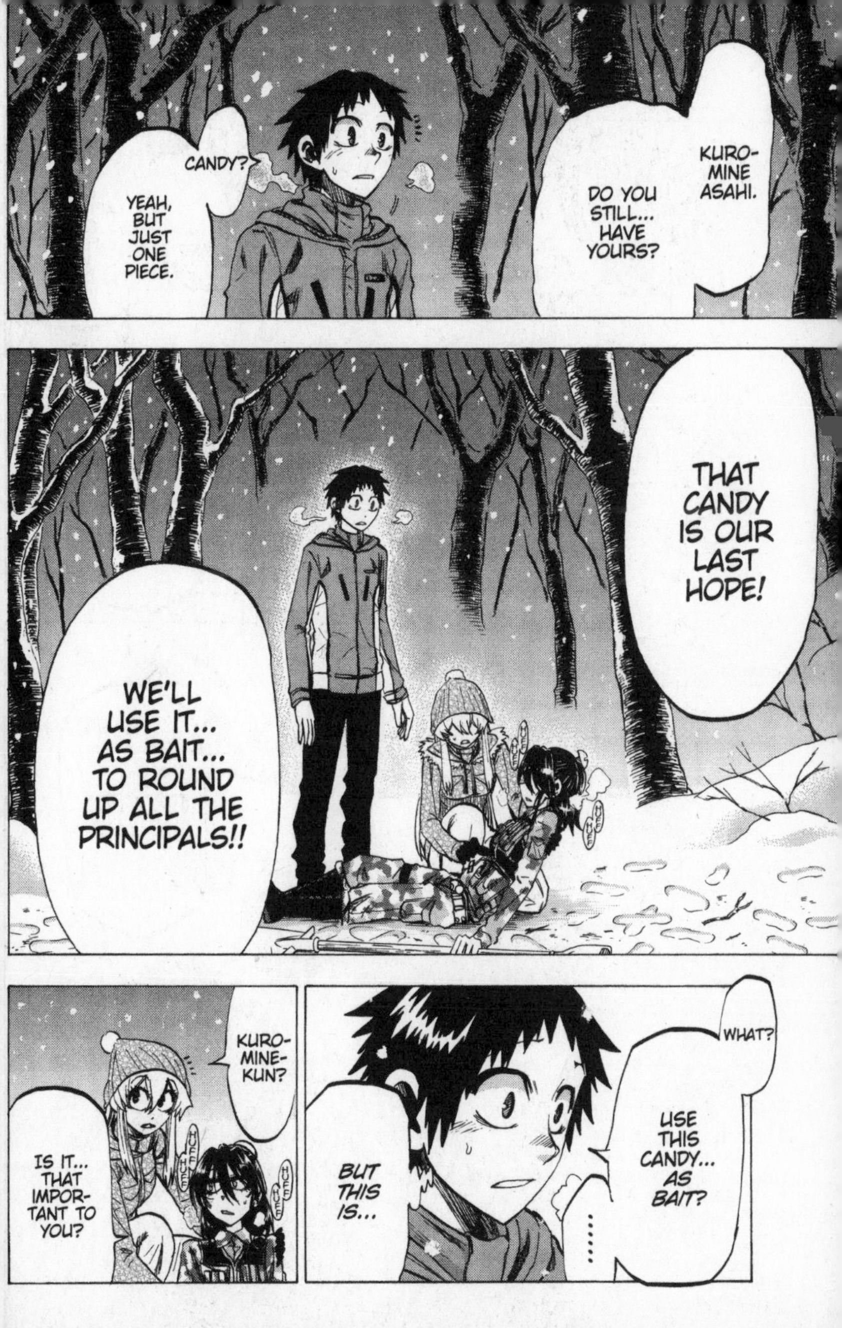
KURO-MINE ASAHI.
DO YOU STILL... HAVE YOURS?
CANDY?
YEAH, BUT JUST ONE PIECE.
THAT CANDY IS OUR LAST HOPE!
WE'LL USE IT... AS BAIT... TO ROUND UP ALL THE PRINCIPALS!!
WHAT?
USE THIS CANDY... AS BAIT?
......
BUT THIS IS...
KURO-MINE-KUN?
IS IT... THAT IMPORTANT TO YOU?

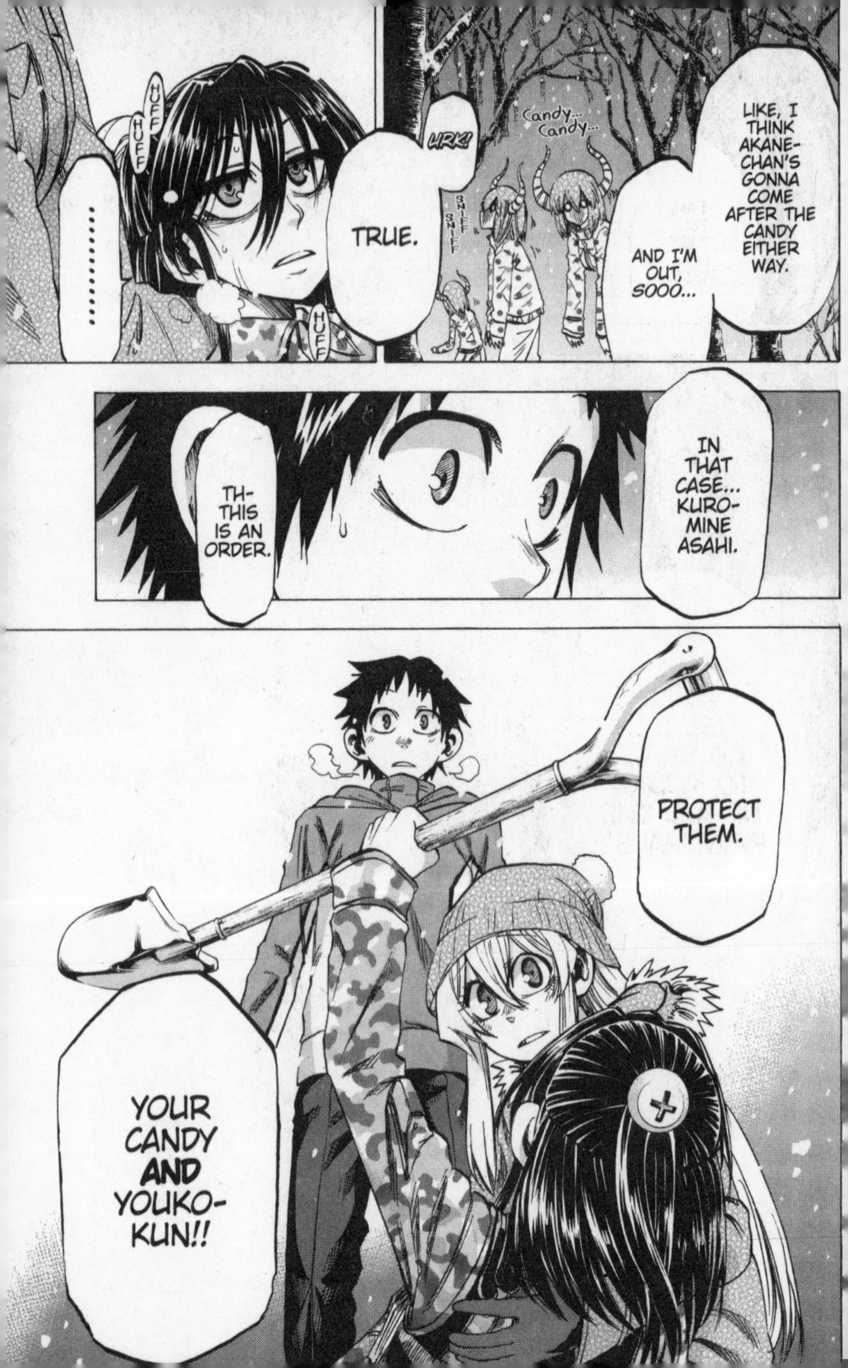
LIKE, I THINK AKANE-CHAN'S GONNA COME AFTER THE CANDY EITHER WAY.
AND I'M OUT, SOOO...
Candy... Candy...
SNIFF SNIFF
URK!
TRUE.
HUFF HUFF
......
HUFF HUFF
IN THAT CASE... KUROMINE ASAHI.
TH-THIS IS AN ORDER.
PROTECT THEM.
YOUR CANDY AND YOUKO-KUN!!

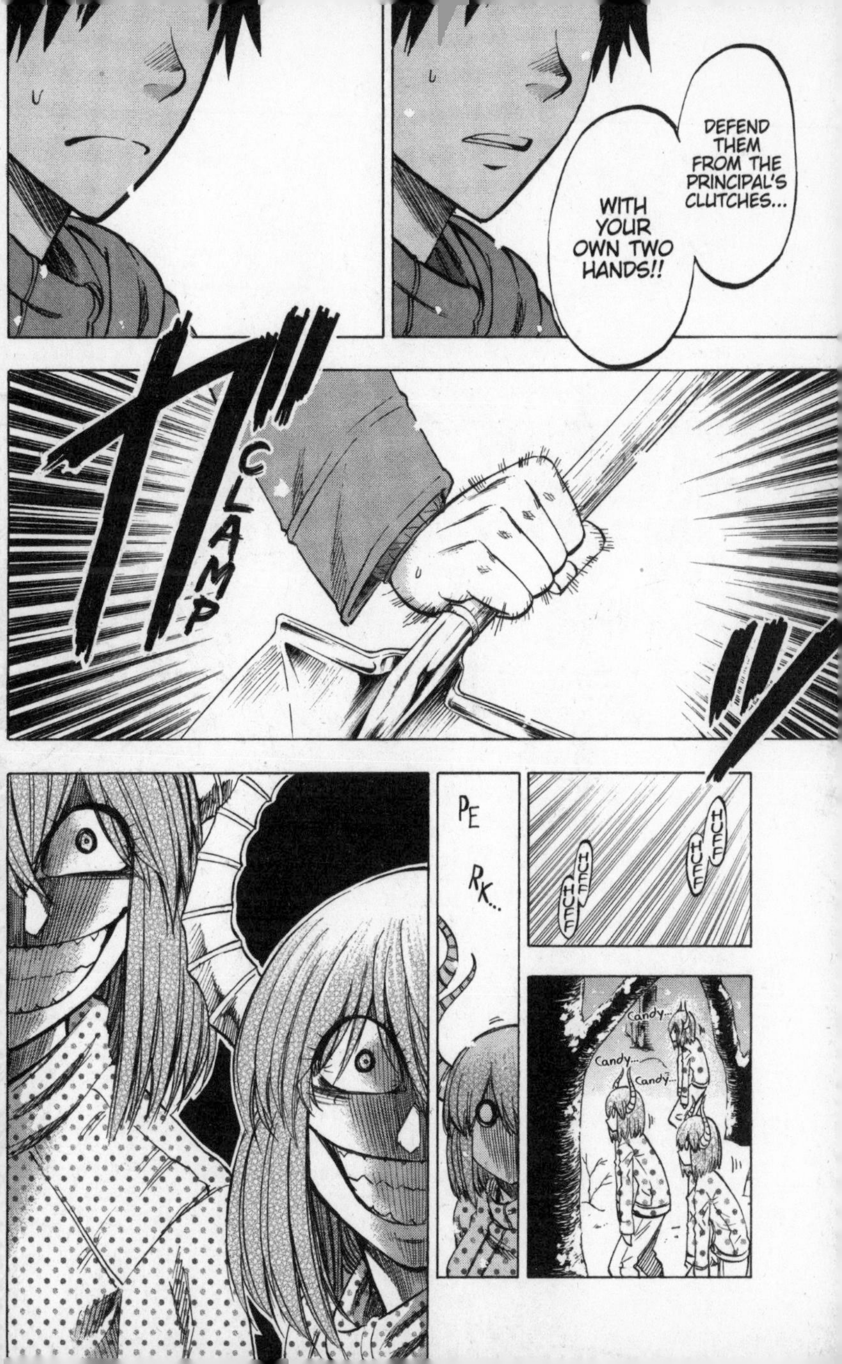
DEFEND THEM FROM THE PRINCIPAL'S CLUTCHES...
WITH YOUR OWN TWO HANDS!!
CLAMP
HUFF HUFF
HUFF HUFF
Candy...
Candy...
Candy...
PERK...

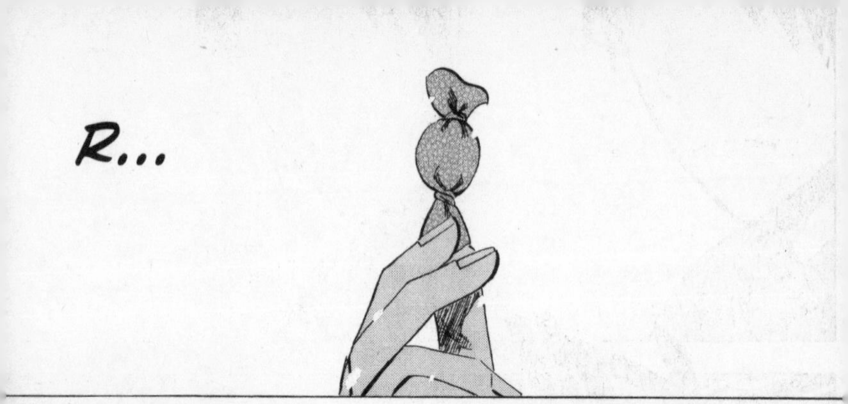
R...

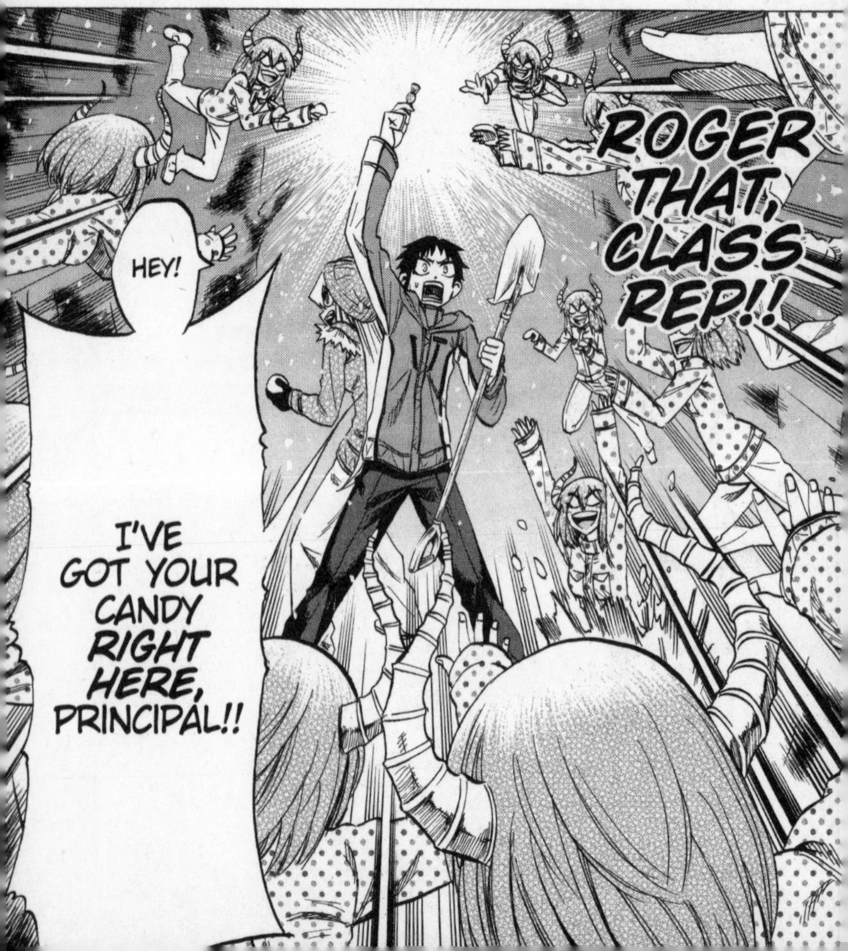
ROGER THAT, CLASS REP!!
HEY!
I'VE GOT YOUR CANDY RIGHT HERE, PRINCIPAL!!

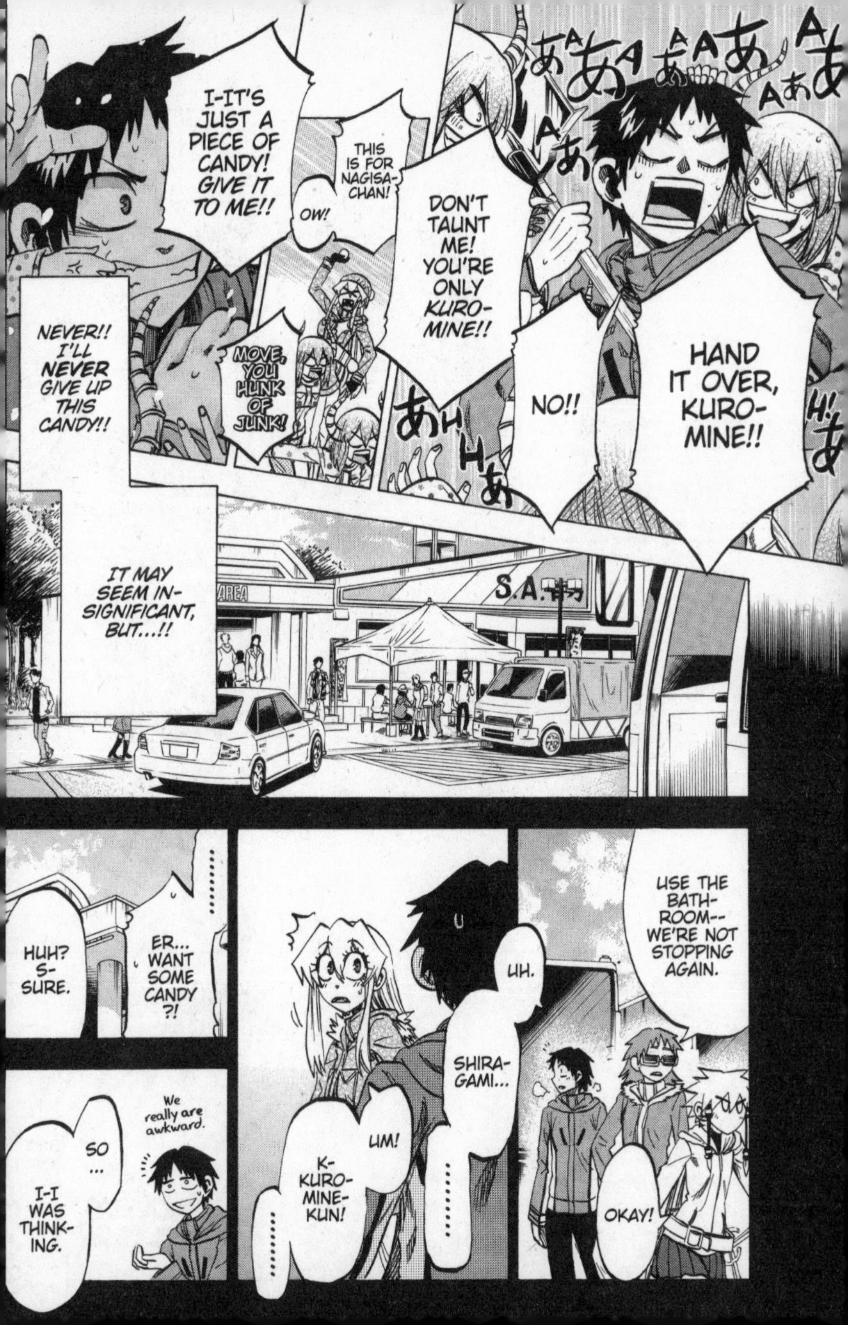
HAND IT OVER, KURO-MINE!!
NO!!
DON'T TAUNT ME! YOU'RE ONLY KURO-MINE!!
THIS IS FOR NAGISA-CHAN!
OW!
MOVE, YOU HUNK OF JUNK!
I-IT'S JUST A PIECE OF CANDY! GIVE IT TO ME!!
NEVER!! I'LL NEVER GIVE UP THIS CANDY!!
S.A.
AREA
IT MAY SEEM IN-SIGNIFICANT, BUT...!!
USE THE BATH-ROOM-- WE'RE NOT STOPPING AGAIN.
OKAY!
UH.
SHIRA-GAMI...
UM!
K-KURO-MINE-KUN!
......
......
......
ER... WANT SOME CANDY ?!
HUH? S-SURE.
We really are awkward.
SO ...
I-I WAS THINK-ING.

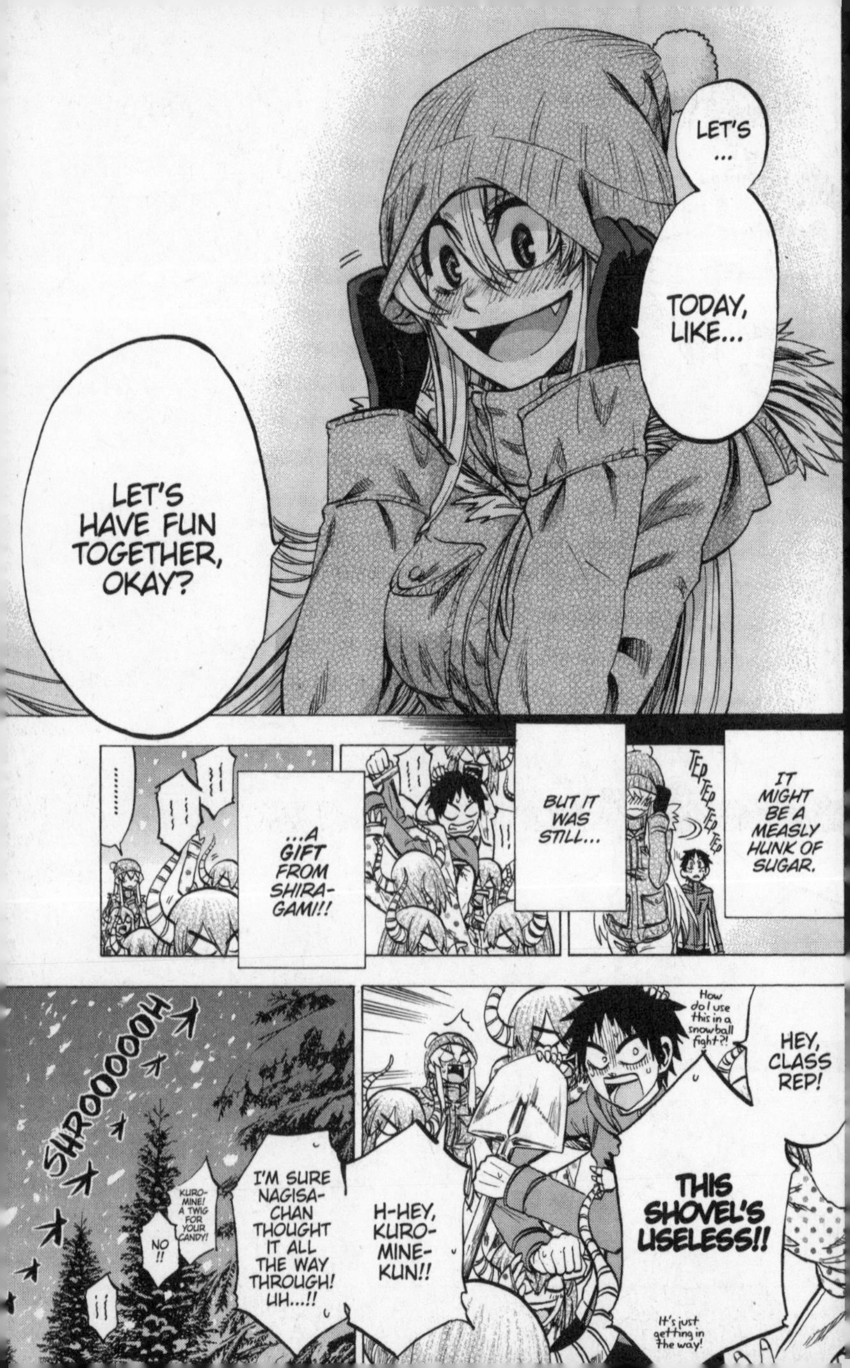
LET'S ...
TODAY, LIKE...
LET'S HAVE FUN TOGETHER, OKAY?
IT MIGHT BE A MEASLY HUNK OF SUGAR.
TEP TEP TEP TEP
BUT IT WAS STILL...
!!
...A GIFT FROM SHIRA-GAMI!!
......
HEY, CLASS REP!
How do I use this in a snowball fight?!
THIS SHOVEL'S USELESS!!
It's just getting in the way!
H-HEY, KURO-MINE-KUN!!
I'M SURE NAGISA-CHAN THOUGHT IT ALL THE WAY THROUGH! UH...!!
SHROOOOOOH
KURO-MINE! A TWIG FOR YOUR CANDY!
NO!!
!!

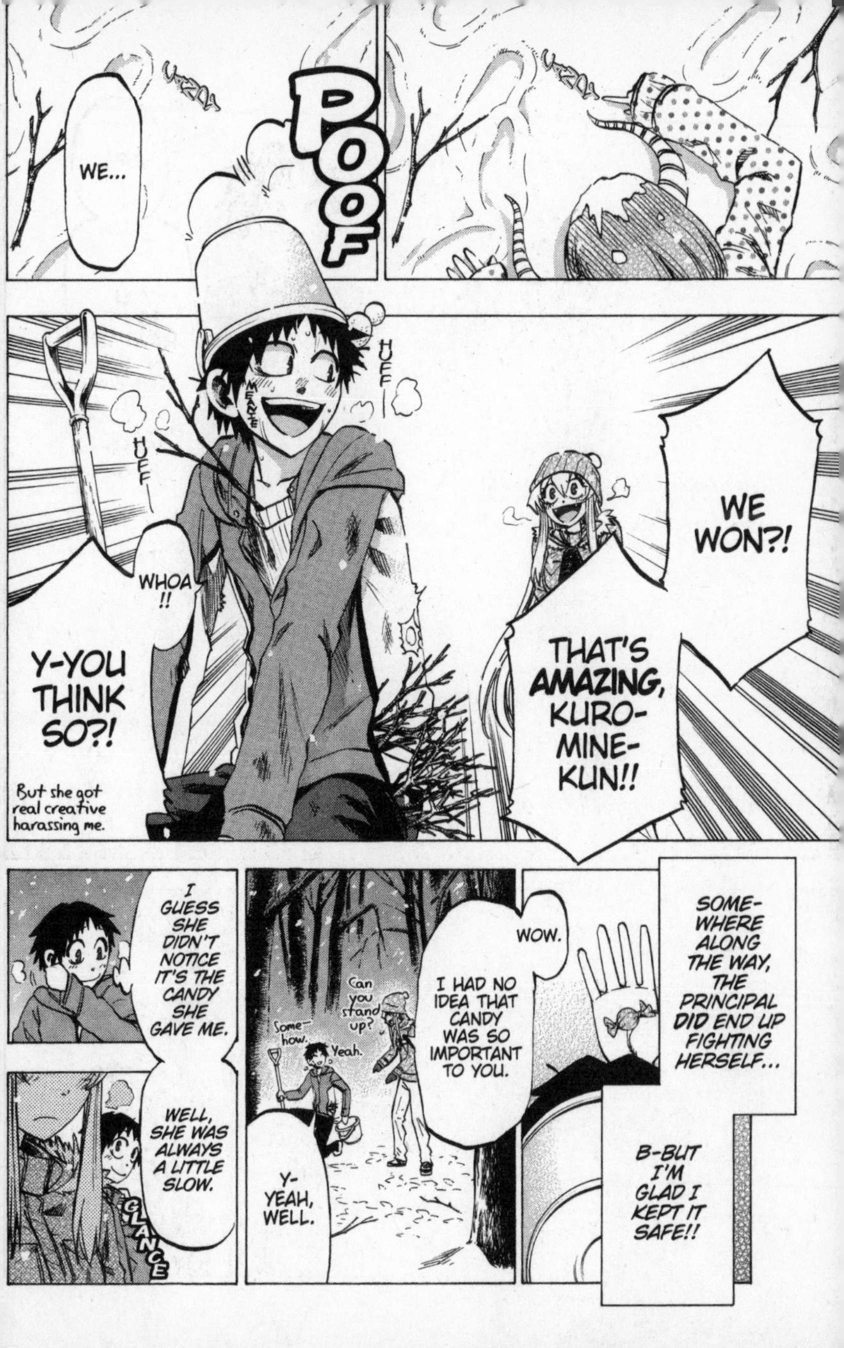
POOF
WE...
WE WON?!
THAT'S AMAZING, KURO-MINE-KUN!!
HUFF
HUFF
WHOA!!
Y-YOU THINK SO?!
But she got real creative harassing me.
SOME-WHERE ALONG THE WAY, THE PRINCIPAL DID END UP FIGHTING HERSELF...
B-BUT I'M GLAD I KEPT IT SAFE!!
WOW.
I HAD NO IDEA THAT CANDY WAS SO IMPORTANT TO YOU.
Can you stand up?
Some-how.
Yeah.
Y-YEAH, WELL.
I GUESS SHE DIDN'T NOTICE IT'S THE CANDY SHE GAVE ME.
WELL, SHE WAS ALWAYS A LITTLE SLOW.
GLANCE

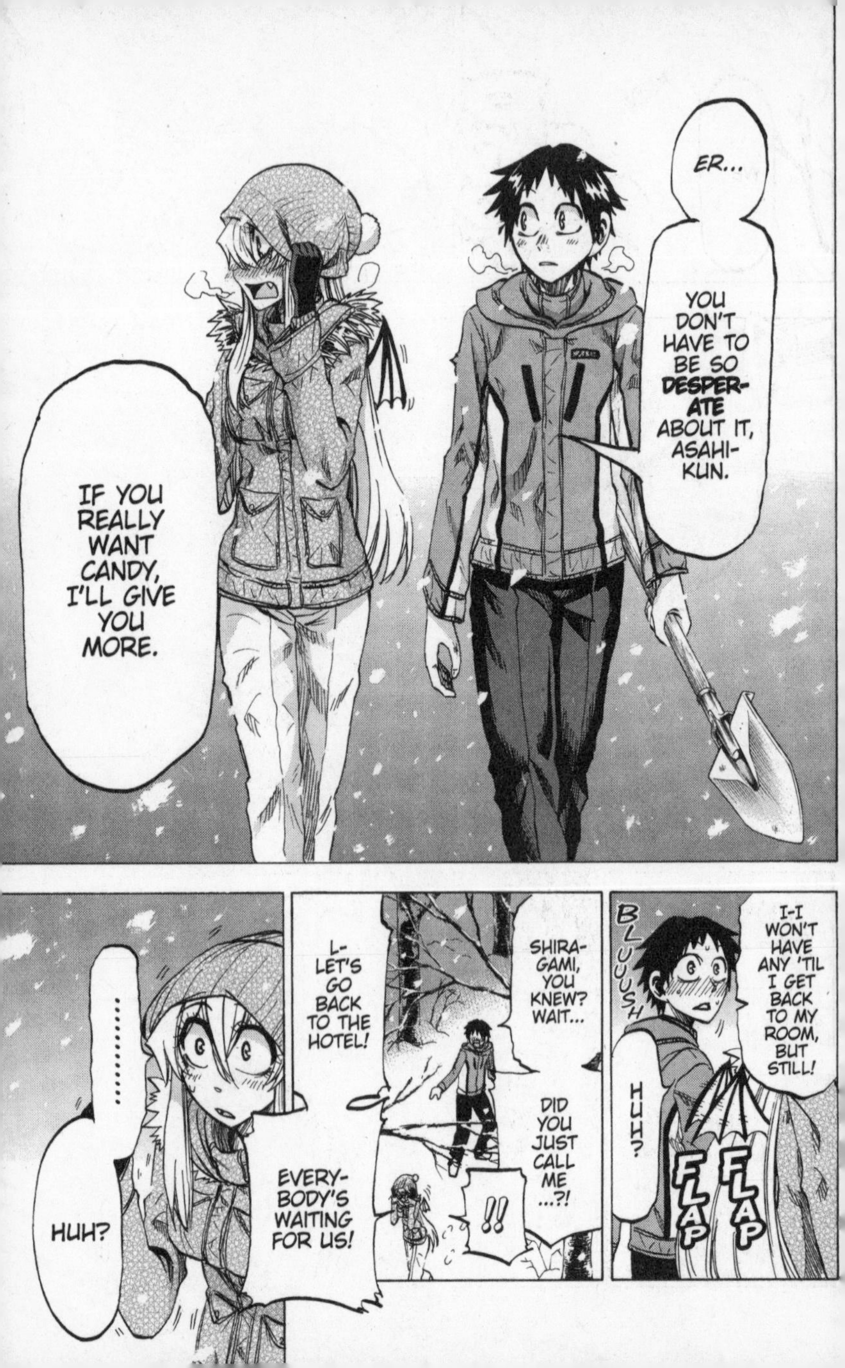
ER...
YOU DON'T HAVE TO BE SO DESPERATE ABOUT IT, ASAHI-KUN.
IF YOU REALLY WANT CANDY, I'LL GIVE YOU MORE.
I-I WON'T HAVE ANY 'TIL I GET BACK TO MY ROOM, BUT STILL!
BLUUUSH
HUH?
FLAP FLAP
SHIRAGAMI, YOU KNEW? WAIT...
DID YOU JUST CALL ME ...?!
!!
L-LET'S GO BACK TO THE HOTEL!
EVERYBODY'S WAITING FOR US!
......
HUH?

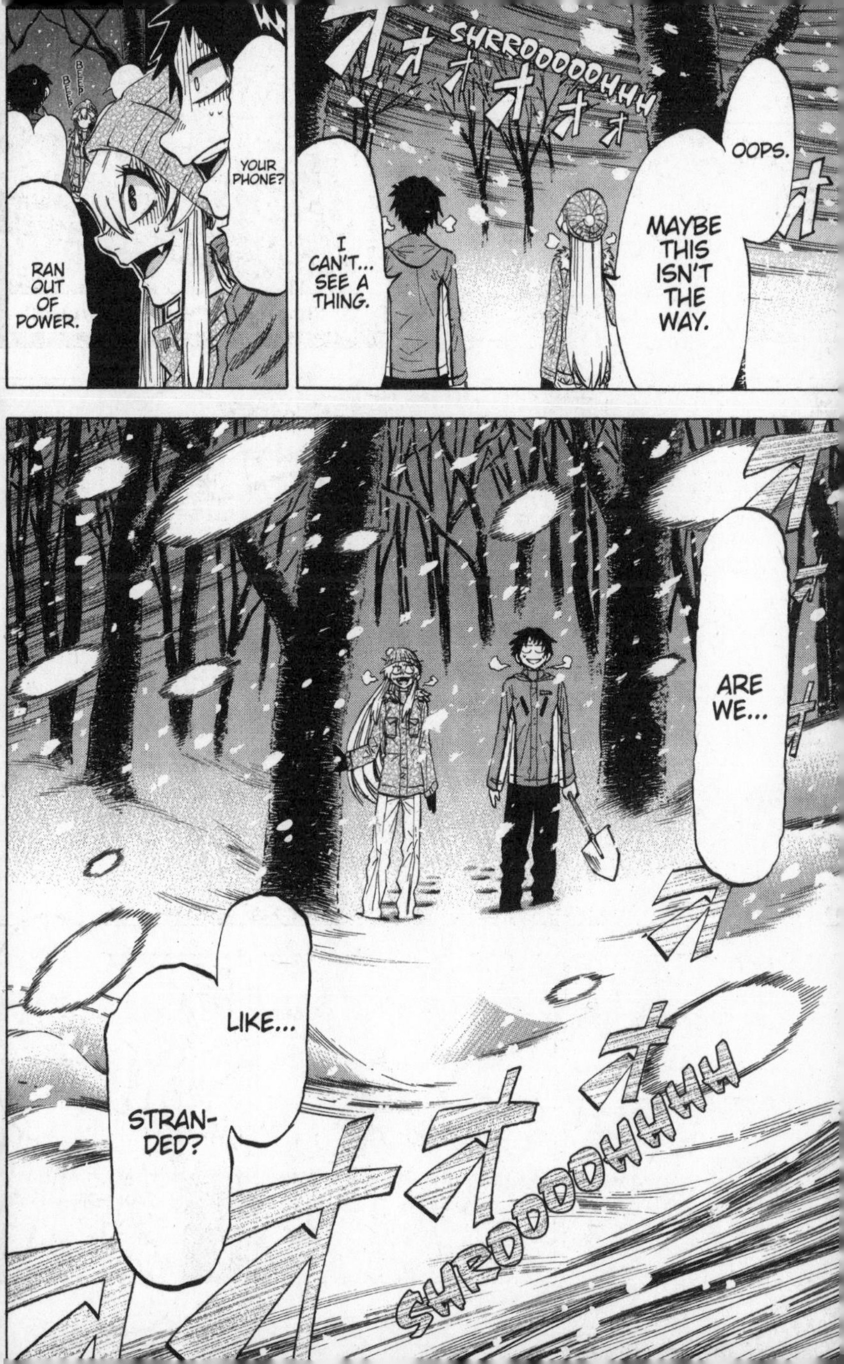
SHRROOOOOOHHH
OOPS.
MAYBE THIS ISN'T THE WAY.
I CAN'T... SEE A THING.
BEEP BEEP
YOUR PHONE?
RAN OUT OF POWER.
ARE WE...
LIKE...
STRAN-DED?
SHROOOOOHHHHH

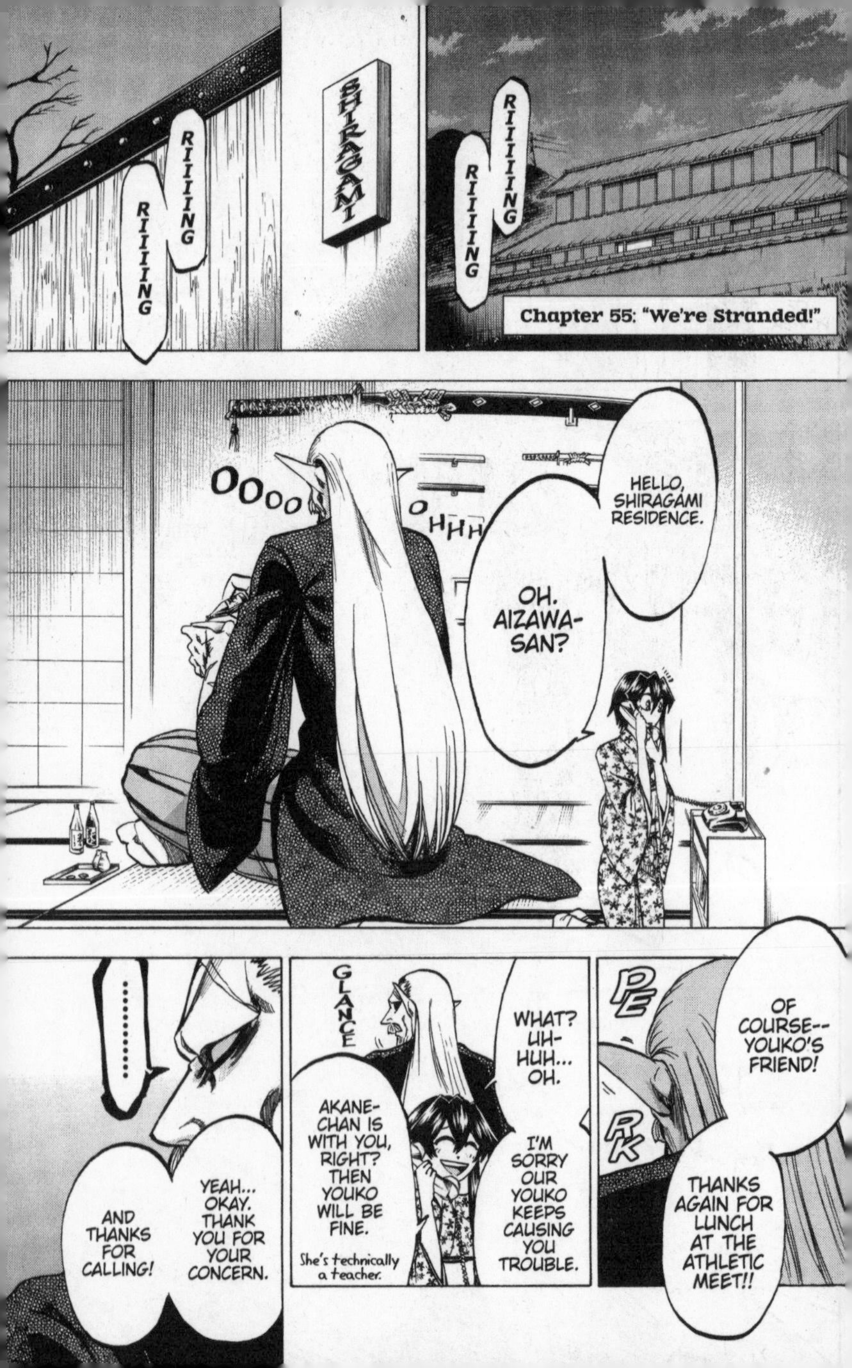
RIIIIING
RIIIIING
Chapter 55: "We're Stranded!"
SHIRAGAMI
RIIIING
RIIIIING
HELLO, SHIRAGAMI RESIDENCE.
OOOOOHHH
OH. AIZAWA-SAN?
OF COURSE--YOUKO'S FRIEND!
PERK
THANKS AGAIN FOR LUNCH AT THE ATHLETIC MEET!!
WHAT? UH-HUH... OH.
GLANCE
I'M SORRY OUR YOUKO KEEPS CAUSING YOU TROUBLE.
AKANE-CHAN IS WITH YOU, RIGHT? THEN YOUKO WILL BE FINE.
She's technically a teacher.
....
YEAH... OKAY. THANK YOU FOR YOUR CONCERN.
AND THANKS FOR CALLING!

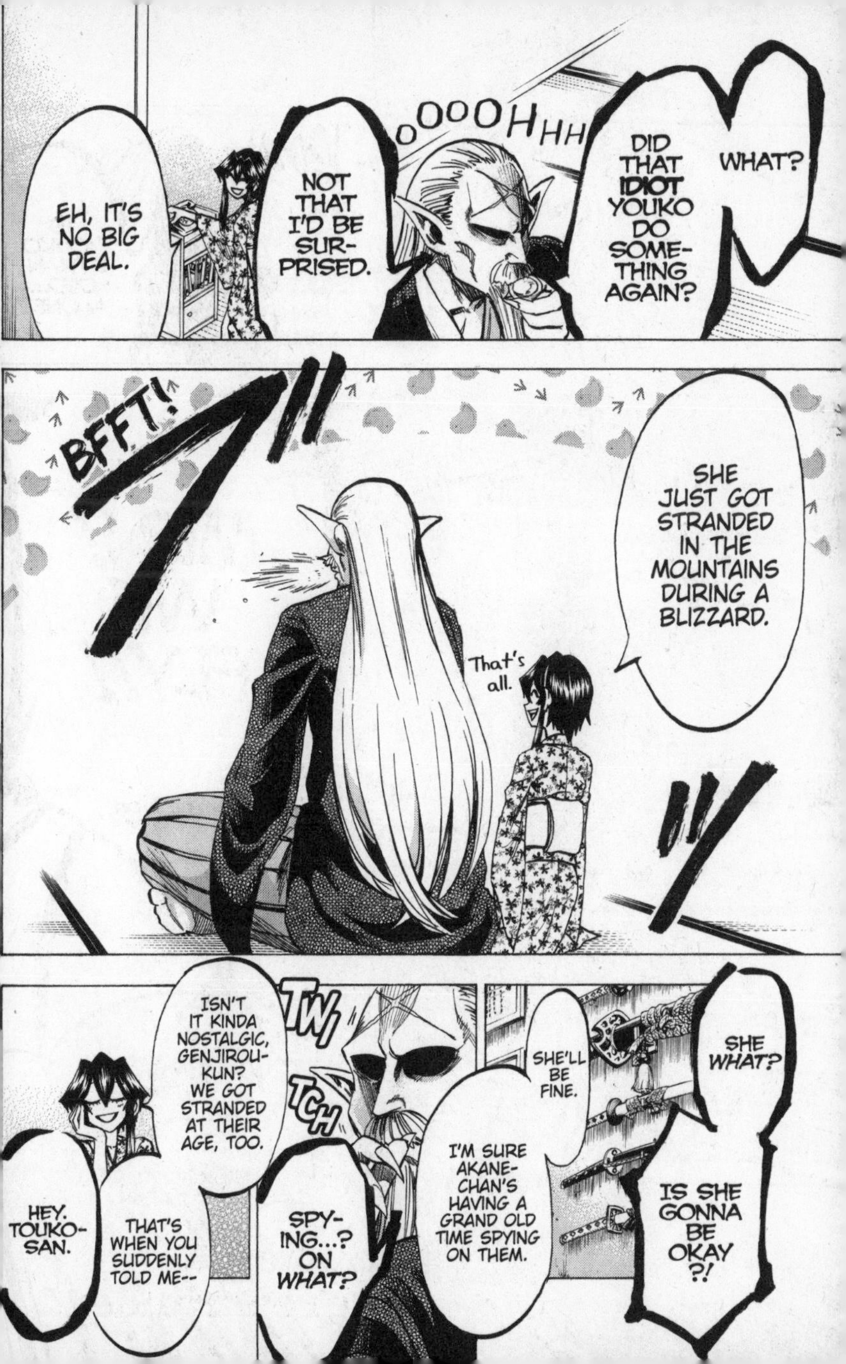
WHAT?
DID THAT IDIOT YOUKO DO SOME-THING AGAIN?
oOOOOHHH
NOT THAT I'D BE SUR-PRISED.
EH, IT'S NO BIG DEAL.
SHE JUST GOT STRANDED IN THE MOUNTAINS DURING A BLIZZARD.
That's all.
BFFT!
SHE WHAT?
IS SHE GONNA BE OKAY?!
SHE'LL BE FINE.
I'M SURE AKANE-CHAN'S HAVING A GRAND OLD TIME SPYING ON THEM.
TWITCH
SPY-ING...? ON WHAT?
ISN'T IT KINDA NOSTALGIC, GENJIROU-KUN? WE GOT STRANDED AT THEIR AGE, TOO.
THAT'S WHEN YOU SUDDENLY TOLD ME--
HEY. TOUKO-SAN.

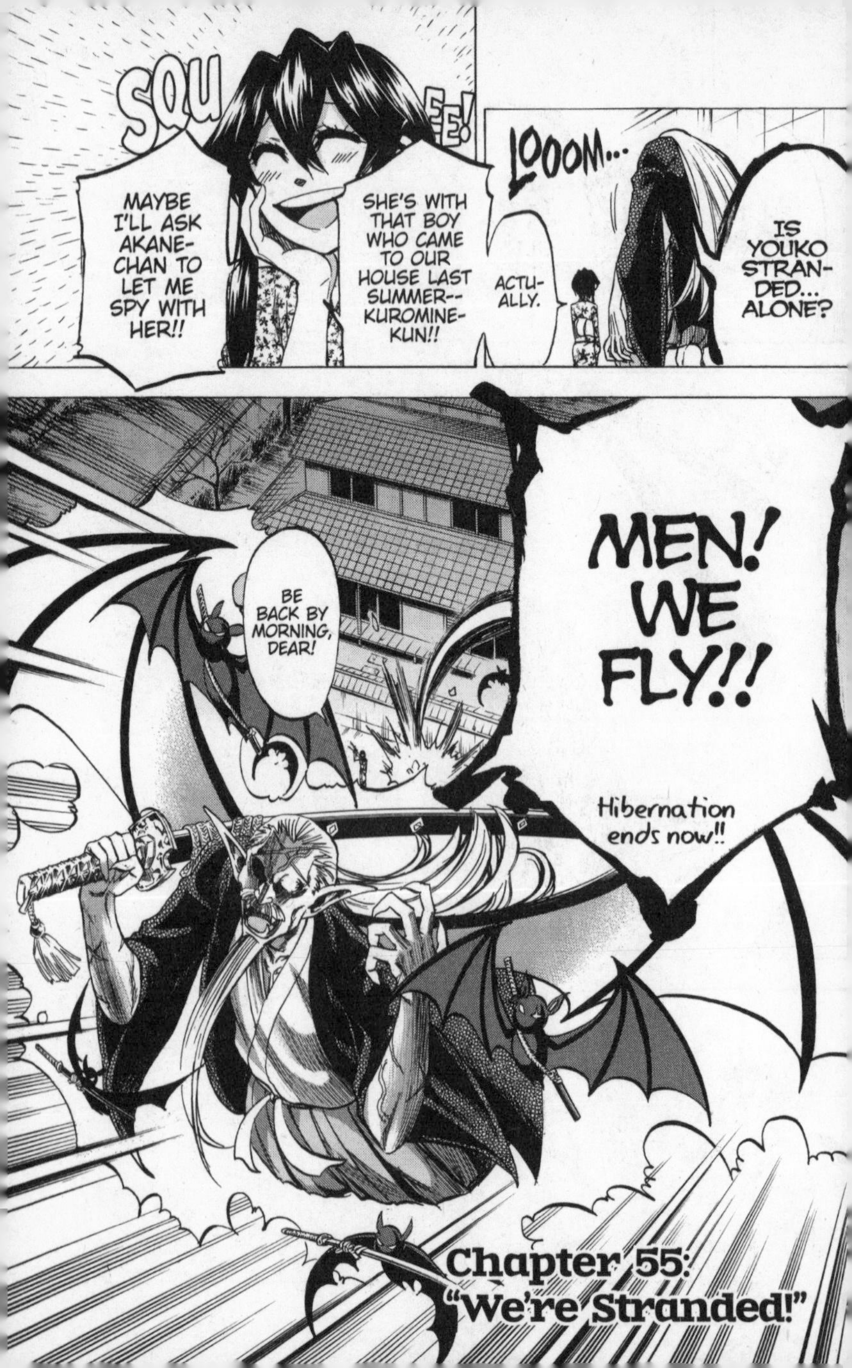
IS YOUKO STRANDED... ALONE?
LOOOM...
ACTU-ALLY.
SHE'S WITH THAT BOY WHO CAME TO OUR HOUSE LAST SUMMER-- KUROMINE-KUN!!
SQU EE!
MAYBE I'LL ASK AKANE-CHAN TO LET ME SPY WITH HER!!
MEN! WE FLY!!
Hibernation ends now!!
BE BACK BY MORNING, DEAR!
Chapter 55: "We're Stranded!"

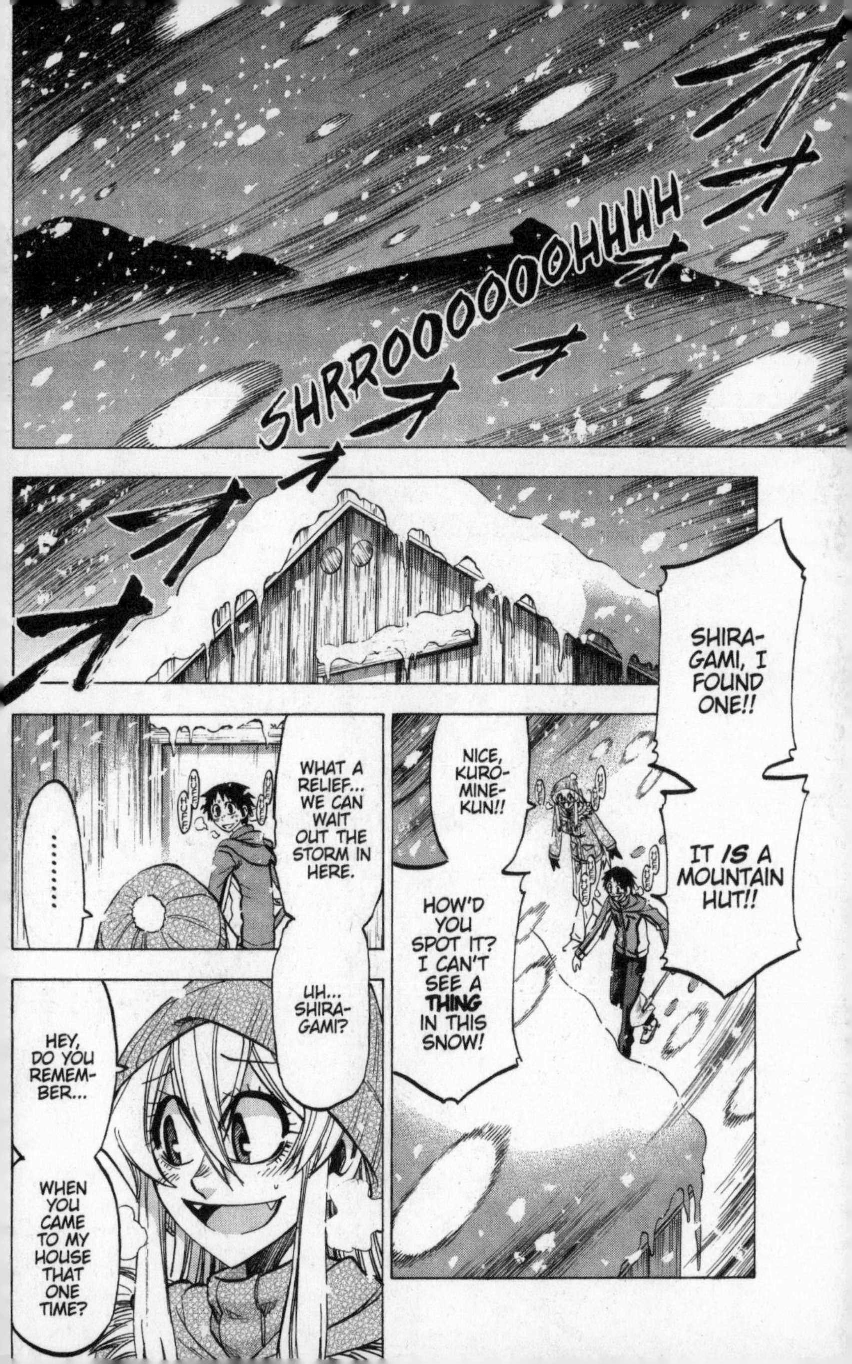
SHRROOOOOOHHHH
SHIRA-GAMI, I FOUND ONE!!
IT *IS* A MOUNTAIN HUT!!
NICE, KURO-MINE-KUN!!
HOW'D YOU SPOT IT? I CAN'T SEE A **THING** IN THIS SNOW!
WHAT A RELIEF... WE CAN WAIT OUT THE STORM IN HERE.
......
UH... SHIRA-GAMI?
HEY, DO YOU REMEMBER...
WHEN YOU CAME TO MY HOUSE THAT ONE TIME?

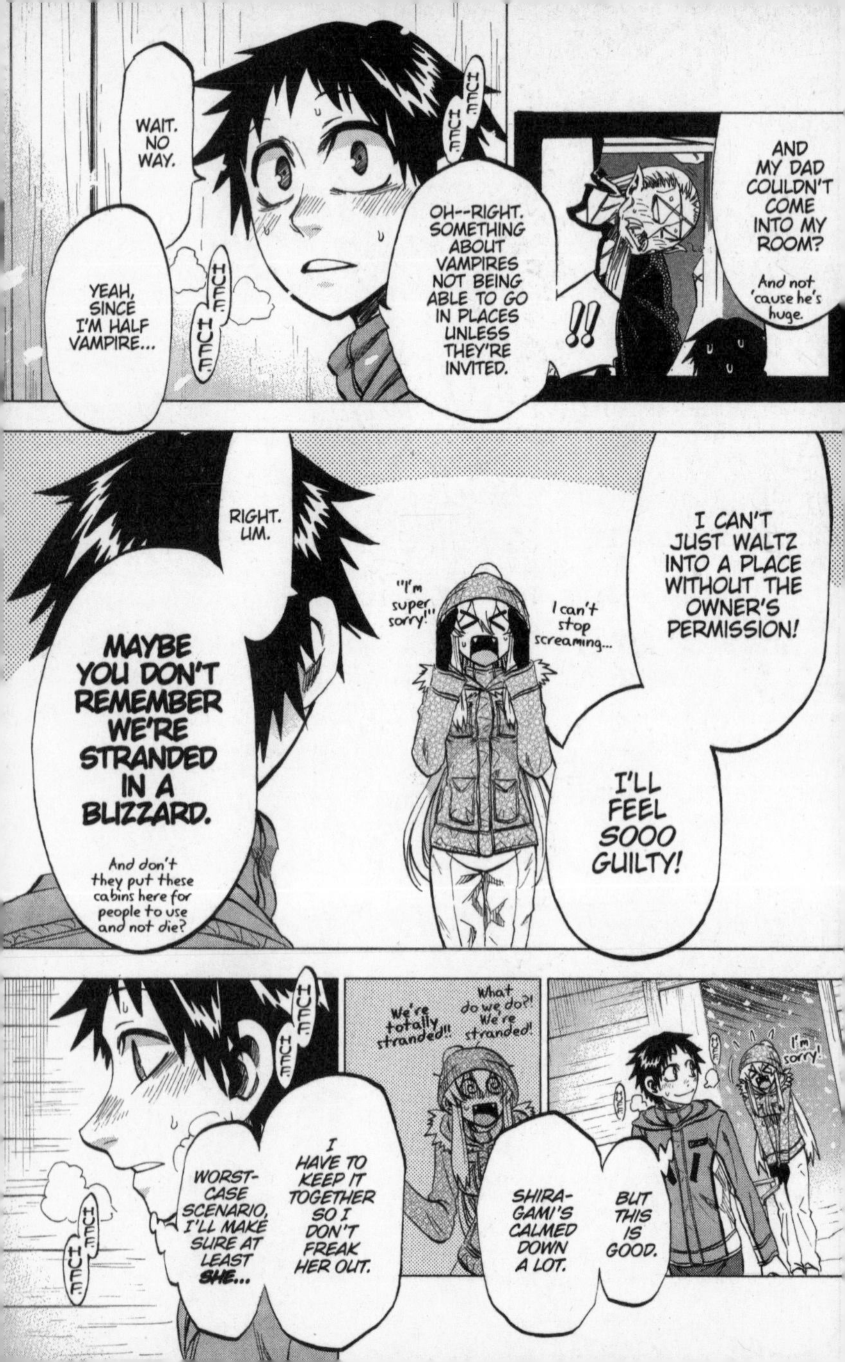
AND MY DAD COULDN'T COME INTO MY ROOM?
And not 'cause he's huge.
!!
HUFF HUFF
WAIT. NO WAY.
OH--RIGHT. SOMETHING ABOUT VAMPIRES NOT BEING ABLE TO GO IN PLACES UNLESS THEY'RE INVITED.
HUFF HUFF
YEAH, SINCE I'M HALF VAMPIRE...
I CAN'T JUST WALTZ INTO A PLACE WITHOUT THE OWNER'S PERMISSION!
I'LL FEEL SOOO GUILTY!
I can't stop screaming...
"I'm super sorry!"
RIGHT. UM.
MAYBE YOU DON'T REMEMBER WE'RE STRANDED IN A BLIZZARD.
And don't they put these cabins here for people to use and not die?
I'm sorry!
BUT THIS IS GOOD.
SHIRA-GAMI'S CALMED DOWN A LOT.
What do we do?! We're stranded!
We're totally stranded!!
HUFF HUFF
I HAVE TO KEEP IT TOGETHER SO I DON'T FREAK HER OUT.
WORST-CASE SCENARIO, I'LL MAKE SURE AT LEAST SHE...
HUFF HUFF

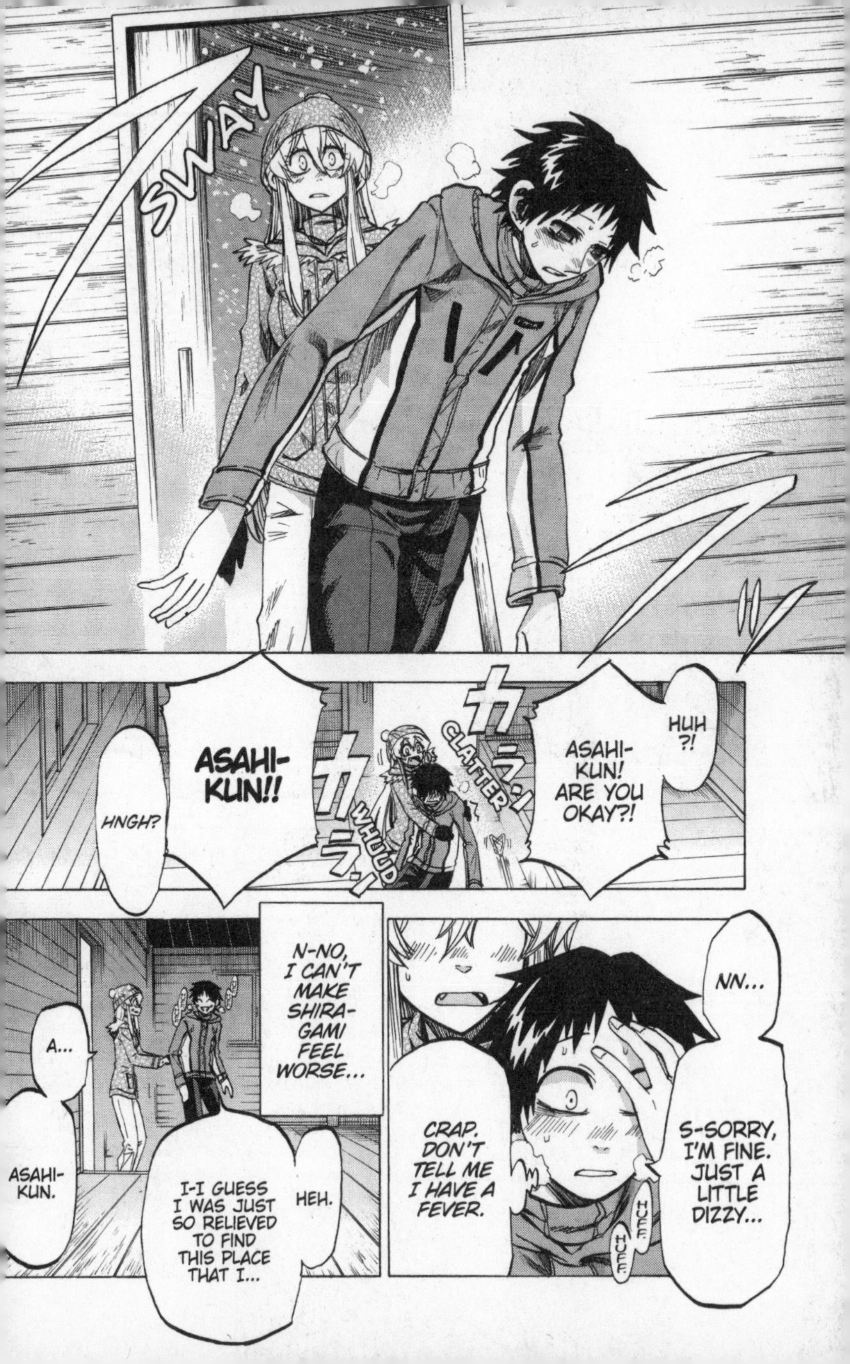
SWAY
HUH ?!
ASAHI-KUN! ARE YOU OKAY?!
カラ
CLATTER
カラ
WHUUD
ASAHI-KUN!!
HNGH?
NN...
S-SORRY, I'M FINE. JUST A LITTLE DIZZY...
HUFF HUFF
CRAP. DON'T TELL ME I HAVE A FEVER.
N-NO, I CAN'T MAKE SHIRA-GAMI FEEL WORSE...
HEH.
I-I GUESS I WAS JUST SO RELIEVED TO FIND THIS PLACE THAT I...
A...
ASAHI-KUN.

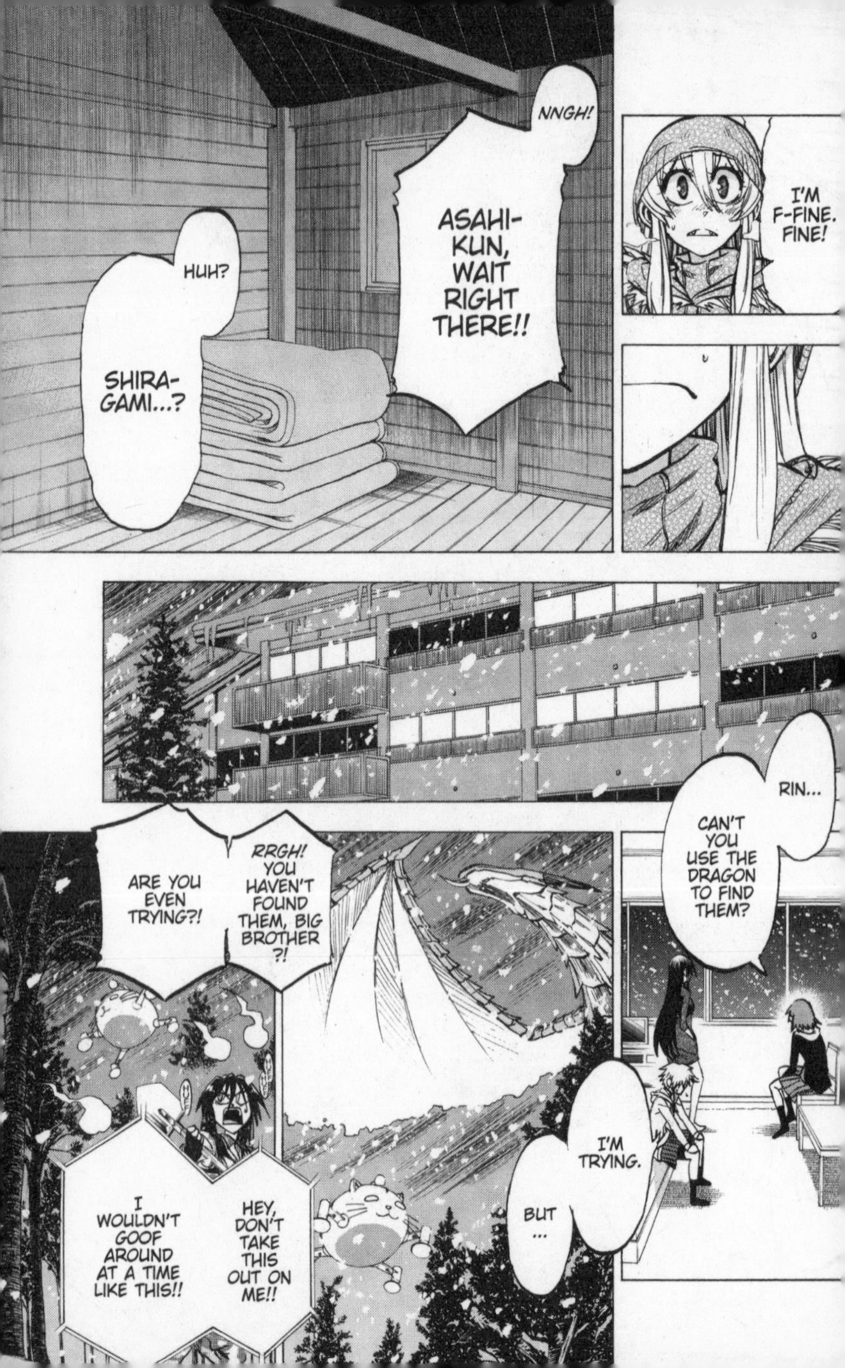
I'M F-FINE. FINE!
NNGH!
ASAHI-KUN, WAIT RIGHT THERE!!
HUH?
SHIRAGAMI...?
RIN...
CAN'T YOU USE THE DRAGON TO FIND THEM?
I'M TRYING.
BUT...
RRGH! YOU HAVEN'T FOUND THEM, BIG BROTHER?!
ARE YOU EVEN TRYING?!
HEY, DON'T TAKE THIS OUT ON ME!!
I WOULDN'T GOOF AROUND AT A TIME LIKE THIS!!

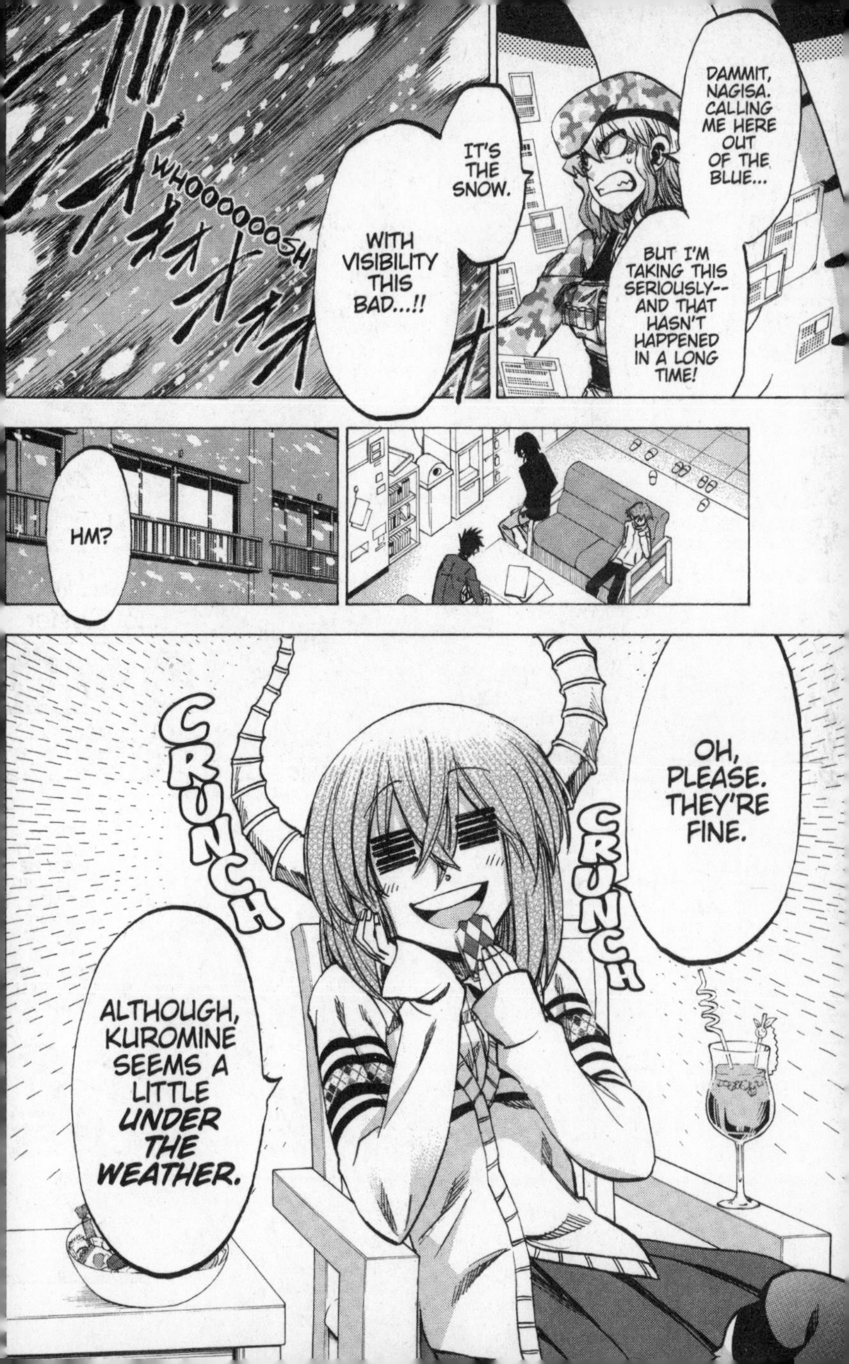
DAMMIT, NAGISA. CALLING ME HERE OUT OF THE BLUE...
BUT I'M TAKING THIS SERIOUSLY--AND THAT HASN'T HAPPENED IN A LONG TIME!
IT'S THE SNOW.
WITH VISIBILITY THIS BAD...!!
WHOOOOOOOSH
HM?
OH, PLEASE. THEY'RE FINE.
CRUNCH
CRUNCH
ALTHOUGH, KUROMINE SEEMS A LITTLE *UNDER THE WEATHER.*

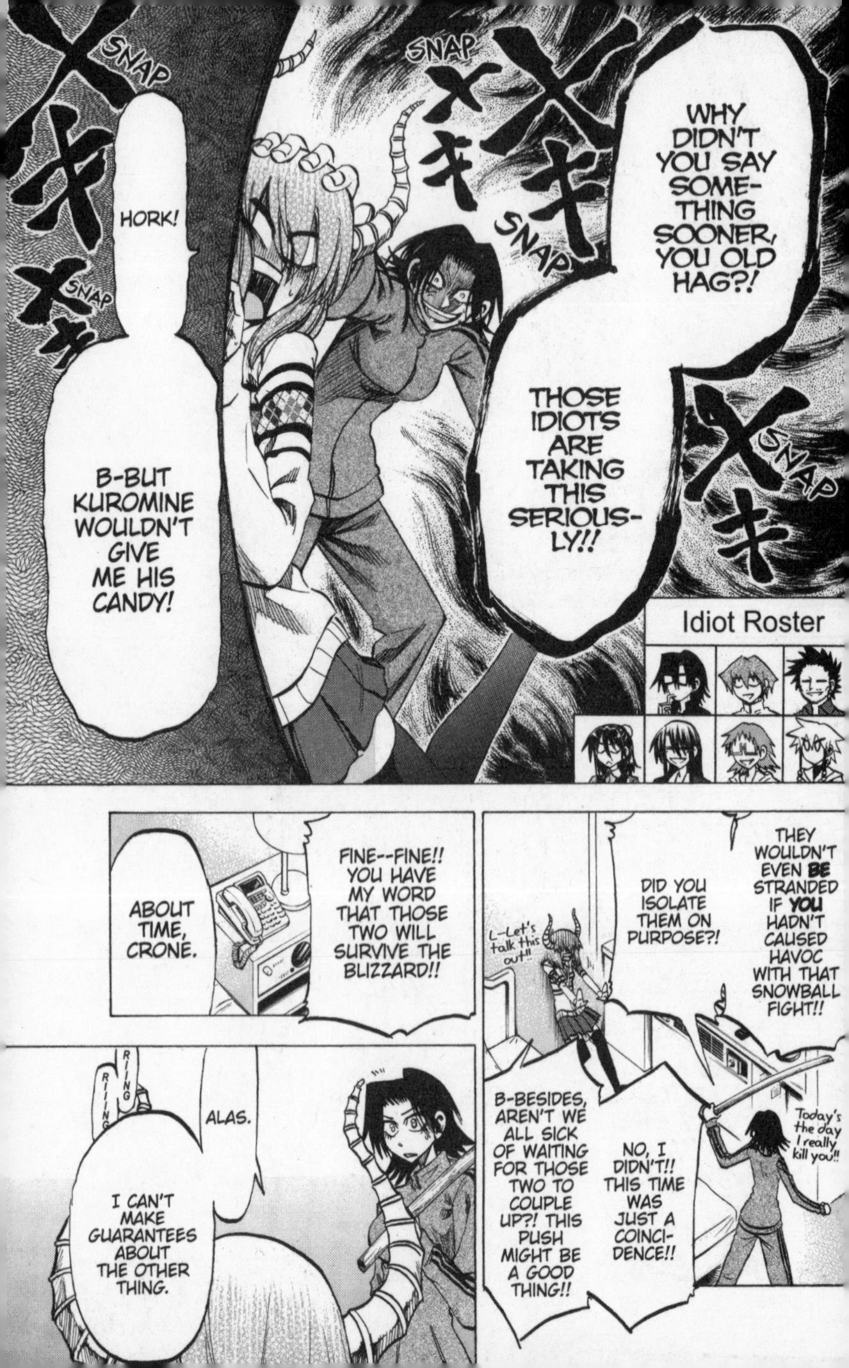
SNAP
WHY DIDN'T YOU SAY SOME-THING SOONER, YOU OLD HAG?!
SNAP
THOSE IDIOTS ARE TAKING THIS SERIOUS-LY!!
SNAP
SNAP
HORK!
SNAP
B-BUT KUROMINE WOULDN'T GIVE ME HIS CANDY!
Idiot Roster
THEY WOULDN'T EVEN BE STRANDED IF YOU HADN'T CAUSED HAVOC WITH THAT SNOWBALL FIGHT!!
Today's the day I really kill you!!
DID YOU ISOLATE THEM ON PURPOSE?!
L-Let's talk this out!!
NO, I DIDN'T!! THIS TIME WAS JUST A COINCI-DENCE!!
B-BESIDES, AREN'T WE ALL SICK OF WAITING FOR THOSE TWO TO COUPLE UP?! THIS PUSH MIGHT BE A GOOD THING!!
FINE--FINE!! YOU HAVE MY WORD THAT THOSE TWO WILL SURVIVE THE BLIZZARD!!
ABOUT TIME, CRONE.
RIING
RIING
ALAS.
I CAN'T MAKE GUARANTEES ABOUT THE OTHER THING.

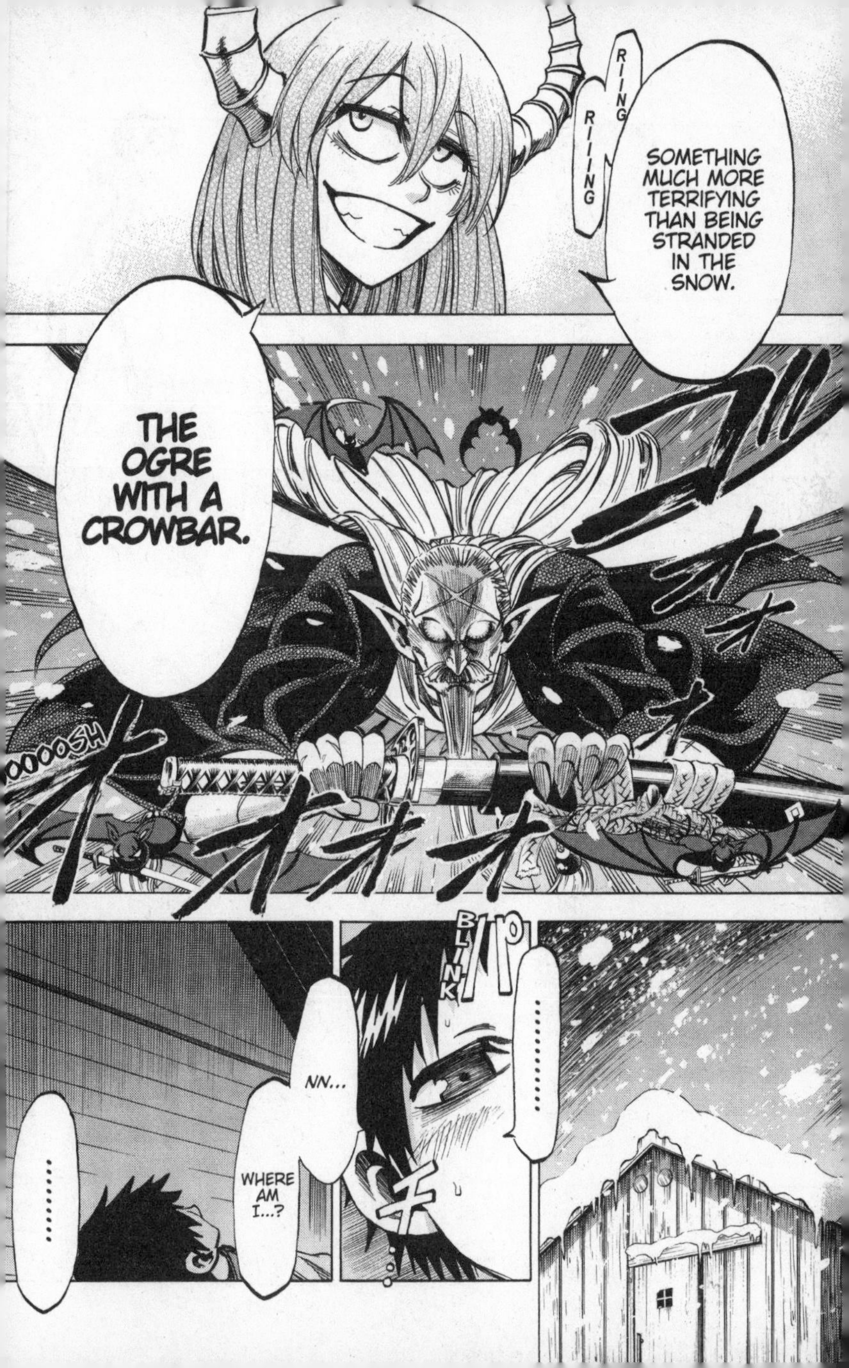
RIIING RIIING
SOMETHING MUCH MORE TERRIFYING THAN BEING STRANDED IN THE SNOW.
THE OGRE WITH A CROWBAR.
WOOOOOSH
BLINK
....
NN...
WHERE AM I...?
....

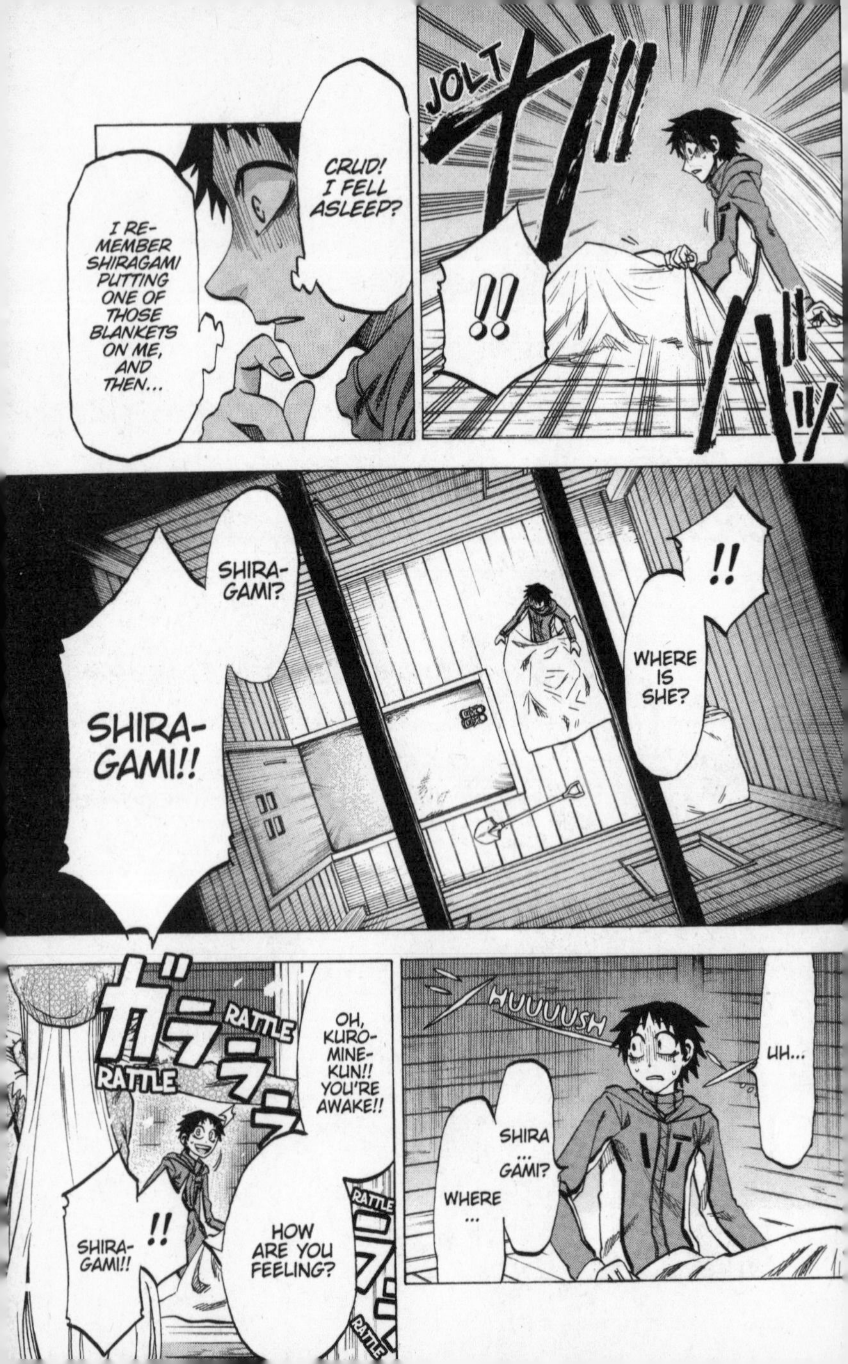
JOLT
!!
CRUD! I FELL ASLEEP?
I RE-MEMBER SHIRAGAMI PUTTING ONE OF THOSE BLANKETS ON ME, AND THEN...
!!
WHERE IS SHE?
SHIRA-GAMI?
SHIRA-GAMI!!
HUUUUSH
UH...
SHIRA... GAMI?
WHERE...
RATTLE
RATTLE
OH, KURO-MINE-KUN!! YOU'RE AWAKE!!
HOW ARE YOU FEELING?
RATTLE
RATTLE
!!
SHIRA-GAMI!!

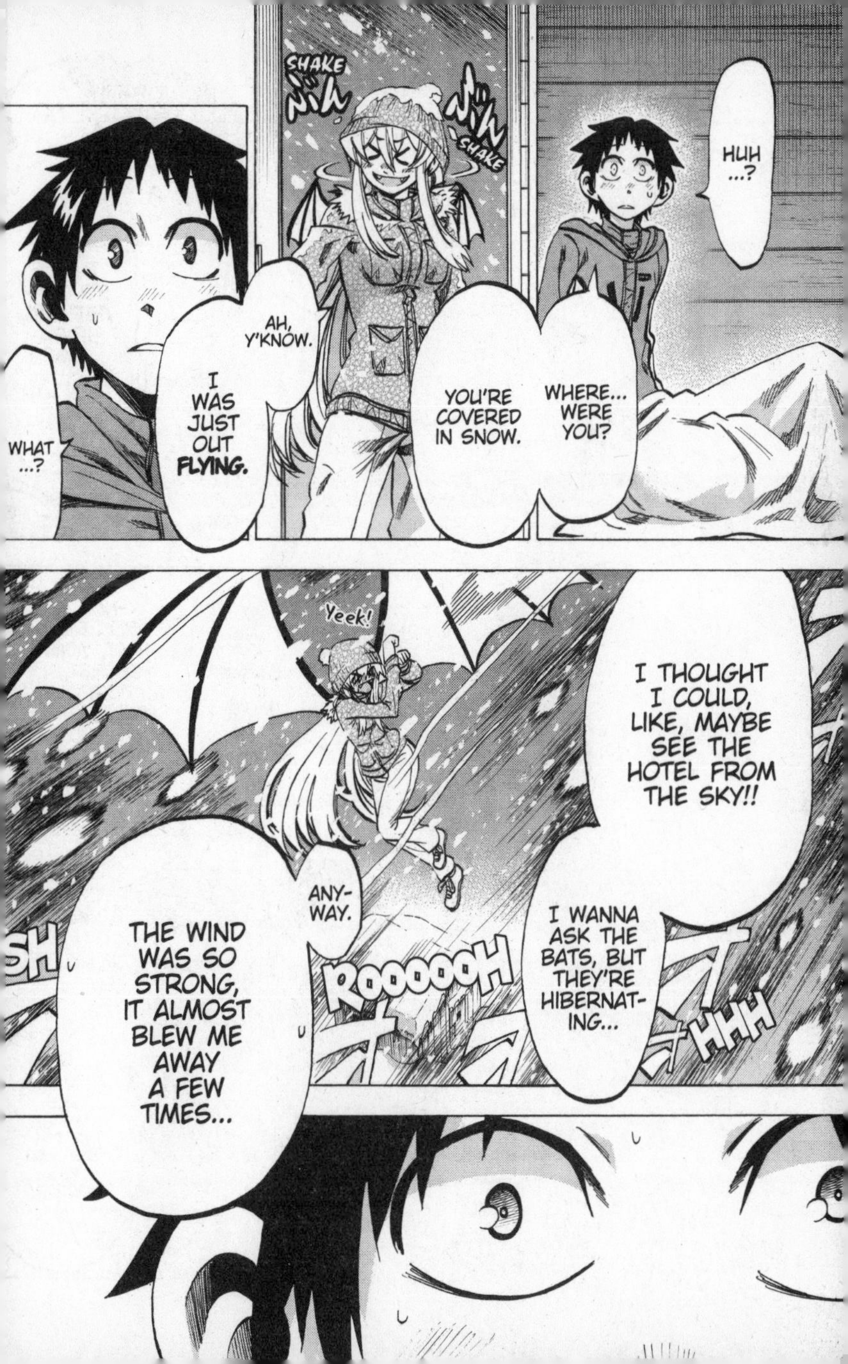
HUH ...?
SHAKE
SHAKE
WHERE... WERE YOU?
YOU'RE COVERED IN SNOW.
AH, Y'KNOW.
I WAS JUST OUT FLYING.
WHAT ...?
I THOUGHT I COULD, LIKE, MAYBE SEE THE HOTEL FROM THE SKY!!
Yeek!
I WANNA ASK THE BATS, BUT THEY'RE HIBERNAT-ING...
ANY-WAY.
SH
ROOOOOH
HHH
THE WIND WAS SO STRONG, IT ALMOST BLEW ME AWAY A FEW TIMES...

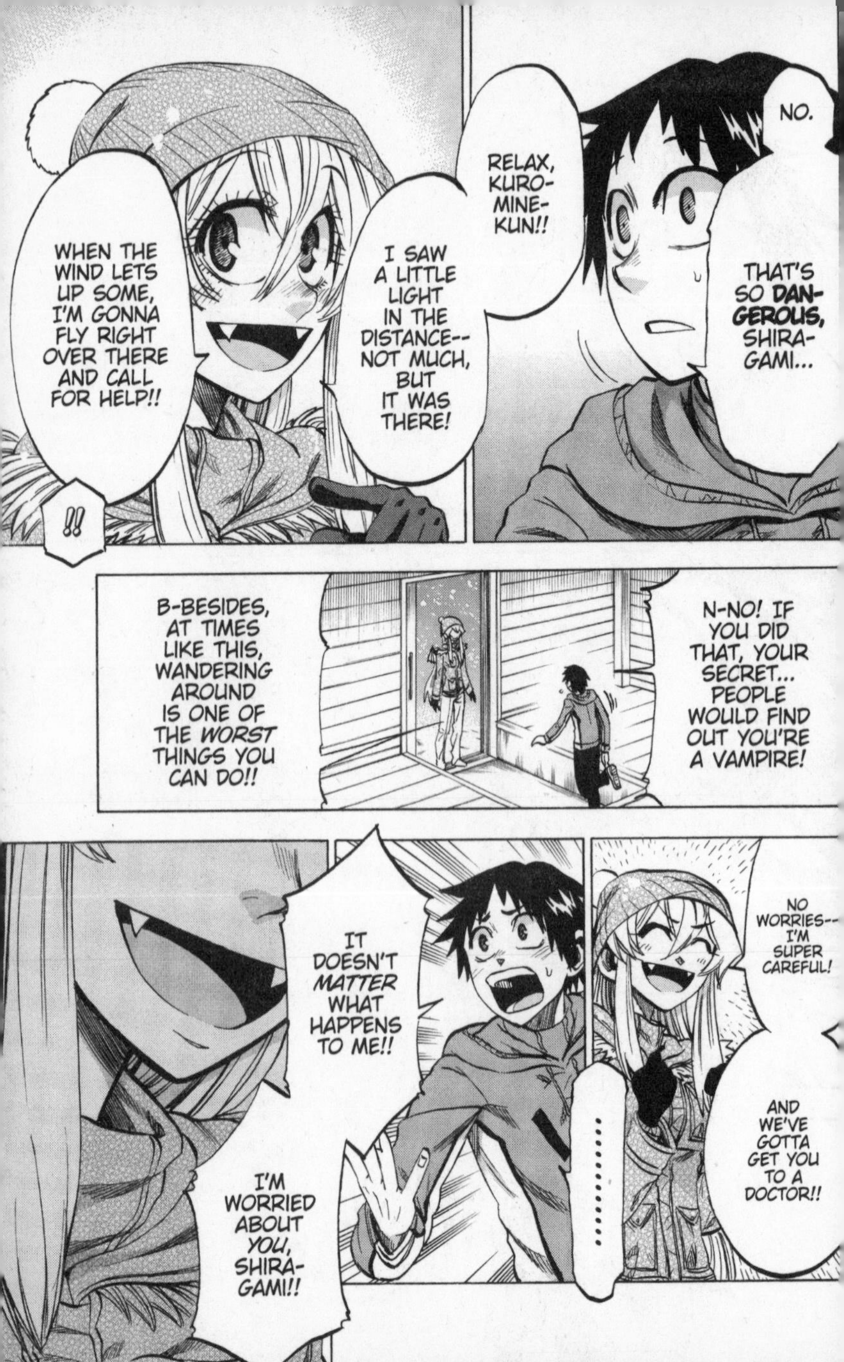
NO.
THAT'S SO DANGEROUS, SHIRAGAMI...
RELAX, KUROMINE-KUN!!
I SAW A LITTLE LIGHT IN THE DISTANCE-- NOT MUCH, BUT IT WAS THERE!
WHEN THE WIND LETS UP SOME, I'M GONNA FLY RIGHT OVER THERE AND CALL FOR HELP!!
!!
N-NO! IF YOU DID THAT, YOUR SECRET... PEOPLE WOULD FIND OUT YOU'RE A VAMPIRE!
B-BESIDES, AT TIMES LIKE THIS, WANDERING AROUND IS ONE OF THE WORST THINGS YOU CAN DO!!
NO WORRIES-- I'M SUPER CAREFUL!
AND WE'VE GOTTA GET YOU TO A DOCTOR!!
IT DOESN'T MATTER WHAT HAPPENS TO ME!!
I'M WORRIED ABOUT YOU, SHIRAGAMI!!
......

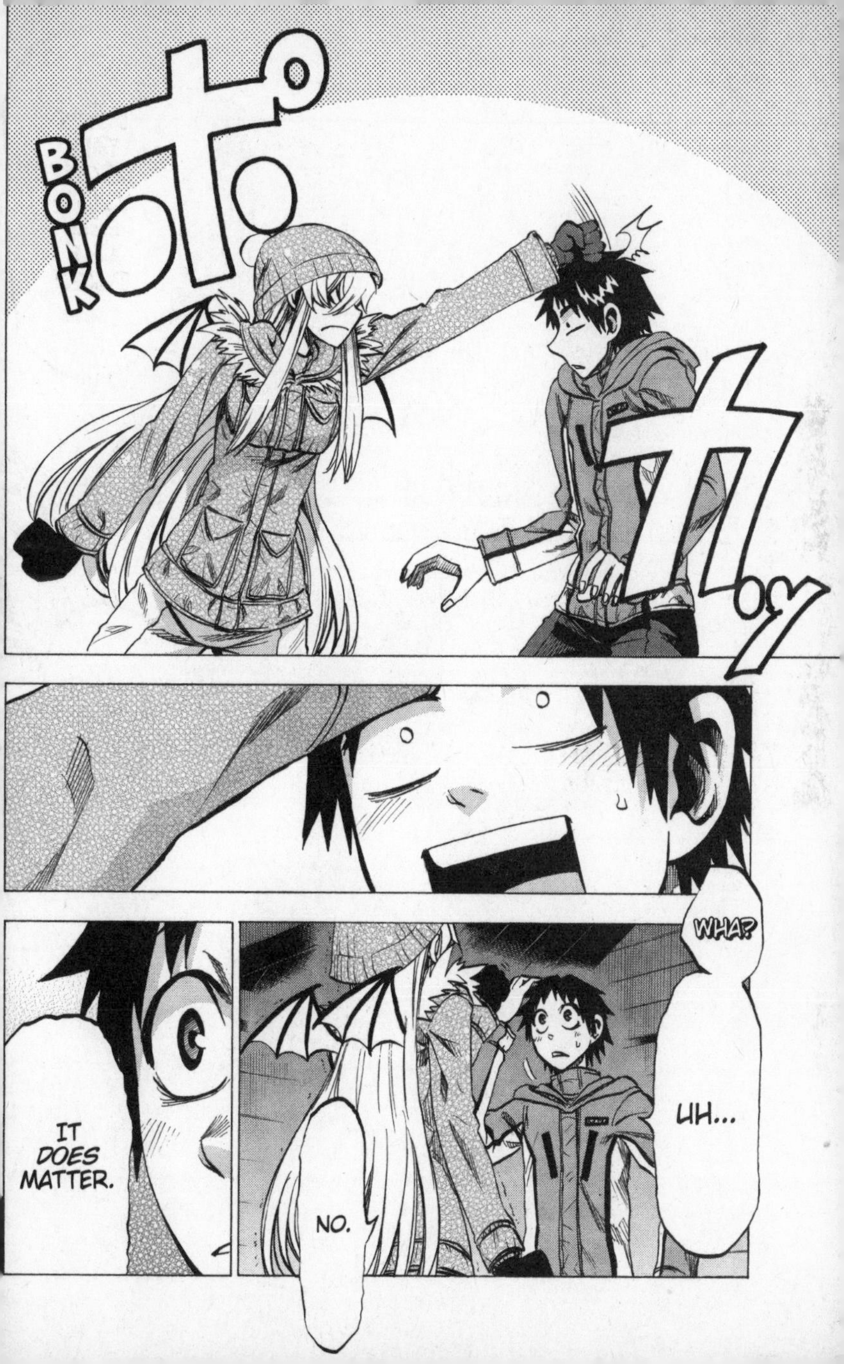
BONK
WHA?
UH...
NO.
IT DOES MATTER.

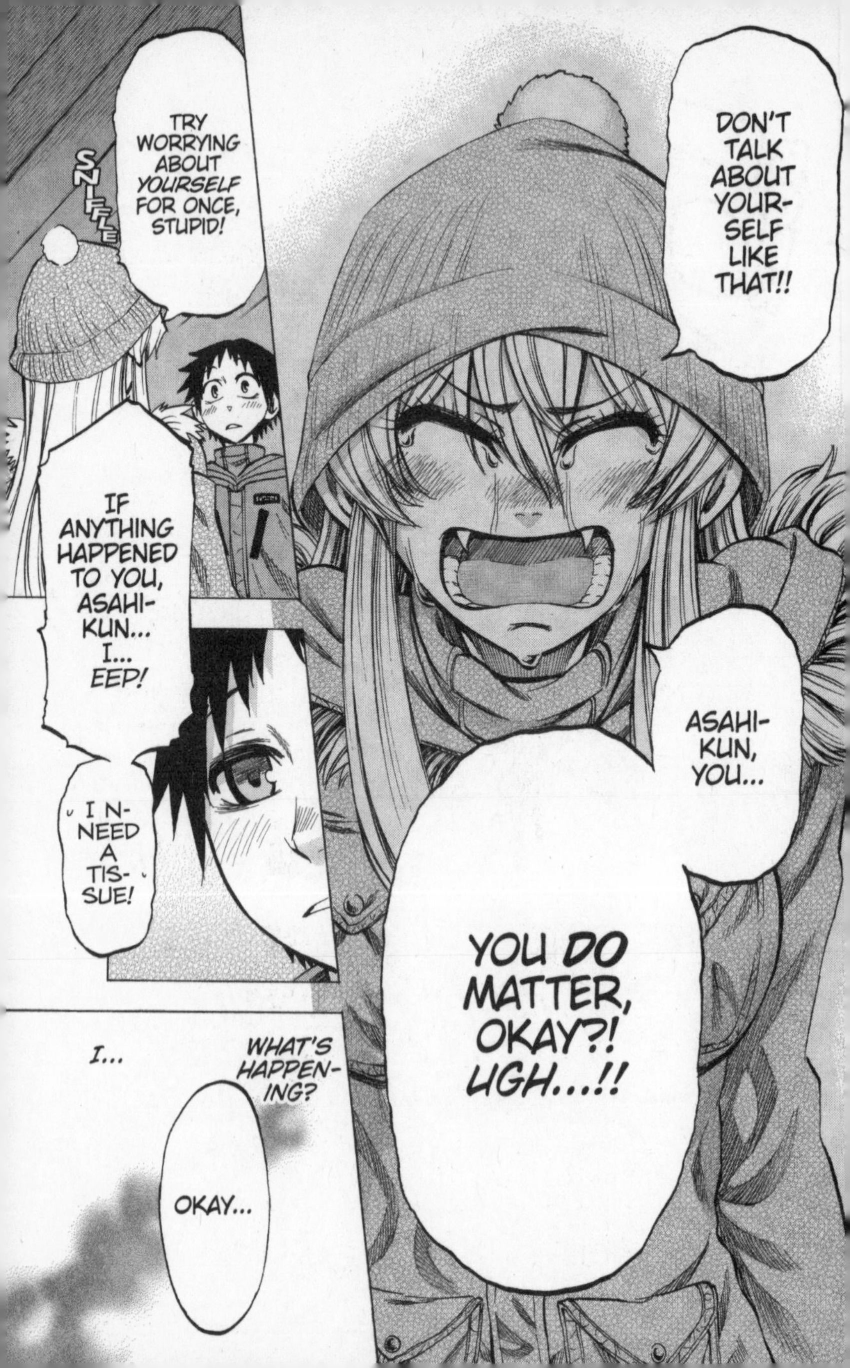
DON'T TALK ABOUT YOUR-SELF LIKE THAT!!
ASAHI-KUN, YOU...
YOU DO MATTER, OKAY?! UGH...!!
TRY WORRYING ABOUT YOURSELF FOR ONCE, STUPID!
SNIFFLE
IF ANYTHING HAPPENED TO YOU, ASAHI-KUN... I... EEP!
I N-NEED A TIS-SUE!
WHAT'S HAPPEN-ING?
I...
OKAY...

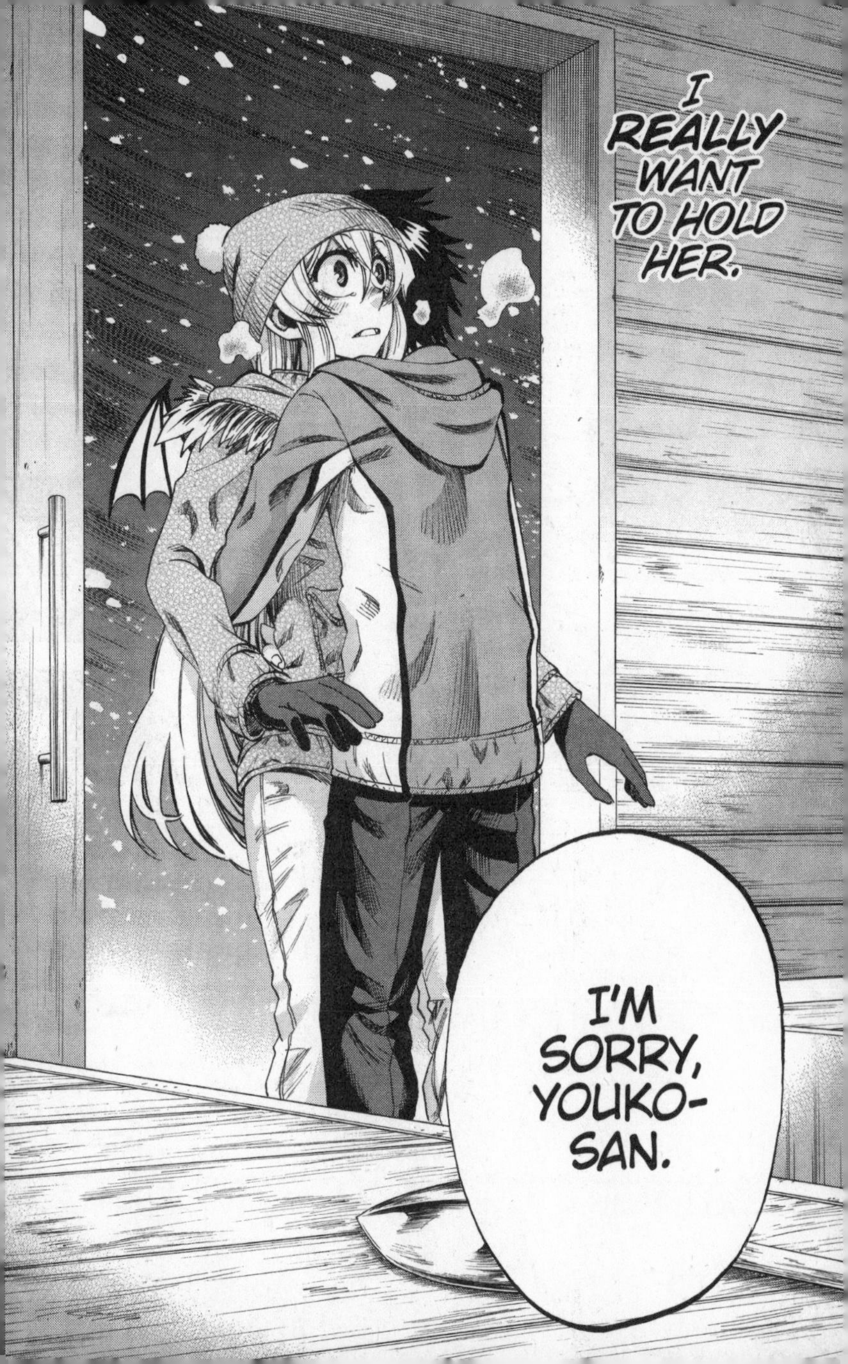
I REALLY WANT TO HOLD HER.
I'M SORRY, YOUKO-SAN.

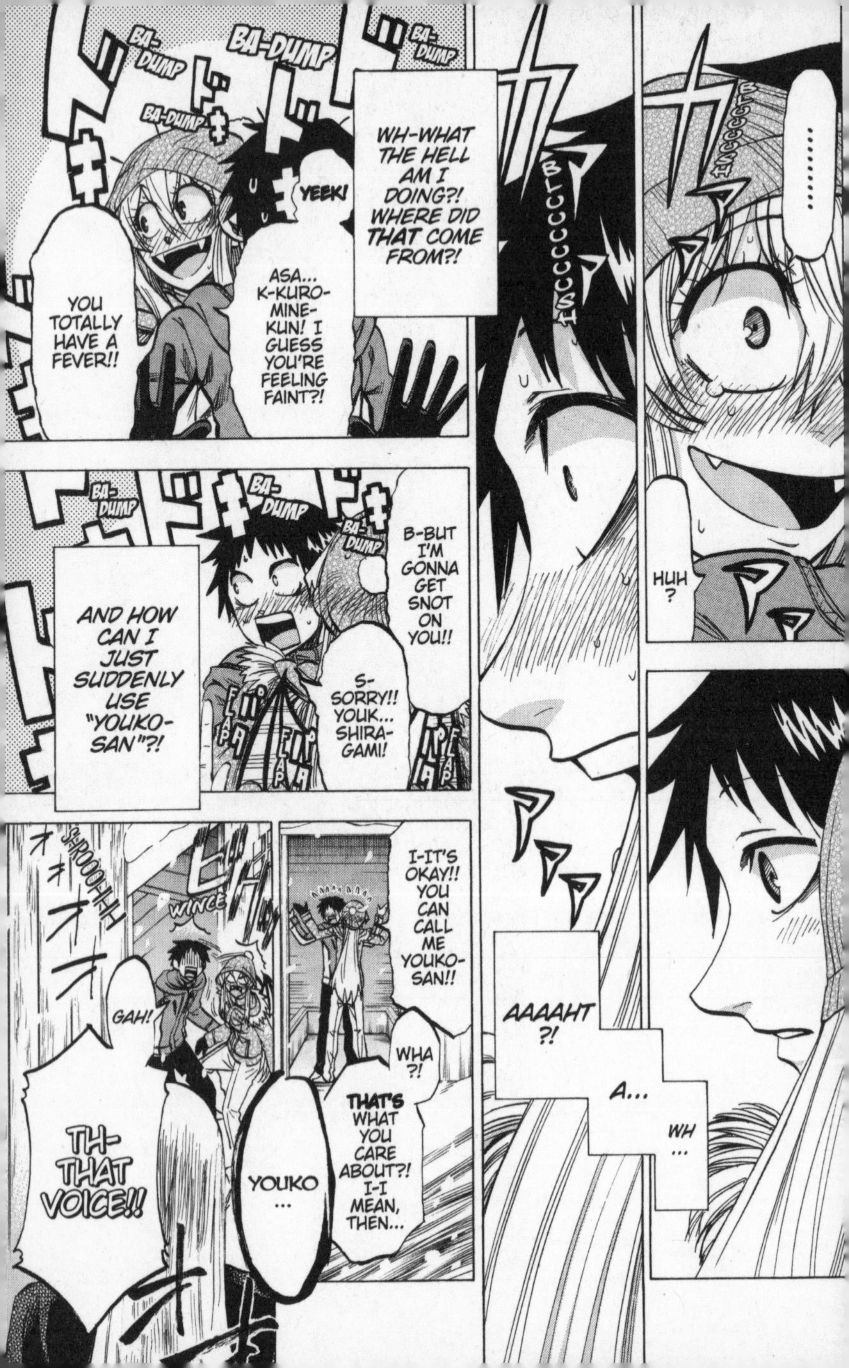
......
HUH?
WH...
A...
AAAAHT?!
BA-DUMP
BA-DUMP
BA-DUMP
BA-DUMP
WH-WHAT THE HELL AM I DOING?! WHERE DID THAT COME FROM?!
YEEK!
ASA... K-KUROMINE-KUN! I GUESS YOU'RE FEELING FAINT?!
YOU TOTALLY HAVE A FEVER!!
BA-DUMP
BA-DUMP
BA-DUMP
B-BUT I'M GONNA GET SNOT ON YOU!!
FLAP
S-SORRY!! YOUK... SHIRAGAMI!
FLAP
FLAP
AND HOW CAN I JUST SUDDENLY USE "YOUKO-SAN"?!
I-IT'S OKAY!! YOU CAN CALL ME YOUKO-SAN!!
WHA?!
THAT'S WHAT YOU CARE ABOUT?! I-I MEAN, THEN...
YOUKO...
WINCE
GAH!
SHROOOHHH
TH-THAT VOICE!!

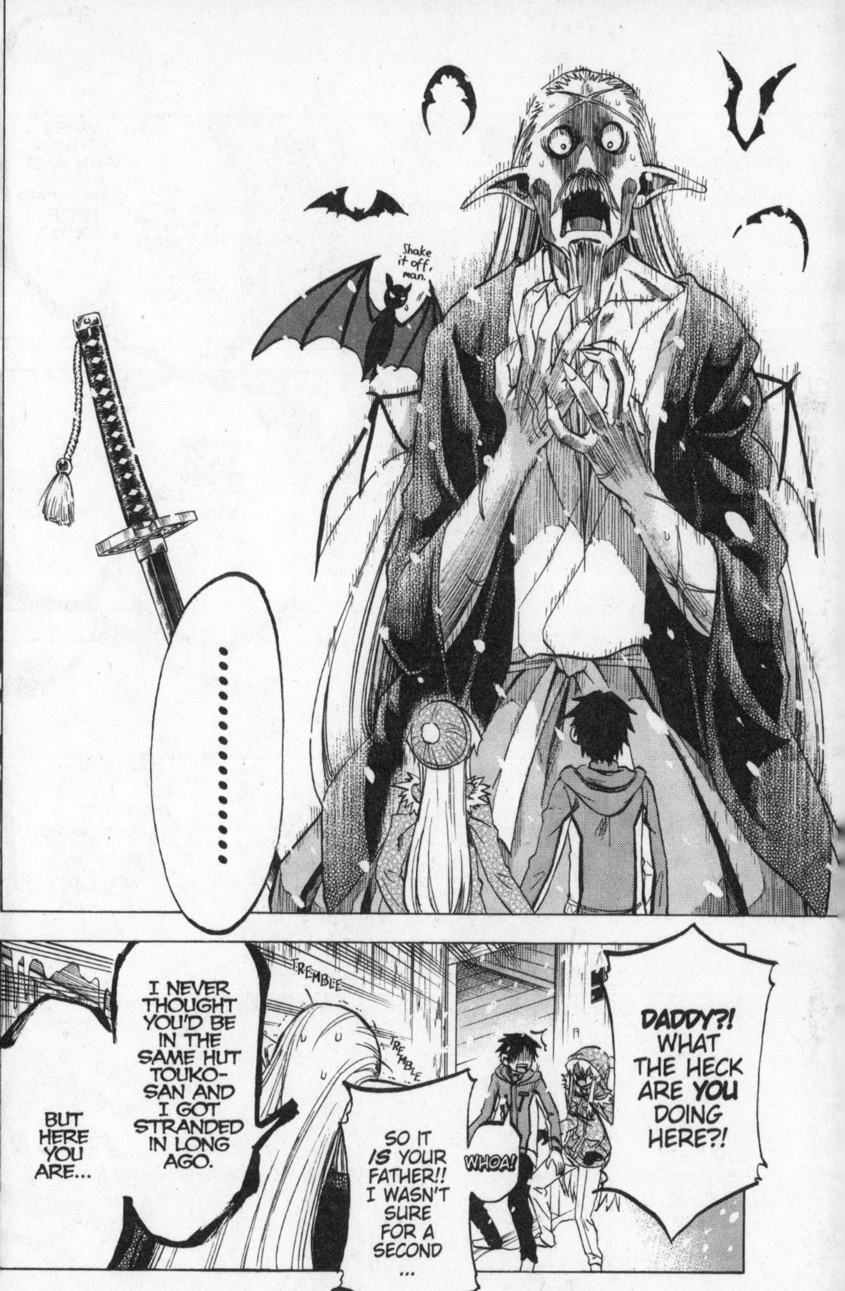
Shake it off, man.
....
DADDY?! WHAT THE HECK ARE YOU DOING HERE?!
WHOA!
SO IT IS YOUR FATHER!! I WASN'T SURE FOR A SECOND ...
TREMBLE
TREMBLE
I NEVER THOUGHT YOU'D BE IN THE SAME HUT TOUKO-SAN AND I GOT STRANDED IN LONG AGO.
BUT HERE YOU ARE...

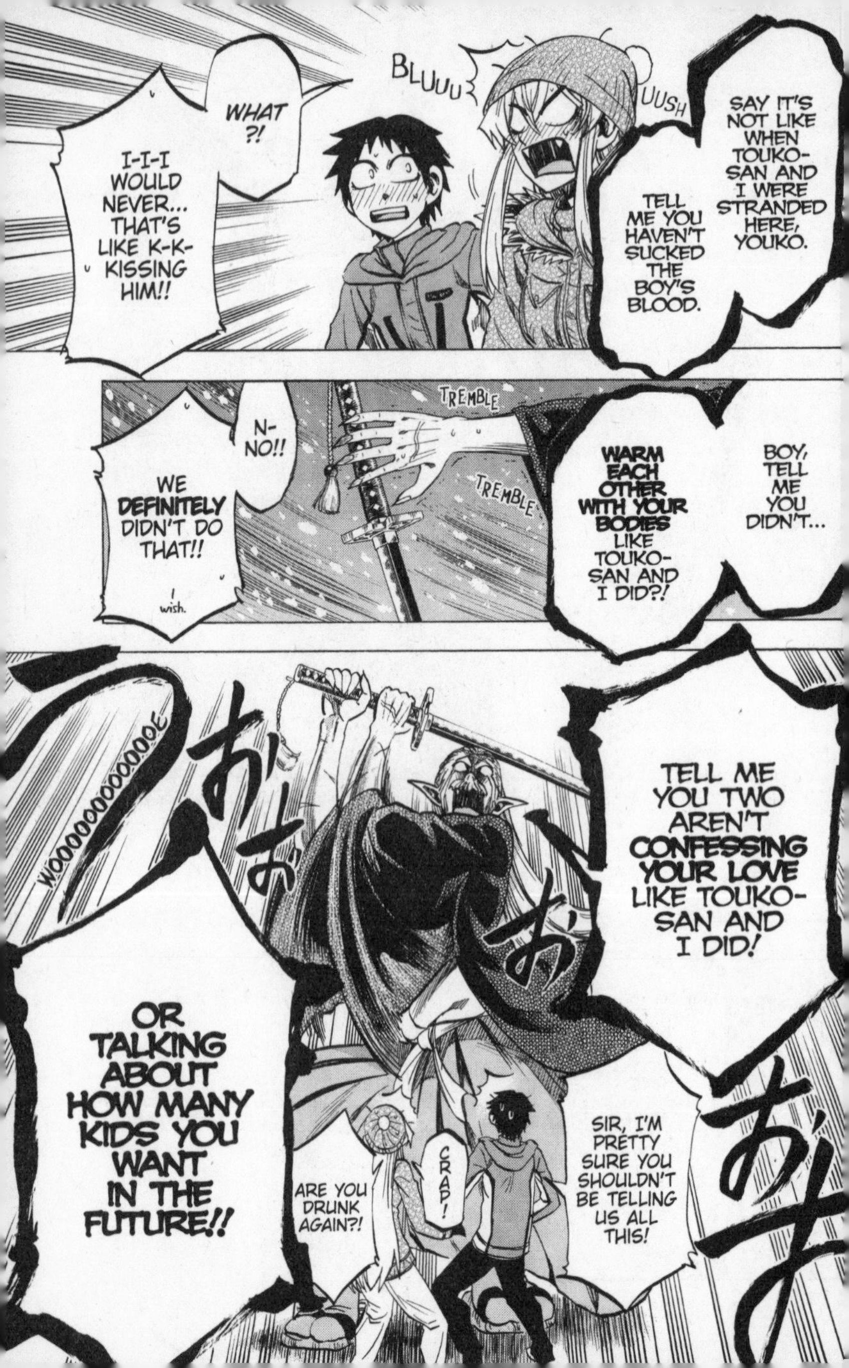
SAY IT'S NOT LIKE WHEN TOUKO-SAN AND I WERE STRANDED HERE, YOUKO.
TELL ME YOU HAVEN'T SUCKED THE BOY'S BLOOD.
BLUUUUUSH
WHAT?!
I-I-I WOULD NEVER... THAT'S LIKE K-K-KISSING HIM!!
BOY, TELL ME YOU DIDN'T...
WARM EACH OTHER WITH YOUR BODIES LIKE TOUKO-SAN AND I DID?!
TREMBLE
TREMBLE
N-NO!!
WE DEFINITELY DIDN'T DO THAT!!
I wish.
TELL ME YOU TWO AREN'T CONFESSING YOUR LOVE LIKE TOUKO-SAN AND I DID!
WOOOOOOOOOOOOE
OR TALKING ABOUT HOW MANY KIDS YOU WANT IN THE FUTURE!!
SIR, I'M PRETTY SURE YOU SHOULDN'T BE TELLING US ALL THIS!
CRAP!
ARE YOU DRUNK AGAIN?!

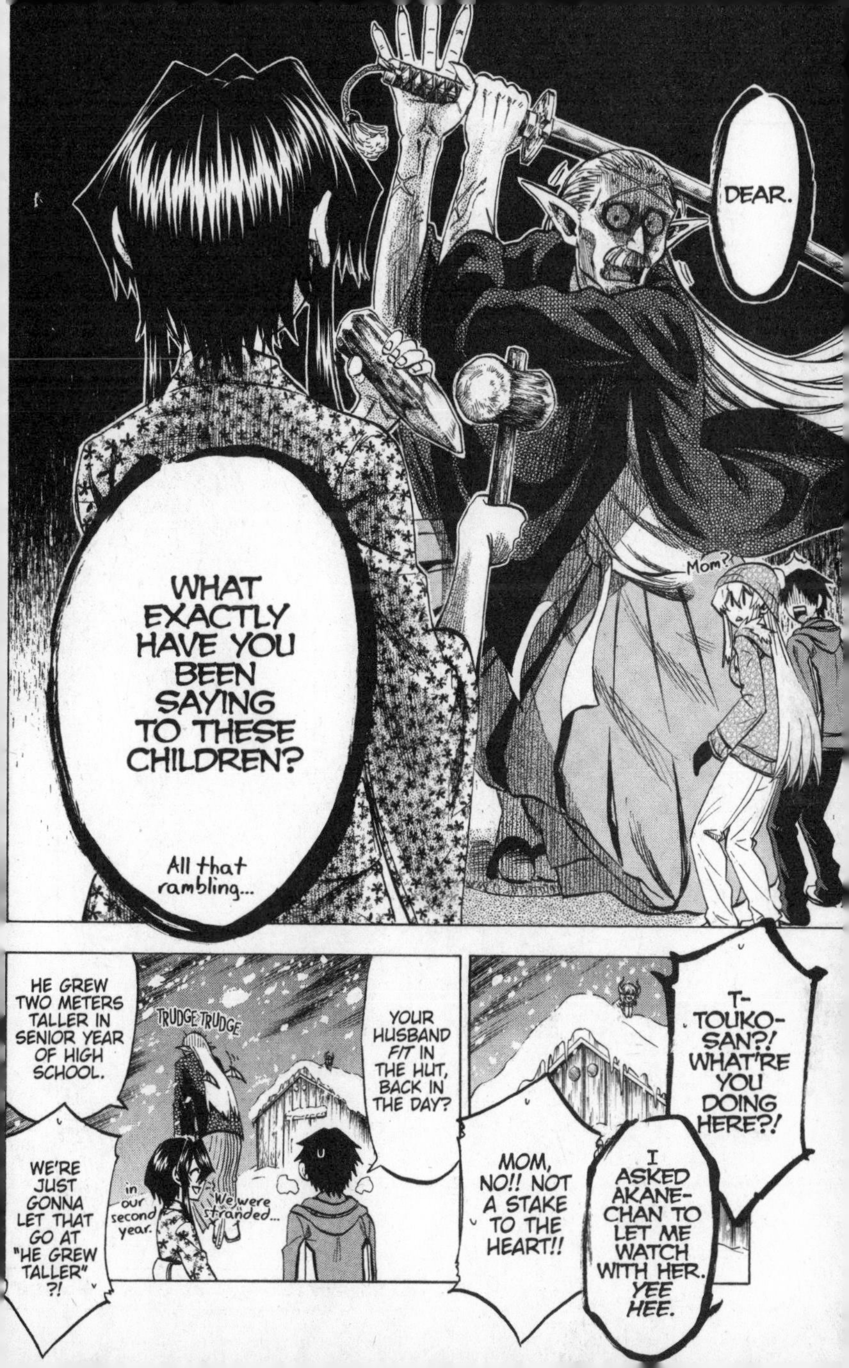
DEAR.
Mom?
WHAT EXACTLY HAVE YOU BEEN SAYING TO THESE CHILDREN?
All that rambling...
T-TOUKO-SAN?! WHAT'RE YOU DOING HERE?!
I ASKED AKANE-CHAN TO LET ME WATCH WITH HER. YEE HEE.
MOM, NO!! NOT A STAKE TO THE HEART!!
YOUR HUSBAND *FIT* IN THE HUT, BACK IN THE DAY?
HE GREW TWO METERS TALLER IN SENIOR YEAR OF HIGH SCHOOL.
TRUDGE TRUDGE
We were stranded...
in our second year.
WE'RE JUST GONNA LET THAT GO AT "HE GREW TALLER"?!

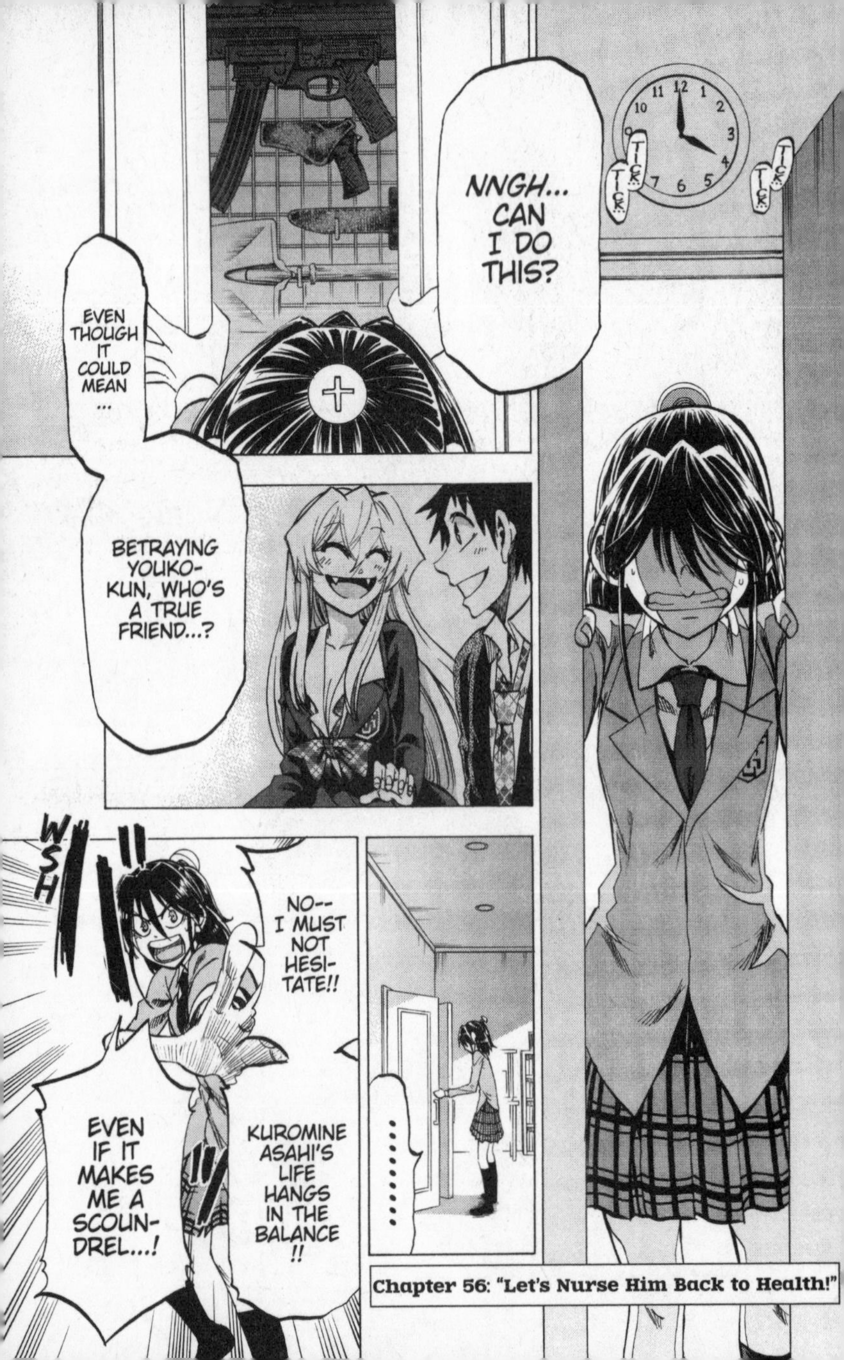
TICK TICK
TICK TICK
Chapter 56: "Let's Nurse Him Back to Health!"
NNGH... CAN I DO THIS?
EVEN THOUGH IT COULD MEAN ...
BETRAYING YOUKO-KUN, WHO'S A TRUE FRIEND...?
......
NO-- I MUST NOT HESITATE!!
WSH
KUROMINE ASAHI'S LIFE HANGS IN THE BALANCE!!
EVEN IF IT MAKES ME A SCOUNDREL...!

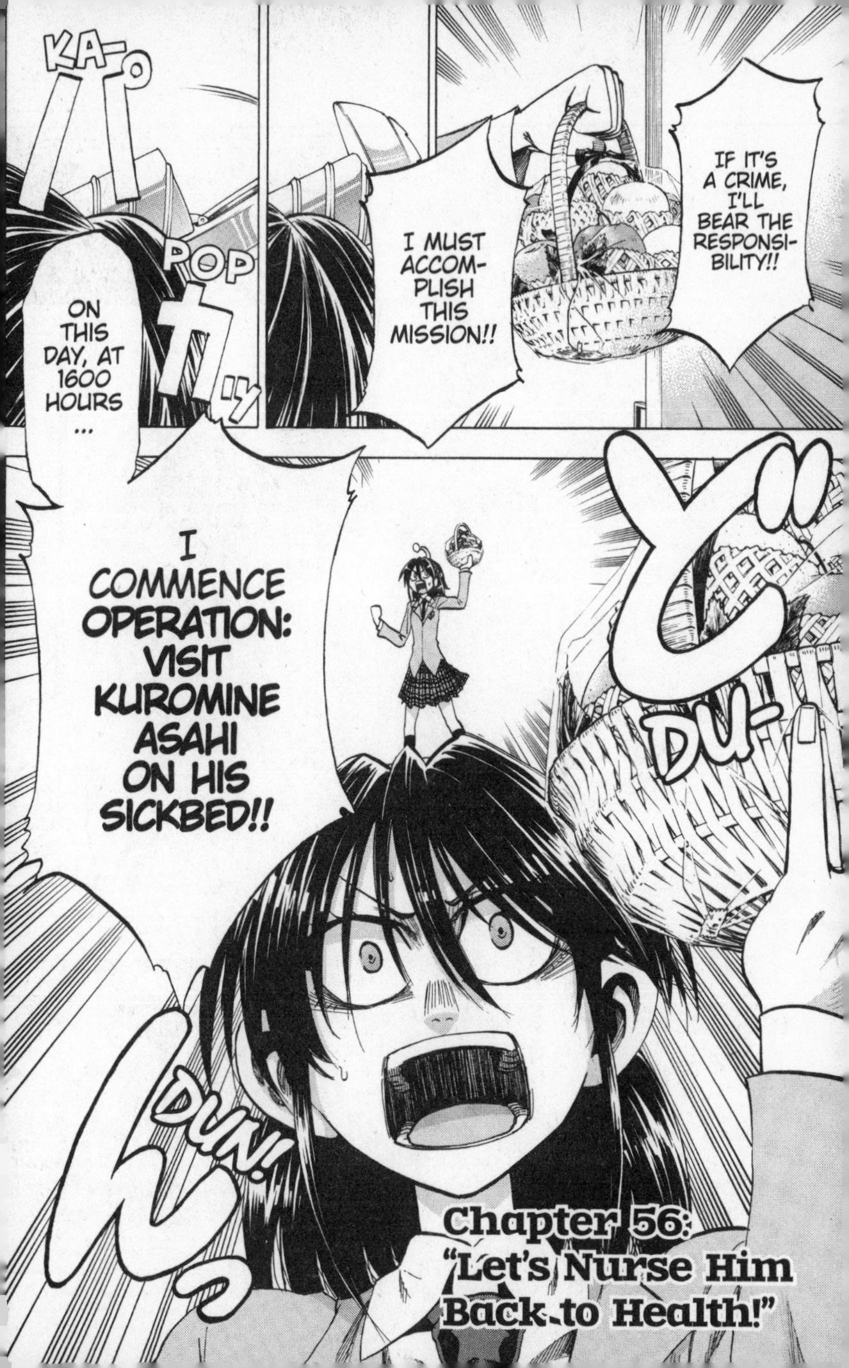
IF IT'S A CRIME, I'LL BEAR THE RESPONSIBILITY!!
I MUST ACCOMPLISH THIS MISSION!!
KA-
POP
ON THIS DAY, AT 1600 HOURS ...
I COMMENCE OPERATION: VISIT KUROMINE ASAHI ON HIS SICKBED!!
DU-
DUN!

Chapter 56: "Let's Nurse Him Back to Health!"

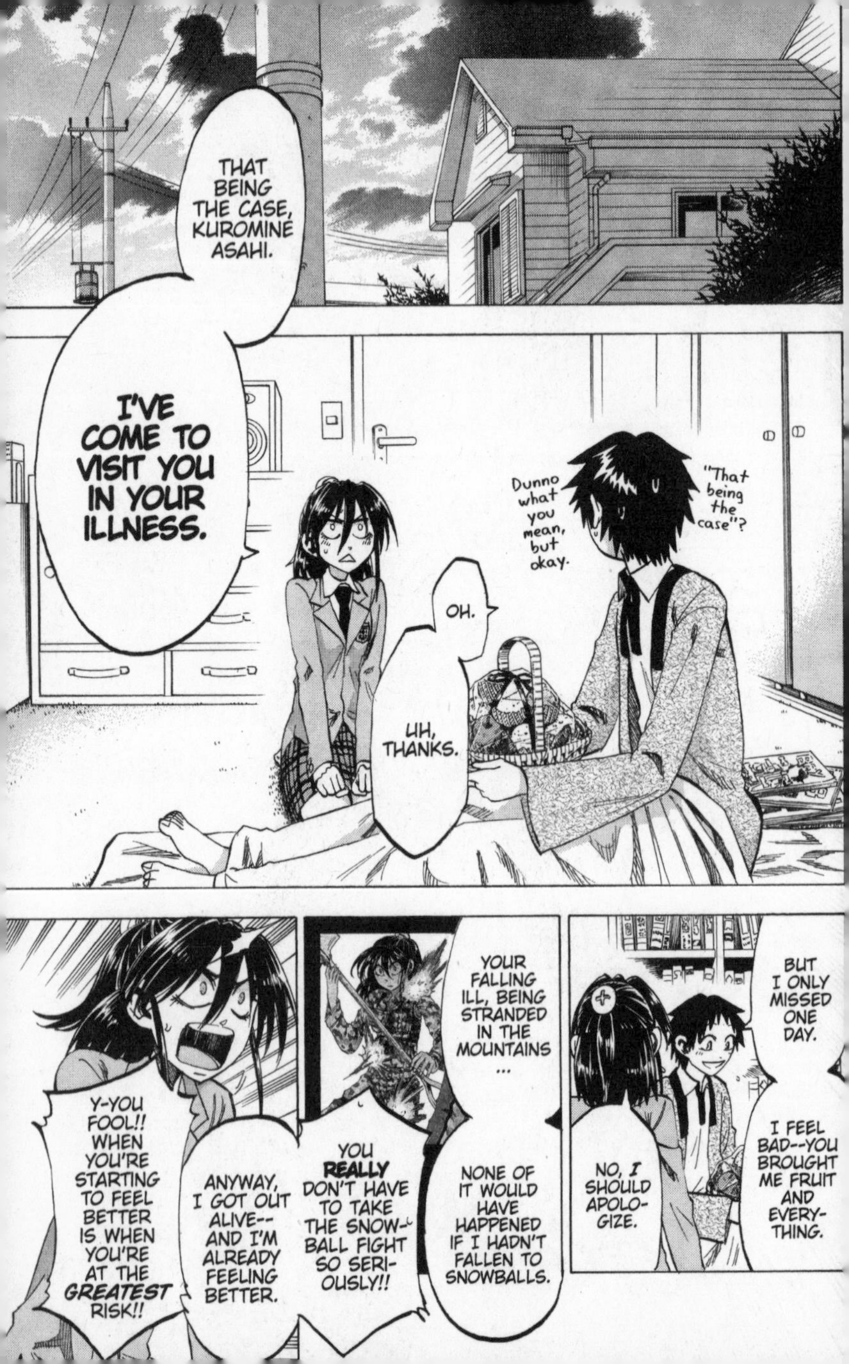
THAT BEING THE CASE, KUROMINE ASAHI.
I'VE COME TO VISIT YOU IN YOUR ILLNESS.
"That being the case"?
Dunno what you mean, but okay.
OH.
UH, THANKS.
BUT I ONLY MISSED ONE DAY.
I FEEL BAD--YOU BROUGHT ME FRUIT AND EVERYTHING.
NO, *I* SHOULD APOLOGIZE.
YOUR FALLING ILL, BEING STRANDED IN THE MOUNTAINS ...
NONE OF IT WOULD HAVE HAPPENED IF I HADN'T FALLEN TO SNOWBALLS.
YOU **REALLY** DON'T HAVE TO TAKE THE SNOWBALL FIGHT SO SERIOUSLY!!
ANYWAY, I GOT OUT ALIVE-- AND I'M ALREADY FEELING BETTER.
Y-YOU FOOL!! WHEN YOU'RE STARTING TO FEEL BETTER IS WHEN YOU'RE AT THE ***GREATEST*** RISK!!

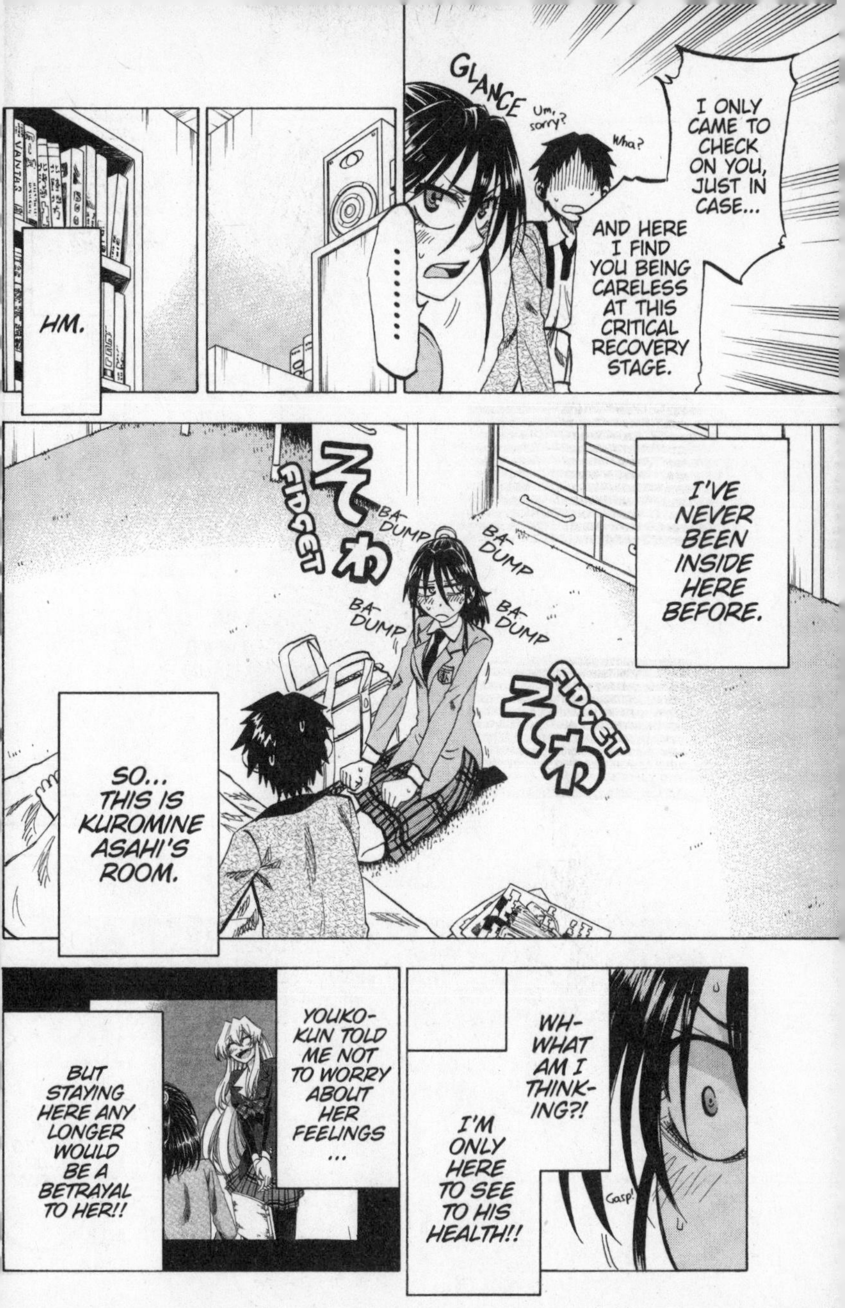
I ONLY CAME TO CHECK ON YOU, JUST IN CASE...
GLANCE
Wha?
Um, sorry?
AND HERE I FIND YOU BEING CARELESS AT THIS CRITICAL RECOVERY STAGE.
HM.
I'VE NEVER BEEN INSIDE HERE BEFORE.
BA-DUMP
BA-DUMP
FIDGET
そわ
BA-DUMP
BA-DUMP
FIDGET
そわ
SO... THIS IS KUROMINE ASAHI'S ROOM.
Gasp!
WH-WHAT AM I THINKING?!
I'M ONLY HERE TO SEE TO HIS HEALTH!!
YOUKO-KUN TOLD ME NOT TO WORRY ABOUT HER FEELINGS...
BUT STAYING HERE ANY LONGER WOULD BE A BETRAYAL TO HER!!

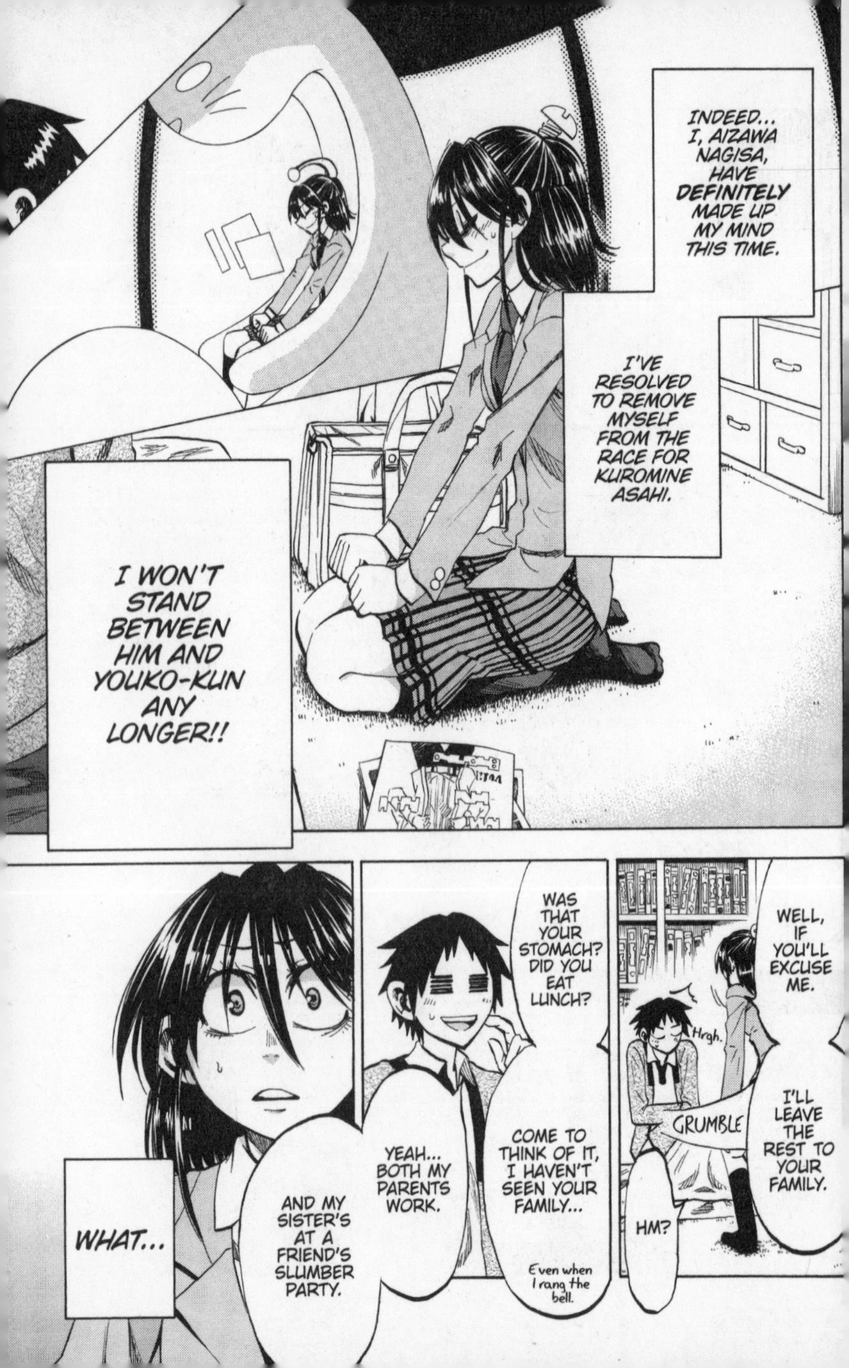
INDEED... I, AIZAWA NAGISA, HAVE DEFINITELY MADE UP MY MIND THIS TIME.
I'VE RESOLVED TO REMOVE MYSELF FROM THE RACE FOR KUROMINE ASAHI.
I WON'T STAND BETWEEN HIM AND YOUKO-KUN ANY LONGER!!
WELL, IF YOU'LL EXCUSE ME.
Hrgh.
GRUMBLE
I'LL LEAVE THE REST TO YOUR FAMILY.
HM?
WAS THAT YOUR STOMACH? DID YOU EAT LUNCH?
COME TO THINK OF IT, I HAVEN'T SEEN YOUR FAMILY...
Even when I rang the bell.
YEAH... BOTH MY PARENTS WORK.
AND MY SISTER'S AT A FRIEND'S SLUMBER PARTY.
WHAT...

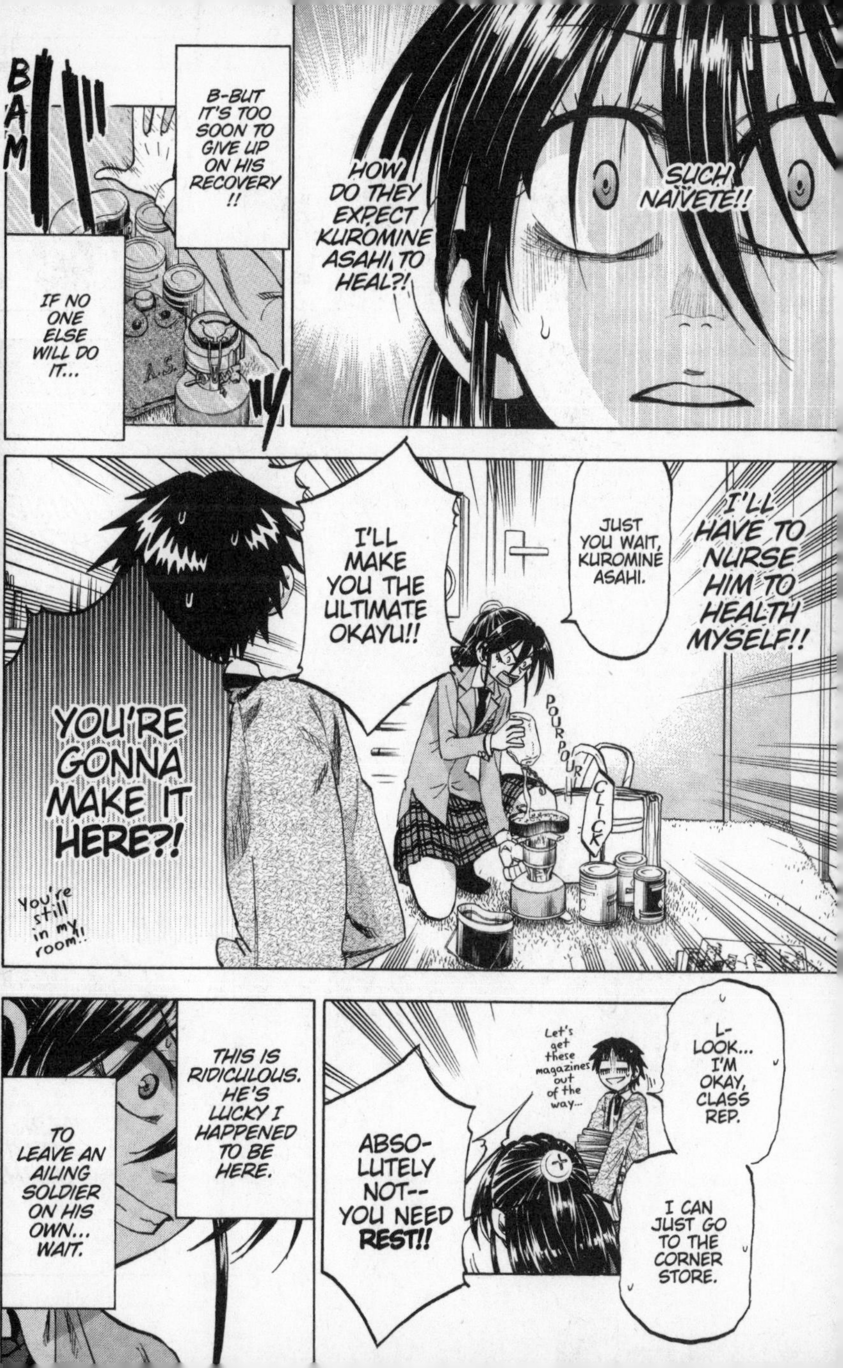
SUCH NAÏVETE!!
HOW DO THEY EXPECT KUROMINE ASAHI TO HEAL?!
B-BUT IT'S TOO SOON TO GIVE UP ON HIS RECOVERY!!
BAM
IF NO ONE ELSE WILL DO IT...
I'LL HAVE TO NURSE HIM TO HEALTH MYSELF!!
JUST YOU WAIT, KUROMINE ASAHI.
I'LL MAKE YOU THE ULTIMATE OKAYU!!
POUR POUR
CLICK
YOU'RE GONNA MAKE IT HERE?!
You're still in my room!!
L-LOOK... I'M OKAY, CLASS REP.
Let's get these magazines out of the way...
I CAN JUST GO TO THE CORNER STORE.
ABSOLUTELY NOT--YOU NEED REST!!
THIS IS RIDICULOUS. HE'S LUCKY I HAPPENED TO BE HERE.
TO LEAVE AN AILING SOLDIER ON HIS OWN... WAIT.

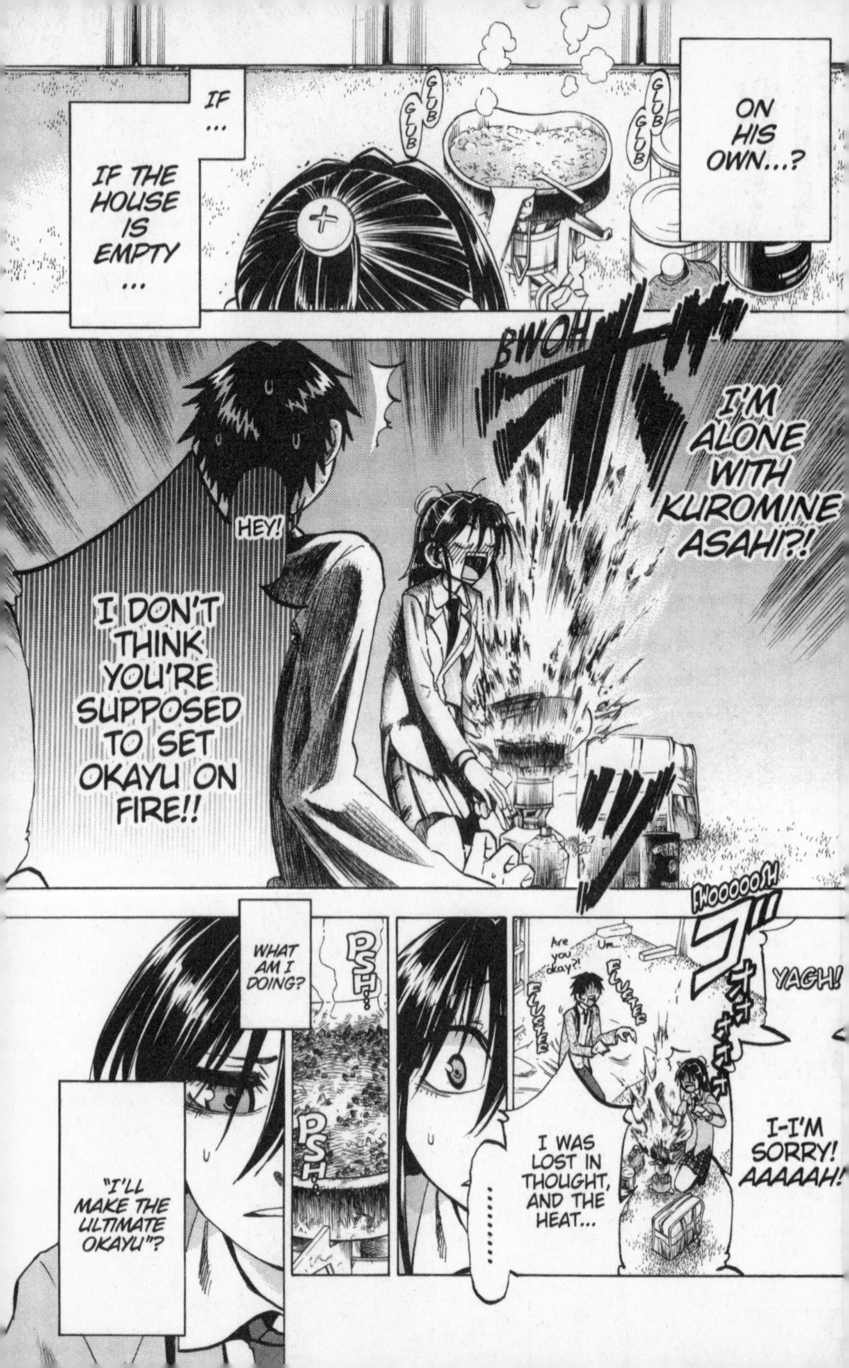
ON HIS OWN...?
GLUB GLUB
GLUB GLUB
IF ...
IF THE HOUSE IS EMPTY ...
BWOH
I'M ALONE WITH KUROMINE ASAHI?!
HEY!
I DON'T THINK YOU'RE SUPPOSED TO SET OKAYU ON FIRE!!
FWOOOOOSH
YAGH!
Are you okay?!
Um...
I-I'M SORRY! AAAAAH!
I WAS LOST IN THOUGHT, AND THE HEAT...
......
PSH...
PSH...
WHAT AM I DOING?
"I'LL MAKE THE ULTIMATE OKAYU"?

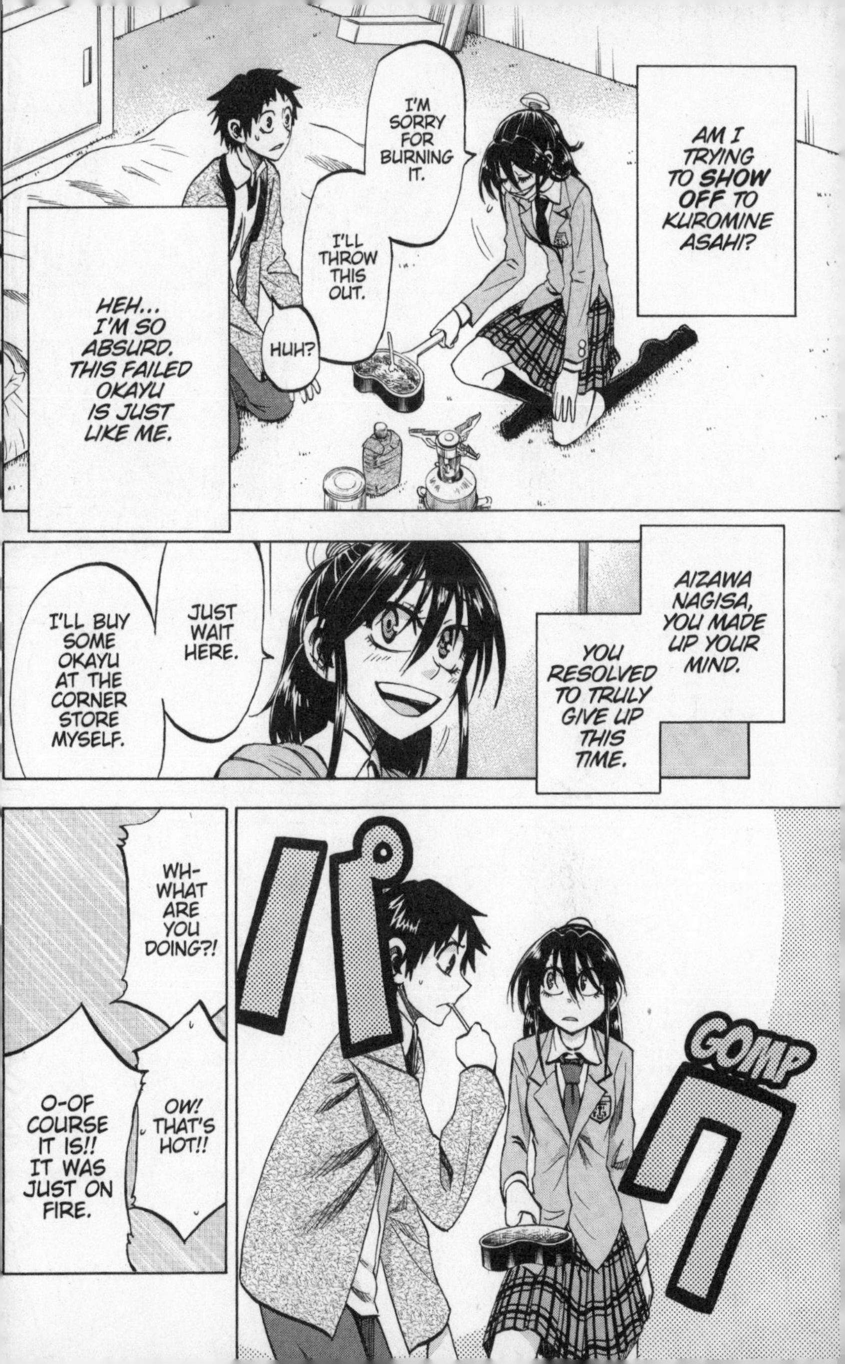
AM I TRYING TO SHOW OFF TO KUROMINE ASAHI?
I'M SORRY FOR BURNING IT.
I'LL THROW THIS OUT.
HUH?
HEH... I'M SO ABSURD. THIS FAILED OKAYU IS JUST LIKE ME.
AIZAWA NAGISA, YOU MADE UP YOUR MIND.
YOU RESOLVED TO TRULY GIVE UP THIS TIME.
JUST WAIT HERE.
I'LL BUY SOME OKAYU AT THE CORNER STORE MYSELF.
GOMP
WH-WHAT ARE YOU DOING?!
OW! THAT'S HOT!!
O-OF COURSE IT IS!! IT WAS JUST ON FIRE.

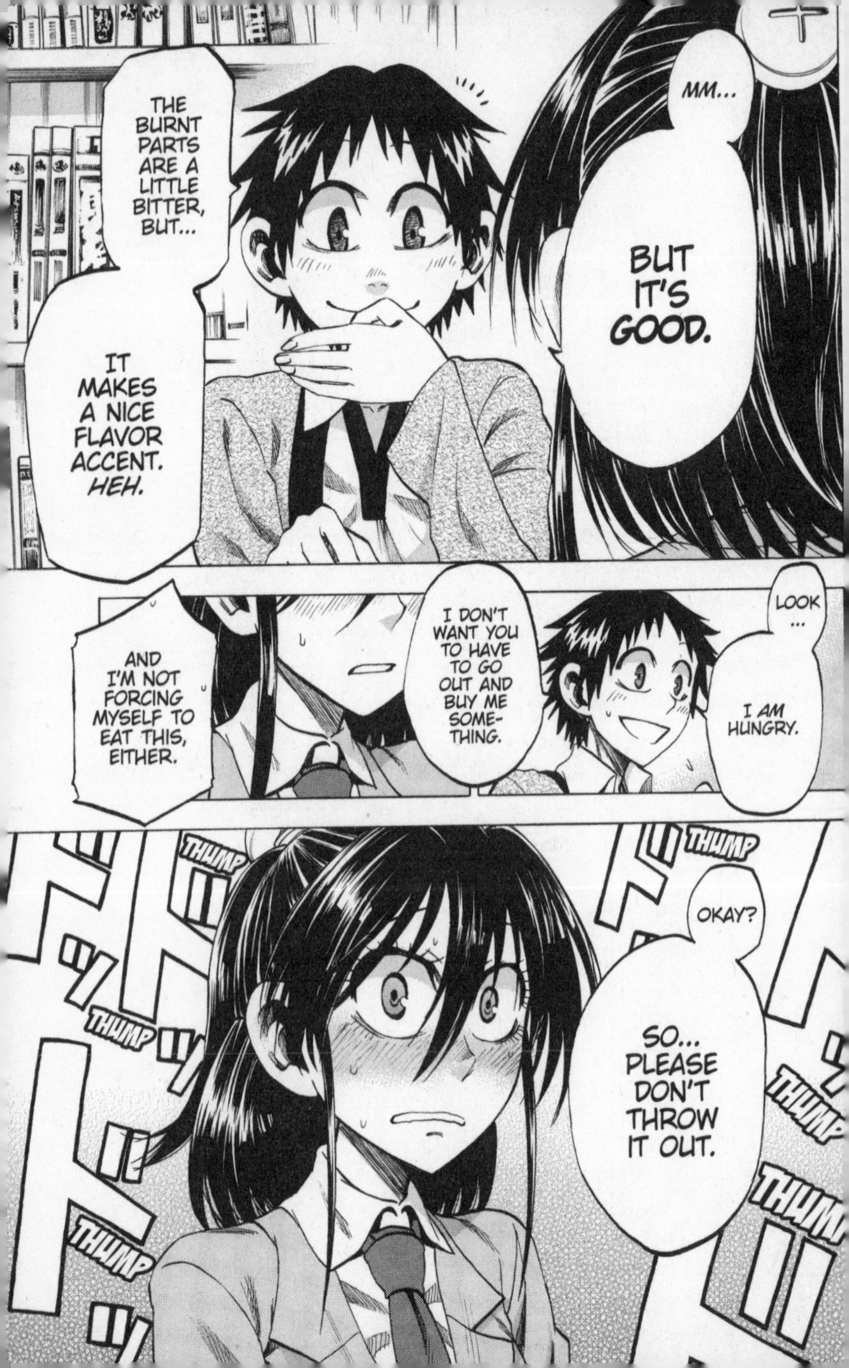
MM...
BUT IT'S GOOD.
THE BURNT PARTS ARE A LITTLE BITTER, BUT...
IT MAKES A NICE FLAVOR ACCENT. *HEH.*
LOOK...
I *AM* HUNGRY.
I DON'T WANT YOU TO HAVE TO GO OUT AND BUY ME SOME-THING.
AND I'M NOT FORCING MYSELF TO EAT THIS, EITHER.
THUMP
THUMP
OKAY?
SO... PLEASE DON'T THROW IT OUT.
THUMP
THUMP
THUMP
THUMP

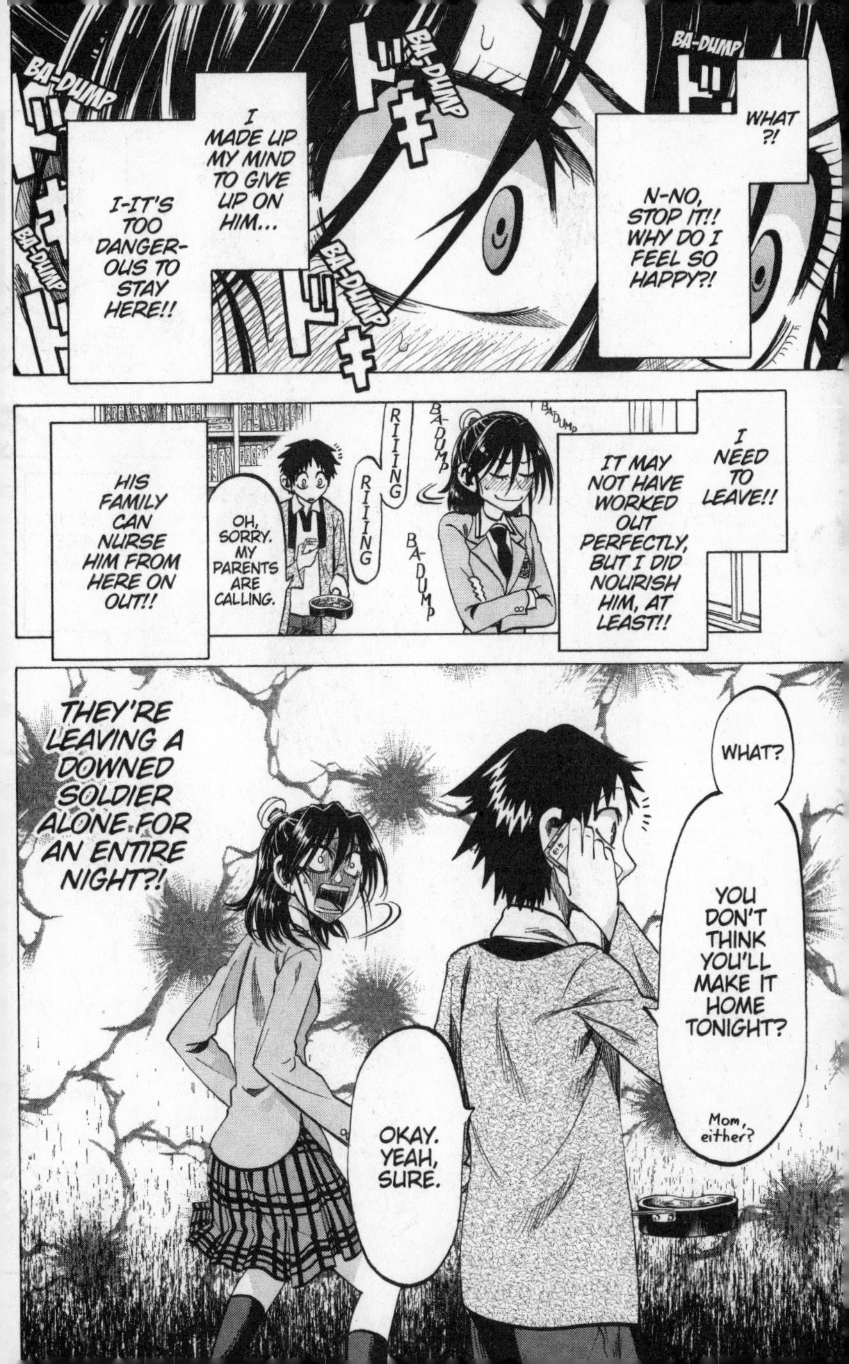
BA-DUMP
BA-DUMP
WHAT?!
N-NO, STOP IT!! WHY DO I FEEL SO HAPPY?!
BA-DUMP
I MADE UP MY MIND TO GIVE UP ON HIM...
I-IT'S TOO DANGER-OUS TO STAY HERE!!
BA-DUMP
BA-DUMP
I NEED TO LEAVE!!
IT MAY NOT HAVE WORKED OUT PERFECTLY, BUT I DID NOURISH HIM, AT LEAST!!
BADUMP
BA-DUMP
BA-DUMP
RIIING
RIIING
OH, SORRY. MY PARENTS ARE CALLING.
HIS FAMILY CAN NURSE HIM FROM HERE ON OUT!!
WHAT?
YOU DON'T THINK YOU'LL MAKE IT HOME TONIGHT?
Mom, either?
OKAY. YEAH, SURE.
THEY'RE LEAVING A DOWNED SOLDIER ALONE FOR AN ENTIRE NIGHT?!

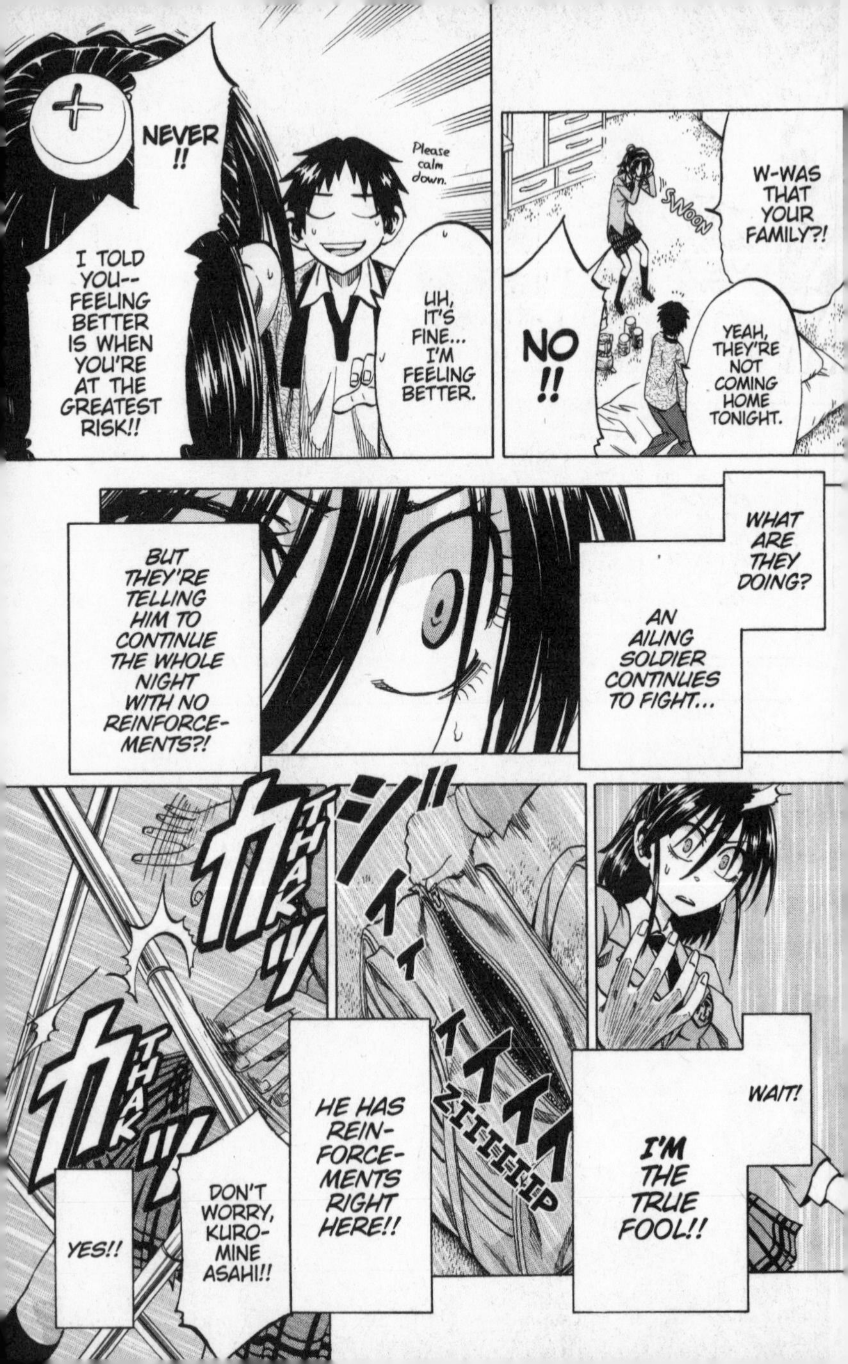
W-WAS THAT YOUR FAMILY?!
SWOON
YEAH, THEY'RE NOT COMING HOME TONIGHT.
NO!!
NEVER!!
Please calm down.
I TOLD YOU-- FEELING BETTER IS WHEN YOU'RE AT THE GREATEST RISK!!
UH, IT'S FINE... I'M FEELING BETTER.
WHAT ARE THEY DOING?
AN AILING SOLDIER CONTINUES TO FIGHT...
BUT THEY'RE TELLING HIM TO CONTINUE THE WHOLE NIGHT WITH NO REINFORCE-MENTS?!
WAIT!
I'M THE TRUE FOOL!!
ZIIIIIIIP
HE HAS REIN-FORCE-MENTS RIGHT HERE!!
THAK!!
THAK!!
DON'T WORRY, KURO-MINE ASAHI!!
YES!!

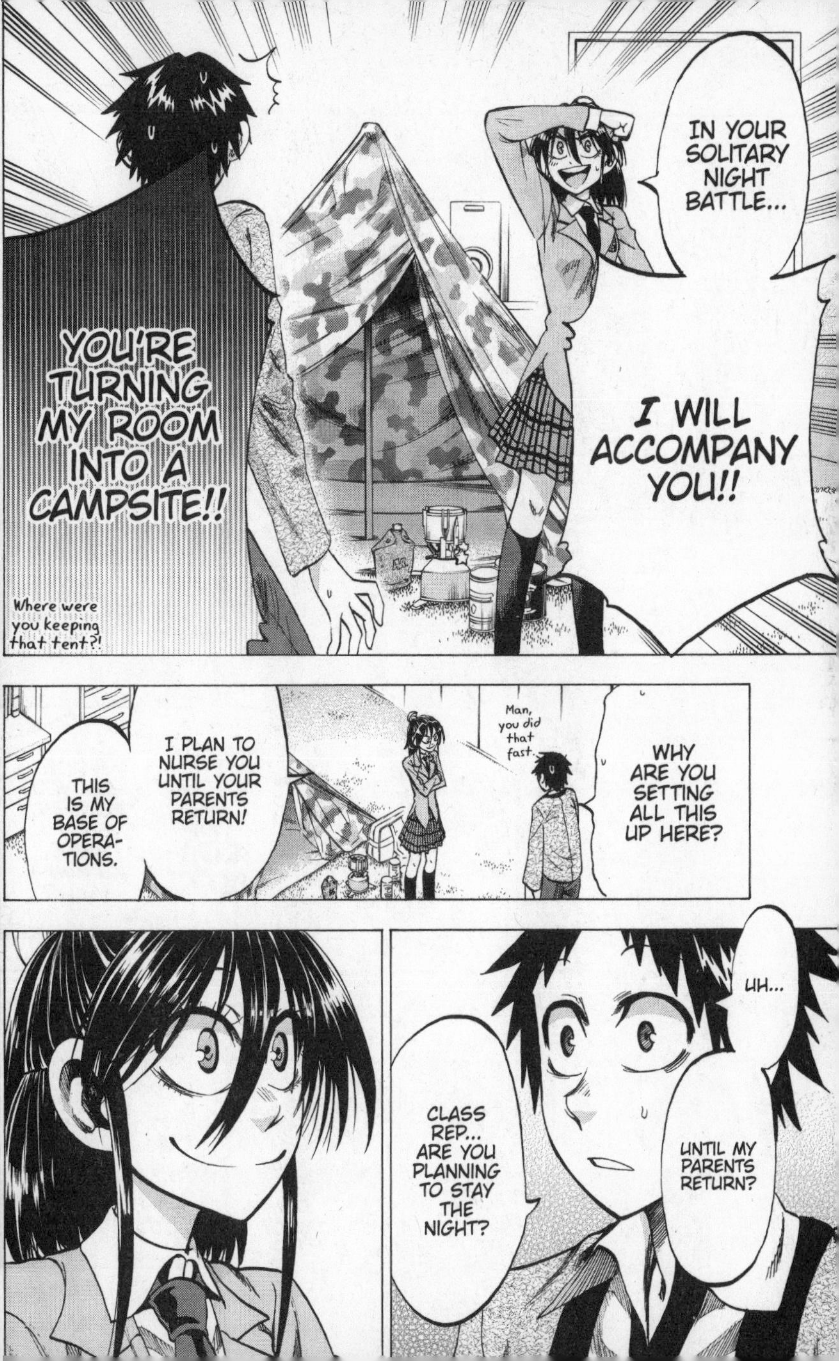
IN YOUR SOLITARY NIGHT BATTLE...
I WILL ACCOMPANY YOU!!
YOU'RE TURNING MY ROOM INTO A CAMPSITE!!
Where were you keeping that tent?!
WHY ARE YOU SETTING ALL THIS UP HERE?
Man, you did that fast.
I PLAN TO NURSE YOU UNTIL YOUR PARENTS RETURN!
THIS IS MY BASE OF OPERA-TIONS.
UH...
UNTIL MY PARENTS RETURN?
CLASS REP... ARE YOU PLANNING TO STAY THE NIGHT?

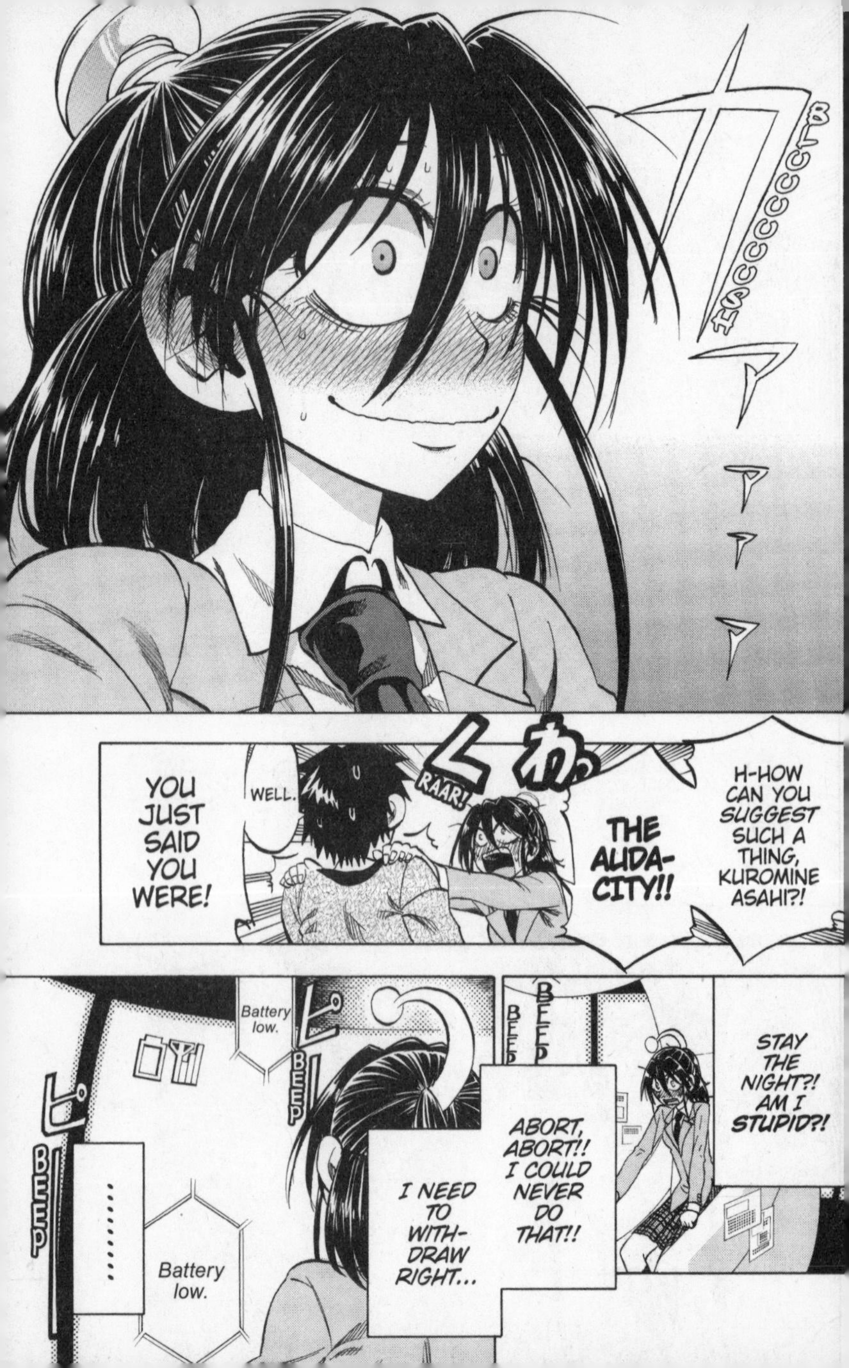
BLUUUUUUSH
H-HOW CAN YOU SUGGEST SUCH A THING, KUROMINE ASAHI?!
THE AUDA-CITY!!
RAAR!
WELL.
YOU JUST SAID YOU WERE!
STAY THE NIGHT?! AM I STUPID?!
ABORT, ABORT!! I COULD NEVER DO THAT!!
I NEED TO WITH-DRAW RIGHT...
BEEP
BEEP
Battery low.
BEEP
......
Battery low.

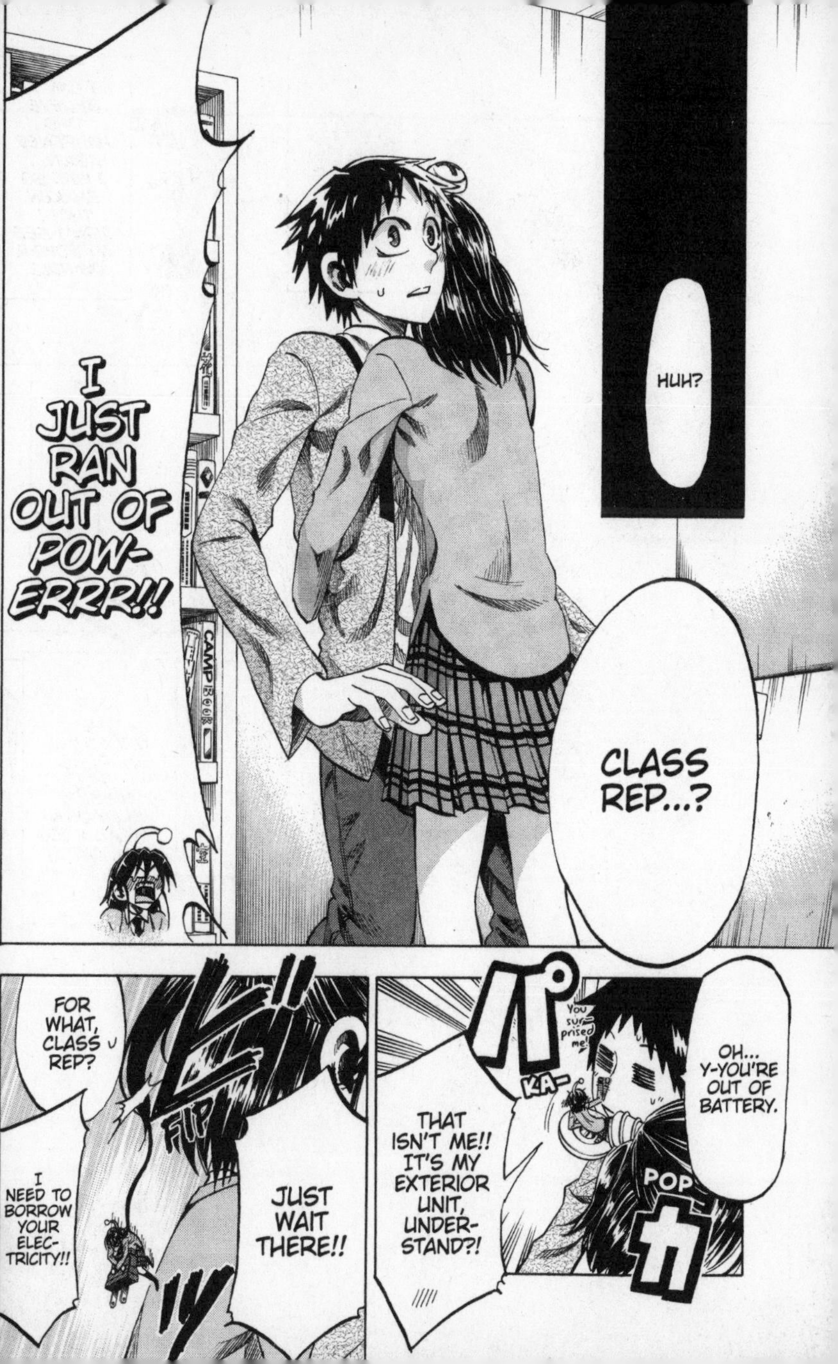
HUH?
CLASS REP...?
I JUST RAN OUT OF POW-ERRR!!
パ
You sur-prised me!
OH... Y-YOU'RE OUT OF BATTERY.
KA-
POP
カ
THAT ISN'T ME!! IT'S MY EXTERIOR UNIT, UNDER-STAND?!
FOR WHAT, CLASS REP?
FLIP
JUST WAIT THERE!!
I NEED TO BORROW YOUR ELEC-TRICITY!!

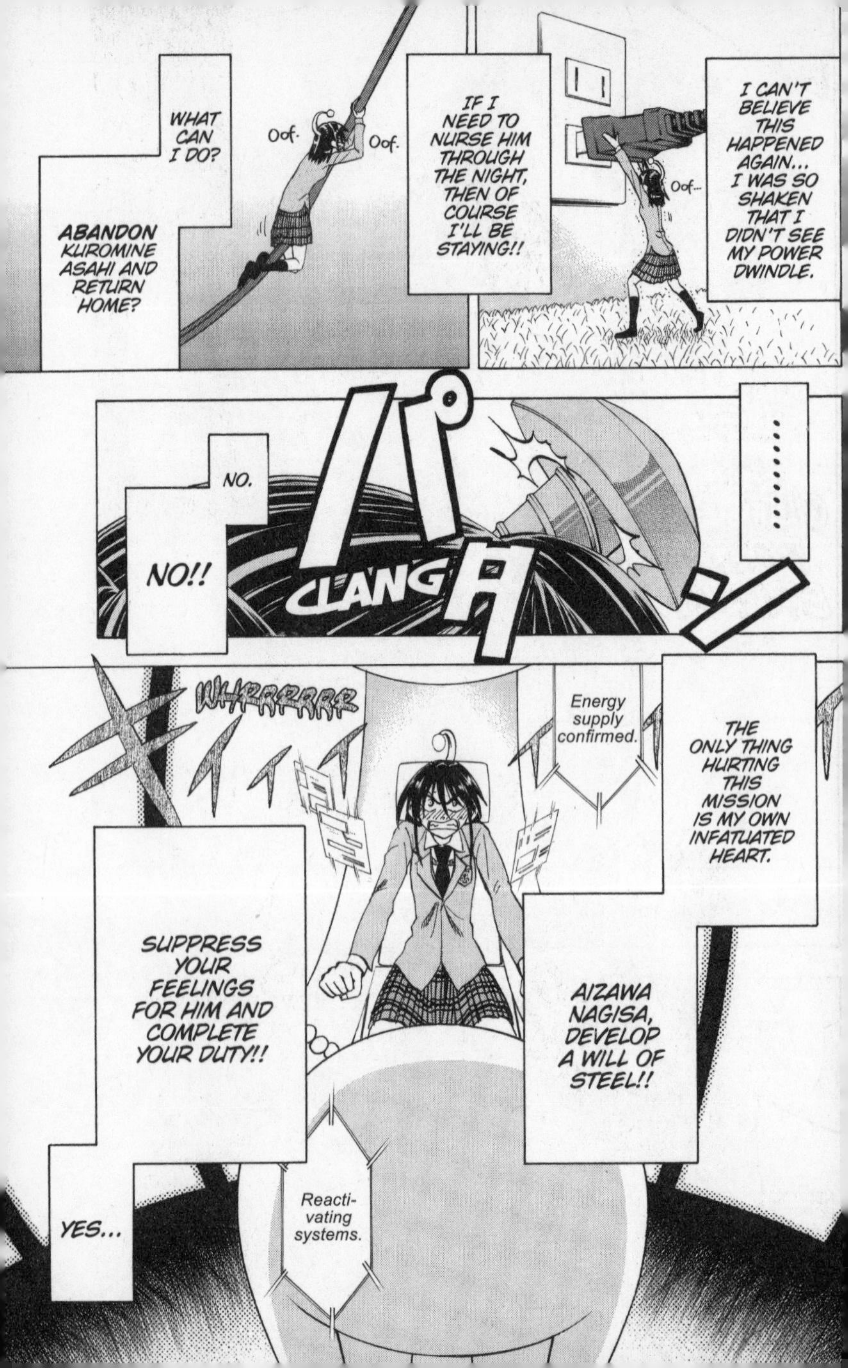
I CAN'T BELIEVE THIS HAPPENED AGAIN... I WAS SO SHAKEN THAT I DIDN'T SEE MY POWER DWINDLE.
Oof...
IF I NEED TO NURSE HIM THROUGH THE NIGHT, THEN OF COURSE I'LL BE STAYING!!
Oof.
Oof.
WHAT CAN I DO?
ABANDON KUROMINE ASAHI AND RETURN HOME?
......
CLANG
NO.
NO!!
THE ONLY THING HURTING THIS MISSION IS MY OWN INFATUATED HEART.
Energy supply confirmed.
WHIRRRRRRR
AIZAWA NAGISA, DEVELOP A WILL OF STEEL!!
SUPPRESS YOUR FEELINGS FOR HIM AND COMPLETE YOUR DUTY!!
Reacti-vating systems.
YES...

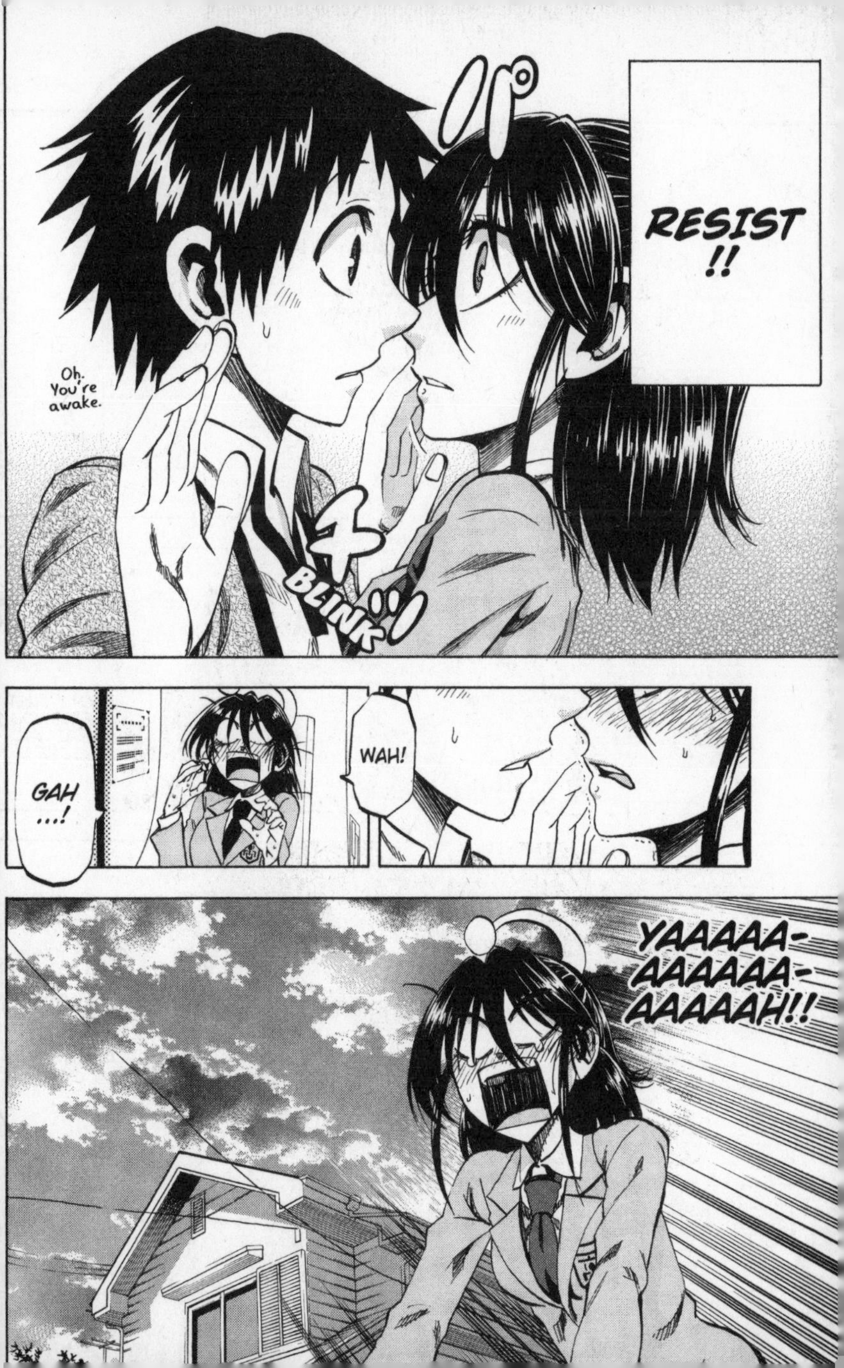
RESIST!!
Oh. You're awake.
BLINK...
WAH!
GAH...!
YAAAAA-AAAAAA-AAAAAH!!

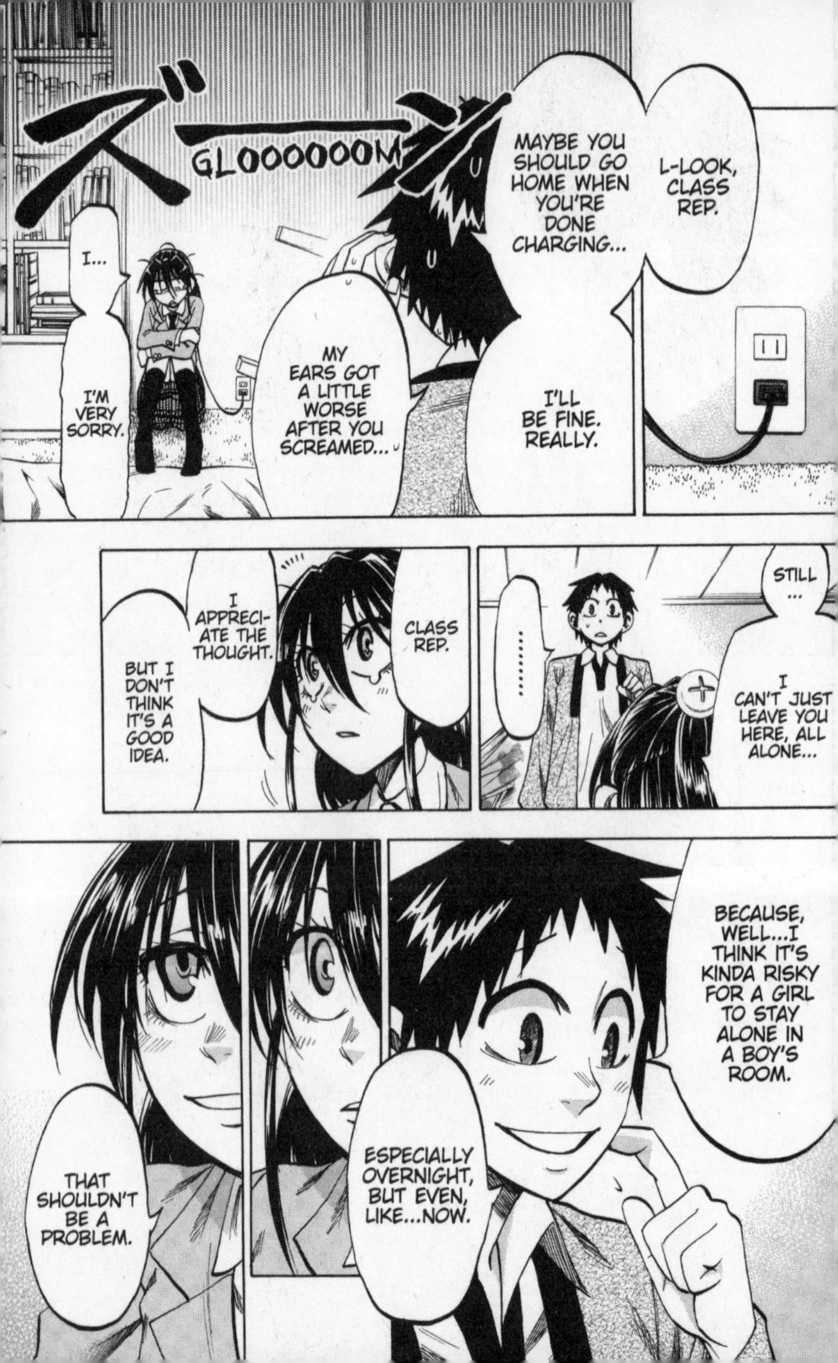
L-LOOK, CLASS REP.
MAYBE YOU SHOULD GO HOME WHEN YOU'RE DONE CHARGING...
I'LL BE FINE. REALLY.
GLOOOOOOM
MY EARS GOT A LITTLE WORSE AFTER YOU SCREAMED...
I...
I'M VERY SORRY.
STILL...
I CAN'T JUST LEAVE YOU HERE, ALL ALONE...
......
CLASS REP.
I APPRECIATE THE THOUGHT.
BUT I DON'T THINK IT'S A GOOD IDEA.
BECAUSE, WELL...I THINK IT'S KINDA RISKY FOR A GIRL TO STAY ALONE IN A BOY'S ROOM.
ESPECIALLY OVERNIGHT, BUT EVEN, LIKE...NOW.
THAT SHOULDN'T BE A PROBLEM.

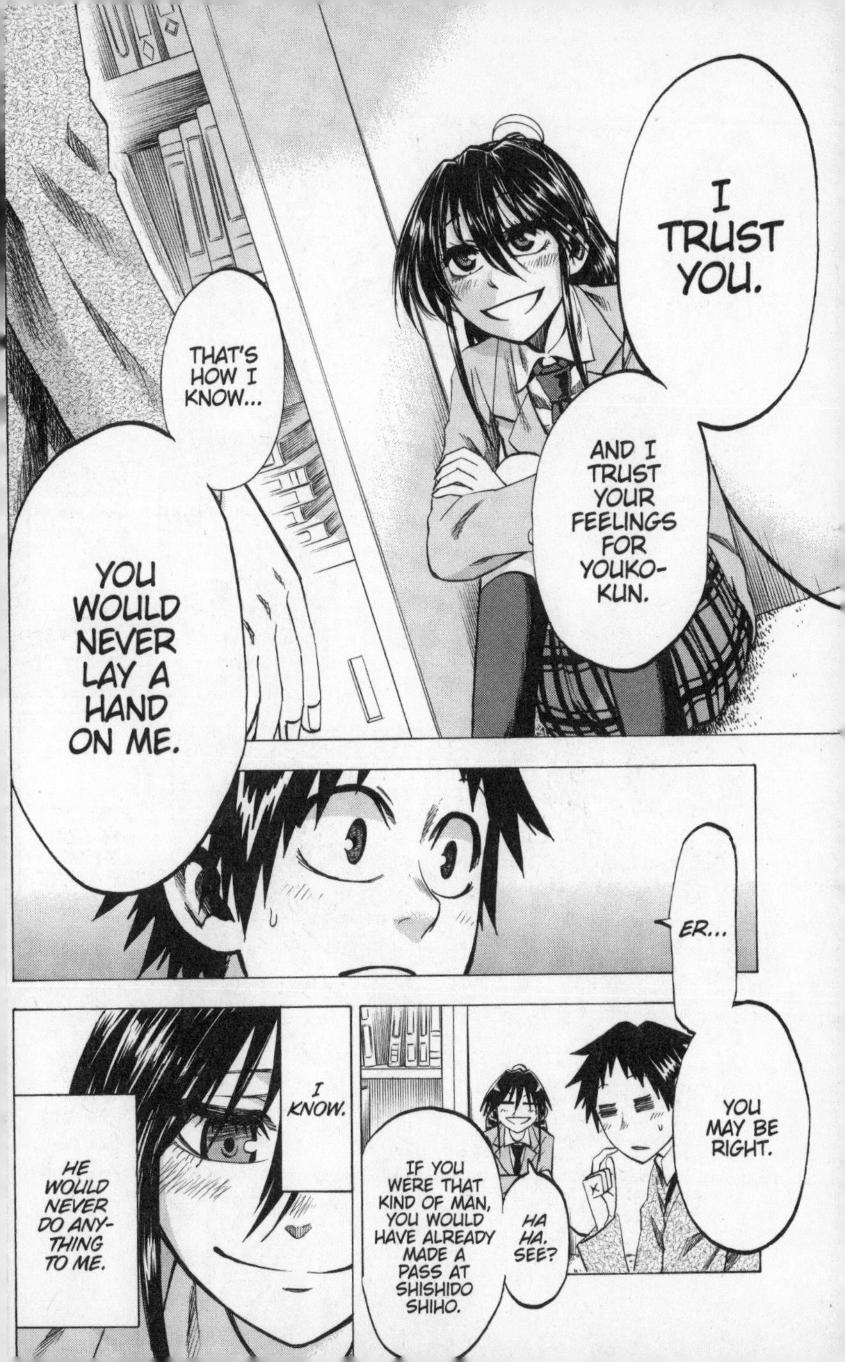
I TRUST YOU.
AND I TRUST YOUR FEELINGS FOR YOUKO-KUN.
THAT'S HOW I KNOW...
YOU WOULD NEVER LAY A HAND ON ME.
ER...
YOU MAY BE RIGHT.
HA HA. SEE?
IF YOU WERE THAT KIND OF MAN, YOU WOULD HAVE ALREADY MADE A PASS AT SHISHIDO SHIHO.
I KNOW.
HE WOULD NEVER DO ANY-THING TO ME.

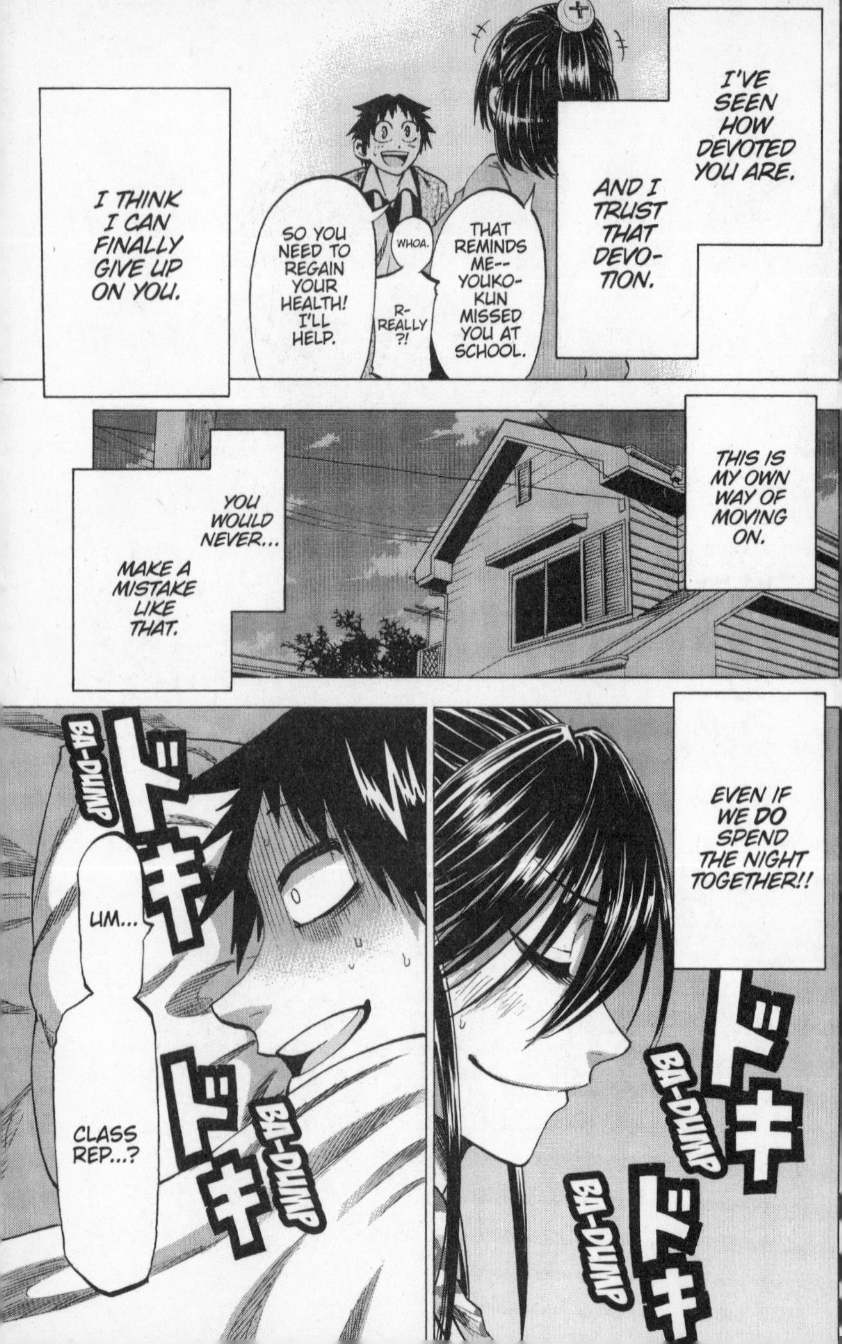
I'VE SEEN HOW DEVOTED YOU ARE.
AND I TRUST THAT DEVO-TION.
THAT REMINDS ME-- YOUKO-KUN MISSED YOU AT SCHOOL.
WHOA.
R-REALLY?!
SO YOU NEED TO REGAIN YOUR HEALTH! I'LL HELP.
I THINK I CAN FINALLY GIVE UP ON YOU.
THIS IS MY OWN WAY OF MOVING ON.
YOU WOULD NEVER...
MAKE A MISTAKE LIKE THAT.
EVEN IF WE DO SPEND THE NIGHT TOGETHER!!
ドキ
BA-DUMP
ドキ
BA-DUMP
ドキ
BA-DUMP
UM...
CLASS REP...?
ドキ
BA-DUMP

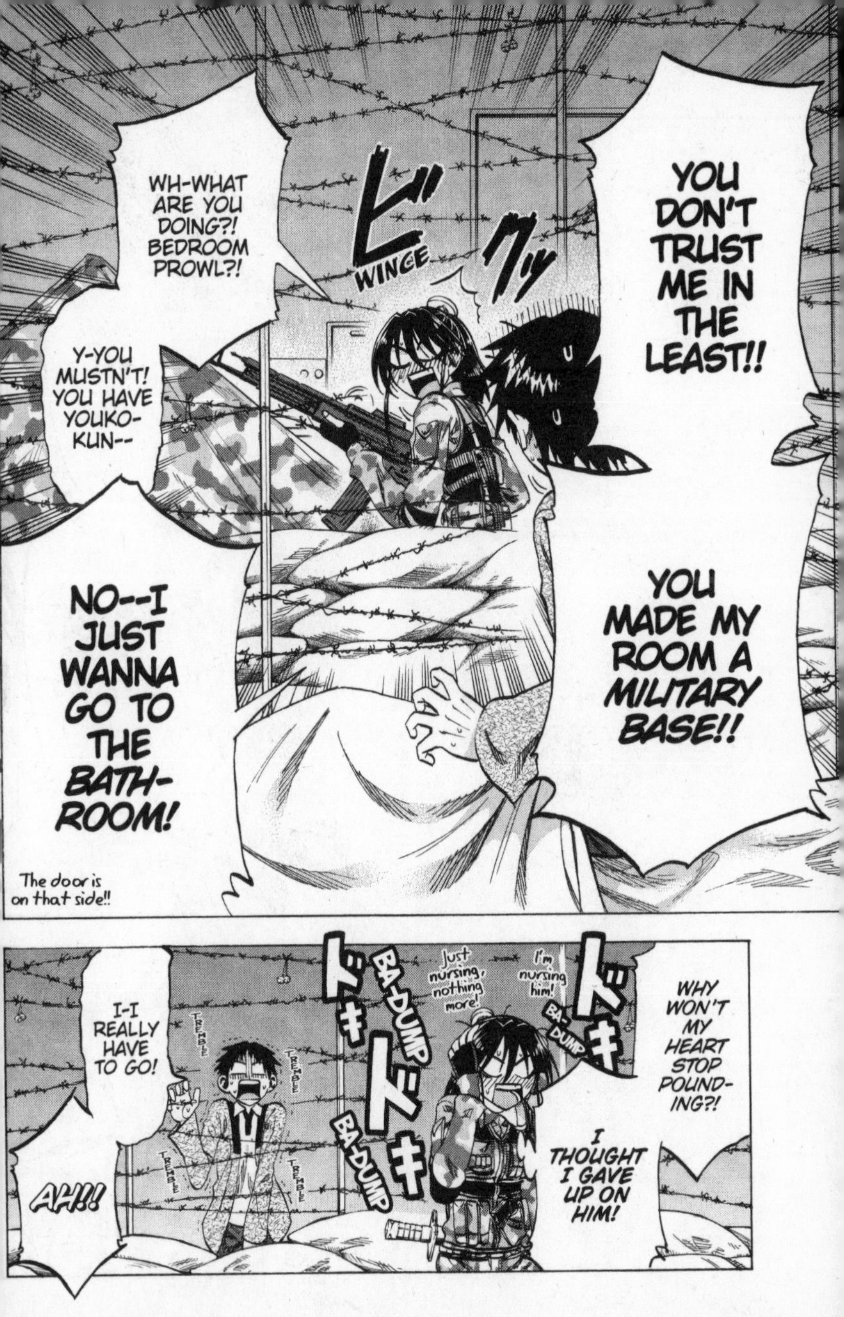
YOU DON'T TRUST ME IN THE LEAST!!
ビクッ
WINCE
WH-WHAT ARE YOU DOING?! BEDROOM PROWL?!
Y-YOU MUSTN'T! YOU HAVE YOUKO-KUN--
YOU MADE MY ROOM A MILITARY BASE!!
NO--I JUST WANNA GO TO THE BATHROOM!
The door is on that side!!
WHY WON'T MY HEART STOP POUNDING?!
I THOUGHT I GAVE UP ON HIM!
I'm nursing him!
ドキ
BA-DUMP
Just nursing, nothing more!
ドキドキ
BA-DUMP
BA-DUMP
TREMBLE
TREMBLE
I-I REALLY HAVE TO GO!
TREMBLE
TREMBLE
AH!!

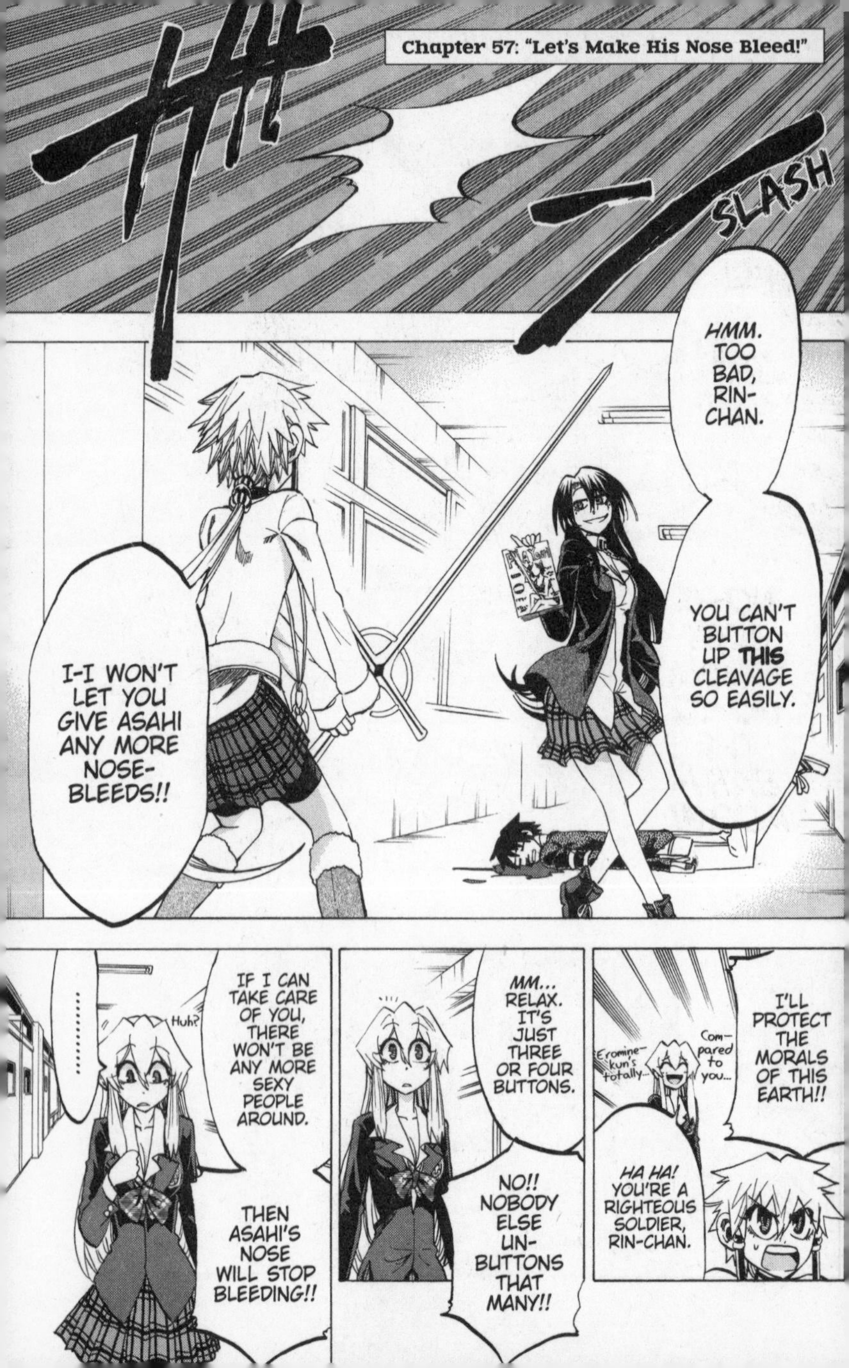
Chapter 57: "Let's Make His Nose Bleed!"
SLASH
HMM. TOO BAD, RIN-CHAN.
YOU CAN'T BUTTON UP **THIS** CLEAVAGE SO EASILY.
I-I WON'T LET YOU GIVE ASAHI ANY MORE NOSE-BLEEDS!!
I'LL PROTECT THE MORALS OF THIS EARTH!!
Compared to you...
Eromine-kun's totally...
HA HA! YOU'RE A RIGHTEOUS SOLDIER, RIN-CHAN.
MM... RELAX. IT'S JUST THREE OR FOUR BUTTONS.
NO!! NOBODY ELSE UN-BUTTONS THAT MANY!!
IF I CAN TAKE CARE OF YOU, THERE WON'T BE ANY MORE SEXY PEOPLE AROUND.
Huh?
......
THEN ASAHI'S NOSE WILL STOP BLEEDING!!

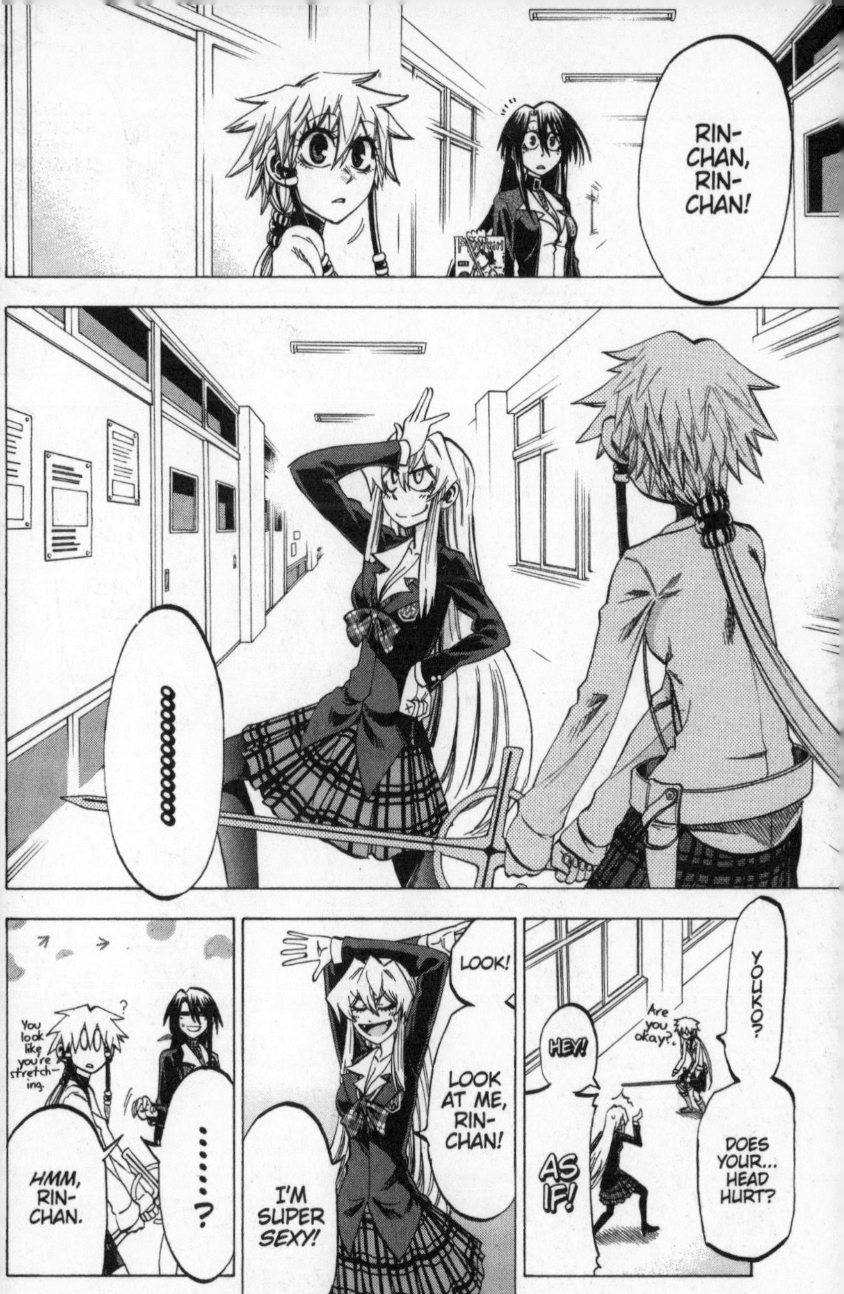
RIN-CHAN, RIN-CHAN!
ooooooooooooo
YOUKO?
Are you okay?
HEY!
DOES YOUR... HEAD HURT?
AS IF!
LOOK!
LOOK AT ME, RIN-CHAN!
I'M SUPER SEXY!
......?
You look like you're stretching.
HMM, RIN-CHAN.

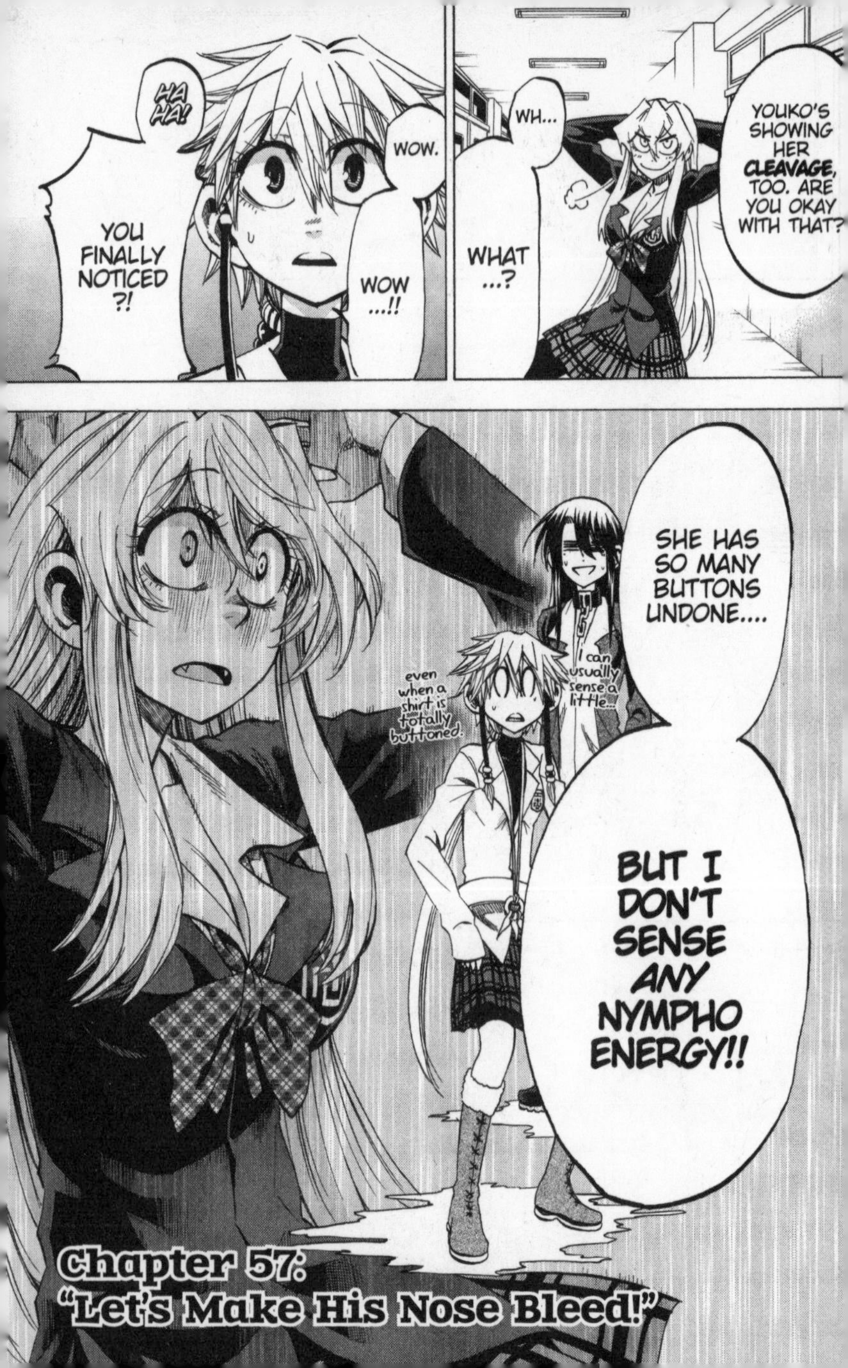
YOUKO'S SHOWING HER CLEAVAGE, TOO. ARE YOU OKAY WITH THAT?
WH...
WHAT ...?
WOW.
WOW ...!!
HA HA!
YOU FINALLY NOTICED ?!
SHE HAS SO MANY BUTTONS UNDONE....
BUT I DON'T SENSE ANY NYMPHO ENERGY!!
I can usually sense a little...
even when a shirt is totally buttoned.
Chapter 57: "Let's Make His Nose Bleed!"

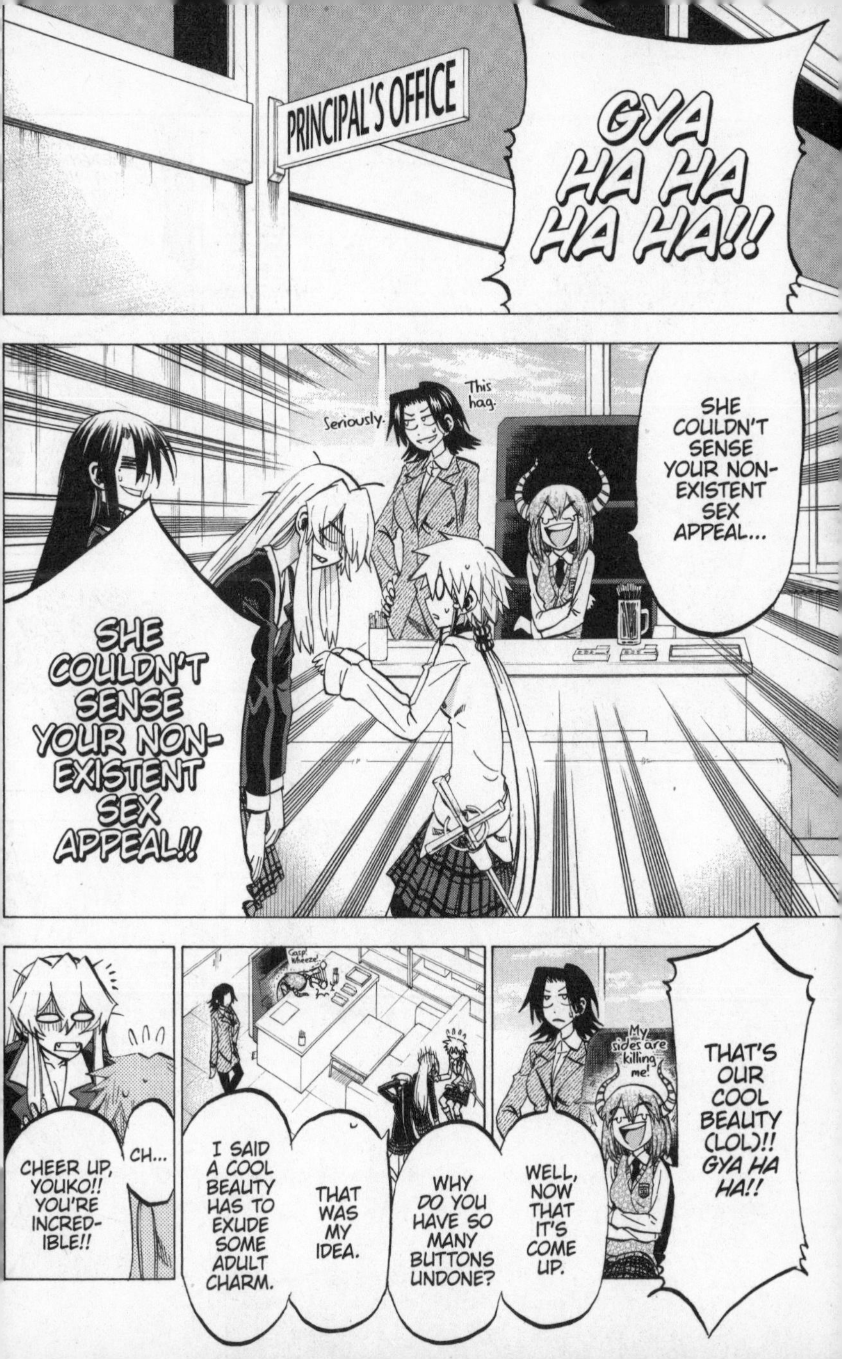
PRINCIPAL'S OFFICE
GYA HA HA HA HA!!
SHE COULDN'T SENSE YOUR NON-EXISTENT SEX APPEAL...
This hag.
Seriously.
SHE COULDN'T SENSE YOUR NON-EXISTENT SEX APPEAL!!
THAT'S OUR COOL BEAUTY (LOL)!! GYA HA HA!!
My sides are killing me!
WELL, NOW THAT IT'S COME UP.
WHY DO YOU HAVE SO MANY BUTTONS UNDONE?
Gasp! Wheeze!
THAT WAS MY IDEA.
I SAID A COOL BEAUTY HAS TO EXUDE SOME ADULT CHARM.
CH...
CHEER UP, YOUKO!! YOU'RE INCRED-IBLE!!

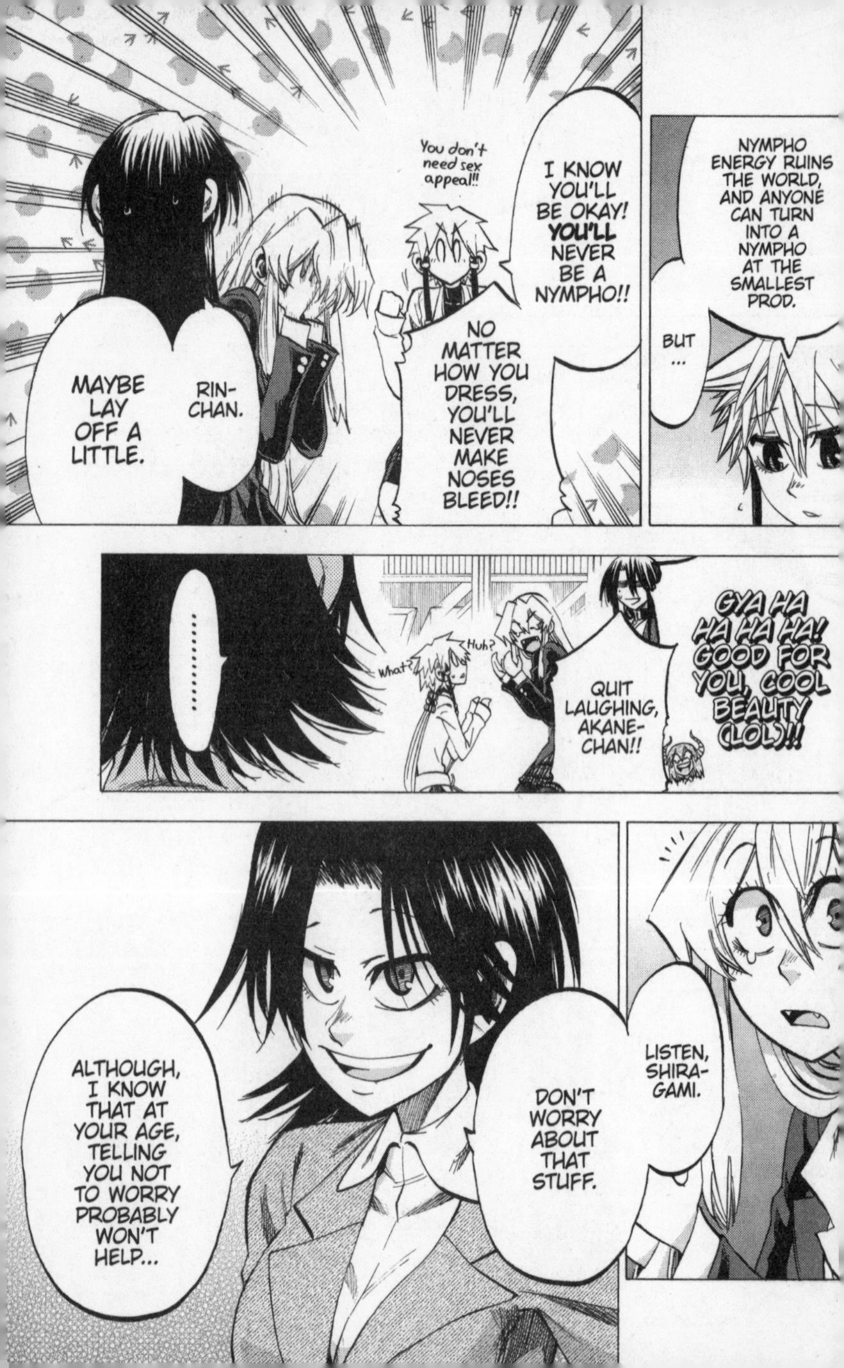
NYMPHO ENERGY RUINS THE WORLD, AND ANYONE CAN TURN INTO A NYMPHO AT THE SMALLEST PROD.
BUT ...
I KNOW YOU'LL BE OKAY! **YOU'LL** NEVER BE A NYMPHO!!
You don't need sex appeal!!
NO MATTER HOW YOU DRESS, YOU'LL NEVER MAKE NOSES BLEED!!
RIN-CHAN.
MAYBE LAY OFF A LITTLE.
GYA HA HA HA HA! GOOD FOR YOU, COOL BEAUTY (LOL)!!
QUIT LAUGHING, AKANE-CHAN!!
Huh?
What?
......
LISTEN, SHIRA-GAMI.
DON'T WORRY ABOUT THAT STUFF.
ALTHOUGH, I KNOW THAT AT YOUR AGE, TELLING YOU NOT TO WORRY PROBABLY WON'T HELP...

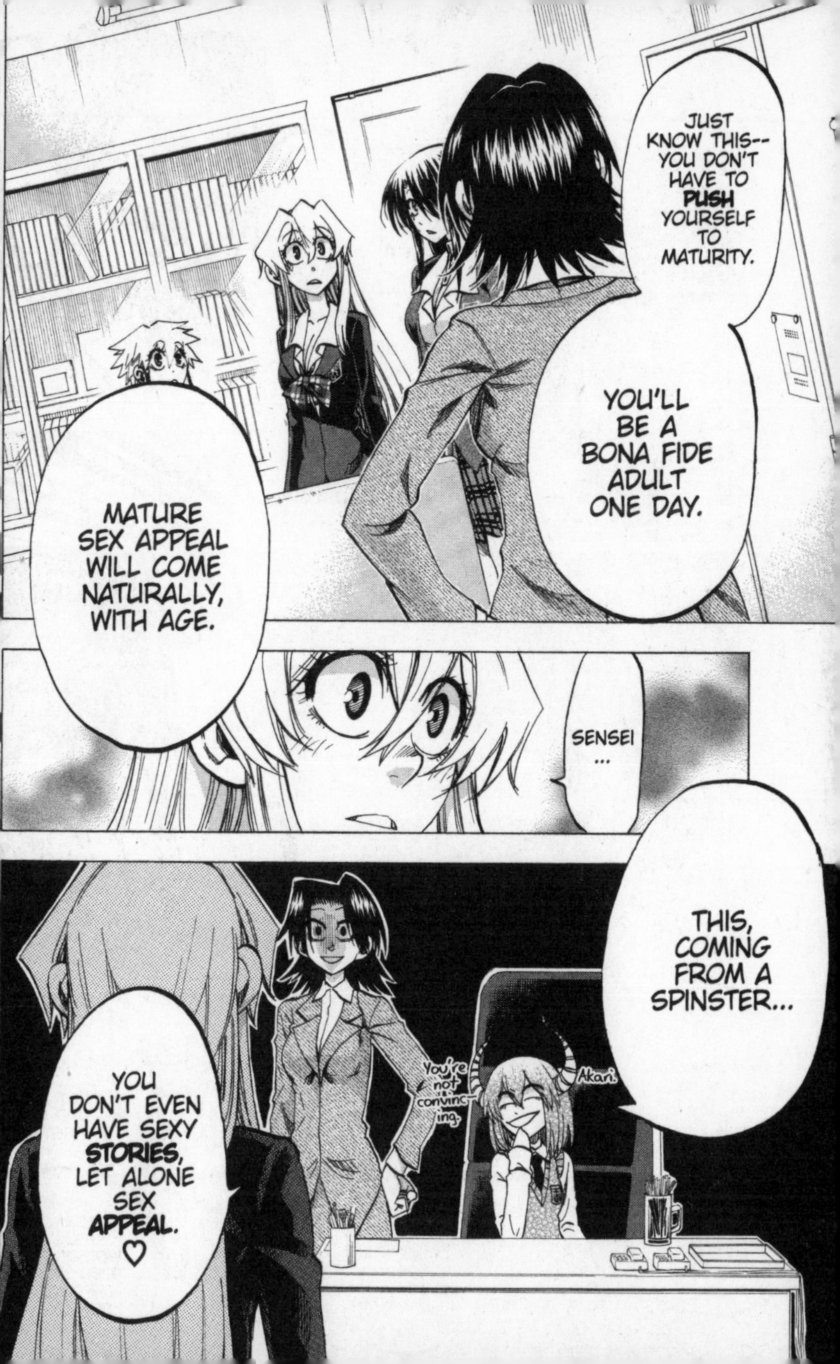
JUST KNOW THIS-- YOU DON'T HAVE TO PUSH YOURSELF TO MATURITY.
YOU'LL BE A BONA FIDE ADULT ONE DAY.
MATURE SEX APPEAL WILL COME NATURALLY, WITH AGE.
SENSEI ...
THIS, COMING FROM A SPINSTER...
Akari.
You're not convincing.
YOU DON'T EVEN HAVE SEXY STORIES, LET ALONE SEX APPEAL. ♡

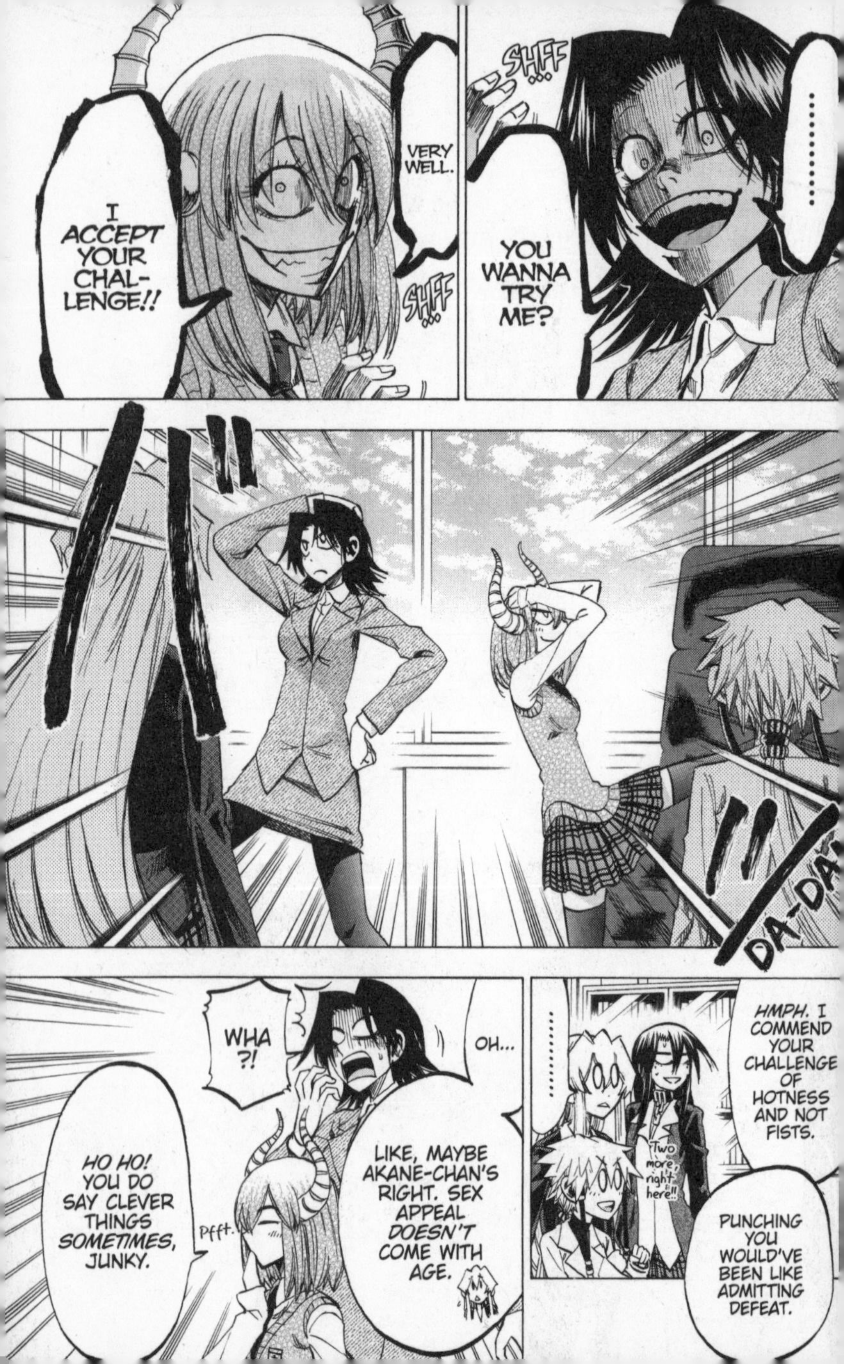
......
SHFF...
YOU WANNA TRY ME?
VERY WELL.
SHFF...
I ACCEPT YOUR CHAL-LENGE!!
DA-DA
HMPH. I COMMEND YOUR CHALLENGE OF HOTNESS AND NOT FISTS.
......
Two more, right here!!
PUNCHING YOU WOULD'VE BEEN LIKE ADMITTING DEFEAT.
OH...
WHA ?!
LIKE, MAYBE AKANE-CHAN'S RIGHT. SEX APPEAL *DOESN'T* COME WITH AGE.
Pfft.
HO HO! YOU DO SAY CLEVER THINGS *SOMETIMES,* JUNKY.

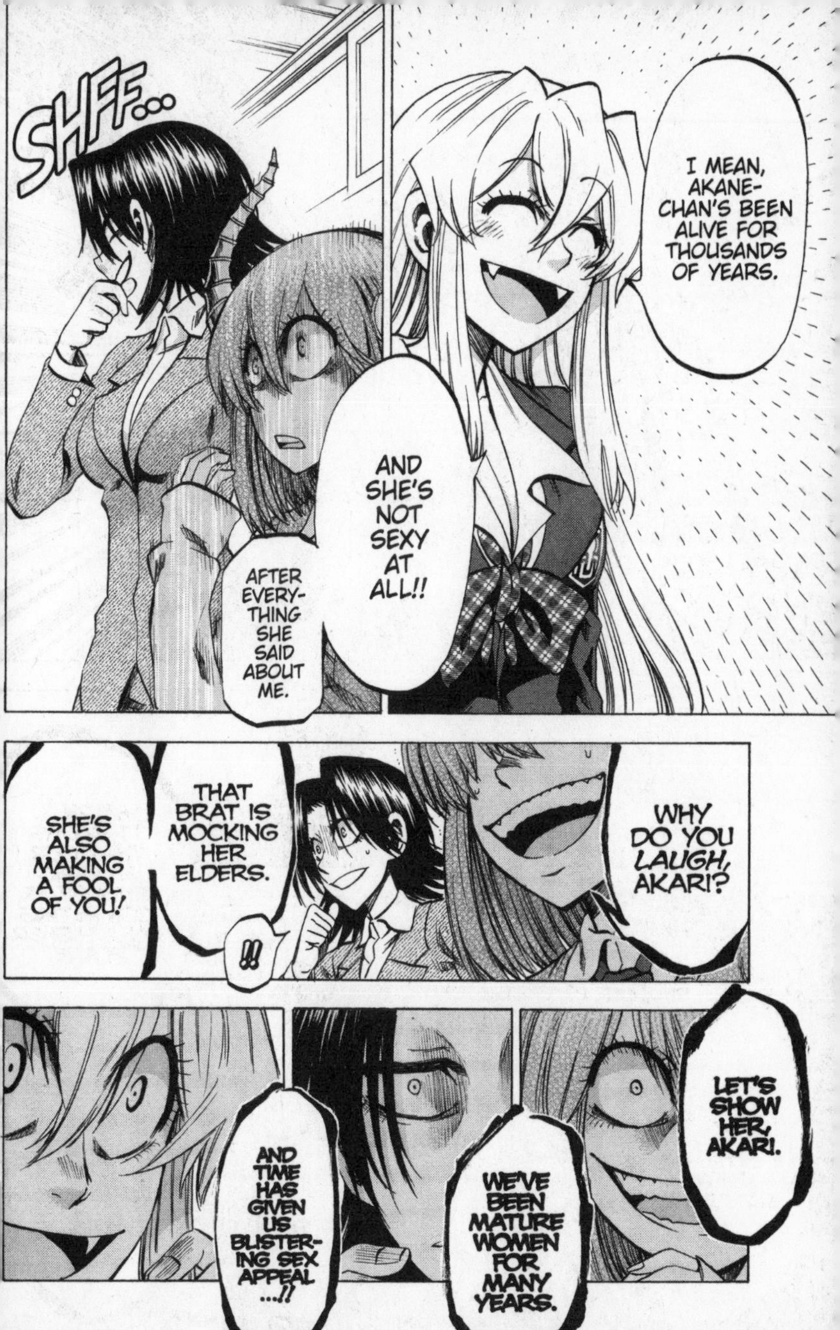
I MEAN, AKANE-CHAN'S BEEN ALIVE FOR THOUSANDS OF YEARS.
AND SHE'S NOT SEXY AT ALL!!
SHFF...
AFTER EVERY-THING SHE SAID ABOUT ME.
WHY DO YOU LAUGH, AKARI?
!!
THAT BRAT IS MOCKING HER ELDERS.
SHE'S ALSO MAKING A FOOL OF YOU!
LET'S SHOW HER, AKARI.
WE'VE BEEN MATURE WOMEN FOR MANY YEARS.
AND TIME HAS GIVEN US BLISTER-ING SEX APPEAL ...!!

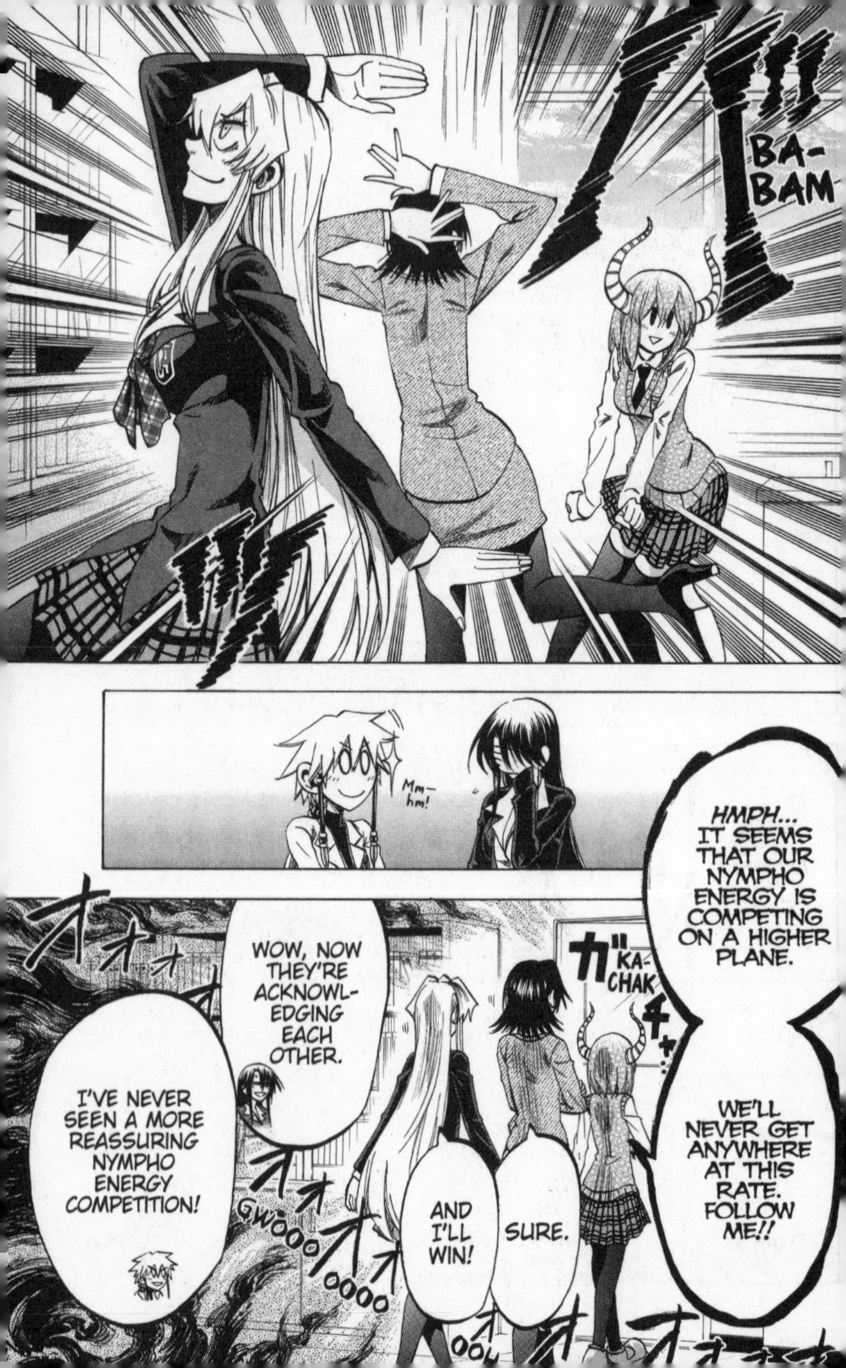
BA-BAM
HMPH... IT SEEMS THAT OUR NYMPHO ENERGY IS COMPETING ON A HIGHER PLANE.
Mm-hm!
KA-CHAK
WE'LL NEVER GET ANYWHERE AT THIS RATE. FOLLOW ME!!
SURE.
AND I'LL WIN!
WOW, NOW THEY'RE ACKNOWL-EDGING EACH OTHER.
I'VE NEVER SEEN A MORE REASSURING NYMPHO ENERGY COMPETITION!
GWOOOO
OOOO

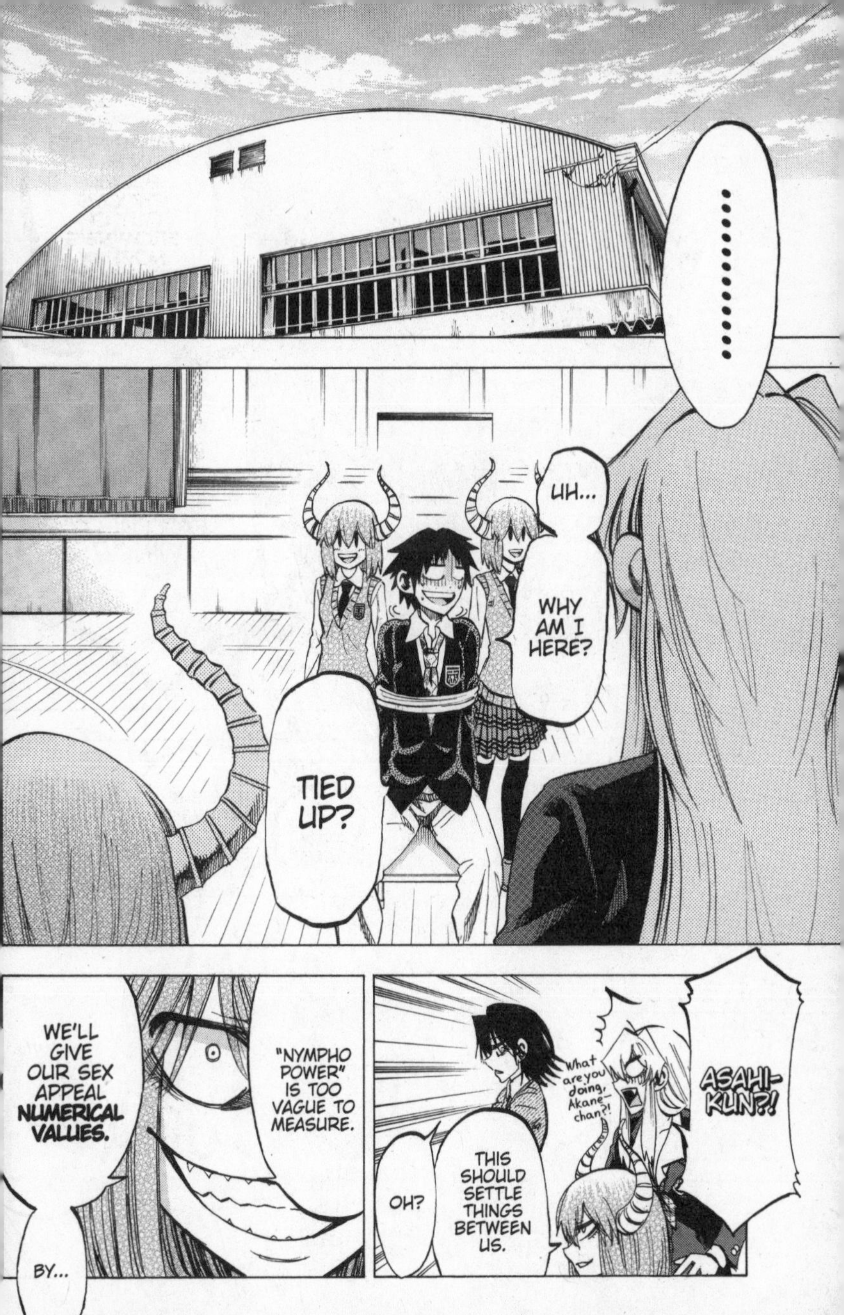
......
UH...
WHY AM I HERE?
TIED UP?
ASAHI-KUN?!
What are you doing, Akane-chan?!
THIS SHOULD SETTLE THINGS BETWEEN US.
OH?
"NYMPHO POWER" IS TOO VAGUE TO MEASURE.
WE'LL GIVE OUR SEX APPEAL NUMERICAL VALUES.
BY...

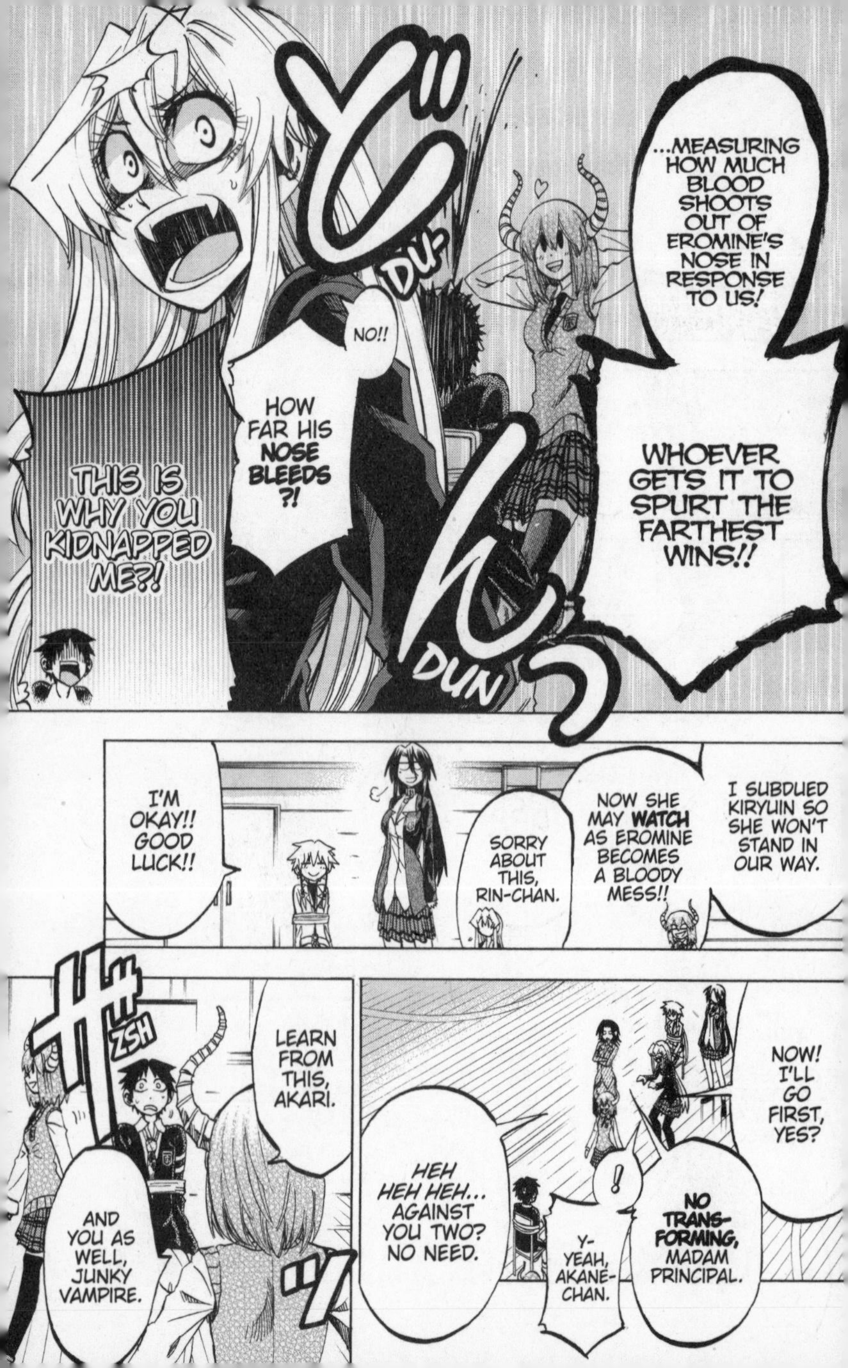
...MEASURING HOW MUCH BLOOD SHOOTS OUT OF EROMINE'S NOSE IN RESPONSE TO US!
WHOEVER GETS IT TO SPURT THE FARTHEST WINS!!
DU-
DUN
NO!!
HOW FAR HIS NOSE BLEEDS?!
THIS IS WHY YOU KIDNAPPED ME?!
I SUBDUED KIRYUIN SO SHE WON'T STAND IN OUR WAY.
NOW SHE MAY WATCH AS EROMINE BECOMES A BLOODY MESS!!
SORRY ABOUT THIS, RIN-CHAN.
I'M OKAY!! GOOD LUCK!!
NOW! I'LL GO FIRST, YES?
NO TRANS-FORMING, MADAM PRINCIPAL.
!
Y-YEAH, AKANE-CHAN.
HEH HEH HEH... AGAINST YOU TWO? NO NEED.
LEARN FROM THIS, AKARI.
ZSH
AND YOU AS WELL, JUNKY VAMPIRE.

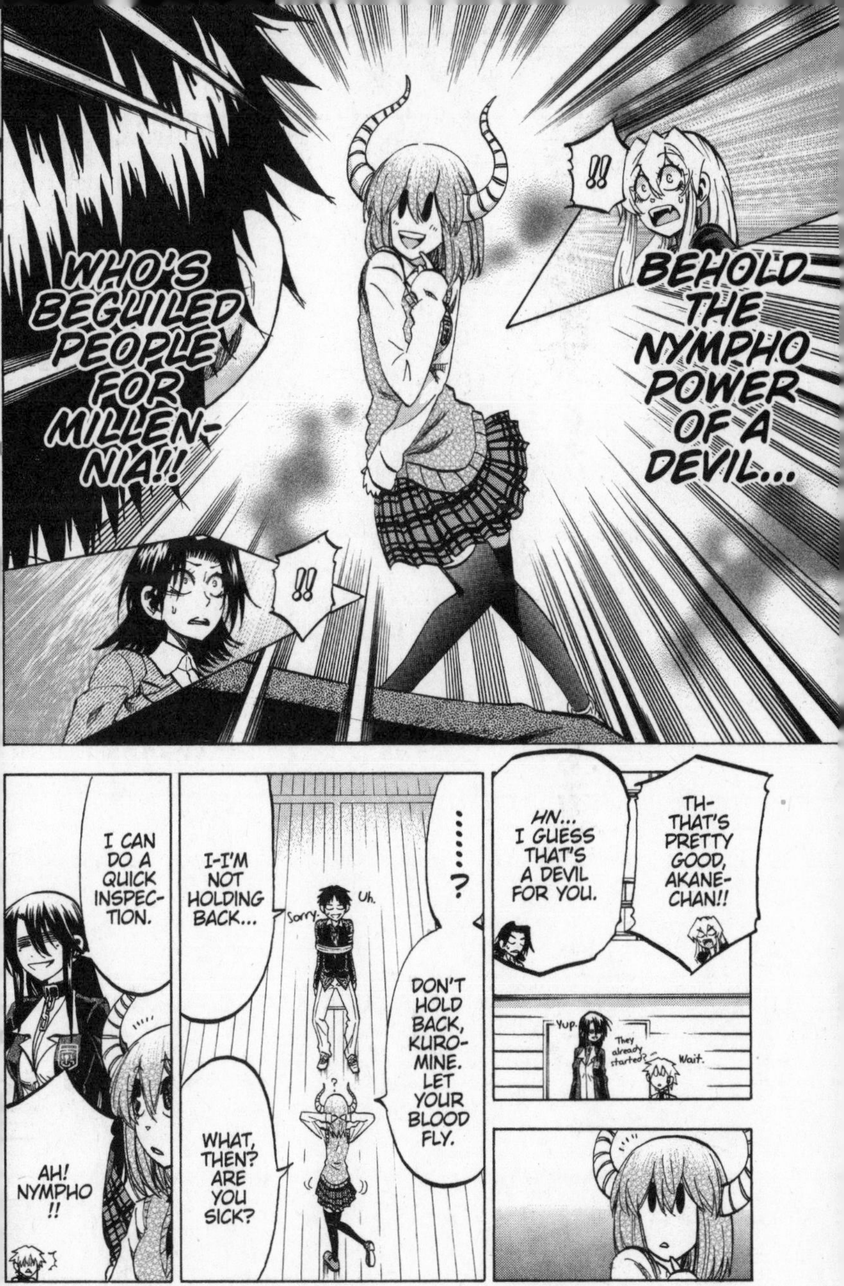
!!
BEHOLD THE NYMPHO POWER OF A DEVIL...
WHO'S BEGUILED PEOPLE FOR MILLEN-NIA!!
!!
TH-THAT'S PRETTY GOOD, AKANE-CHAN!!
HN... I GUESS THAT'S A DEVIL FOR YOU.
They already started?
Wait.
Yup.
......?
DON'T HOLD BACK, KURO-MINE. LET YOUR BLOOD FLY.
Uh.
Sorry.
I-I'M NOT HOLDING BACK...
WHAT, THEN? ARE YOU SICK?
I CAN DO A QUICK INSPEC-TION.
AH! NYMPHO!!

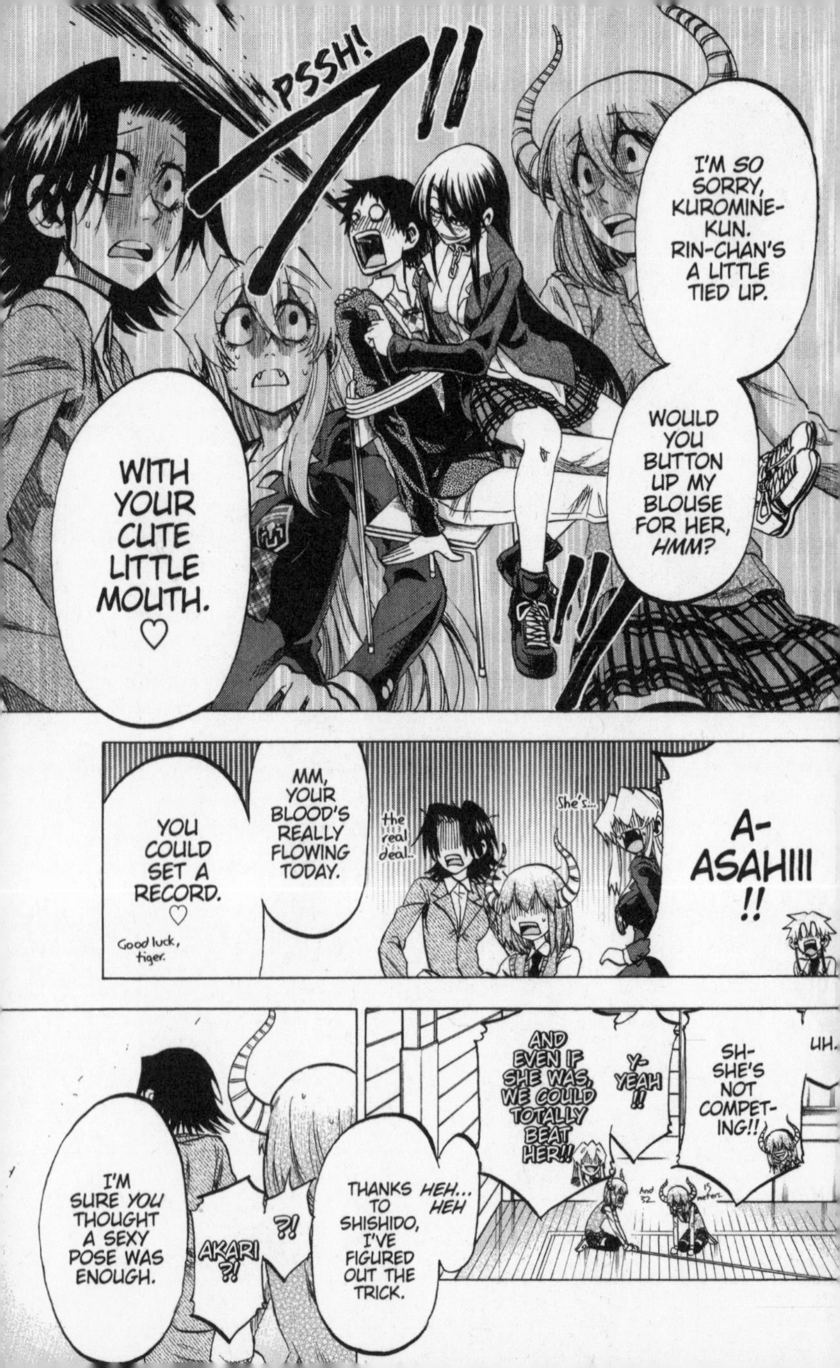
PSSH!
I'M SO SORRY, KUROMINE-KUN. RIN-CHAN'S A LITTLE TIED UP.
WOULD YOU BUTTON UP MY BLOUSE FOR HER, HMM?
WITH YOUR CUTE LITTLE MOUTH. ♡
A-ASAHIIII!!
She's...
the real deal..
MM, YOUR BLOOD'S REALLY FLOWING TODAY.
YOU COULD SET A RECORD. ♡
Good luck, tiger.
UH.
SH-SHE'S NOT COMPETING!!
15 meters.
Y-YEAH!!
AND EVEN IF SHE WAS, WE COULD TOTALLY BEAT HER!!
And 32
HEH... HEH
THANKS TO SHISHIDO, I'VE FIGURED OUT THE TRICK.
?!
AKARI?!
I'M SURE YOU THOUGHT A SEXY POSE WAS ENOUGH.

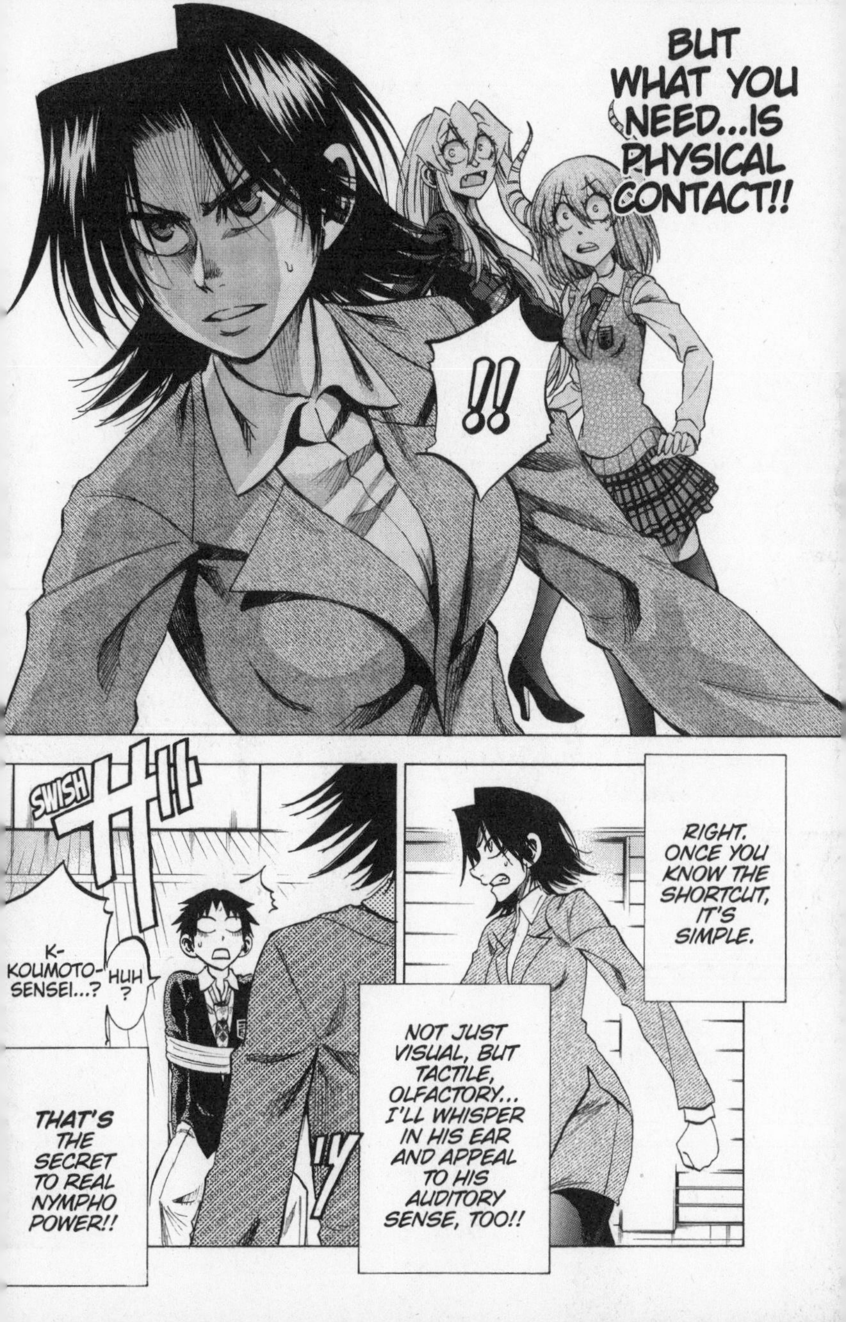
BUT WHAT YOU NEED...IS PHYSICAL CONTACT!!
!!
RIGHT. ONCE YOU KNOW THE SHORTCUT, IT'S SIMPLE.
NOT JUST VISUAL, BUT TACTILE, OLFACTORY... I'LL WHISPER IN HIS EAR AND APPEAL TO HIS AUDITORY SENSE, TOO!!
SWISH
HUH ?
K-KOUMOTO-SENSEI...?
THAT'S THE SECRET TO REAL NYMPHO POWER!!

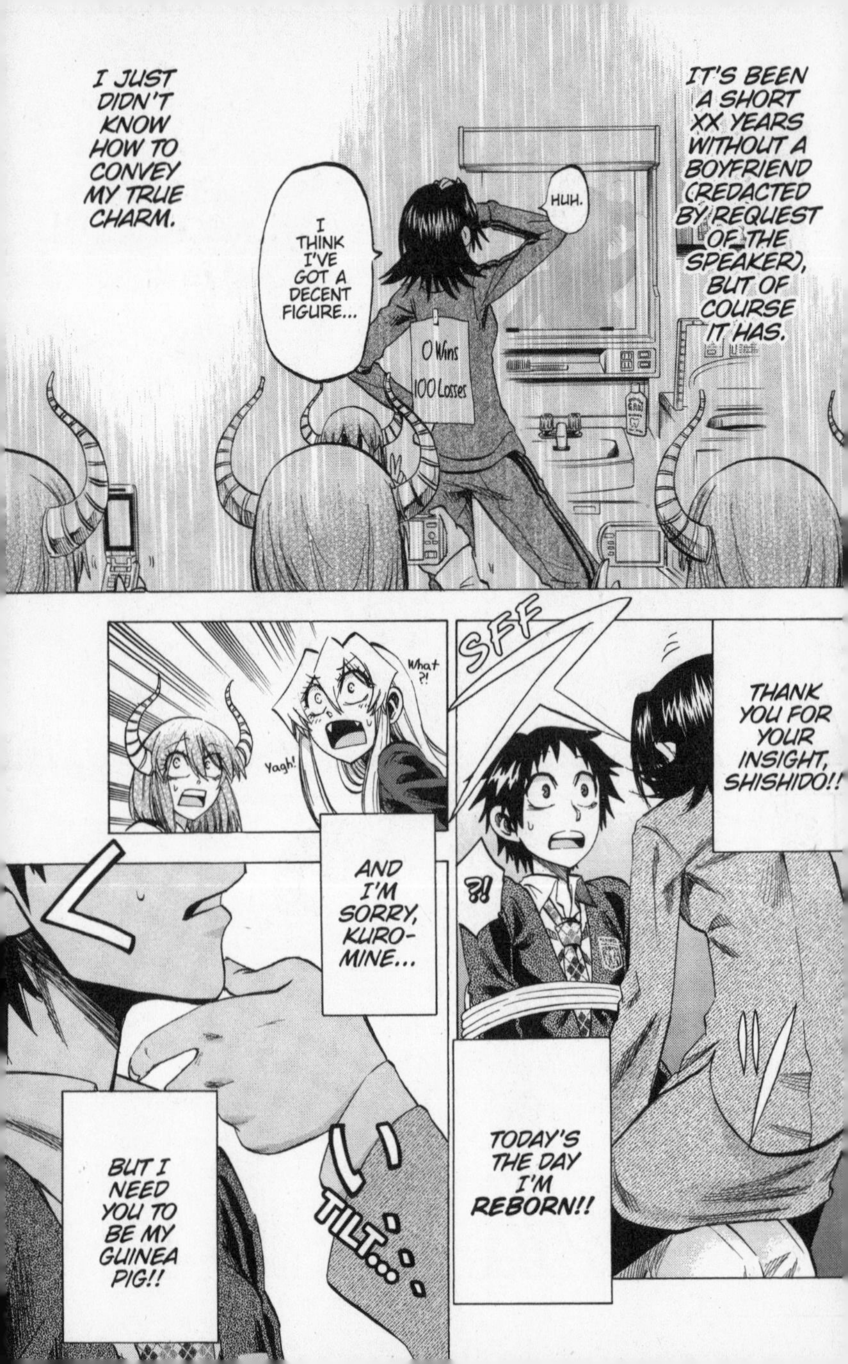
IT'S BEEN A SHORT XX YEARS WITHOUT A BOYFRIEND (REDACTED BY REQUEST OF THE SPEAKER), BUT OF COURSE IT HAS.
HUH.
I THINK I'VE GOT A DECENT FIGURE...
0 Wins 100 Losses
I JUST DIDN'T KNOW HOW TO CONVEY MY TRUE CHARM.
SFF
THANK YOU FOR YOUR INSIGHT, SHISHIDO!!
?!
What ?!
Yagh!
AND I'M SORRY, KURO-MINE...
TODAY'S THE DAY I'M REBORN!!
TILT...
BUT I NEED YOU TO BE MY GUINEA PIG!!

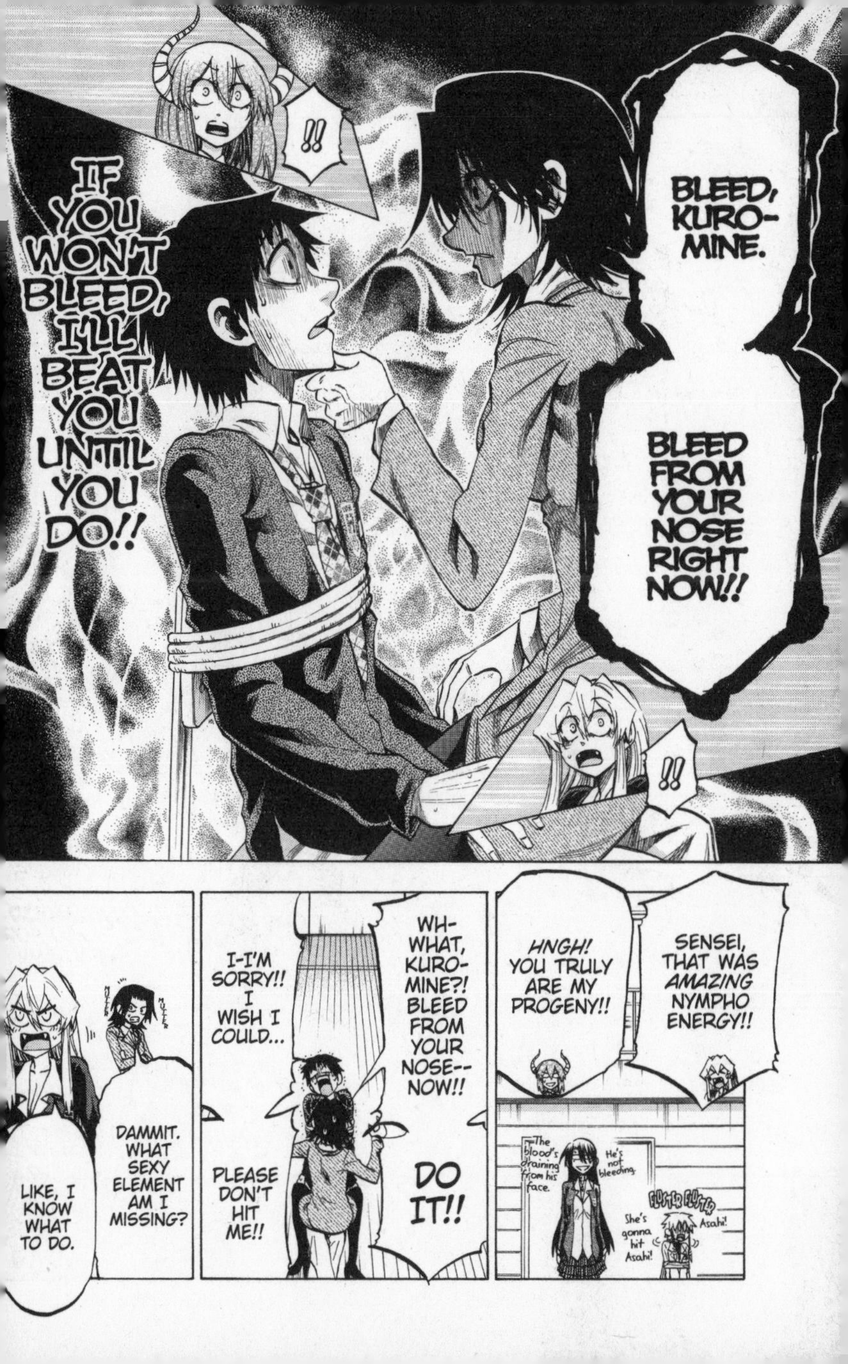
BLEED, KURO-MINE.
!!
BLEED FROM YOUR NOSE RIGHT NOW!!
IF YOU WON'T BLEED, I'LL BEAT YOU UNTIL YOU DO!!
!!
SENSEI, THAT WAS AMAZING NYMPHO ENERGY!!
HNGH! YOU TRULY ARE MY PROGENY!!
He's not bleeding.
The blood's draining from his face.
FLUSTER FLUSTER
Asahi!
She's gonna hit Asahi!
WH-WHAT, KURO-MINE?! BLEED FROM YOUR NOSE--NOW!!
I-I'M SORRY!! I WISH I COULD...
DO IT!!
PLEASE DON'T HIT ME!!
MUTTER MUTTER
DAMMIT. WHAT SEXY ELEMENT AM I MISSING?
LIKE, I KNOW WHAT TO DO.

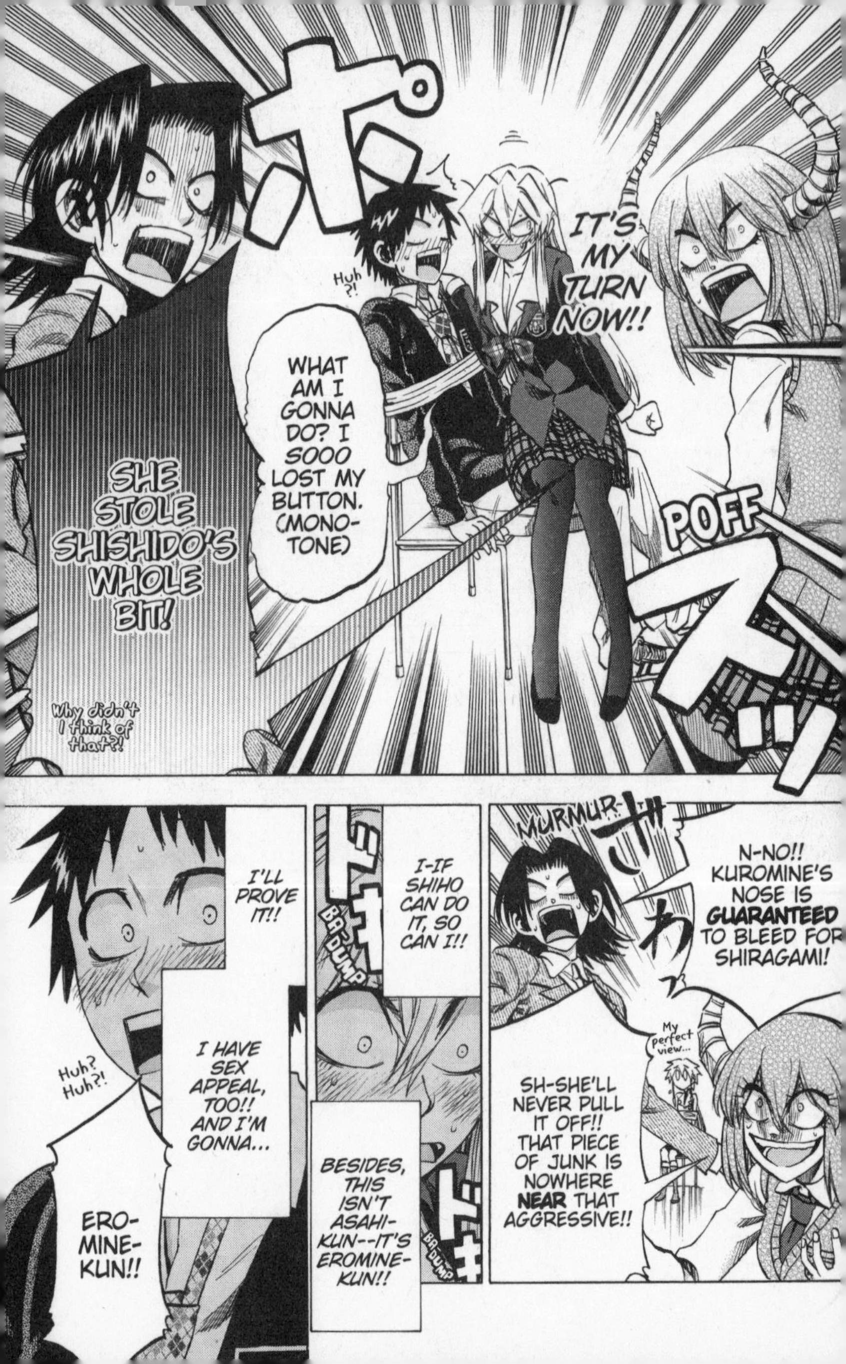
IT'S MY TURN NOW!!
POFF
Huh ?!
WHAT AM I GONNA DO? I SOOO LOST MY BUTTON. (MONOTONE)
SHE STOLE SHISHIDO'S WHOLE BIT!
Why didn't I think of that?!
MURMUR
N-NO!! KUROMINE'S NOSE IS **GUARANTEED** TO BLEED FOR SHIRAGAMI!
My perfect view...
SH-SHE'LL NEVER PULL IT OFF!! THAT PIECE OF JUNK IS NOWHERE **NEAR** THAT AGGRESSIVE!!
BA-DUMP
I-IF SHIHO CAN DO IT, SO CAN I!!
BESIDES, THIS ISN'T ASAHI-KUN--IT'S EROMINE-KUN!!
BA-DUMP
I'LL PROVE IT!!
I HAVE SEX APPEAL, TOO!! AND I'M GONNA...
Huh? Huh?!
EROMINE-KUN!!

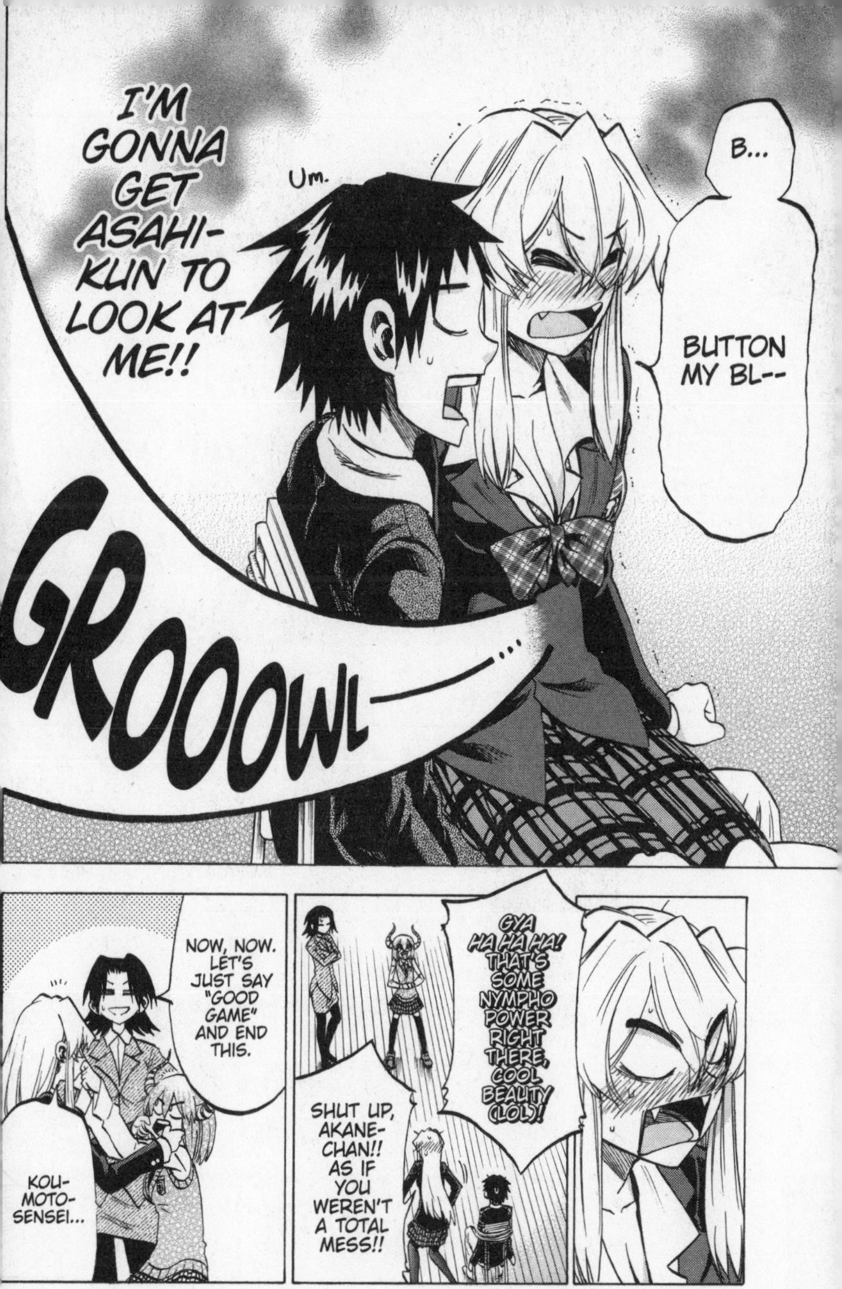
B...
BUTTON MY BL--
Um.
I'M GONNA GET ASAHI-KUN TO LOOK AT ME!!
GROOOWL—...
GYA HA HA HA! THAT'S SOME NYMPHO POWER RIGHT THERE, COOL BEAUTY (LOL)!
SHUT UP, AKANE-CHAN!! AS IF YOU WEREN'T A TOTAL MESS!!
NOW, NOW. LET'S JUST SAY "GOOD GAME" AND END THIS.
KOU-MOTO-SENSEI...

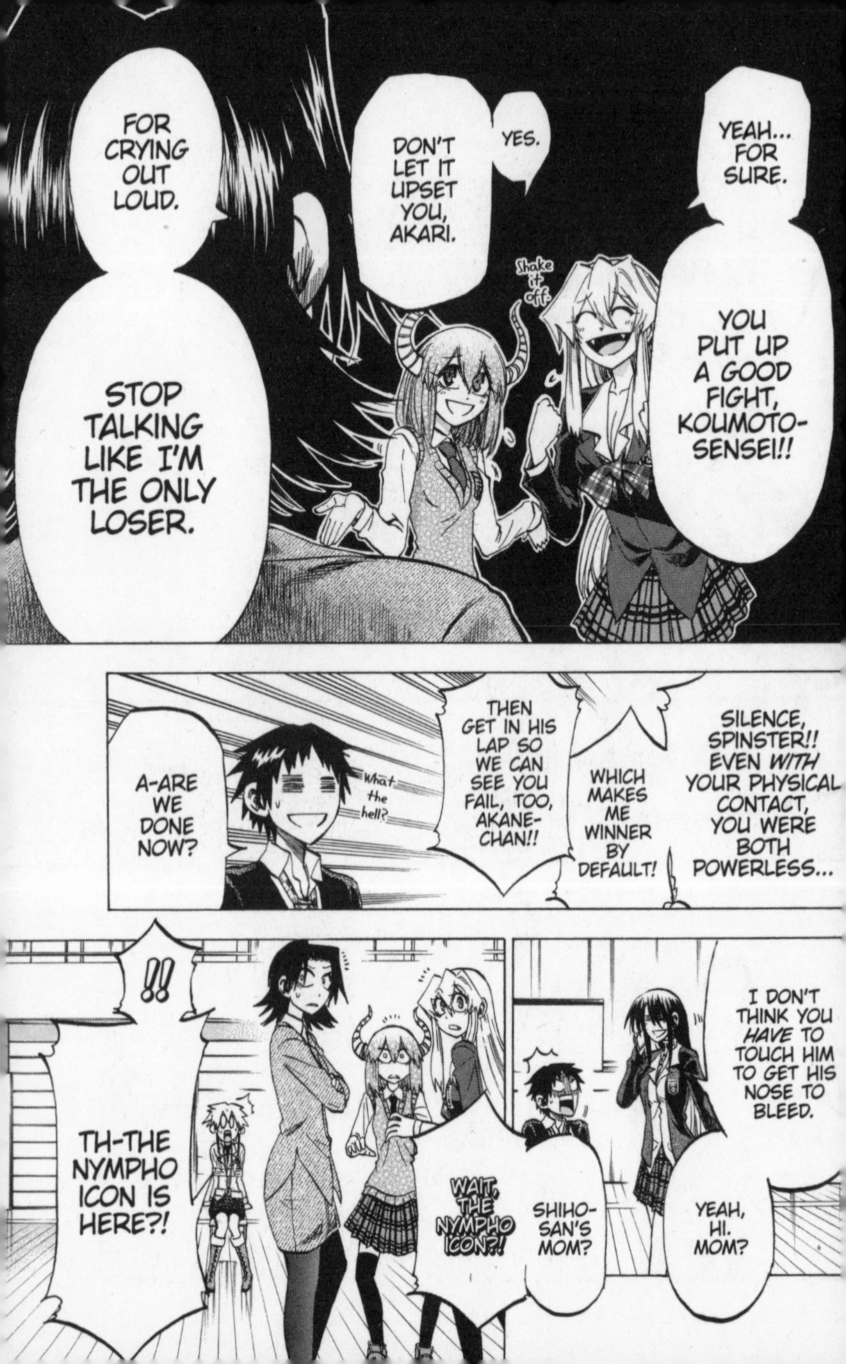
YEAH... FOR SURE.
YOU PUT UP A GOOD FIGHT, KOUMOTO-SENSEI!!
YES.
Shake it off.
DON'T LET IT UPSET YOU, AKARI.
FOR CRYING OUT LOUD.
STOP TALKING LIKE I'M THE ONLY LOSER.
SILENCE, SPINSTER!! EVEN *WITH* YOUR PHYSICAL CONTACT, YOU WERE BOTH POWERLESS...
WHICH MAKES ME WINNER BY DEFAULT!
THEN GET IN HIS LAP SO WE CAN SEE YOU FAIL, TOO, AKANE-CHAN!!
What the hell?
A-ARE WE DONE NOW?
I DON'T THINK YOU *HAVE* TO TOUCH HIM TO GET HIS NOSE TO BLEED.
YEAH, HI. MOM?
SHIHO-SAN'S MOM?
WAIT, THE NYMPHO ICON?!
!!
TH-THE NYMPHO ICON IS HERE?!

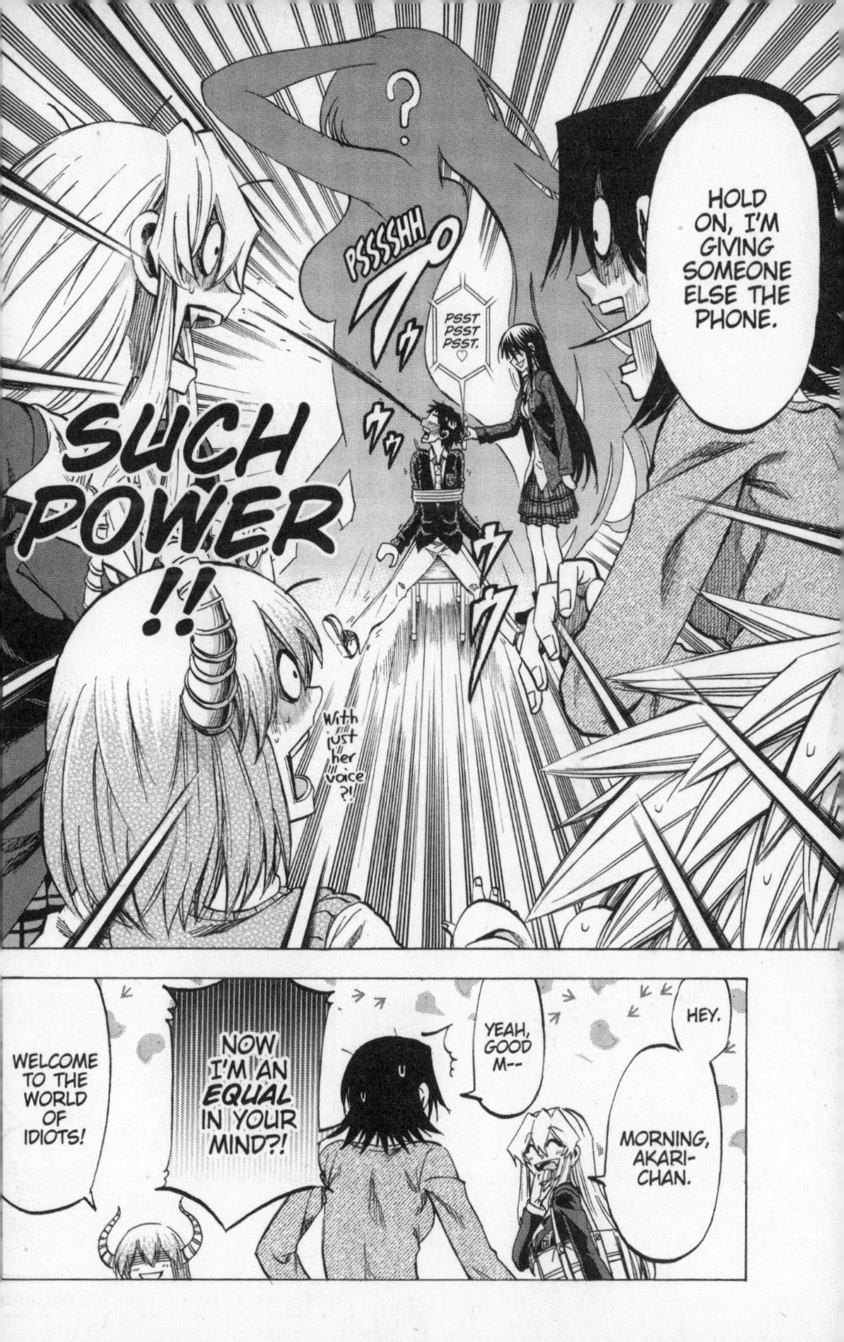
HOLD ON, I'M GIVING SOMEONE ELSE THE PHONE.
PSSSSHH
PSST PSST PSST. ♡
SUCH POWER!!
With just her voice?!
HEY.
MORNING, AKARI-CHAN.
YEAH, GOOD M--
NOW I'M AN *EQUAL* IN YOUR MIND?!
WELCOME TO THE WORLD OF IDIOTS!

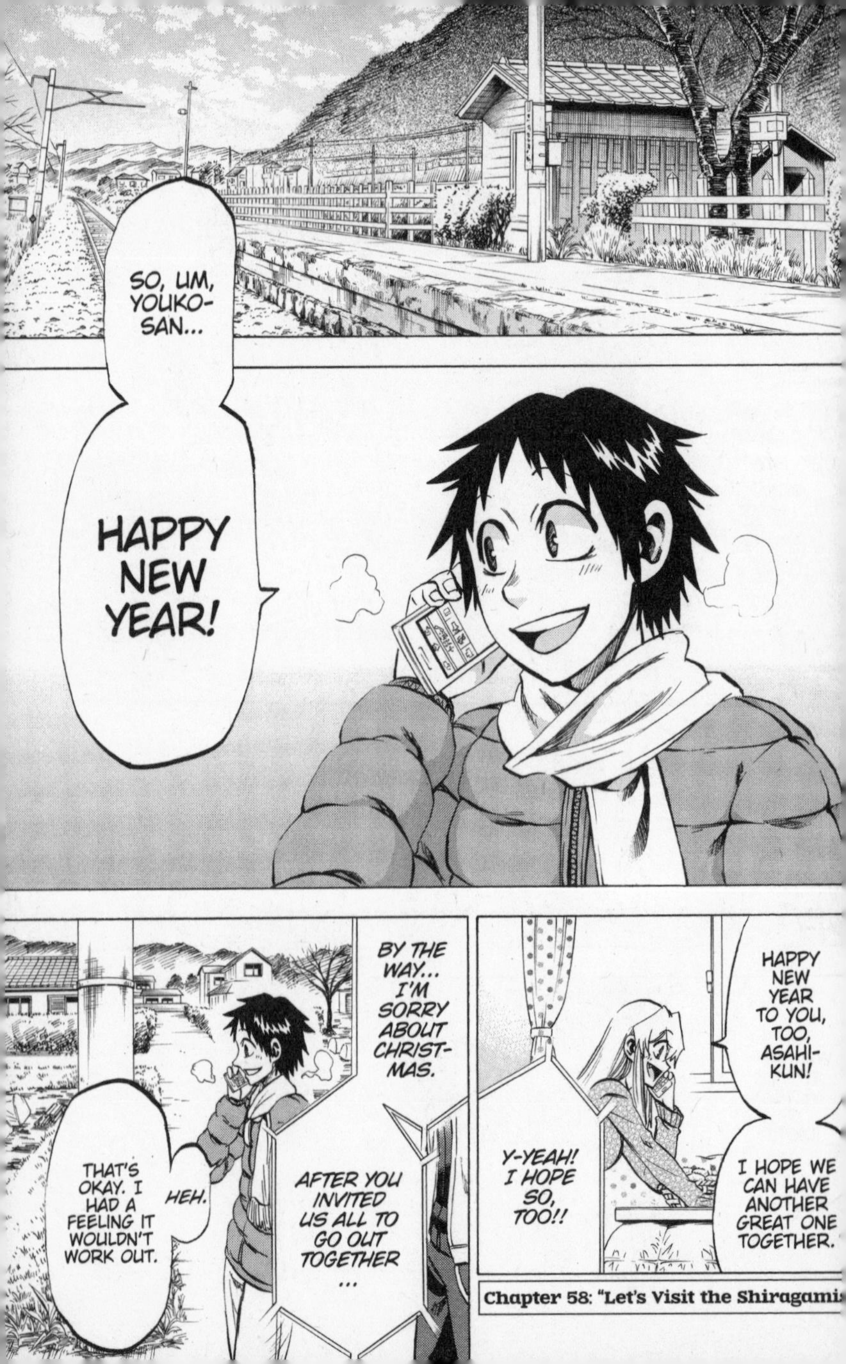
SO, UM, YOUKO-SAN...
HAPPY NEW YEAR!
HAPPY NEW YEAR TO YOU, TOO, ASAHI-KUN!
I HOPE WE CAN HAVE ANOTHER GREAT ONE TOGETHER.
Y-YEAH! I HOPE SO, TOO!!
Chapter 58: “Let's Visit the Shiragami
BY THE WAY... I'M SORRY ABOUT CHRIST-MAS.
AFTER YOU INVITED US ALL TO GO OUT TOGETHER ...
THAT'S OKAY. I HAD A FEELING IT WOULDN'T WORK OUT.
HEH.

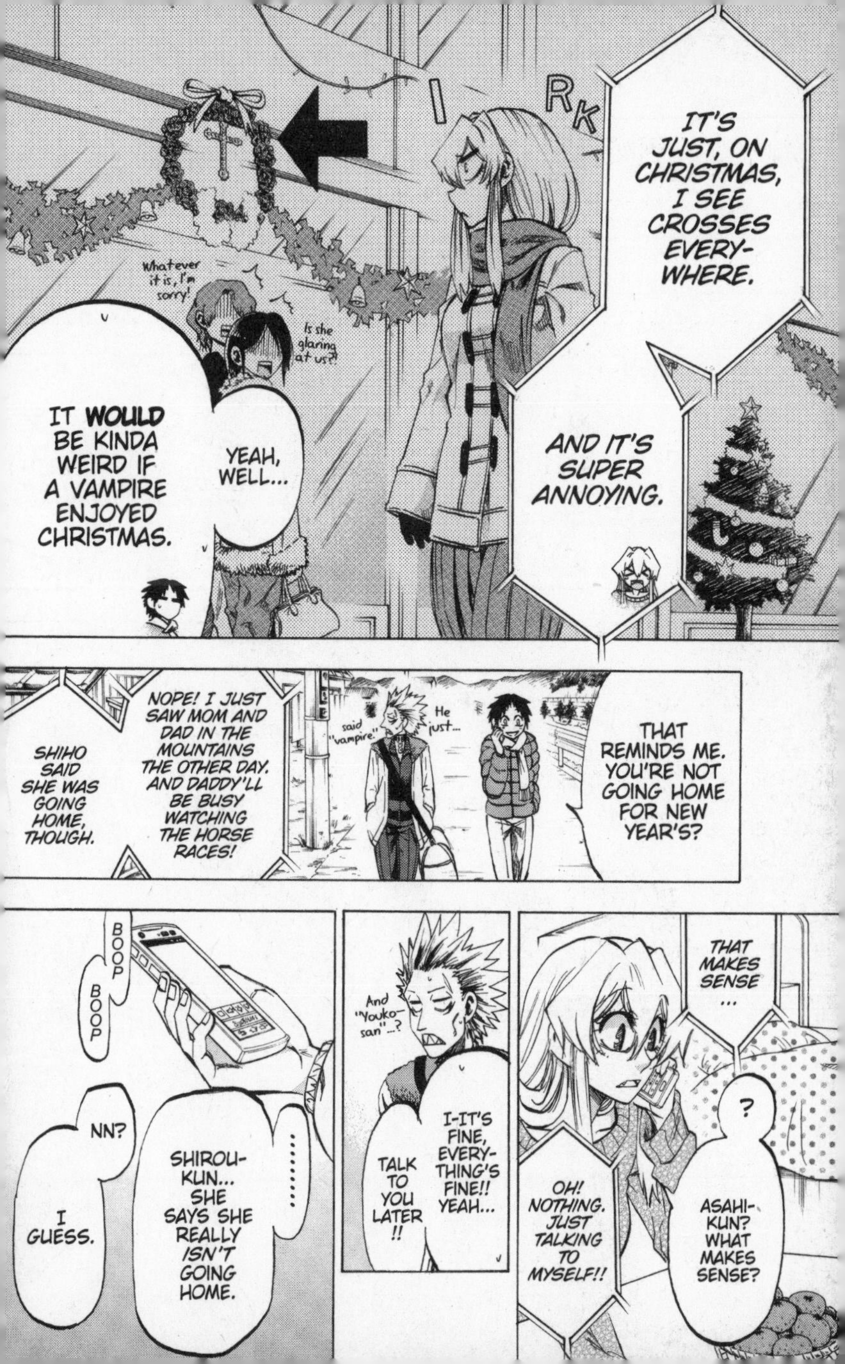
IRK
IT'S JUST, ON CHRISTMAS, I SEE CROSSES EVERY-WHERE.
AND IT'S SUPER ANNOYING.
Whatever it is, I'm sorry!
Is she glaring at us?
YEAH, WELL...
IT **WOULD** BE KINDA WEIRD IF A VAMPIRE ENJOYED CHRISTMAS.
THAT REMINDS ME. YOU'RE NOT GOING HOME FOR NEW YEAR'S?
He just... said "vampire."
NOPE! I JUST SAW MOM AND DAD IN THE MOUNTAINS THE OTHER DAY. AND DADDY'LL BE BUSY WATCHING THE HORSE RACES!
SHIHO SAID SHE WAS GOING HOME, THOUGH.
THAT MAKES SENSE ...
?
ASAHI-KUN? WHAT MAKES SENSE?
OH! NOTHING. JUST TALKING TO MYSELF!!
And "Youko-san"...?
I-IT'S FINE, EVERY-THING'S FINE!! YEAH...
TALK TO YOU LATER !!
BOOP
BOOP
......
SHIROU-KUN... SHE SAYS SHE REALLY *ISN'T* GOING HOME.
NN?
I GUESS.

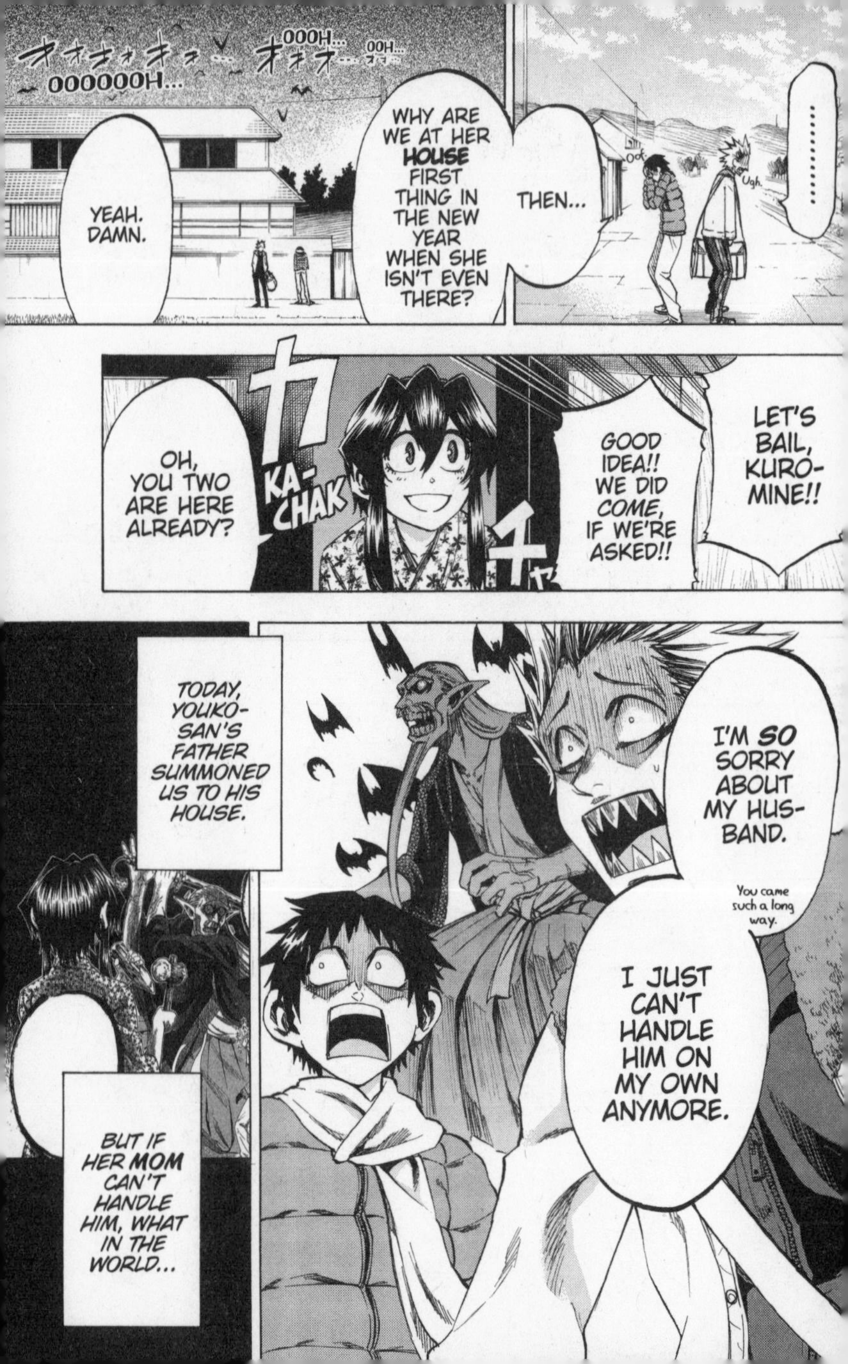
......
Oof.
Ugh.
THEN...
WHY ARE WE AT HER HOUSE FIRST THING IN THE NEW YEAR WHEN SHE ISN'T EVEN THERE?
OOOH...
OOH...
OOOOOOH...
YEAH. DAMN.
LET'S BAIL, KURO-MINE!!
GOOD IDEA!! WE DID COME, IF WE'RE ASKED!!
KA-CHAK
OH, YOU TWO ARE HERE ALREADY?
I'M SO SORRY ABOUT MY HUS-BAND.
You came such a long way.
I JUST CAN'T HANDLE HIM ON MY OWN ANYMORE.
TODAY, YOUKO-SAN'S FATHER SUMMONED US TO HIS HOUSE.
BUT IF HER MOM CAN'T HANDLE HIM, WHAT IN THE WORLD...

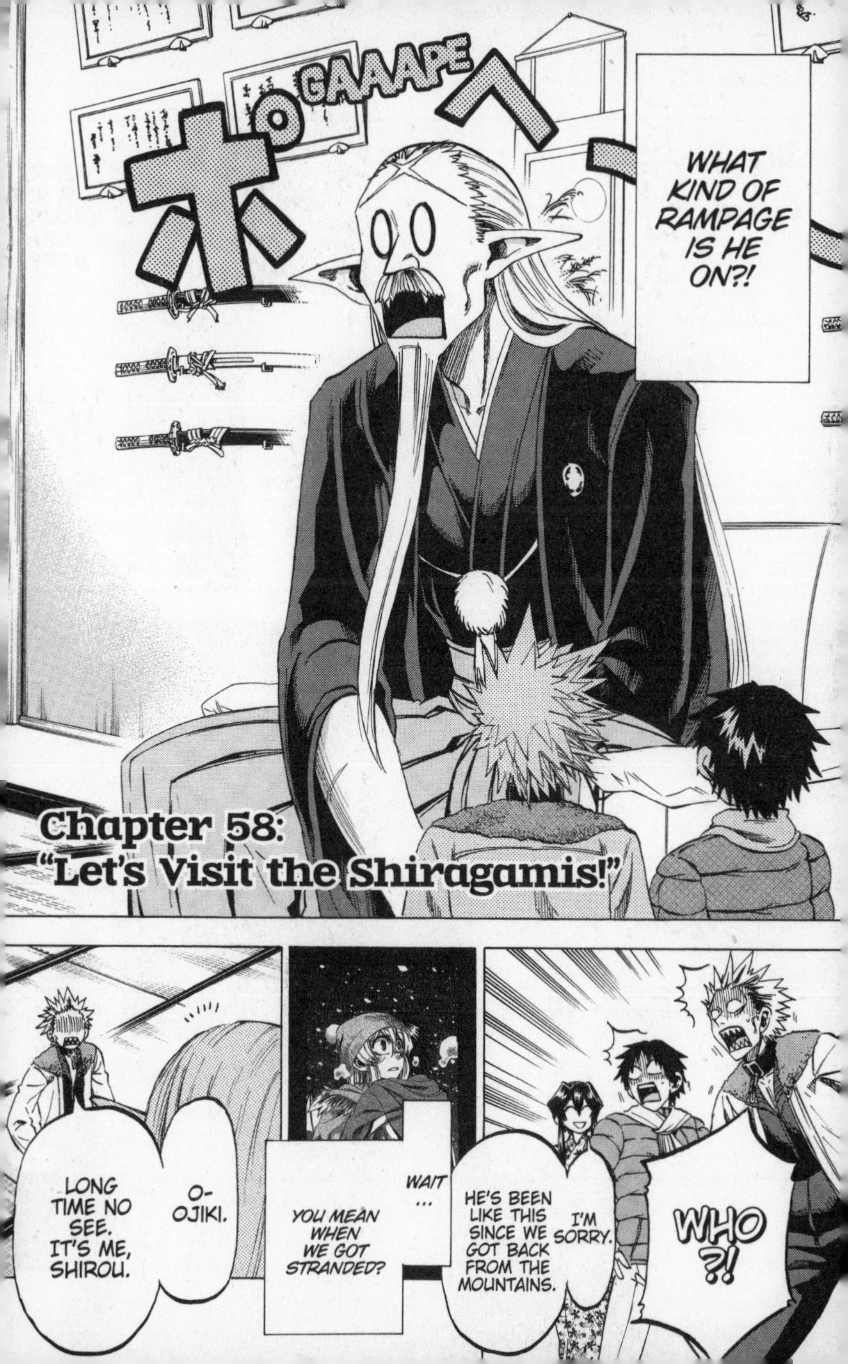
WHAT KIND OF RAMPAGE IS HE ON?!
ホ GAAAPE へ
Chapter 58: "Let's Visit the Shiragamis!"
WHO ?!
I'M SORRY.
HE'S BEEN LIKE THIS SINCE WE GOT BACK FROM THE MOUNTAINS.
WAIT ...
YOU MEAN WHEN WE GOT STRANDED?
O-OJIKI.
LONG TIME NO SEE. IT'S ME, SHIROU.

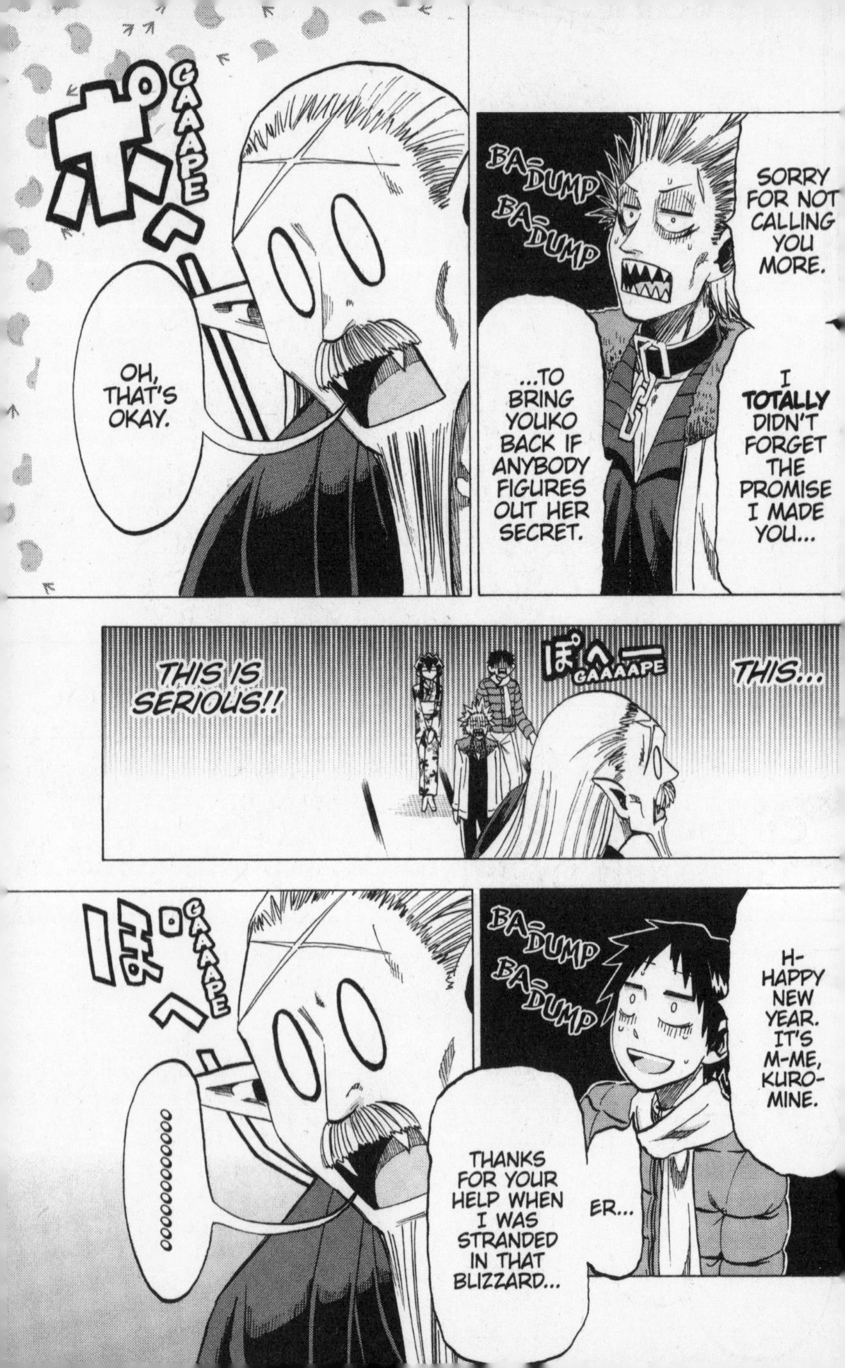
BA-DUMP BA-DUMP
SORRY FOR NOT CALLING YOU MORE.
I **TOTALLY** DIDN'T FORGET THE PROMISE I MADE YOU...
...TO BRING YOUKO BACK IF ANYBODY FIGURES OUT HER SECRET.
ポへー
GAAAPE
OH, THAT'S OKAY.
THIS...
ぽへー
GAAAAPE
THIS IS SERIOUS!!
BA-DUMP BA-DUMP
H-HAPPY NEW YEAR. IT'S M-ME, KURO-MINE.
ER...
THANKS FOR YOUR HELP WHEN I WAS STRANDED IN THAT BLIZZARD...
ぽへー
GAAAAPE
OOOOOOOOOOOOOO...

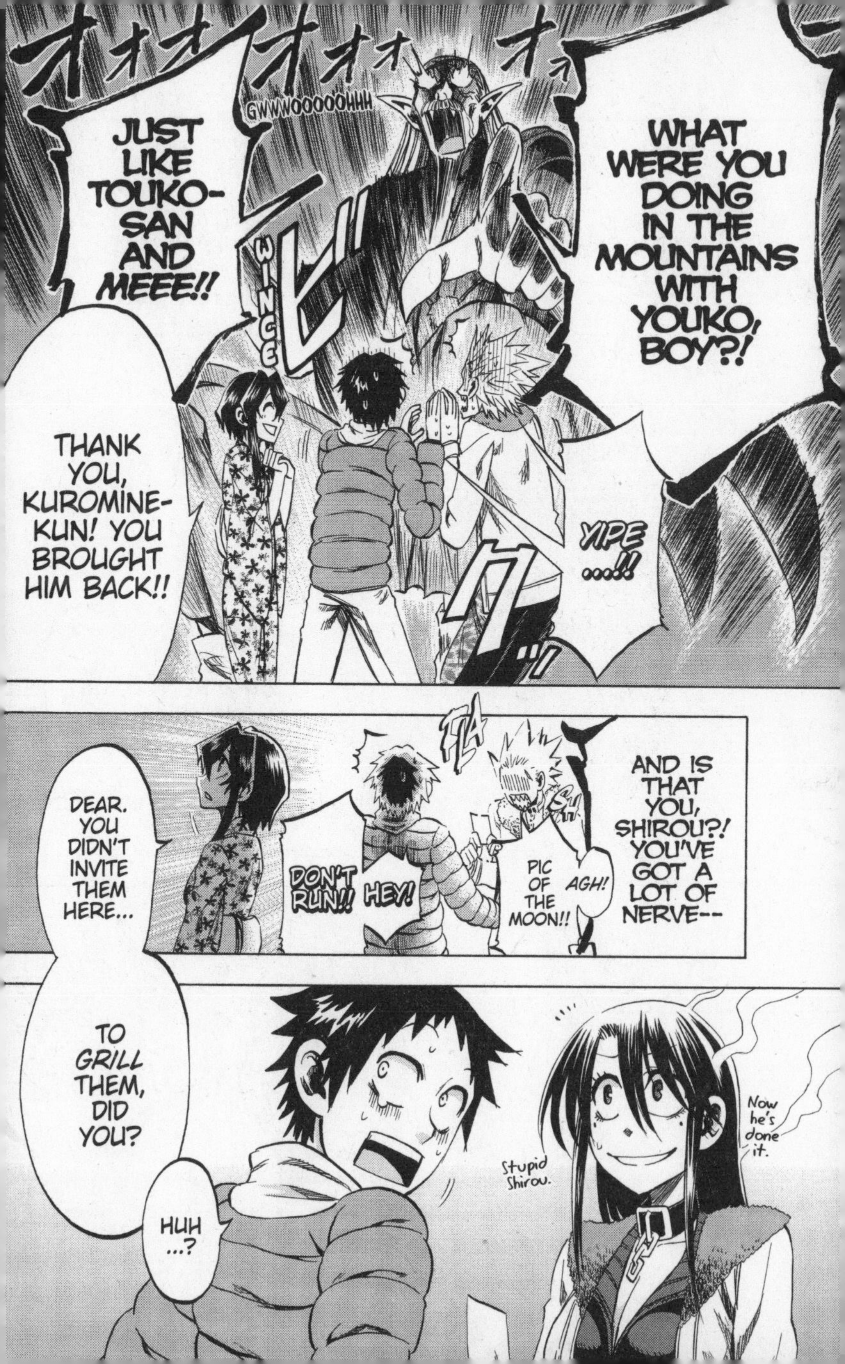
WHAT WERE YOU DOING IN THE MOUNTAINS WITH YOUKO, BOY?!
GWWWOOOOOHHH
JUST LIKE TOUKO-SAN AND MEEE!!
WINCE
YIPE ....!!
THANK YOU, KUROMINE-KUN! YOU BROUGHT HIM BACK!!
AND IS THAT YOU, SHIROU?! YOU'VE GOT A LOT OF NERVE--
AGH!
PIC OF THE MOON!!
HEY!
DON'T RUN!!
DEAR. YOU DIDN'T INVITE THEM HERE...
Now he's done it.
Stupid Shirou.
TO GRILL THEM, DID YOU?
HUH ...?

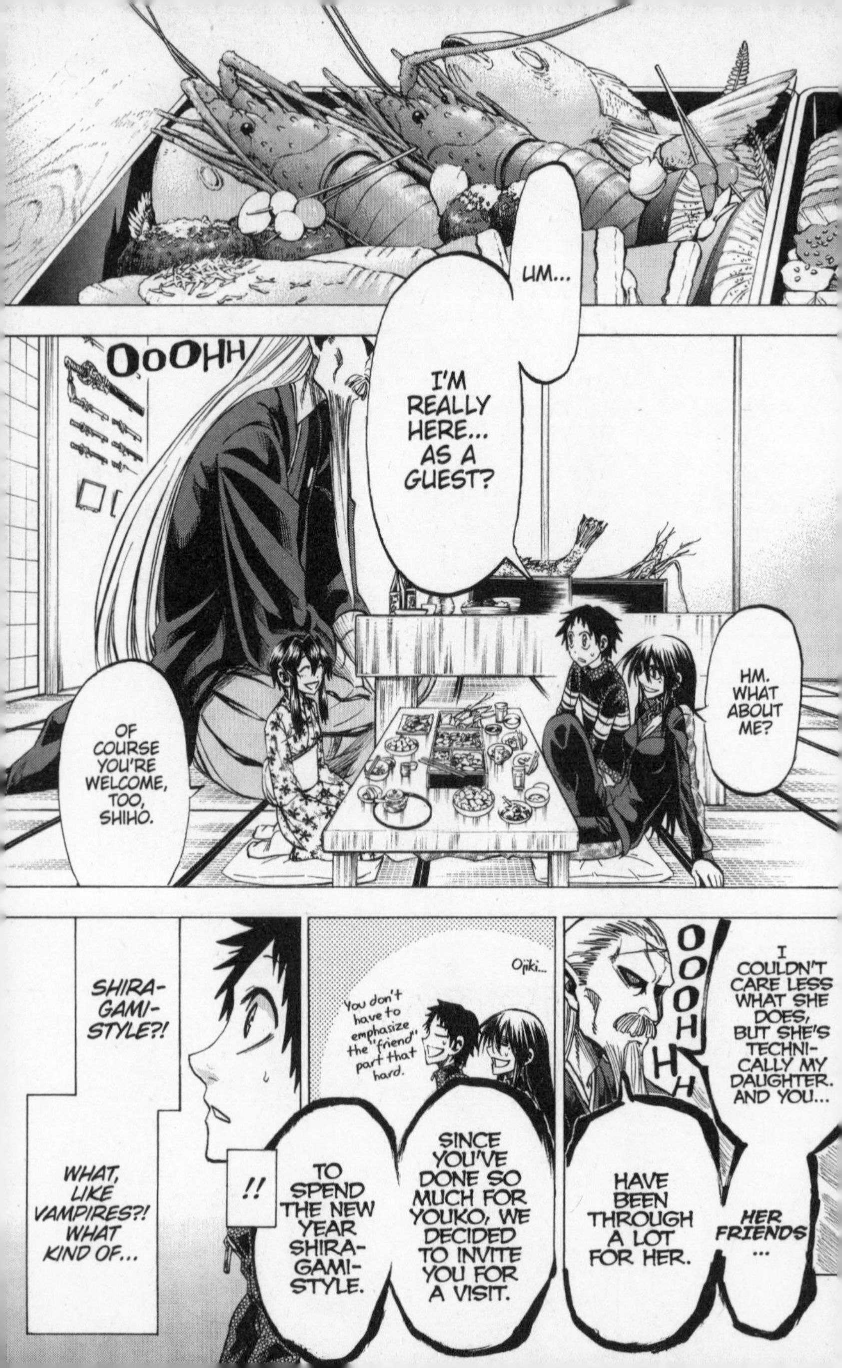
UM...
I'M REALLY HERE... AS A GUEST?
HM. WHAT ABOUT ME?
OOOHH
OF COURSE YOU'RE WELCOME, TOO, SHIHO.
I COULDN'T CARE LESS WHAT SHE DOES, BUT SHE'S TECHNICALLY MY DAUGHTER. AND YOU...
OOOHHH
HAVE BEEN THROUGH A LOT FOR HER.
HER FRIENDS...
SINCE YOU'VE DONE SO MUCH FOR YOUKO, WE DECIDED TO INVITE YOU FOR A VISIT.
TO SPEND THE NEW YEAR SHIRA-GAMI-STYLE.
Ojiki...
You don't have to emphasize the "friend" part that hard.
!!
SHIRA-GAMI-STYLE?!
WHAT, LIKE VAMPIRES?! WHAT KIND OF...

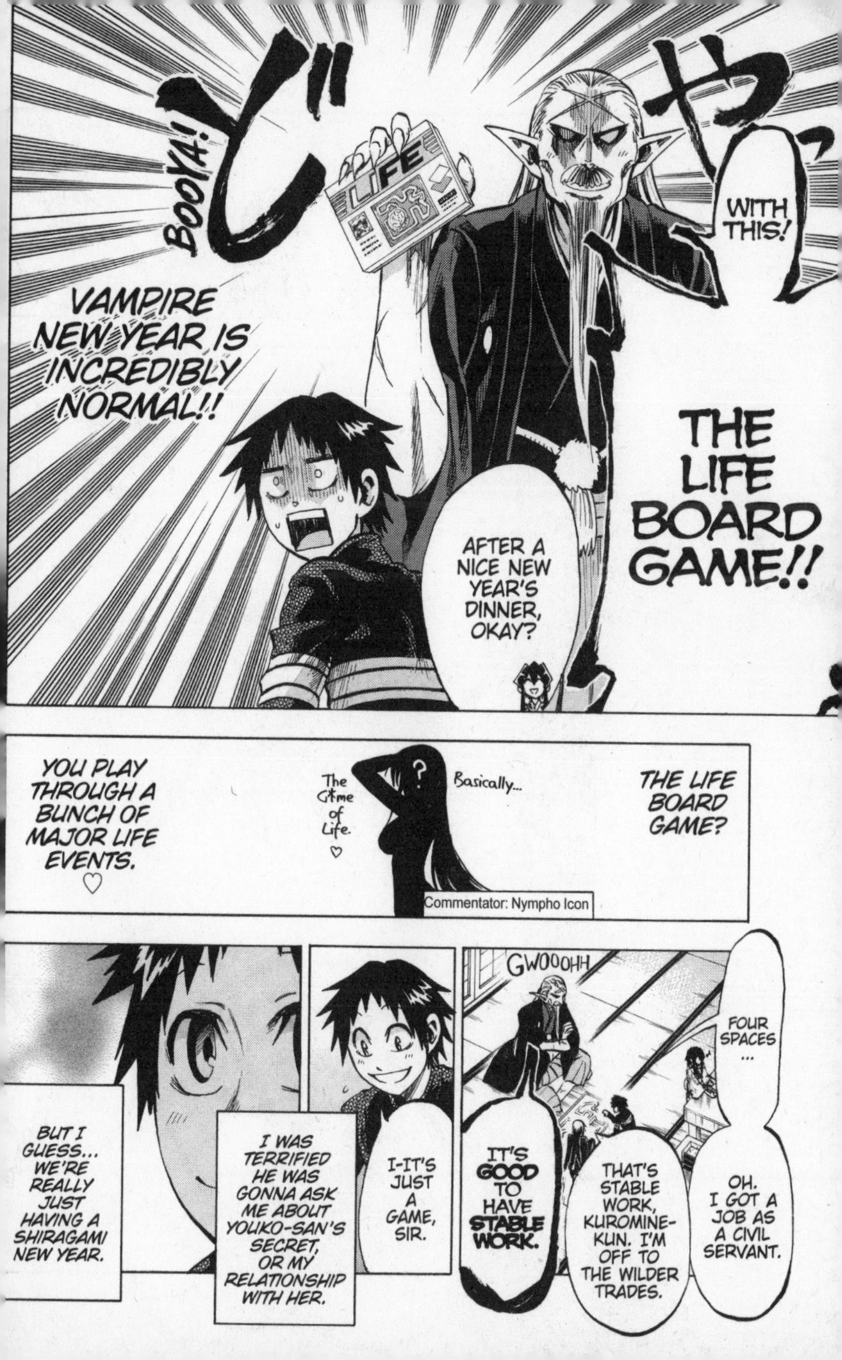
WITH THIS!
BOOYA!
THE LIFE BOARD GAME!!
AFTER A NICE NEW YEAR'S DINNER, OKAY?
VAMPIRE NEW YEAR IS INCREDIBLY NORMAL!!
THE LIFE BOARD GAME?
Basically...
The Game of Life. ♡
YOU PLAY THROUGH A BUNCH OF MAJOR LIFE EVENTS. ♡
Commentator: Nympho Icon
FOUR SPACES ...
GWOOOHH
OH. I GOT A JOB AS A CIVIL SERVANT.
THAT'S STABLE WORK, KUROMINE-KUN. I'M OFF TO THE WILDER TRADES.
IT'S GOOD TO HAVE STABLE WORK.
I-IT'S JUST A GAME, SIR.
I WAS TERRIFIED HE WAS GONNA ASK ME ABOUT YOUKO-SAN'S SECRET, OR MY RELATIONSHIP WITH HER.
BUT I GUESS... WE'RE REALLY JUST HAVING A SHIRAGAMI NEW YEAR.

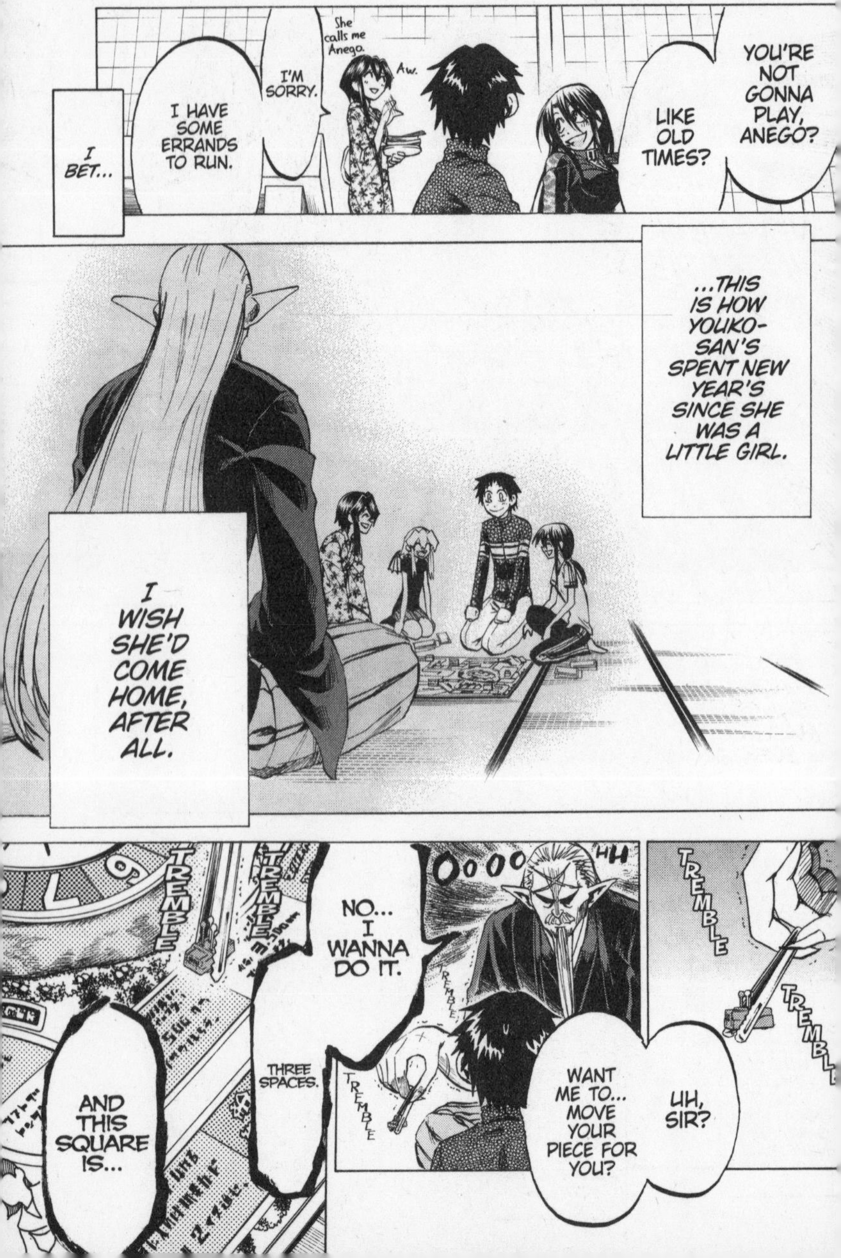
YOU'RE NOT GONNA PLAY, ANEGO?
LIKE OLD TIMES?
Aw.
She calls me Anego.
I'M SORRY.
I HAVE SOME ERRANDS TO RUN.
I BET...
...THIS IS HOW YOUKO-SAN'S SPENT NEW YEAR'S SINCE SHE WAS A LITTLE GIRL.
I WISH SHE'D COME HOME, AFTER ALL.
TREMBLE
TREMBLE
UH, SIR?
OOOOHH
WANT ME TO... MOVE YOUR PIECE FOR YOU?
TREMBLE
NO... I WANNA DO IT.
TREMBLE
THREE SPACES.
TREMBLE
TREMBLE
AND THIS SQUARE IS...

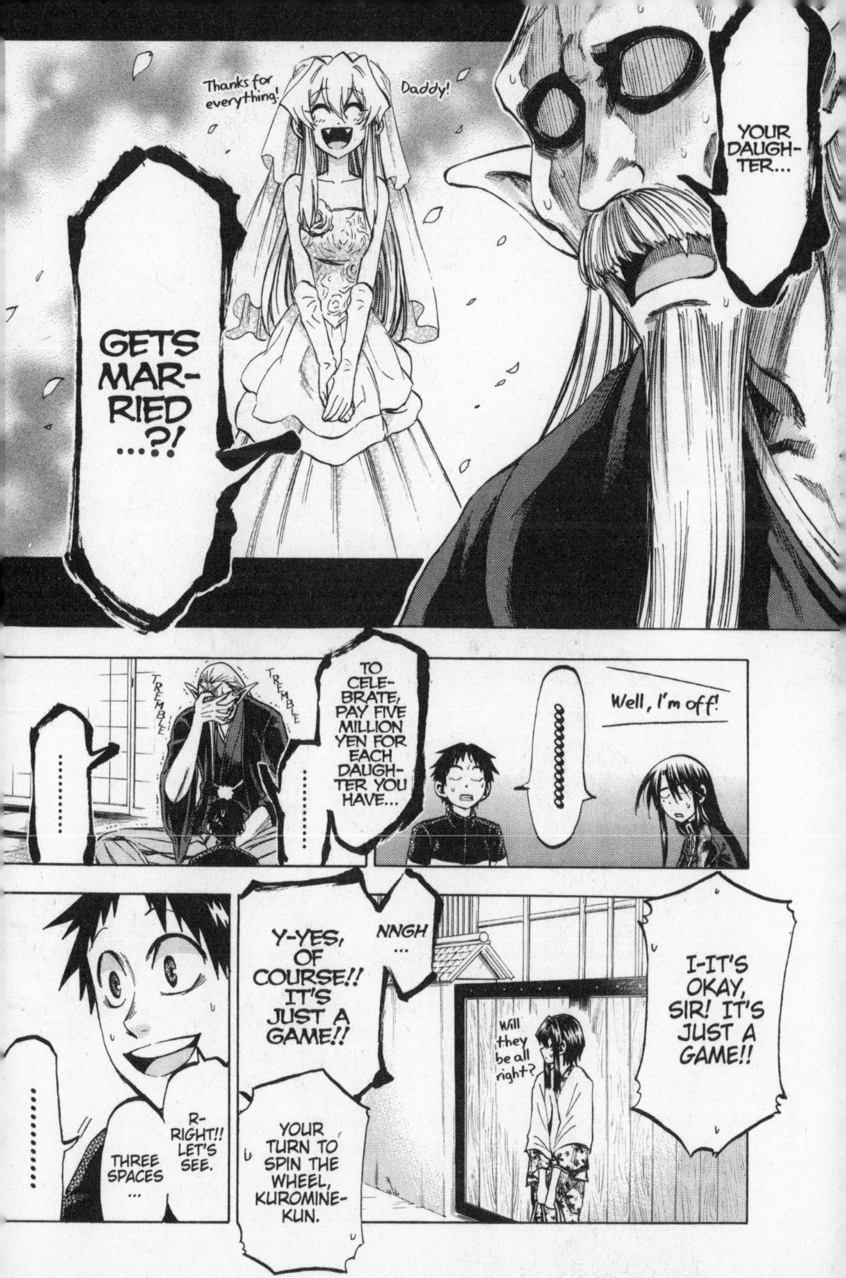
YOUR DAUGHTER...
Thanks for everything! Daddy!
GETS MARRIED...?!
Well, I'm off!
....
TO CELEBRATE, PAY FIVE MILLION YEN FOR EACH DAUGHTER YOU HAVE...
TREMBLE
TREMBLE
......
......
I-IT'S OKAY, SIR! IT'S JUST A GAME!!
Will they be all right?
NNGH...
Y-YES, OF COURSE!! IT'S JUST A GAME!!
YOUR TURN TO SPIN THE WHEEL, KUROMINE-KUN.
R-RIGHT!! LET'S SEE.
THREE SPACES...
....

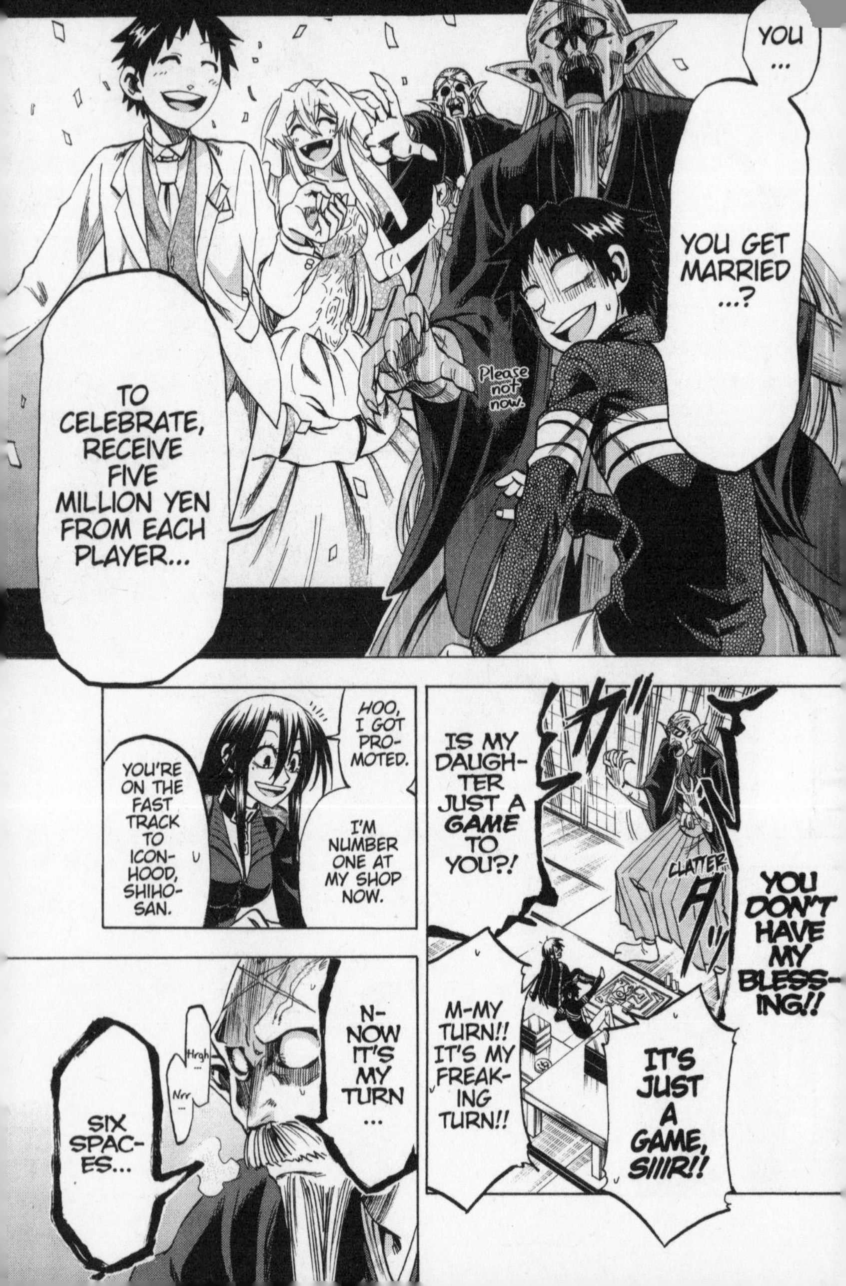
YOU ...
YOU GET MARRIED ...?
Please not now.
TO CELEBRATE, RECEIVE FIVE MILLION YEN FROM EACH PLAYER...
YOU DON'T HAVE MY BLESS-ING!!
IS MY DAUGH-TER JUST A GAME TO YOU?!
CLATTER
IT'S JUST A GAME, SIIIR!!
M-MY TURN!! IT'S MY FREAK-ING TURN!!
HOO, I GOT PRO-MOTED.
I'M NUMBER ONE AT MY SHOP NOW.
YOU'RE ON THE FAST TRACK TO ICON-HOOD, SHIHO-SAN.
N-NOW IT'S MY TURN ...
Hrgh ...
Nrr ...
SIX SPAC-ES...

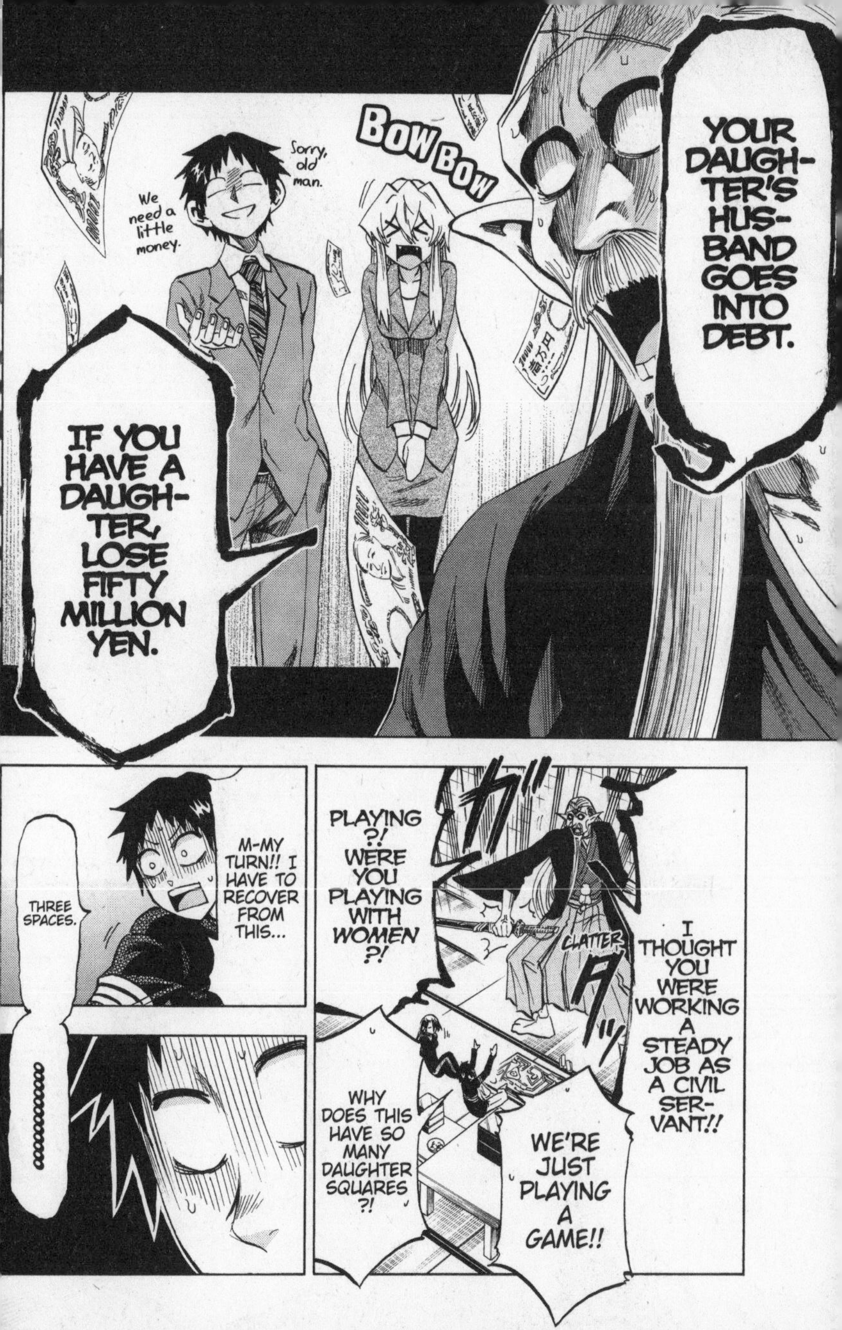
YOUR DAUGHTER'S HUSBAND GOES INTO DEBT.
BOW BOW
Sorry, old man.
We need a little money.
IF YOU HAVE A DAUGHTER, LOSE FIFTY MILLION YEN.
I THOUGHT YOU WERE WORKING A STEADY JOB AS A CIVIL SERVANT!!
CLATTER
PLAYING?! WERE YOU PLAYING WITH WOMEN?!
WE'RE JUST PLAYING A GAME!!
WHY DOES THIS HAVE SO MANY DAUGHTER SQUARES?!
M-MY TURN!! I HAVE TO RECOVER FROM THIS...
THREE SPACES.
oooooooooo

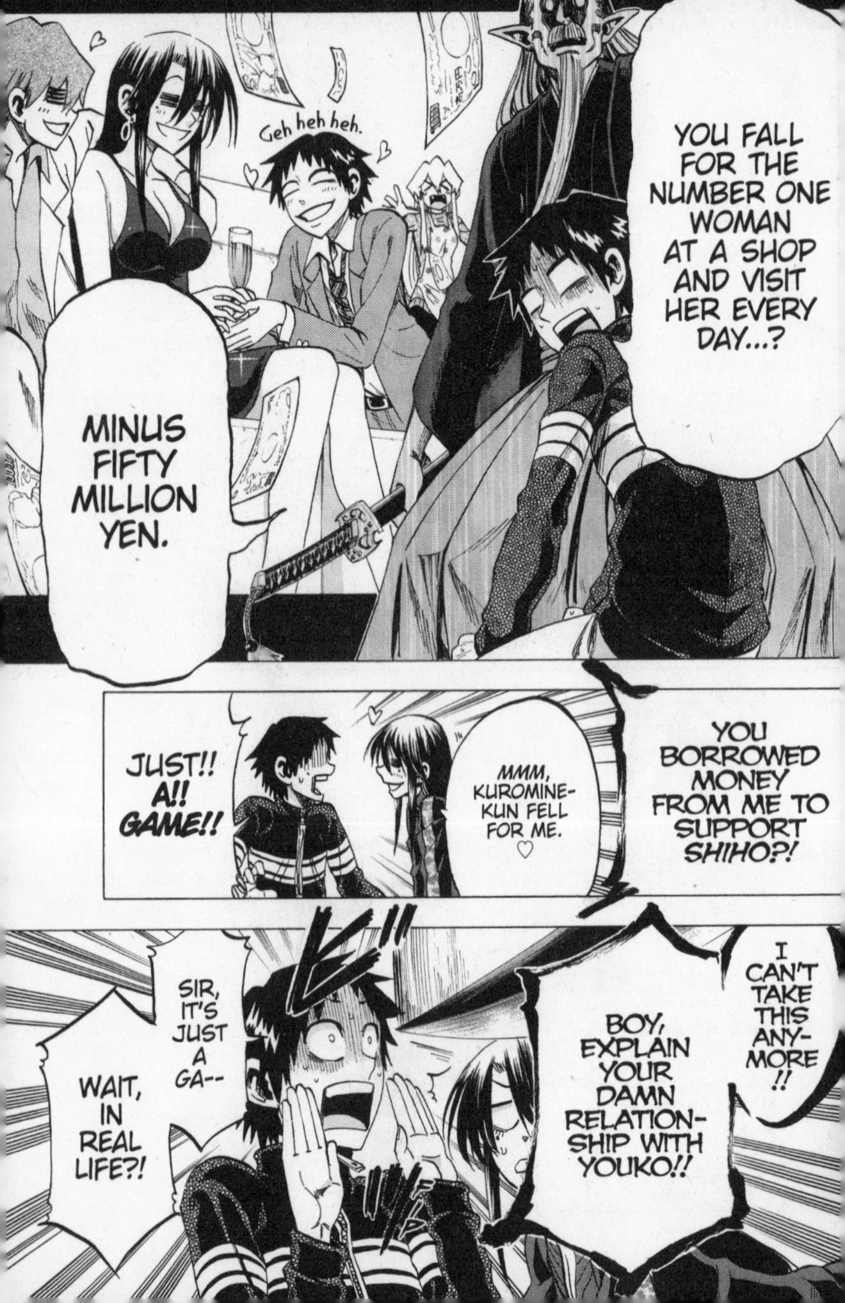
YOU FALL FOR THE NUMBER ONE WOMAN AT A SHOP AND VISIT HER EVERY DAY...?
Geh heh heh.
MINUS FIFTY MILLION YEN.
YOU BORROWED MONEY FROM ME TO SUPPORT SHIHO?!
MMM, KUROMINE-KUN FELL FOR ME. ♡
JUST!! A!! GAME!!
I CAN'T TAKE THIS ANYMORE!!
BOY, EXPLAIN YOUR DAMN RELATIONSHIP WITH YOUKO!!
SIR, IT'S JUST A GA--
WAIT, IN REAL LIFE?!

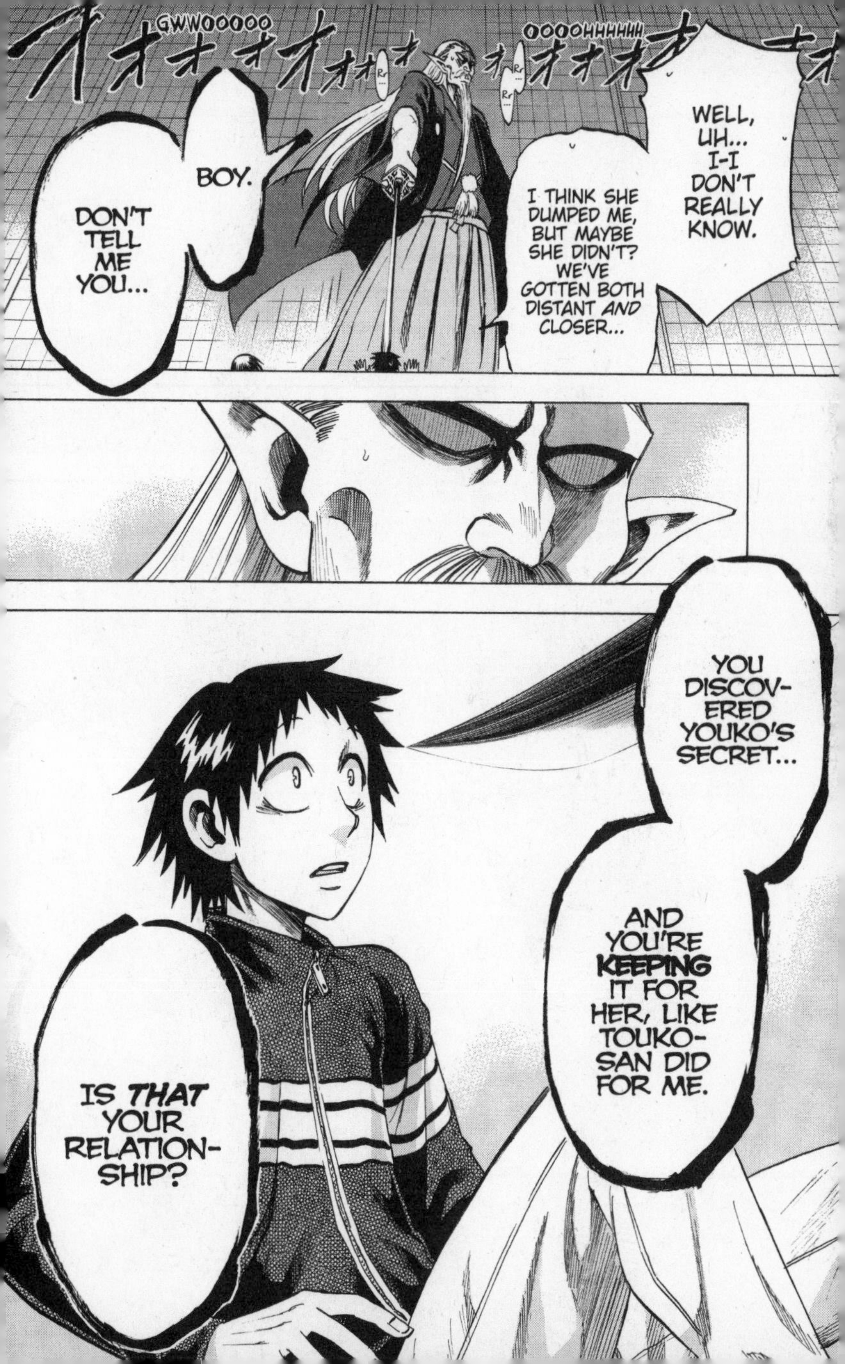
GWWOOOOO
OOOOHHHHHH
Rr...
Rr...
Rr...
WELL, UH... I-I DON'T REALLY KNOW.
I THINK SHE DUMPED ME, BUT MAYBE SHE DIDN'T? WE'VE GOTTEN BOTH DISTANT *AND* CLOSER...
BOY.
DON'T TELL ME YOU...
YOU DISCOV-ERED YOUKO'S SECRET...
AND YOU'RE **KEEPING** IT FOR HER, LIKE TOUKO-SAN DID FOR ME.
IS *THAT* YOUR RELATION-SHIP?

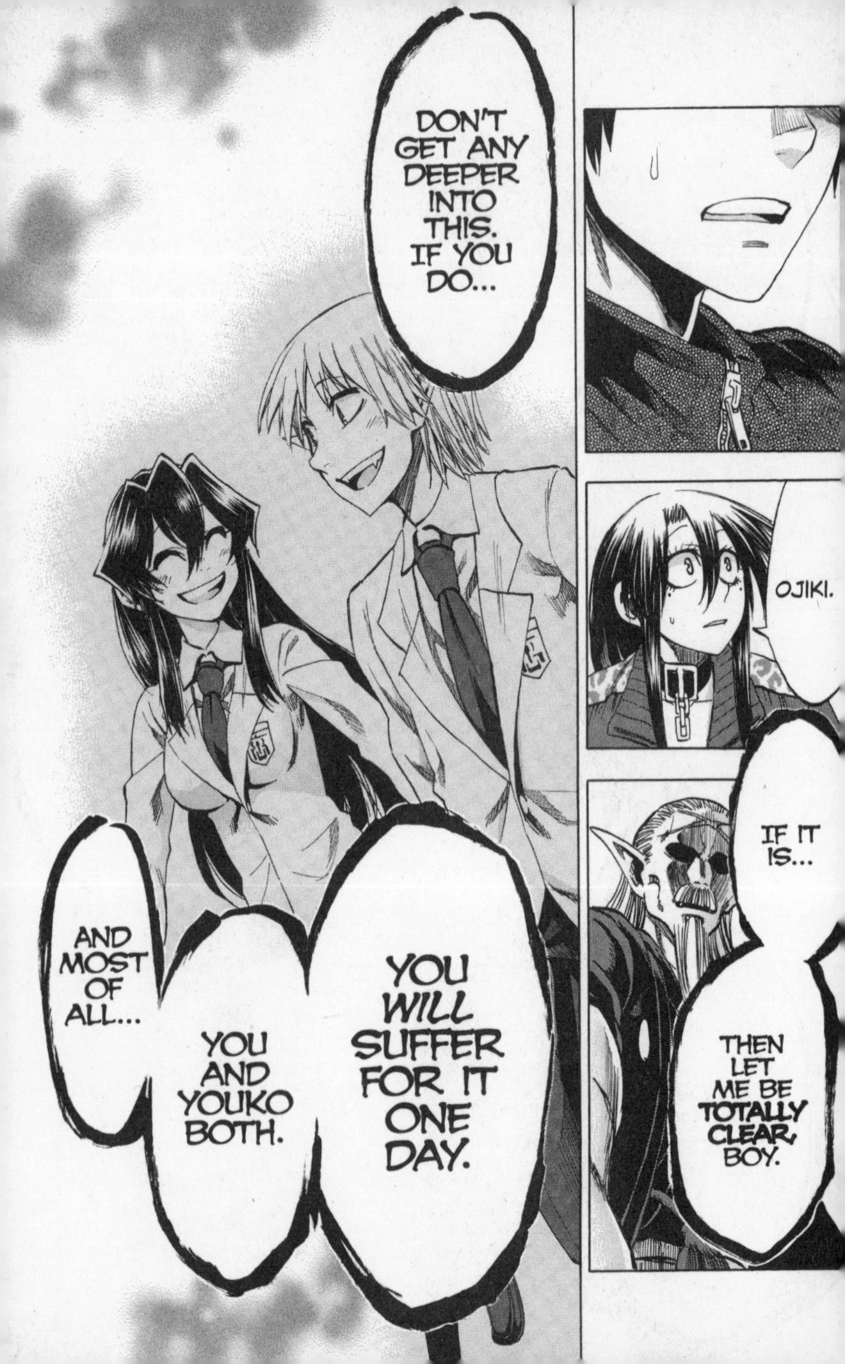
OJIKI.
IF IT IS...
THEN LET ME BE TOTALLY CLEAR, BOY.
DON'T GET ANY DEEPER INTO THIS. IF YOU DO...
YOU WILL SUFFER FOR IT ONE DAY.
YOU AND YOUKO BOTH.
AND MOST OF ALL...

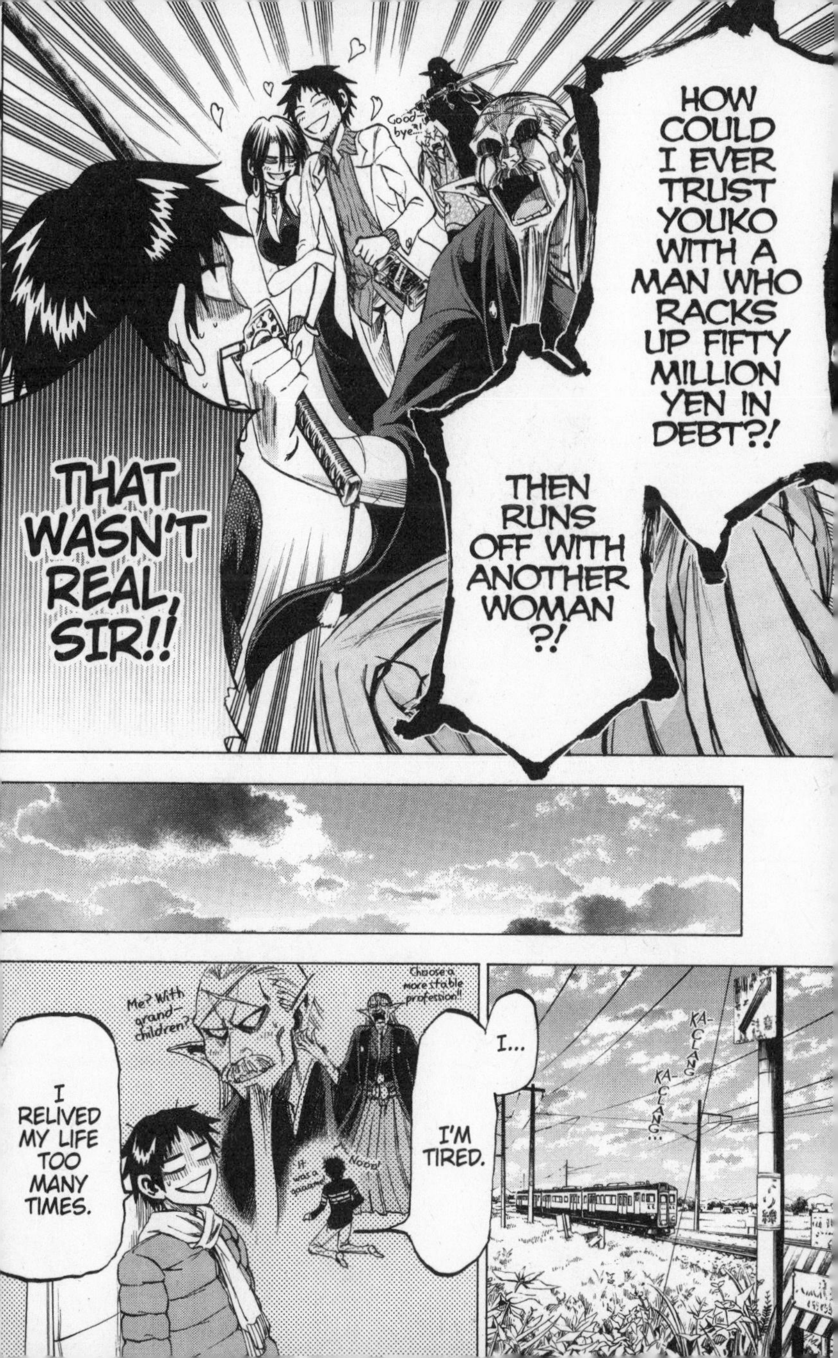
HOW COULD I EVER TRUST YOUKO WITH A MAN WHO RACKS UP FIFTY MILLION YEN IN DEBT?!
Good-bye...?!
THEN RUNS OFF WITH ANOTHER WOMAN?!
THAT WASN'T REAL, SIR!!
KA-CLANG
KA-CLANG...
I...
I'M TIRED.
Choose a more stable profession!!
Me? With grand-children?
Nooo!
It was a gaaame!
I RELIVED MY LIFE TOO MANY TIMES.

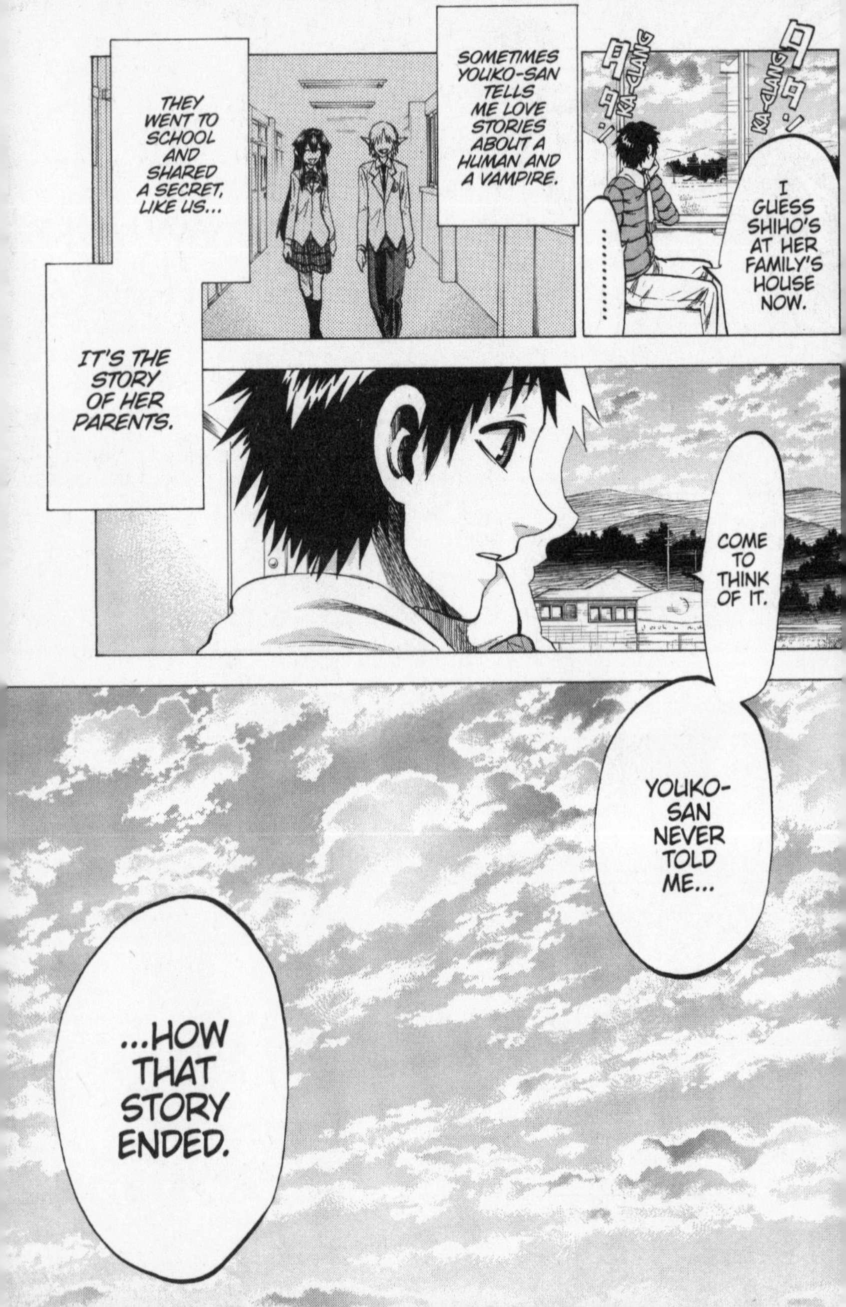
KA-CLANG
KA-CLANG
I GUESS SHIHO'S AT HER FAMILY'S HOUSE NOW.
......
SOMETIMES YOUKO-SAN TELLS ME LOVE STORIES ABOUT A HUMAN AND A VAMPIRE.
THEY WENT TO SCHOOL AND SHARED A SECRET, LIKE US...
IT'S THE STORY OF HER PARENTS.
COME TO THINK OF IT.
YOUKO-SAN NEVER TOLD ME...
...HOW THAT STORY ENDED.

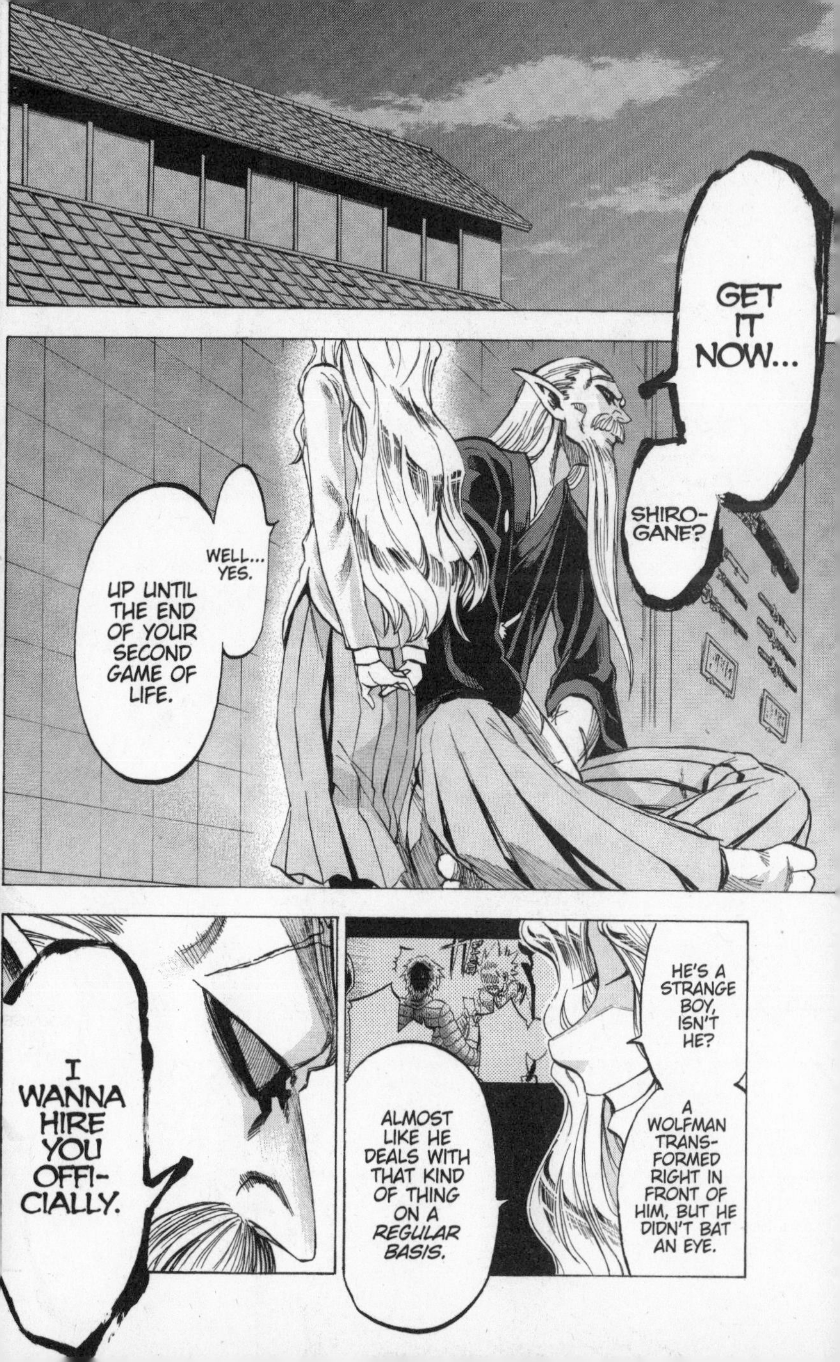
GET IT NOW... SHIROGANE?
WELL... YES. UP UNTIL THE END OF YOUR SECOND GAME OF LIFE.
HE'S A STRANGE BOY, ISN'T HE? A WOLFMAN TRANSFORMED RIGHT IN FRONT OF HIM, BUT HE DIDN'T BAT AN EYE.
ALMOST LIKE HE DEALS WITH THAT KIND OF THING ON A *REGULAR BASIS.*
I WANNA HIRE YOU OFFICIALLY.

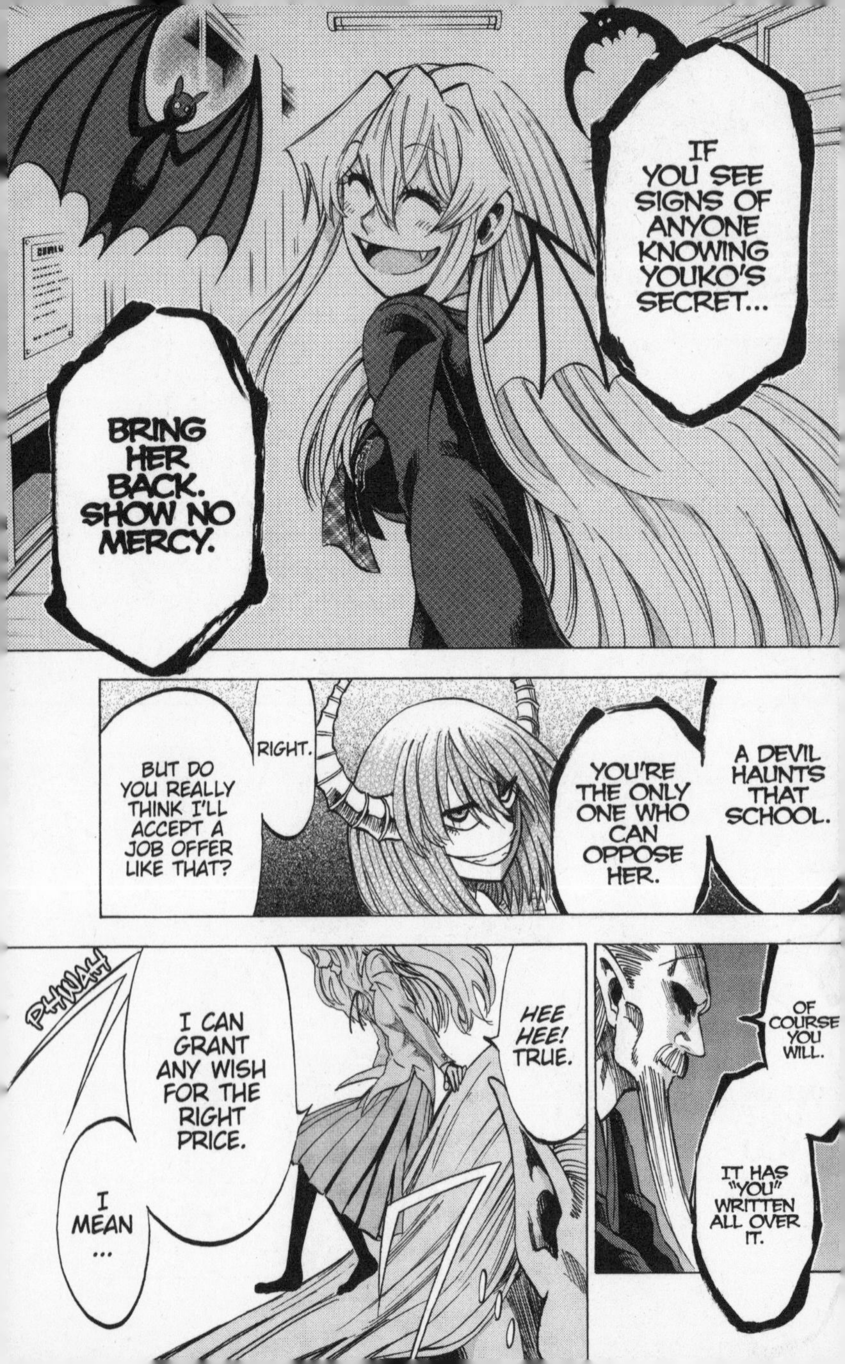
IF YOU SEE SIGNS OF ANYONE KNOWING YOUKO'S SECRET...
BRING HER BACK. SHOW NO MERCY.
A DEVIL HAUNTS THAT SCHOOL.
YOU'RE THE ONLY ONE WHO CAN OPPOSE HER.
RIGHT.
BUT DO YOU REALLY THINK I'LL ACCEPT A JOB OFFER LIKE THAT?
OF COURSE YOU WILL.
IT HAS "YOU" WRITTEN ALL OVER IT.
HEE HEE! TRUE.
I CAN GRANT ANY WISH FOR THE RIGHT PRICE.
I MEAN...
PHWAH

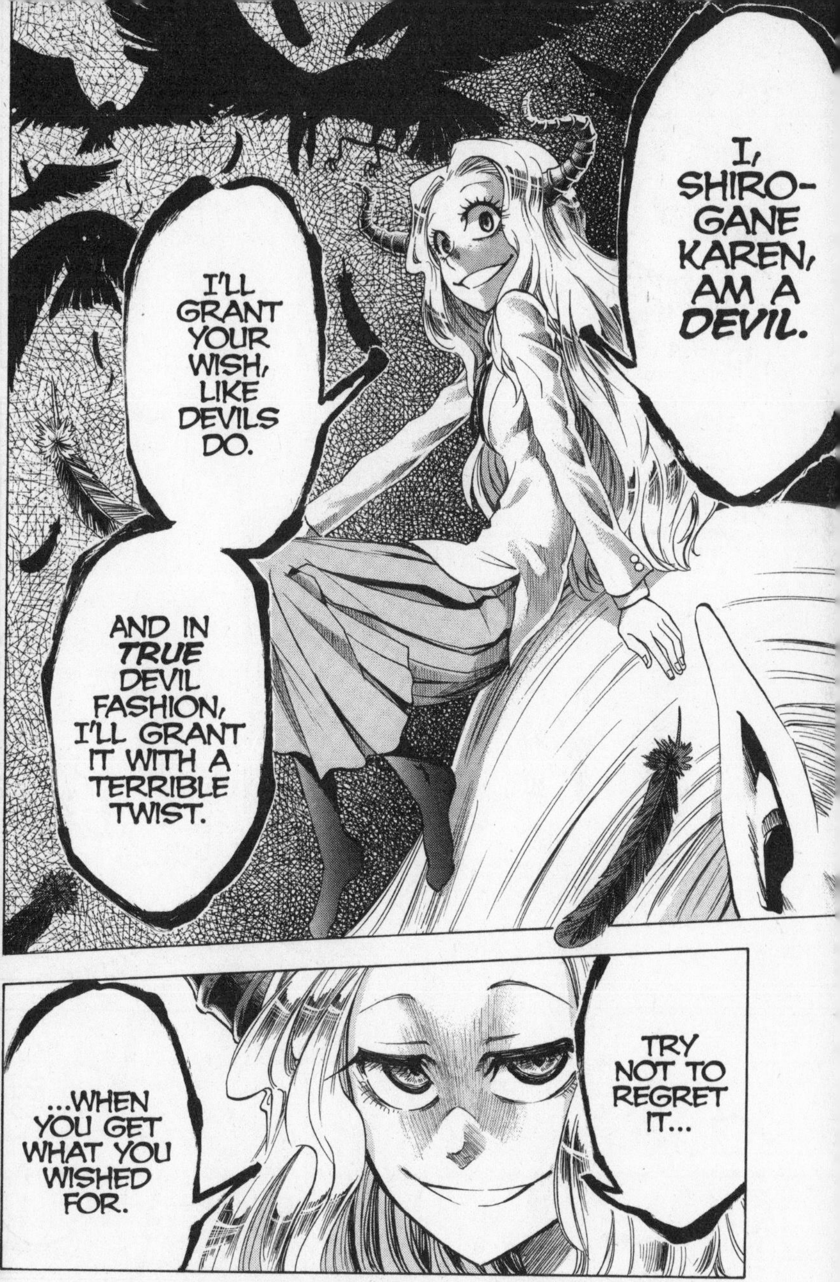
I, SHIRO-GANE KAREN, AM A DEVIL.
I'LL GRANT YOUR WISH, LIKE DEVILS DO.
AND IN TRUE DEVIL FASHION, I'LL GRANT IT WITH A TERRIBLE TWIST.
TRY NOT TO REGRET IT...
...WHEN YOU GET WHAT YOU WISHED FOR.

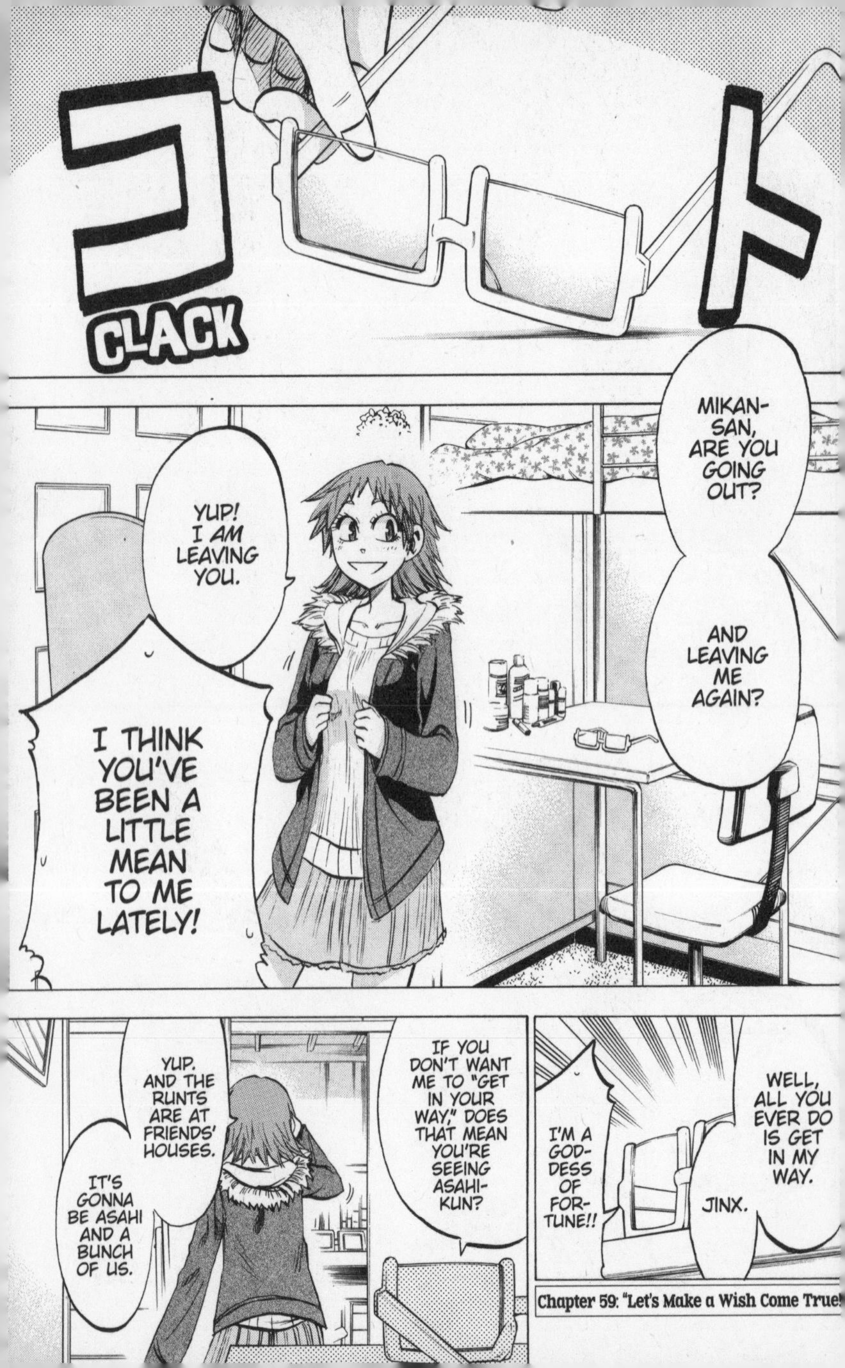
コト
CLACK
MIKAN-SAN, ARE YOU GOING OUT?
AND LEAVING ME AGAIN?
YUP! I AM LEAVING YOU.
I THINK YOU'VE BEEN A LITTLE MEAN TO ME LATELY!
WELL, ALL YOU EVER DO IS GET IN MY WAY.
JINX.
I'M A GOD-DESS OF FOR-TUNE!!
IF YOU DON'T WANT ME TO "GET IN YOUR WAY," DOES THAT MEAN YOU'RE SEEING ASAHI-KUN?
YUP. AND THE RUNTS ARE AT FRIENDS' HOUSES.
IT'S GONNA BE ASAHI AND A BUNCH OF US.

Chapter 59: "Let's Make a Wish Come True!"

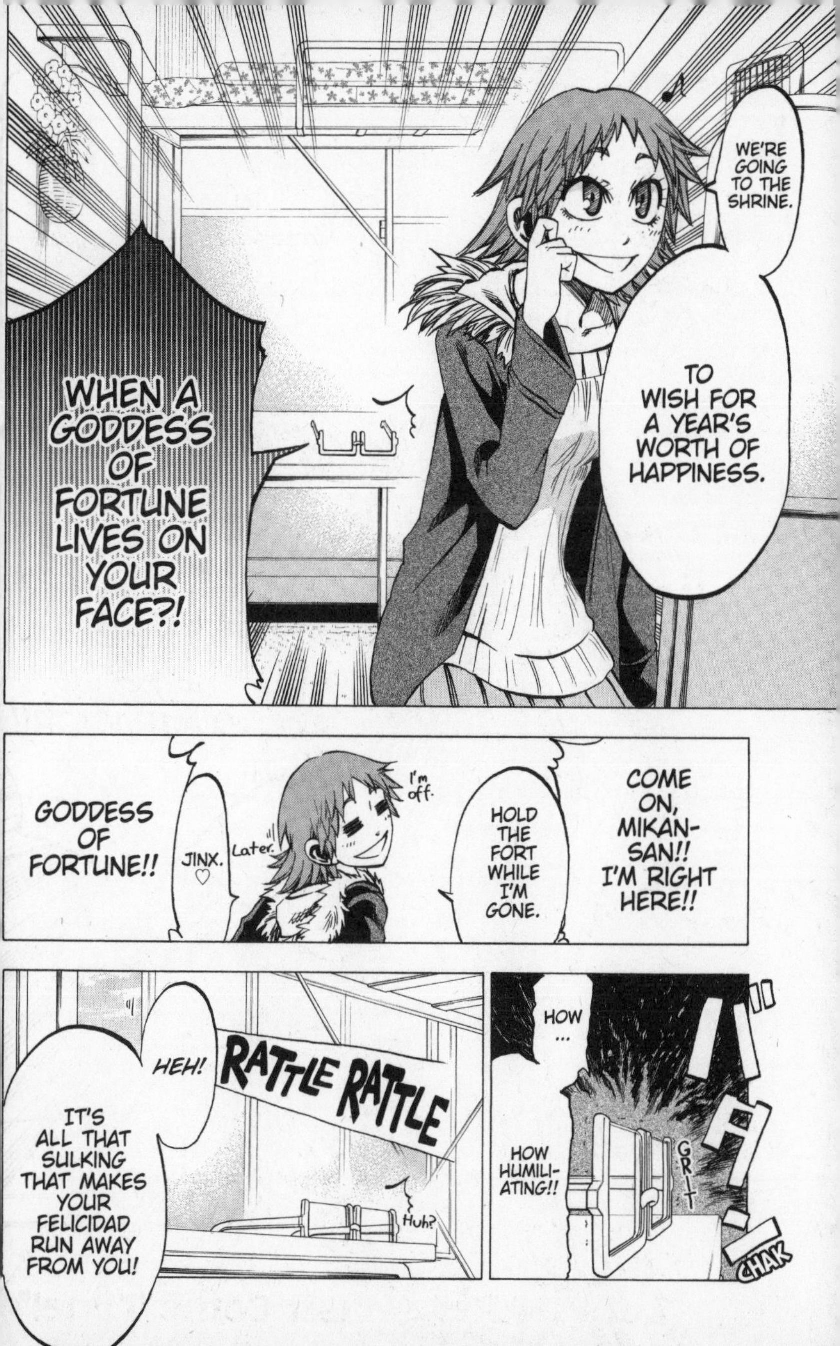
WE'RE GOING TO THE SHRINE.
TO WISH FOR A YEAR'S WORTH OF HAPPINESS.
WHEN A GODDESS OF FORTUNE LIVES ON YOUR FACE?!
COME ON, MIKAN-SAN!! I'M RIGHT HERE!!
HOLD THE FORT WHILE I'M GONE.
I'm off.
Later.
JINX. ♡
GODDESS OF FORTUNE!!
HOW ...
HOW HUMILI-ATING!!
GRIT
CHAK
RATTLE RATTLE
Huh?
HEH!
IT'S ALL THAT SULKING THAT MAKES YOUR FELICIDAD RUN AWAY FROM YOU!

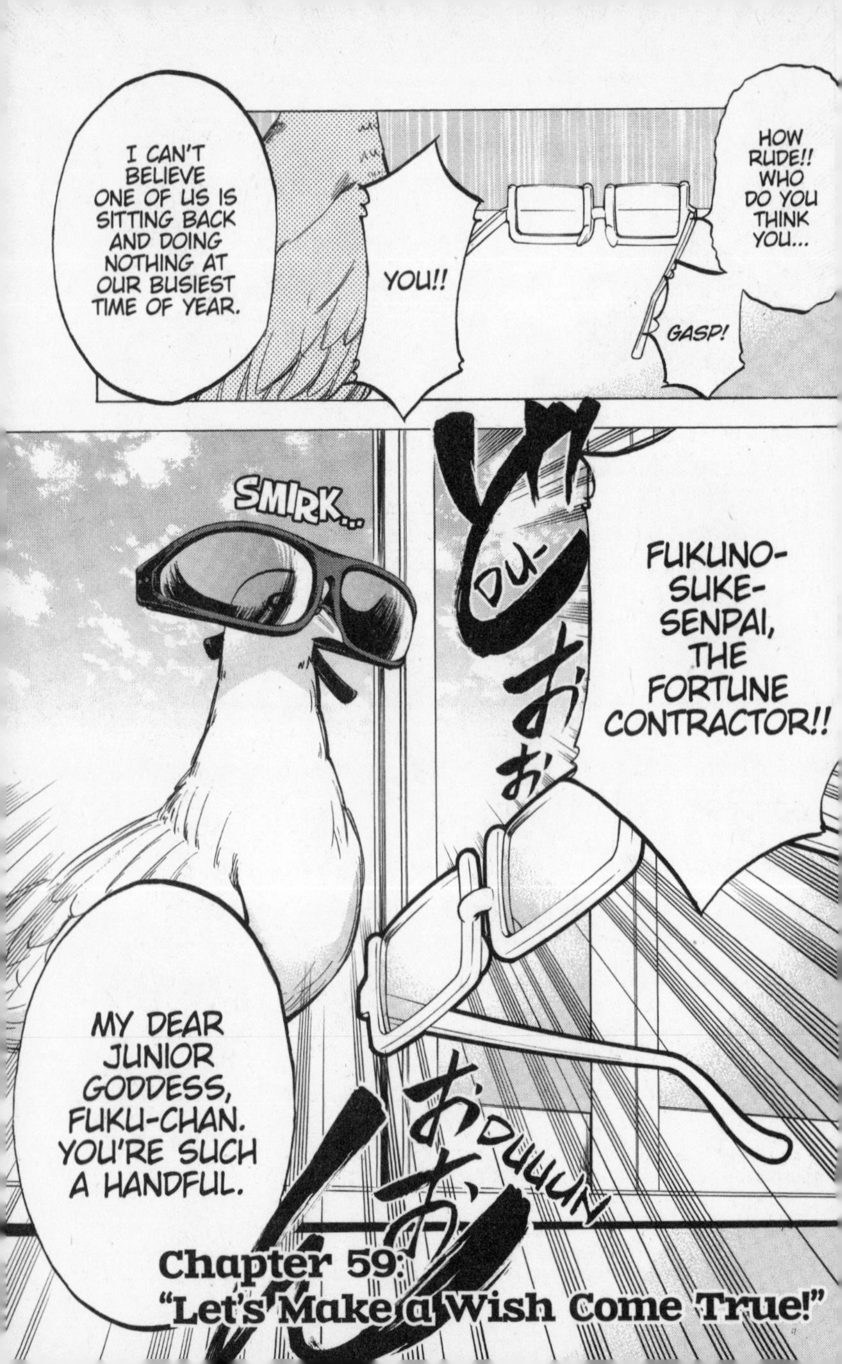
HOW RUDE!! WHO DO YOU THINK YOU...
GASP!
YOU!!
I CAN'T BELIEVE ONE OF US IS SITTING BACK AND DOING NOTHING AT OUR BUSIEST TIME OF YEAR.
FUKUNO-SUKE-SENPAI, THE FORTUNE CONTRACTOR!!
DU-
SMIRK...
DUUUUN
MY DEAR JUNIOR GODDESS, FUKU-CHAN. YOU'RE SUCH A HANDFUL.

Chapter 59: "Let's Make a Wish Come True!"

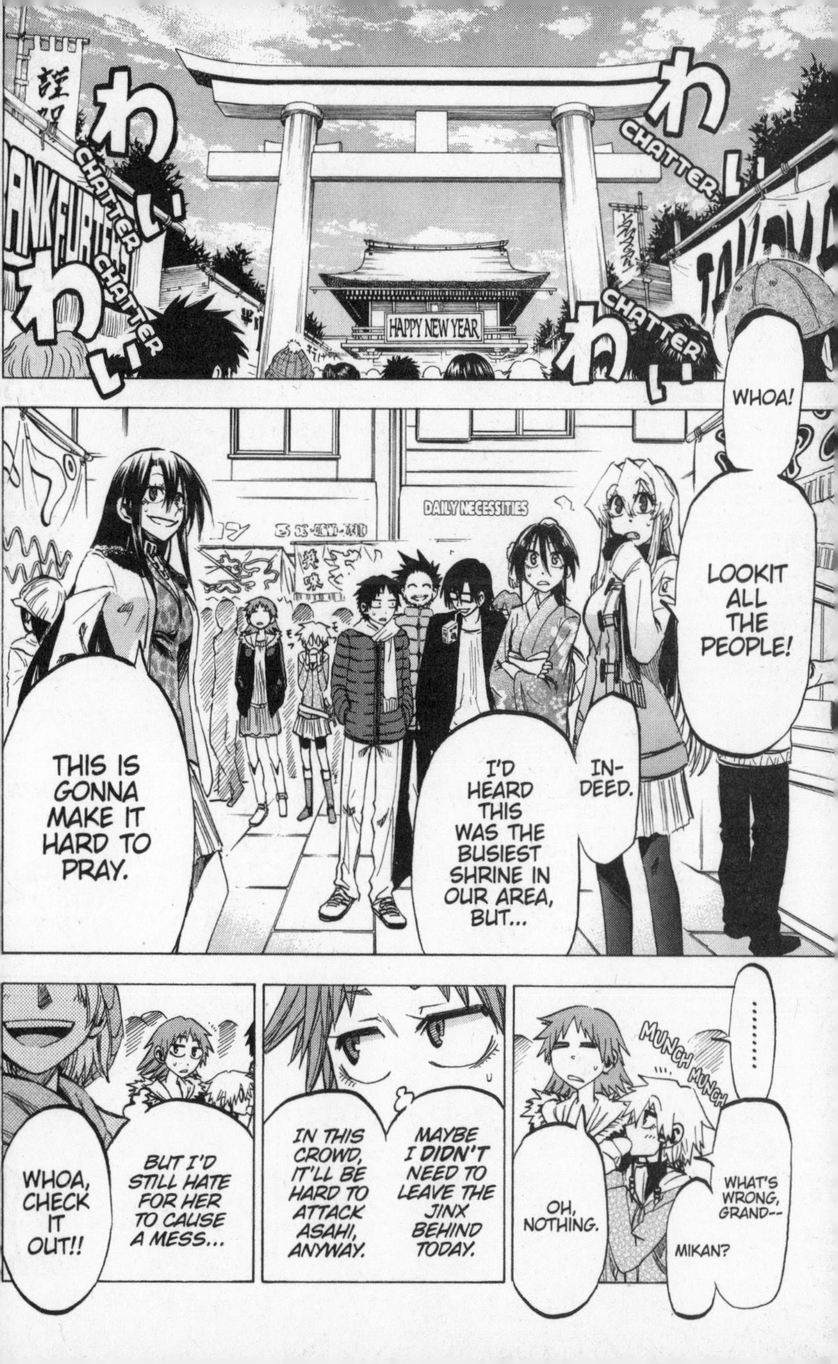
わい
CHATTER
わい
CHATTER
HAPPY NEW YEAR
わい
CHATTER CHATTER
わい
謹賀
WHOA!
LOOKIT ALL THE PEOPLE!
DAILY NECESSITIES
INDEED.
I'D HEARD THIS WAS THE BUSIEST SHRINE IN OUR AREA, BUT...
THIS IS GONNA MAKE IT HARD TO PRAY.
......
MUNCH MUNCH
WHAT'S WRONG, GRAND--
MIKAN?
OH, NOTHING.
MAYBE I DIDN'T NEED TO LEAVE THE JINX BEHIND TODAY.
IN THIS CROWD, IT'LL BE HARD TO ATTACK ASAHI, ANYWAY.
BUT I'D STILL HATE FOR HER TO CAUSE A MESS...
WHOA, CHECK IT OUT!!

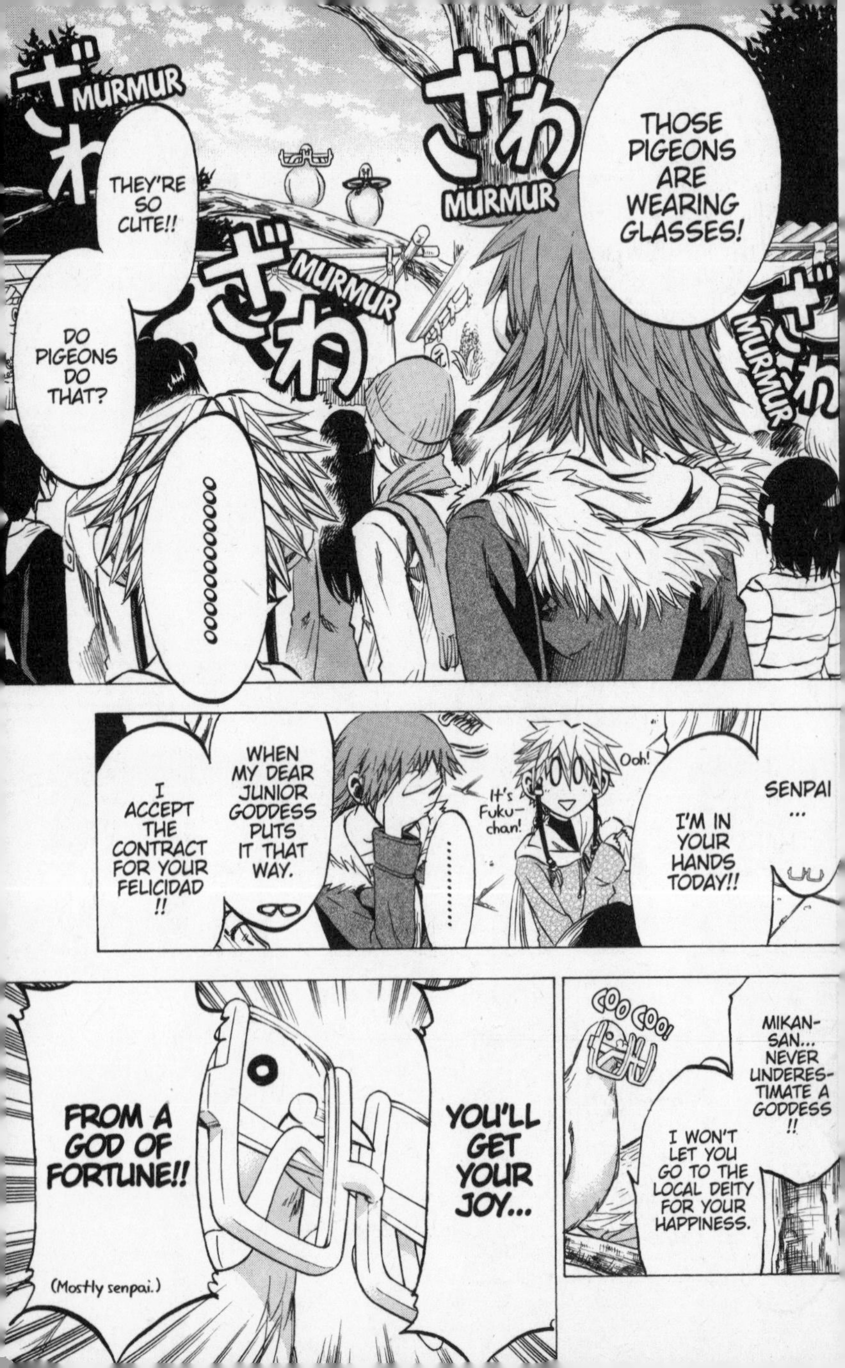
ざわ
MURMUR
THOSE PIGEONS ARE WEARING GLASSES!
ざわ
MURMUR
ざわ
MURMUR
THEY'RE SO CUTE!!
ざわ
MURMUR
DO PIGEONS DO THAT?
OOOOOOOOOOOO
SENPAI ...
I'M IN YOUR HANDS TODAY!!
Ooh!
It's Fuku-chan!
......
WHEN MY DEAR JUNIOR GODDESS PUTS IT THAT WAY.
I ACCEPT THE CONTRACT FOR YOUR FELICIDAD !!
MIKAN-SAN... NEVER UNDERESTIMATE A GODDESS !!
COO COO!
I WON'T LET YOU GO TO THE LOCAL DEITY FOR YOUR HAPPINESS.
YOU'LL GET YOUR JOY...
FROM A GOD OF FORTUNE!!
(Mostly senpai.)

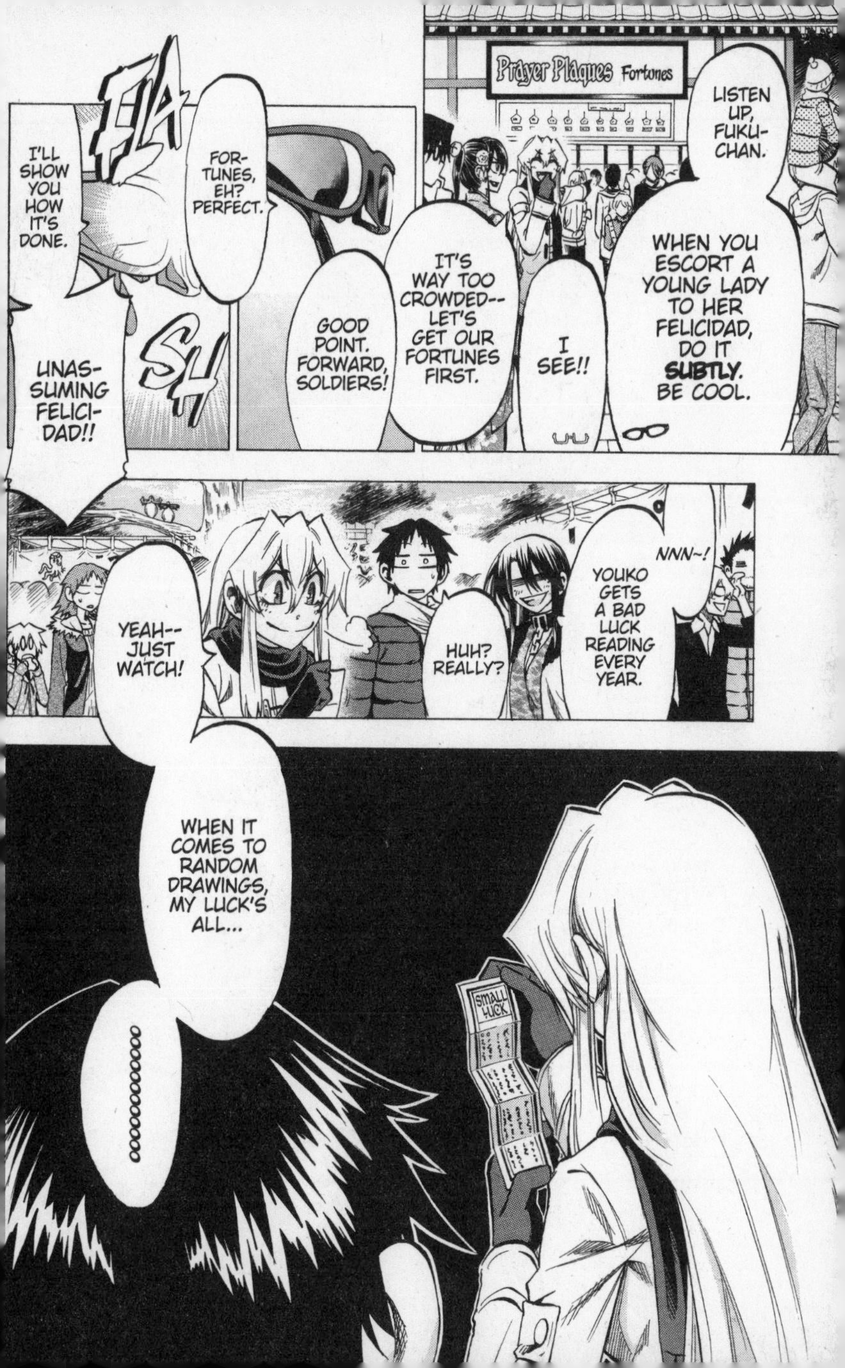
Prayer Plaques Fortunes
LISTEN UP, FUKU-CHAN.
WHEN YOU ESCORT A YOUNG LADY TO HER FELICIDAD, DO IT **SUBTLY**. BE COOL.
I SEE!!
IT'S WAY TOO CROWDED-- LET'S GET OUR FORTUNES FIRST.
GOOD POINT. FORWARD, SOLDIERS!
FOR-TUNES, EH? PERFECT.
I'LL SHOW YOU HOW IT'S DONE.
SH
UNAS-SUMING FELICI-DAD!!
NNN~!
YOUKO GETS A BAD LUCK READING EVERY YEAR.
HUH? REALLY?
YEAH-- JUST WATCH!
WHEN IT COMES TO RANDOM DRAWINGS, MY LUCK'S ALL...
SMALL LUCK
OOOOOOOOOOOOO......

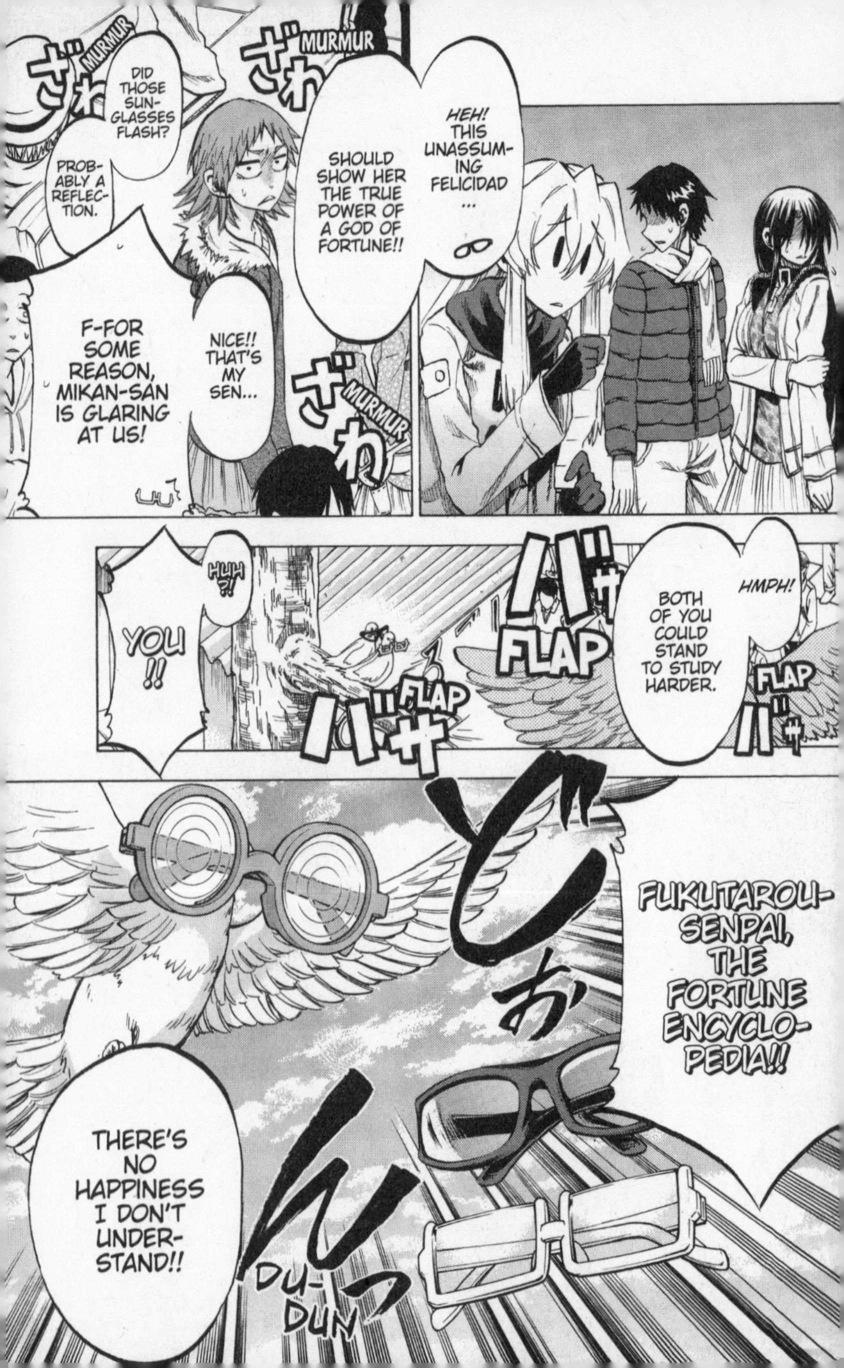
HEH! THIS UNASSUMING FELICIDAD...
SHOULD SHOW HER THE TRUE POWER OF A GOD OF FORTUNE!!
MURMUR
MURMUR
DID THOSE SUNGLASSES FLASH?
PROBABLY A REFLECTION.
NICE!! THAT'S MY SEN...
MURMUR
F-FOR SOME REASON, MIKAN-SAN IS GLARING AT US!
HMPH!
BOTH OF YOU COULD STAND TO STUDY HARDER.
FLAP
FLAP
FLAP
HUH?!
YOU!!
FUKUTAROU-SENPAI, THE FORTUNE ENCYCLOPEDIA!!
THERE'S NO HAPPINESS I DON'T UNDERSTAND!!
DU-DUN

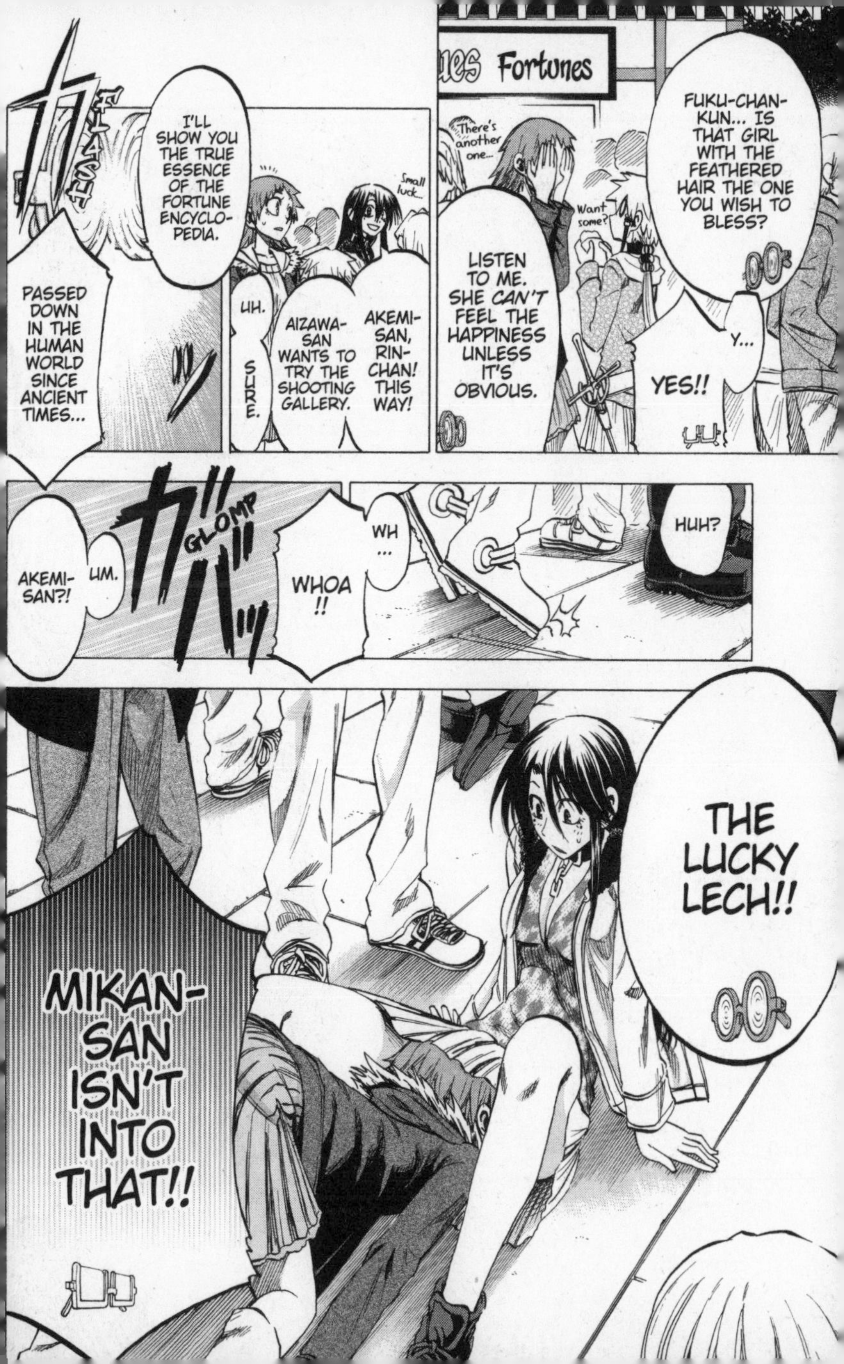
Fortunes
FUKU-CHAN-KUN... IS THAT GIRL WITH THE FEATHERED HAIR THE ONE YOU WISH TO BLESS?
Y...
YES!!
There's another one...
Want some?
LISTEN TO ME. SHE CAN'T FEEL THE HAPPINESS UNLESS IT'S OBVIOUS.
I'LL SHOW YOU THE TRUE ESSENCE OF THE FORTUNE ENCYCLOPEDIA.
Small luck...
AKEMI-SAN, RIN-CHAN! THIS WAY!
AIZAWA-SAN WANTS TO TRY THE SHOOTING GALLERY.
UH. SURE.
FLASH
PASSED DOWN IN THE HUMAN WORLD SINCE ANCIENT TIMES...
HUH?
WH...
WHOA!!
GLOMP
UM.
AKEMI-SAN?!
THE LUCKY LECH!!
MIKAN-SAN ISN'T INTO THAT!!

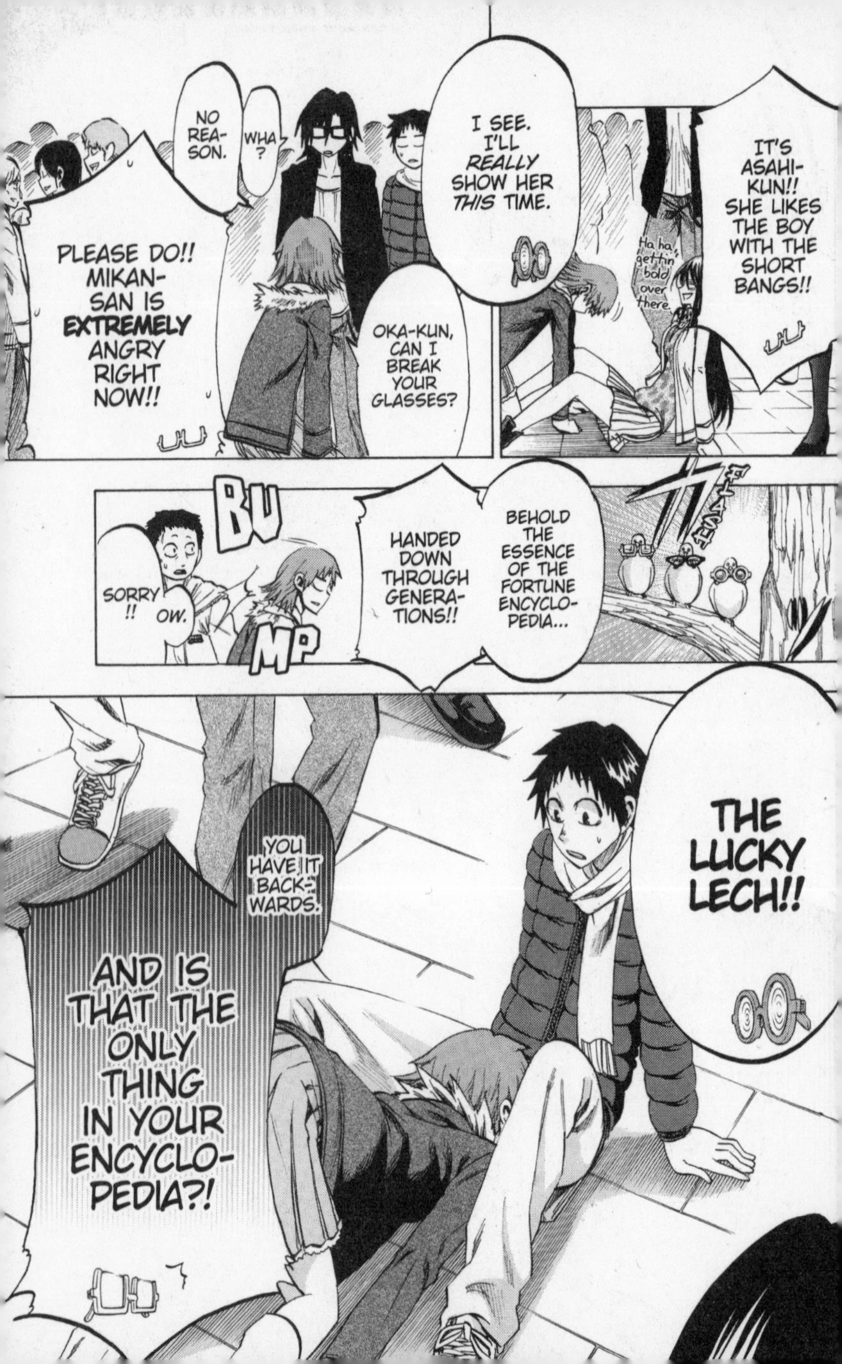
IT'S ASAHI-KUN!! SHE LIKES THE BOY WITH THE SHORT BANGS!!
Ha ha, gettin' bold over there.
I SEE. I'LL REALLY SHOW HER THIS TIME.
OKA-KUN, CAN I BREAK YOUR GLASSES?
WHA?
NO REASON.
PLEASE DO!! MIKAN-SAN IS EXTREMELY ANGRY RIGHT NOW!!
BEHOLD THE ESSENCE OF THE FORTUNE ENCYCLOPEDIA...
HANDED DOWN THROUGH GENERATIONS!!
BUMP
OW.
SORRY!!
THE LUCKY LECH!!
YOU HAVE IT BACKWARDS.
AND IS THAT THE ONLY THING IN YOUR ENCYCLOPEDIA?!

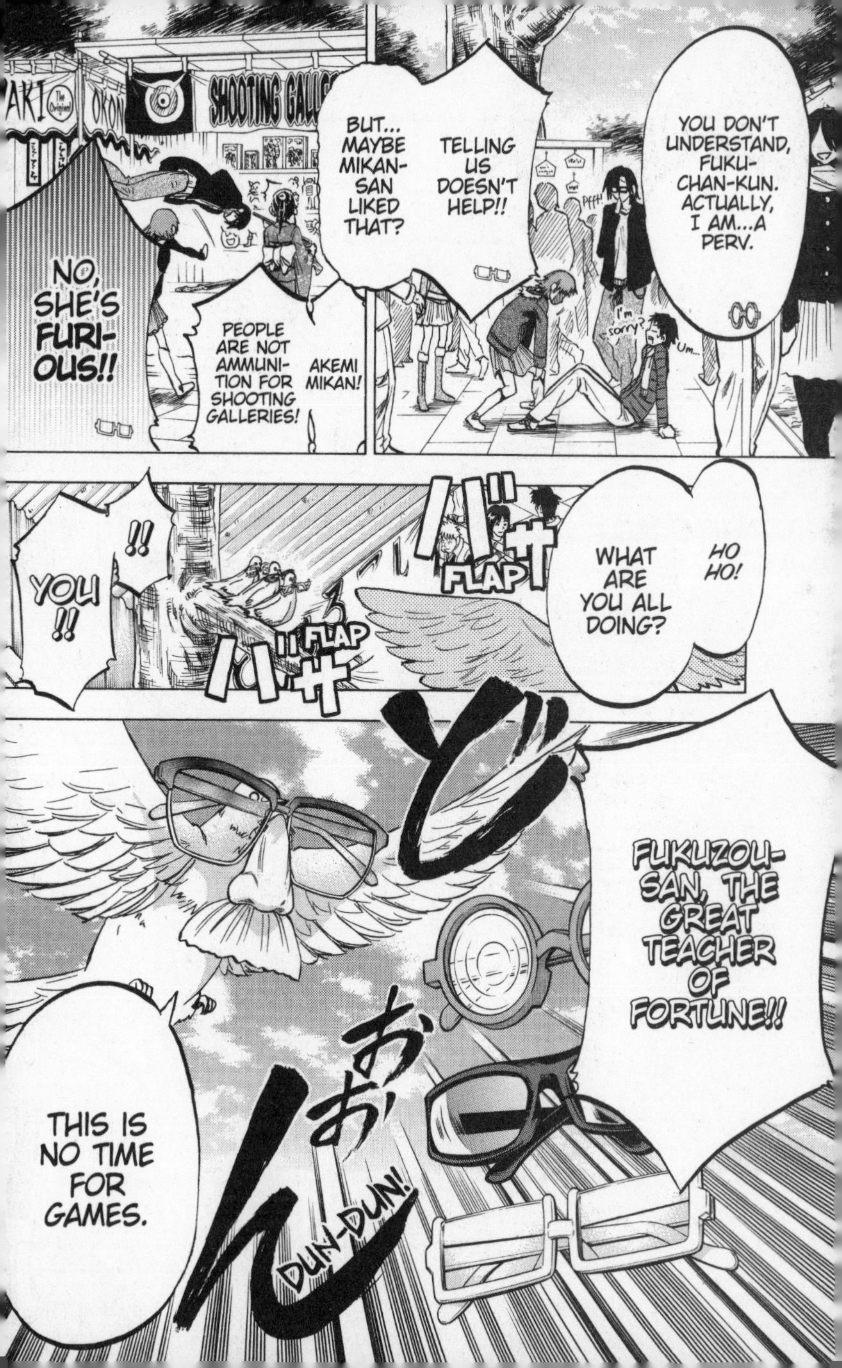
YOU DON'T UNDERSTAND, FUKU-CHAN-KUN. ACTUALLY, I AM...A PERV.
Pfft
I'm sorry?
Um...
TELLING US DOESN'T HELP!!
BUT... MAYBE MIKAN-SAN LIKED THAT?
AKEMI MIKAN!
PEOPLE ARE NOT AMMUNITION FOR SHOOTING GALLERIES!
NO, SHE'S FURIOUS!!
HO HO!
WHAT ARE YOU ALL DOING?
FLAP
FLAP
!!
YOU!!
FUKUZOU-SAN, THE GREAT TEACHER OF FORTUNE!!
DUN-DUN!
THIS IS NO TIME FOR GAMES.

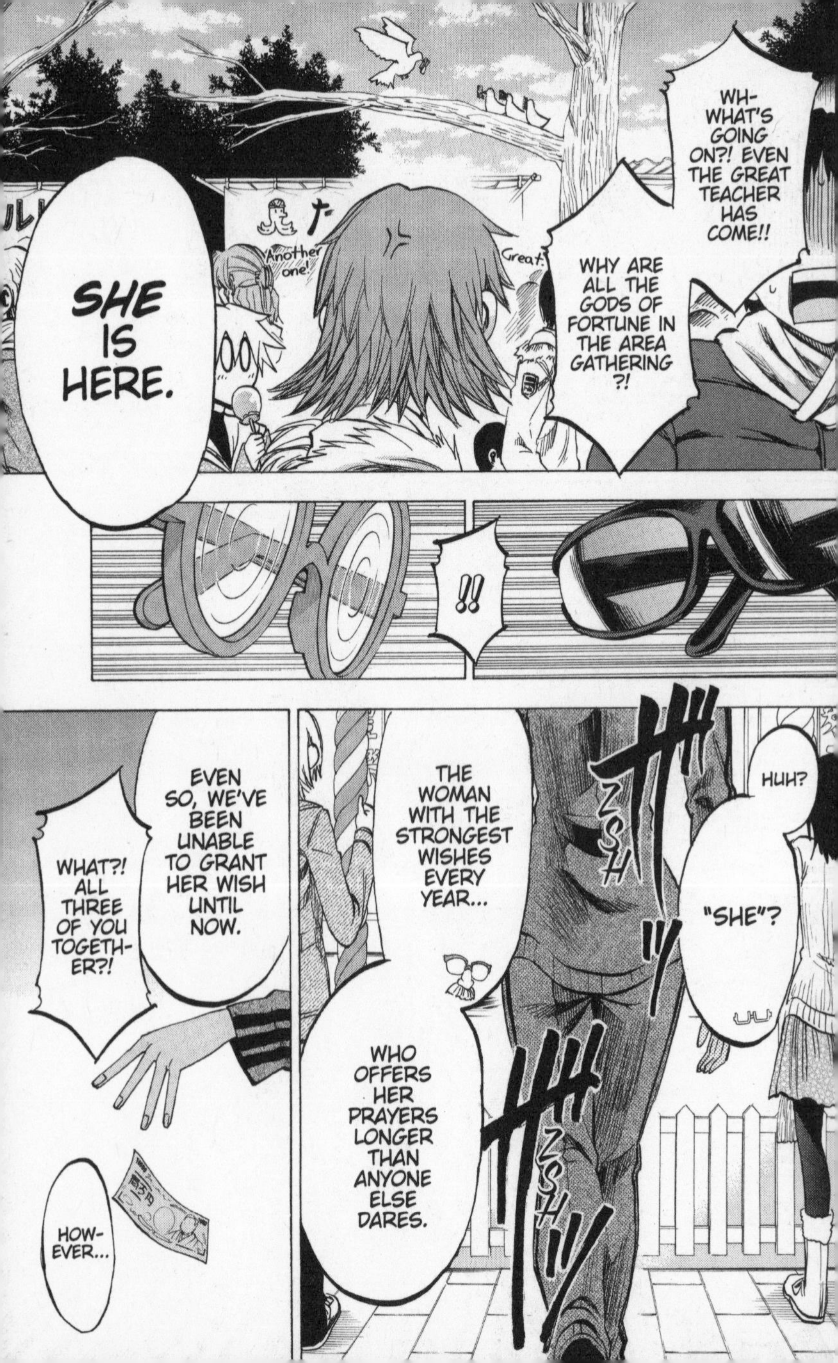
WH- WHAT'S GOING ON?! EVEN THE GREAT TEACHER HAS COME!!
WHY ARE ALL THE GODS OF FORTUNE IN THE AREA GATHERING?!
Great.
Another one!
SHE IS HERE.
!!
HUH?
"SHE"?
ZSH
ZSH
THE WOMAN WITH THE STRONGEST WISHES EVERY YEAR...
WHO OFFERS HER PRAYERS LONGER THAN ANYONE ELSE DARES.
EVEN SO, WE'VE BEEN UNABLE TO GRANT HER WISH UNTIL NOW.
WHAT?! ALL THREE OF YOU TOGETHER?!
HOW-EVER...

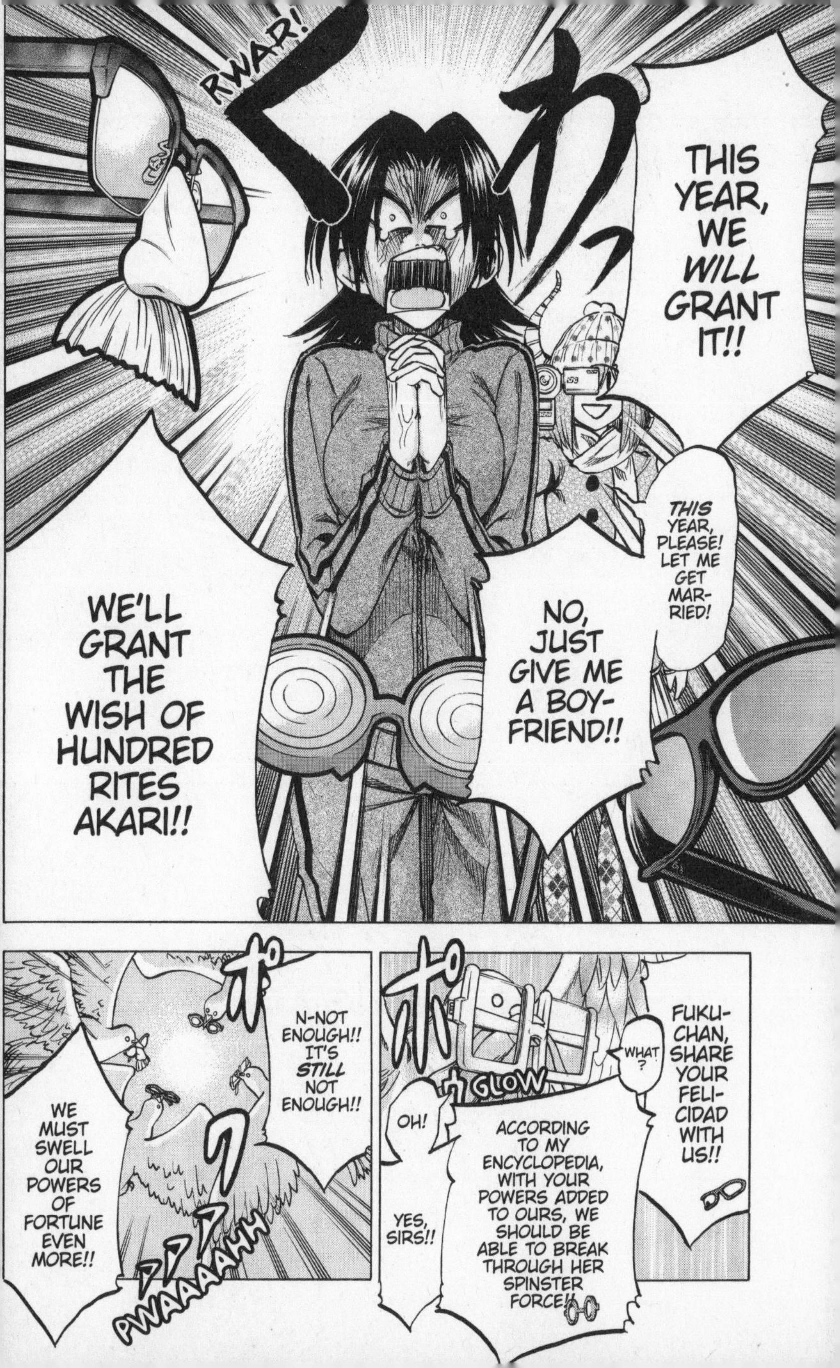
RWAR!
THIS YEAR, WE *WILL* GRANT IT!!
THIS YEAR, PLEASE! LET ME GET MAR-RIED!
NO, JUST GIVE ME A BOY-FRIEND!!
WE'LL GRANT THE WISH OF HUNDRED RITES AKARI!!
FUKU-CHAN, SHARE YOUR FELI-CIDAD WITH US!!
WHAT?
GLOW
OH!
ACCORDING TO MY ENCYCLOPEDIA, WITH YOUR POWERS ADDED TO OURS, WE SHOULD BE ABLE TO BREAK THROUGH HER SPINSTER FORCE!!
YES, SIRS!!
N-NOT ENOUGH!! IT'S *STILL* NOT ENOUGH!!
WE MUST SWELL OUR POWERS OF FORTUNE EVEN MORE!!
PWAAAAAHH

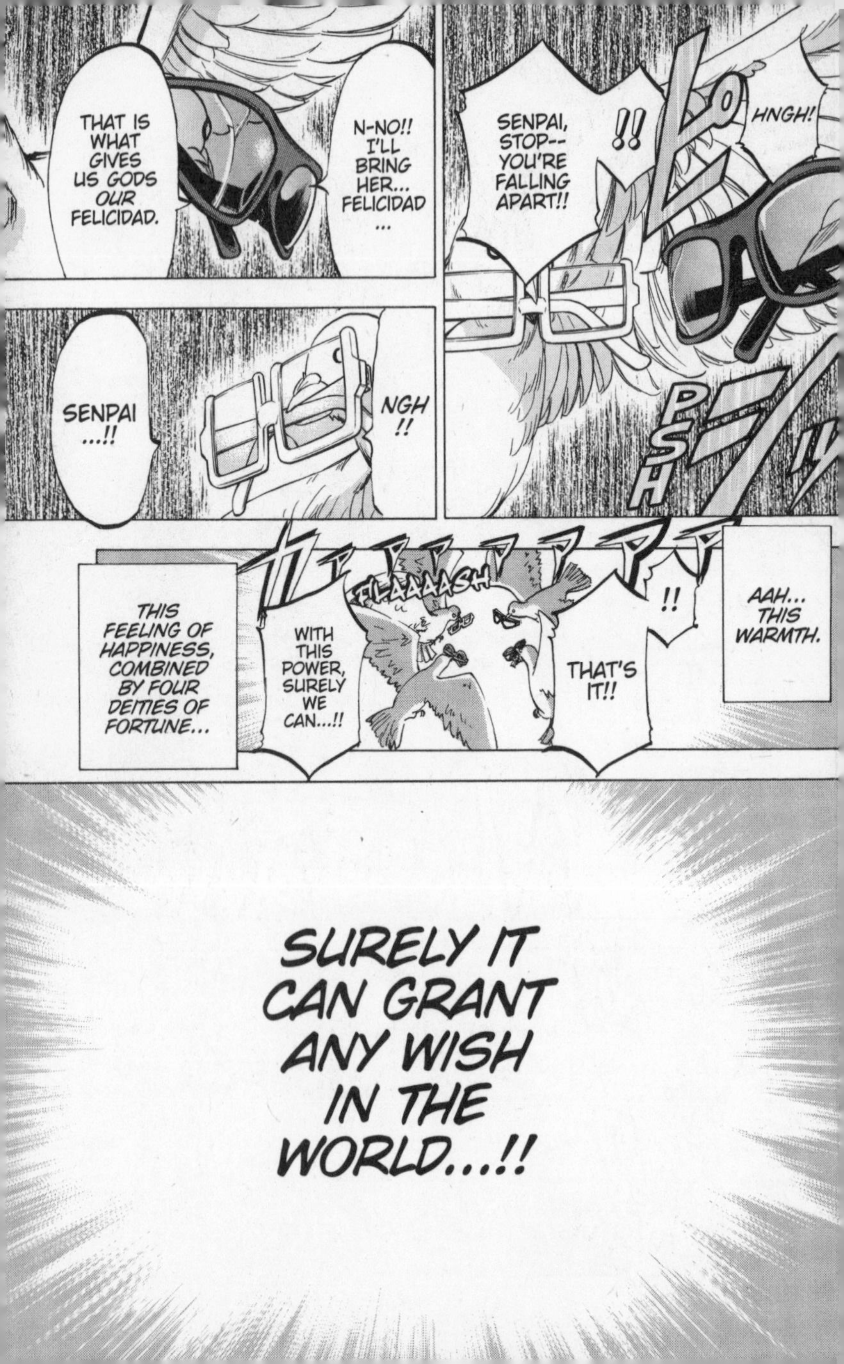
HNGH!
!!
SENPAI, STOP-- YOU'RE FALLING APART!!
PSH
N-NO!! I'LL BRING HER... FELICIDAD...
THAT IS WHAT GIVES US GODS OUR FELICIDAD.
NGH!!
SENPAI...!!
AAH... THIS WARMTH.
!!
FLAAAASH
THAT'S IT!!
WITH THIS POWER, SURELY WE CAN...!!
THIS FEELING OF HAPPINESS, COMBINED BY FOUR DEITIES OF FORTUNE...
SURELY IT CAN GRANT ANY WISH IN THE WORLD...!!

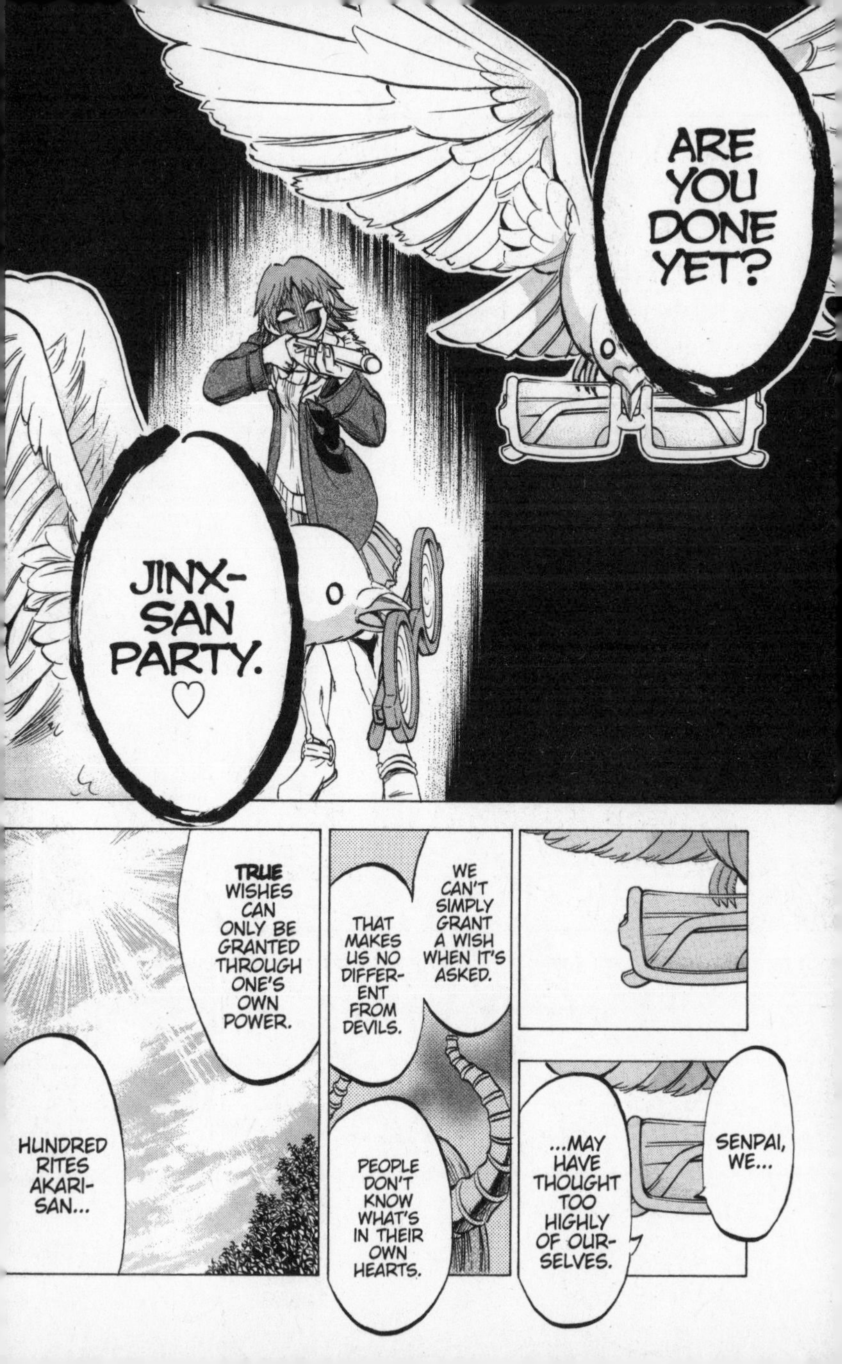
ARE YOU DONE YET?
JINX-SAN PARTY. ♡
SENPAI, WE...
...MAY HAVE THOUGHT TOO HIGHLY OF OURSELVES.
WE CAN'T SIMPLY GRANT A WISH WHEN IT'S ASKED.
THAT MAKES US NO DIFFERENT FROM DEVILS.
PEOPLE DON'T KNOW WHAT'S IN THEIR OWN HEARTS.
TRUE WISHES CAN ONLY BE GRANTED THROUGH ONE'S OWN POWER.
HUNDRED RITES AKARI-SAN...

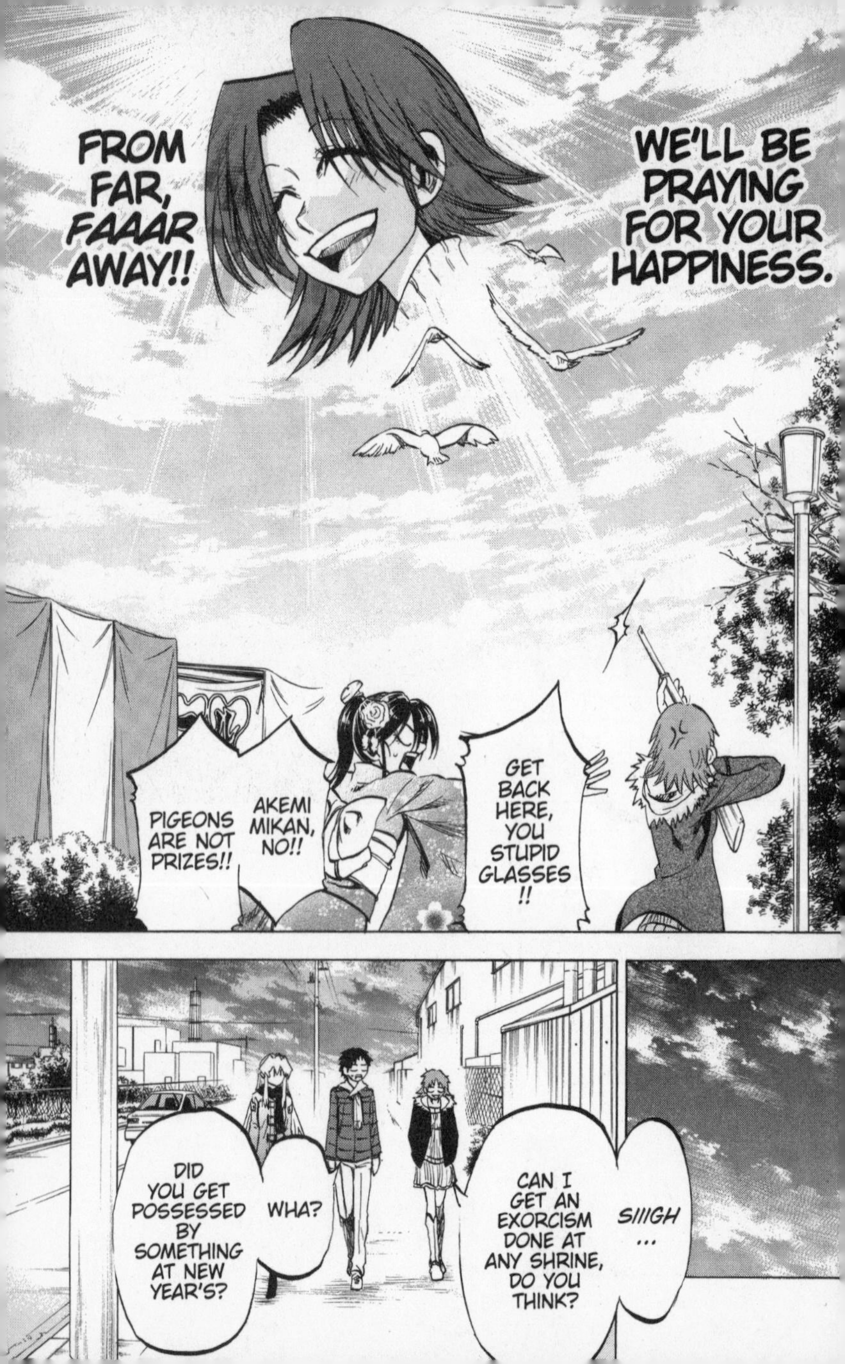
WE'LL BE PRAYING FOR YOUR HAPPINESS.
FROM FAR, FAAAR AWAY!!
GET BACK HERE, YOU STUPID GLASSES!!
AKEMI MIKAN, NO!!
PIGEONS ARE NOT PRIZES!!
SIIIGH...
CAN I GET AN EXORCISM DONE AT ANY SHRINE, DO YOU THINK?
WHA?
DID YOU GET POSSESSED BY SOMETHING AT NEW YEAR'S?

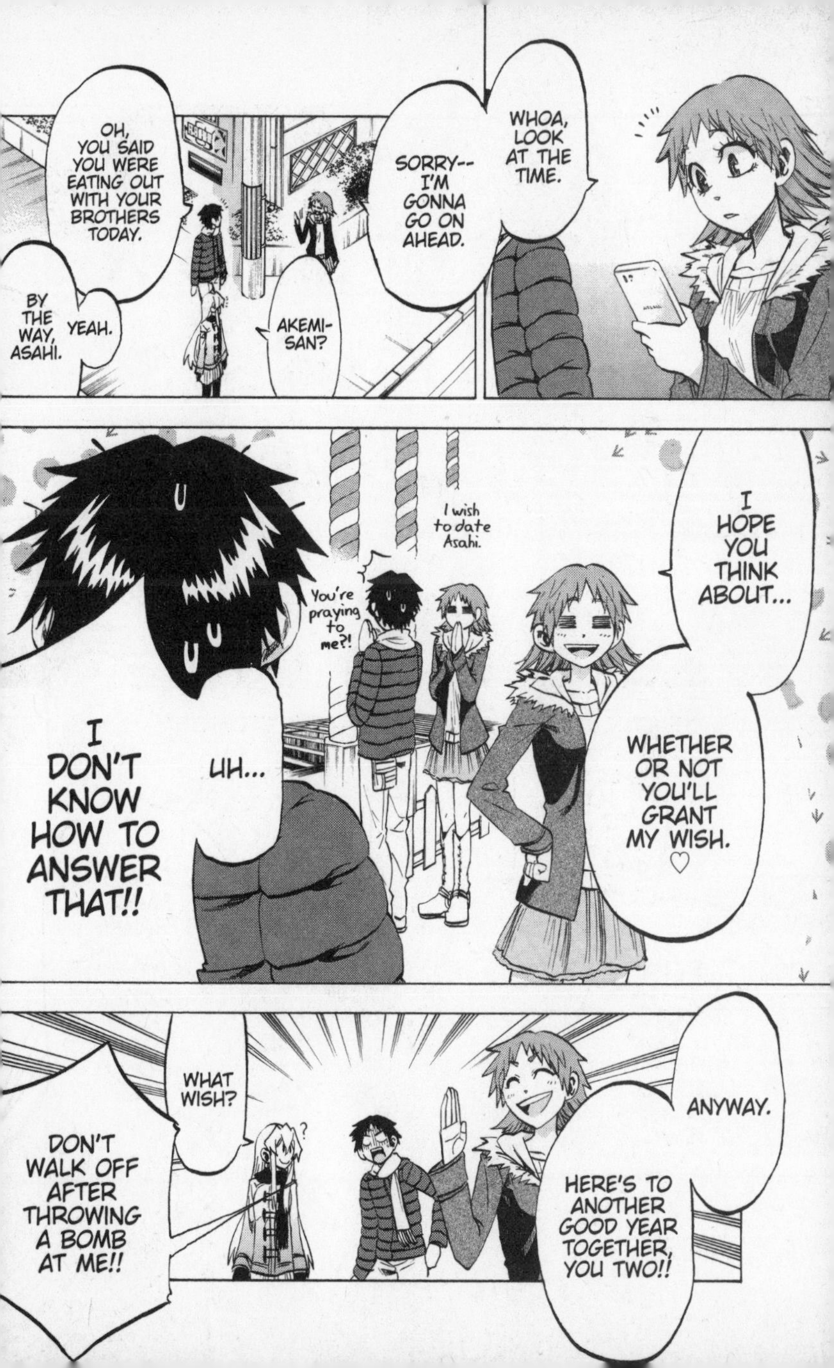
WHOA, LOOK AT THE TIME.
SORRY-- I'M GONNA GO ON AHEAD.
AKEMI-SAN?
OH, YOU SAID YOU WERE EATING OUT WITH YOUR BROTHERS TODAY.
YEAH.
BY THE WAY, ASAHI.
I HOPE YOU THINK ABOUT...
WHETHER OR NOT YOU'LL GRANT MY WISH. ♡
I wish to date Asahi.
You're praying to me?!
UH...
I DON'T KNOW HOW TO ANSWER THAT!!
ANYWAY.
HERE'S TO ANOTHER GOOD YEAR TOGETHER, YOU TWO!!
WHAT WISH?
DON'T WALK OFF AFTER THROWING A BOMB AT ME!!

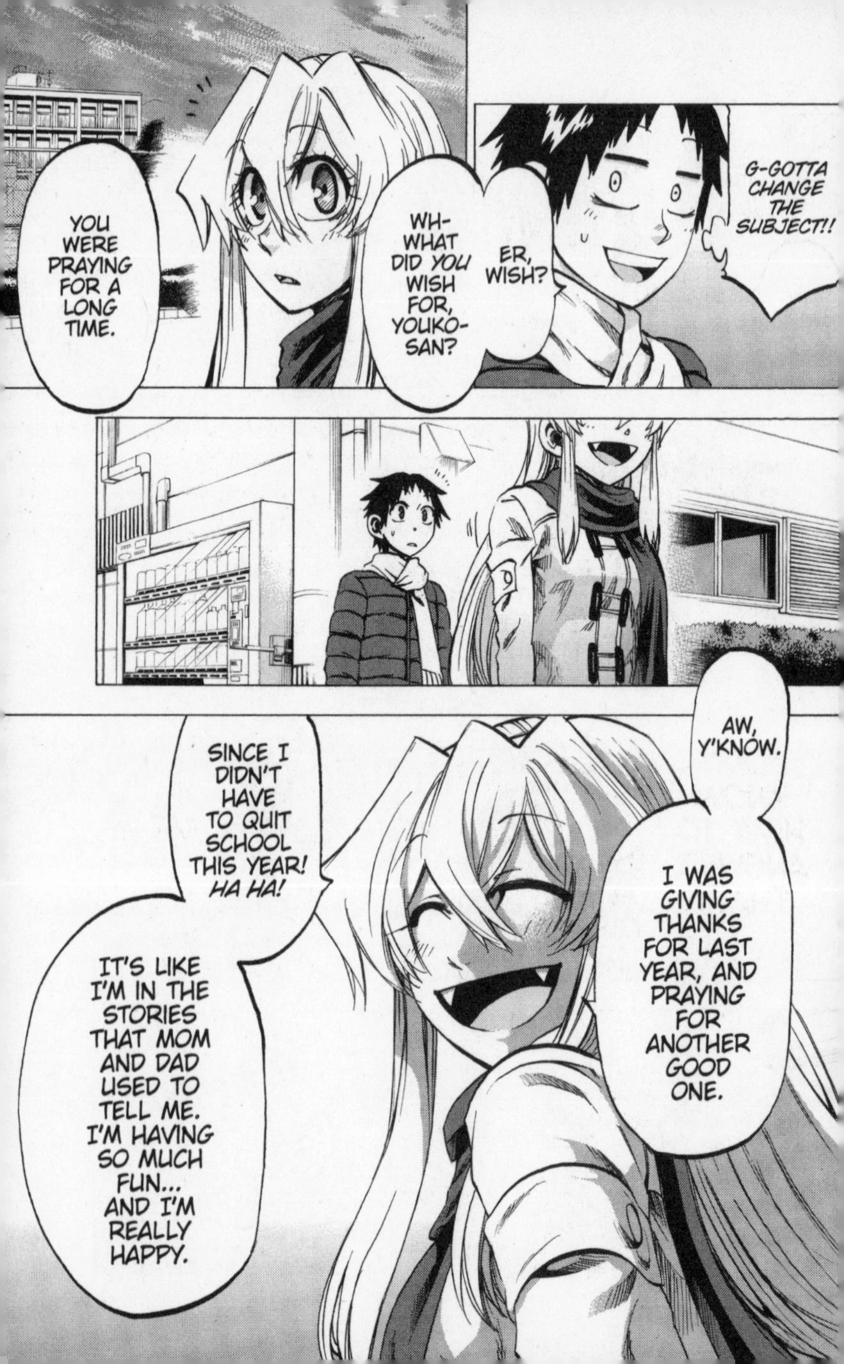
G-GOTTA CHANGE THE SUBJECT!!
ER, WISH?
WH-WHAT DID *YOU* WISH FOR, YOUKO-SAN?
YOU WERE PRAYING FOR A LONG TIME.
AW, Y'KNOW.
I WAS GIVING THANKS FOR LAST YEAR, AND PRAYING FOR ANOTHER GOOD ONE.
SINCE I DIDN'T HAVE TO QUIT SCHOOL THIS YEAR! *HA HA!*
IT'S LIKE I'M IN THE STORIES THAT MOM AND DAD USED TO TELL ME. I'M HAVING SO MUCH FUN... AND I'M REALLY HAPPY.

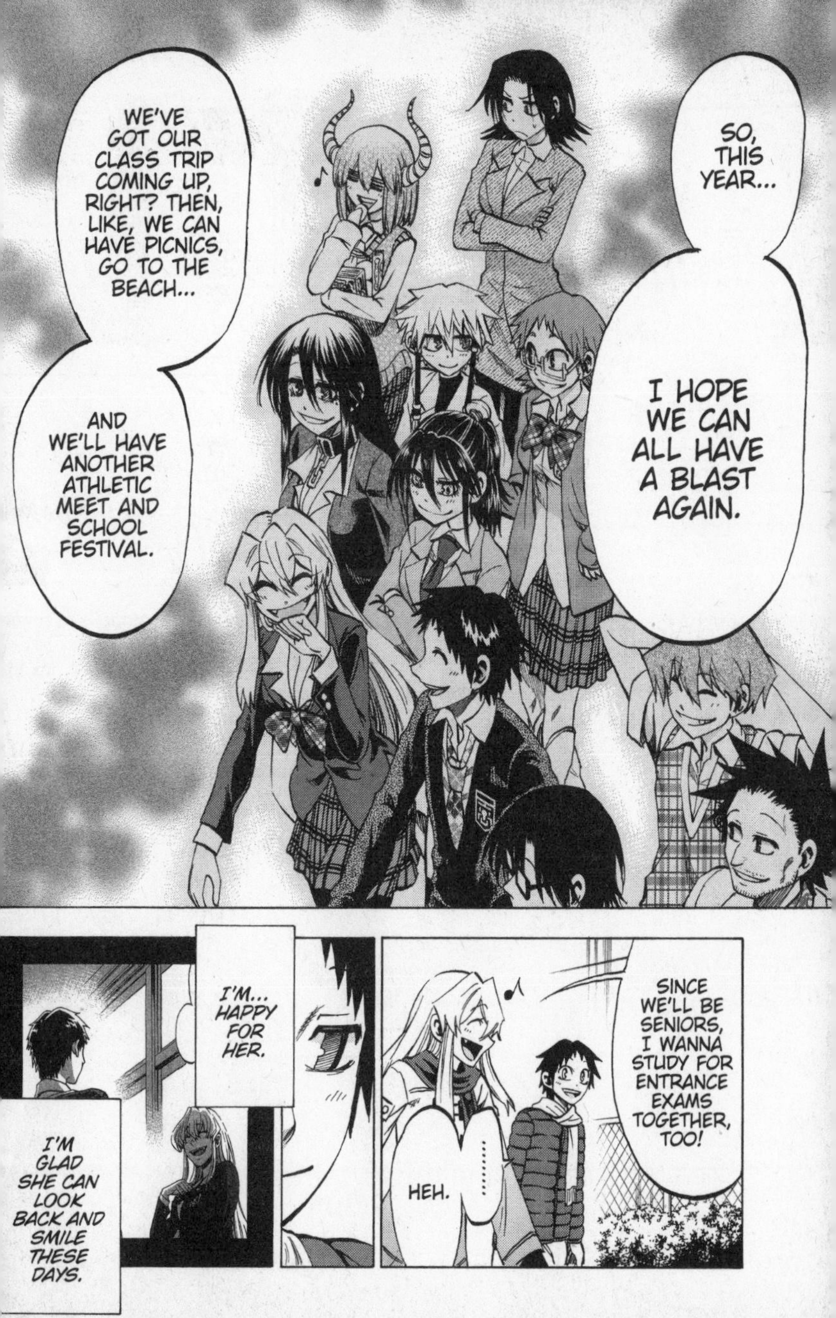
SO, THIS YEAR...
WE'VE GOT OUR CLASS TRIP COMING UP, RIGHT? THEN, LIKE, WE CAN HAVE PICNICS, GO TO THE BEACH...
AND WE'LL HAVE ANOTHER ATHLETIC MEET AND SCHOOL FESTIVAL.
I HOPE WE CAN ALL HAVE A BLAST AGAIN.
SINCE WE'LL BE SENIORS, I WANNA STUDY FOR ENTRANCE EXAMS TOGETHER, TOO!
......
HEH.
I'M... HAPPY FOR HER.
I'M GLAD SHE CAN LOOK BACK AND SMILE THESE DAYS.

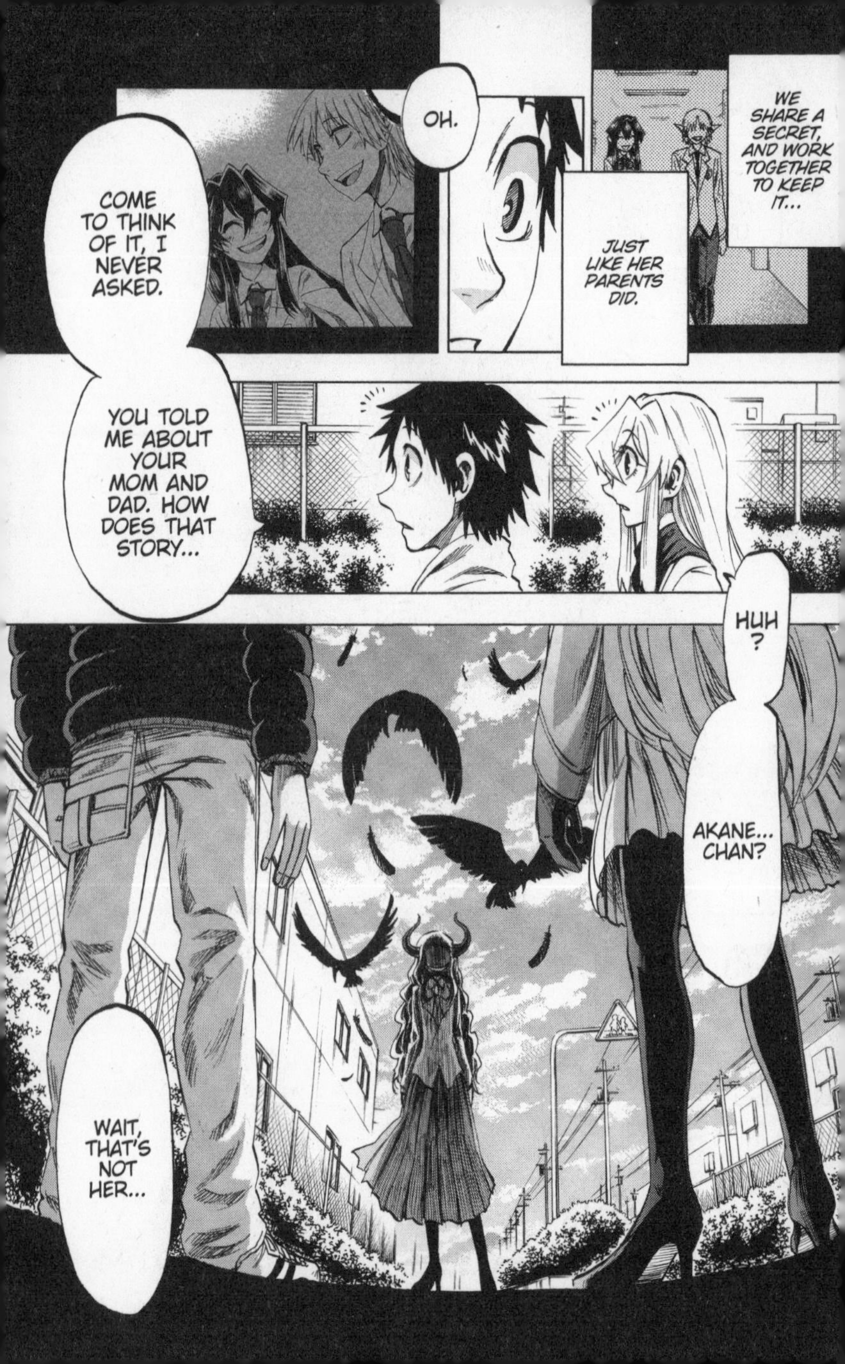
WE SHARE A SECRET, AND WORK TOGETHER TO KEEP IT...
JUST LIKE HER PARENTS DID.
OH.
COME TO THINK OF IT, I NEVER ASKED.
YOU TOLD ME ABOUT YOUR MOM AND DAD. HOW DOES THAT STORY...
HUH?
AKANE... CHAN?
WAIT, THAT'S NOT HER...

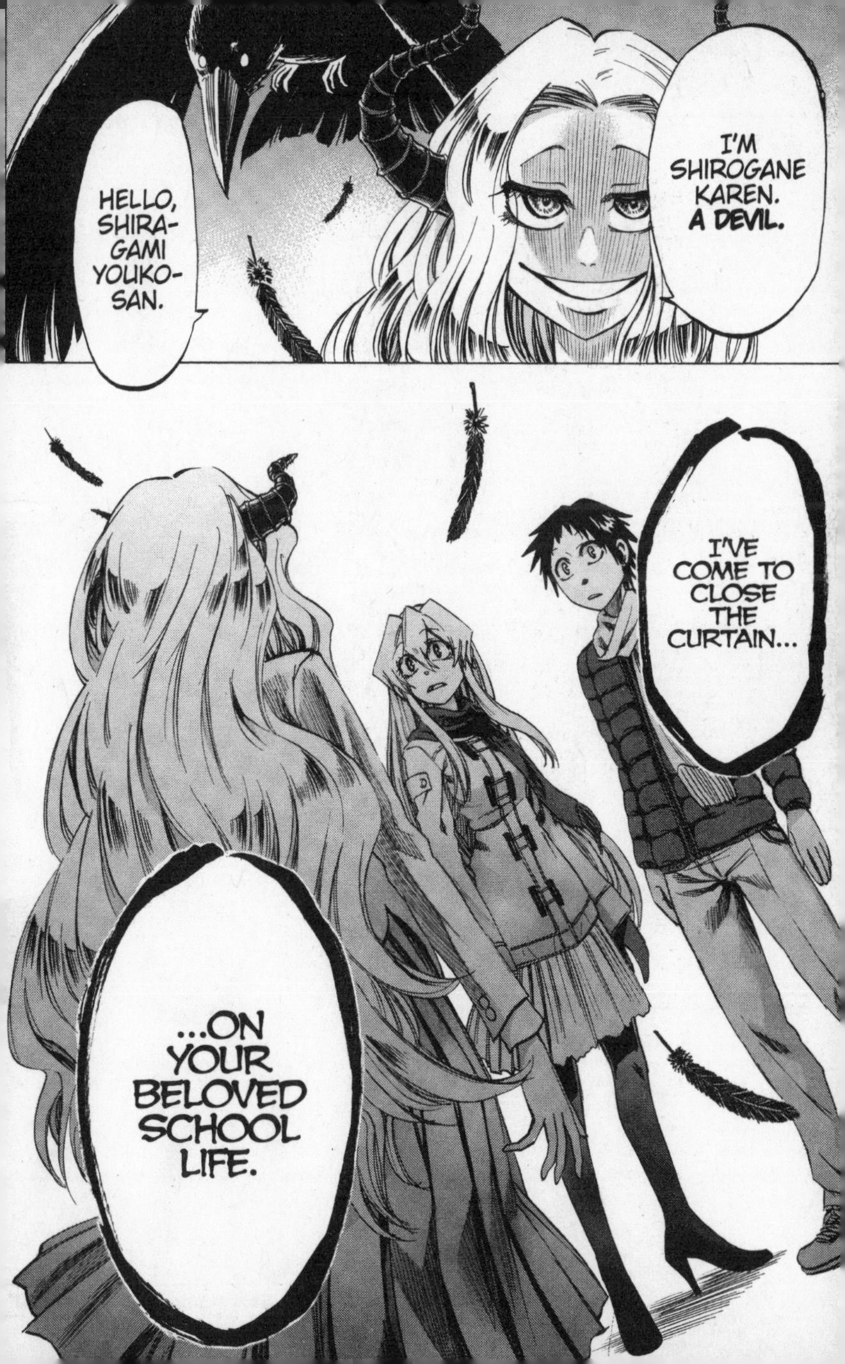
I'M SHIROGANE KAREN. A DEVIL.
HELLO, SHIRAGAMI YOUKO-SAN.
I'VE COME TO CLOSE THE CURTAIN...
...ON YOUR BELOVED SCHOOL LIFE.

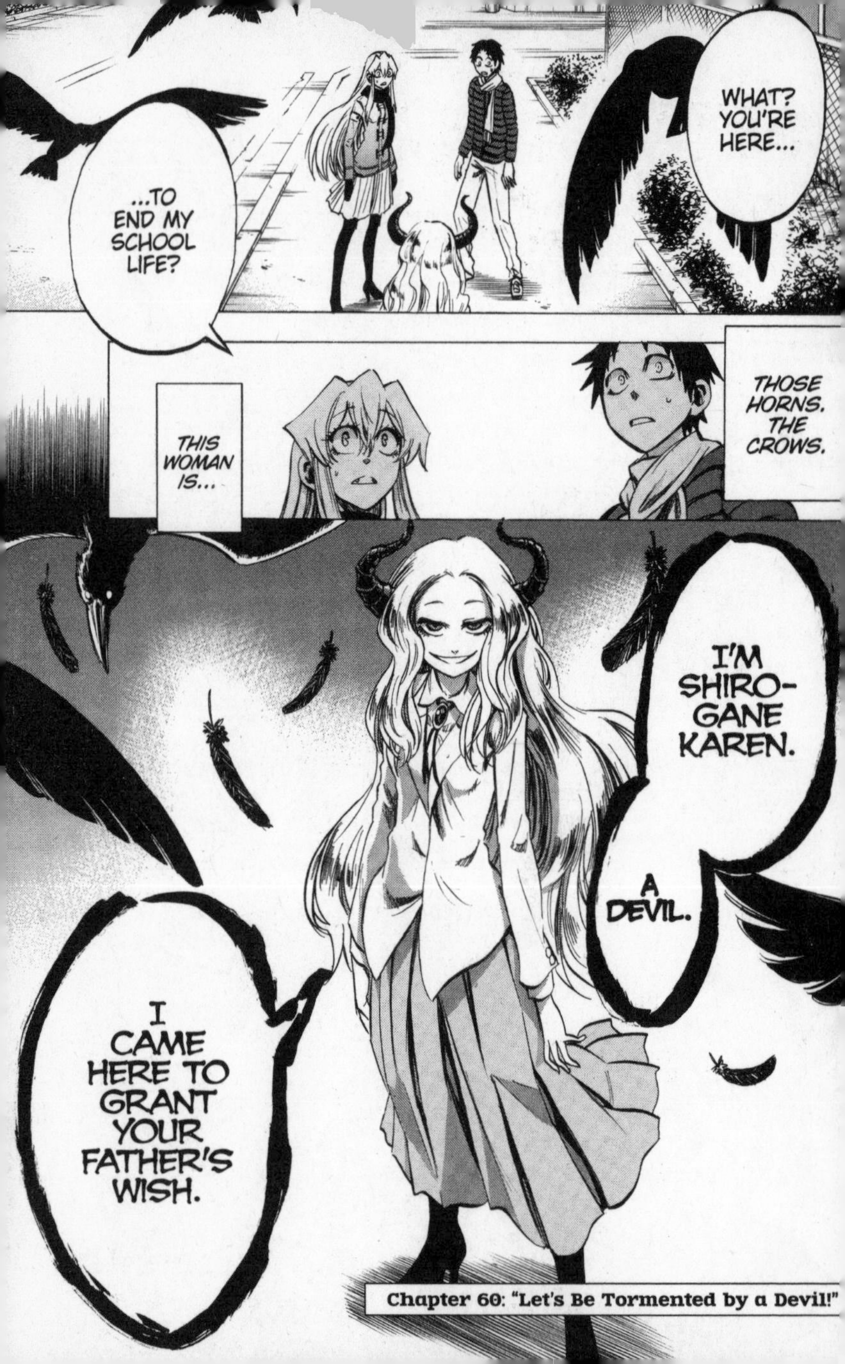
WHAT? YOU'RE HERE...
...TO END MY SCHOOL LIFE?
THOSE HORNS. THE CROWS.
THIS WOMAN IS...
I'M SHIRO-GANE KAREN.
A DEVIL.
I CAME HERE TO GRANT YOUR FATHER'S WISH.

Chapter 60: "Let's Be Tormented by a Devil!"

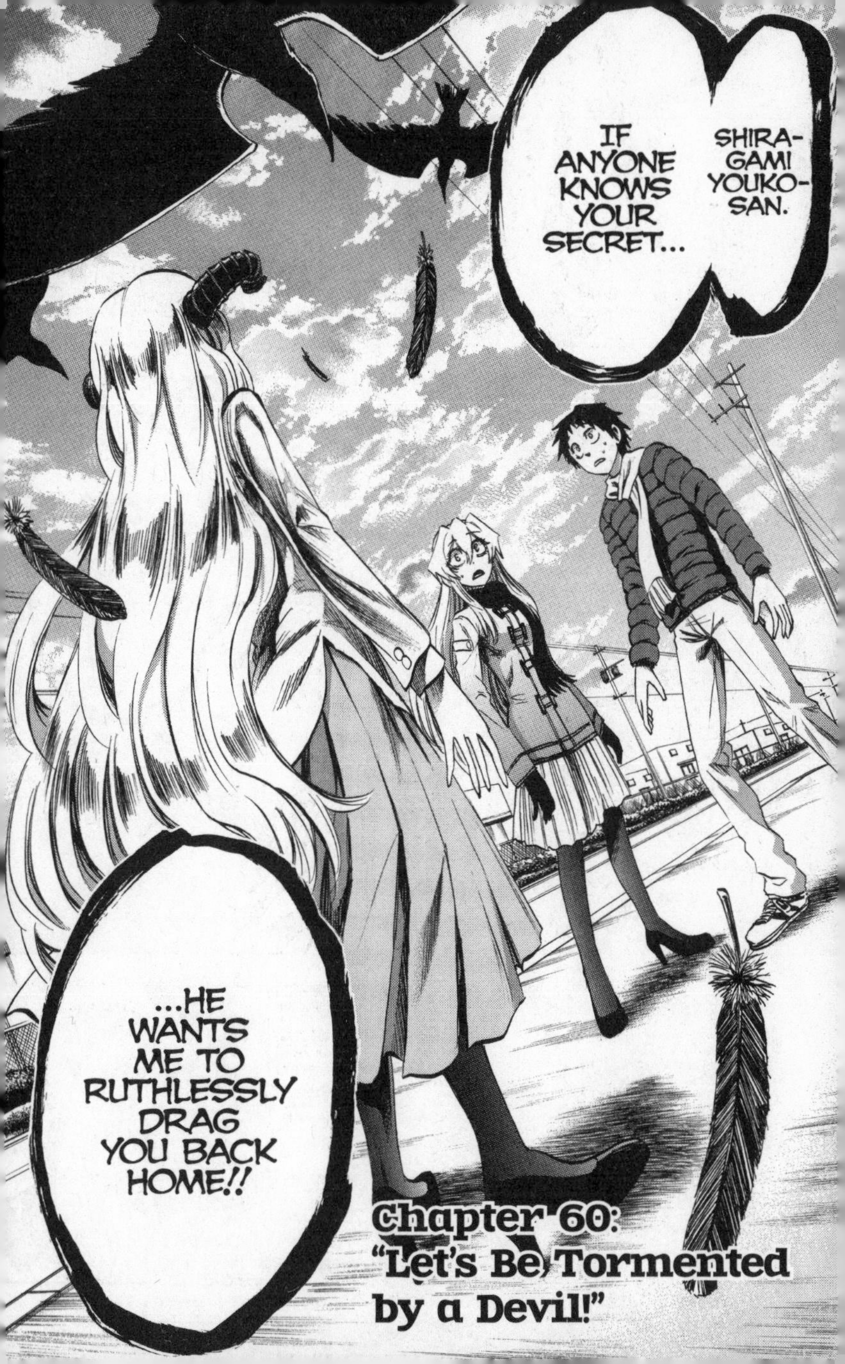
SHIRAGAMI YOUKO-SAN.
IF ANYONE KNOWS YOUR SECRET...
...HE WANTS ME TO RUTHLESSLY DRAG YOU BACK HOME!!
Chapter 60: "Let's Be Tormented by a Devil!"

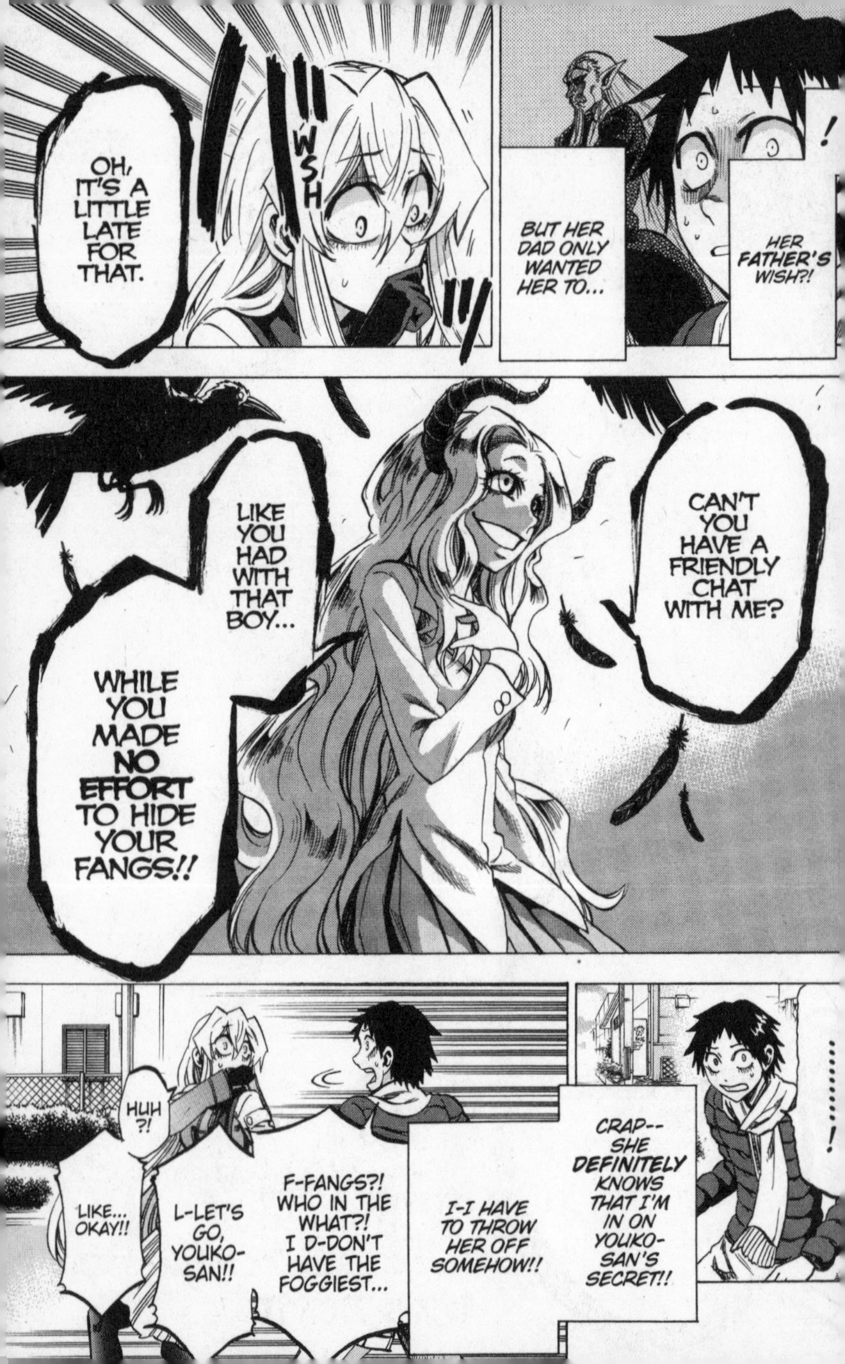
!
HER FATHER'S WISH?!
BUT HER DAD ONLY WANTED HER TO...
WSH
OH, IT'S A LITTLE LATE FOR THAT.
CAN'T YOU HAVE A FRIENDLY CHAT WITH ME?
LIKE YOU HAD WITH THAT BOY...
WHILE YOU MADE NO EFFORT TO HIDE YOUR FANGS!!
......!
CRAP-- SHE DEFINITELY KNOWS THAT I'M IN ON YOUKO-SAN'S SECRET!!
I-I HAVE TO THROW HER OFF SOMEHOW!!
F-FANGS?! WHO IN THE WHAT?! I D-DON'T HAVE THE FOGGIEST...
L-LET'S GO, YOUKO-SAN!!
HUH?!
LIKE... OKAY!!

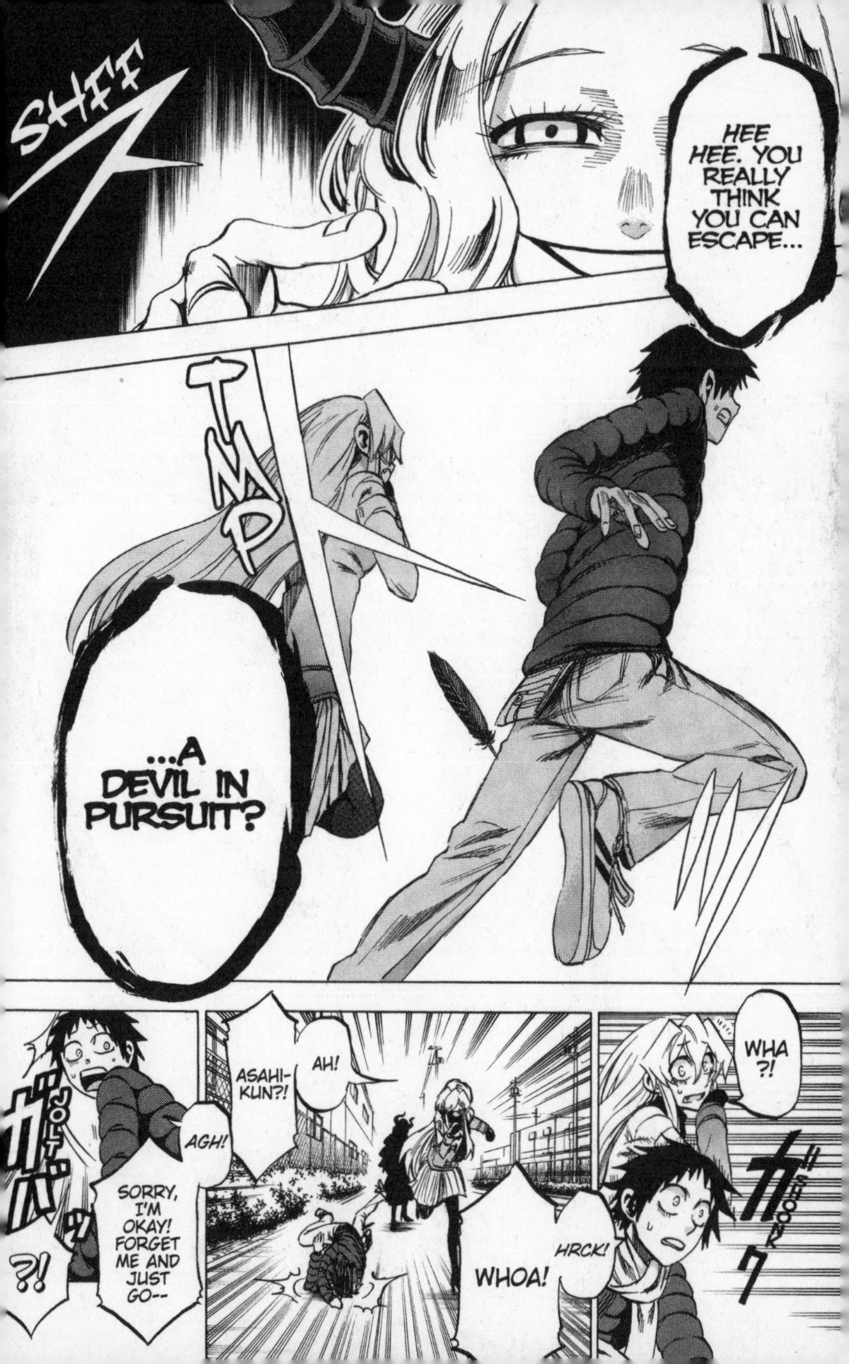
SHFF
HEE HEE. YOU REALLY THINK YOU CAN ESCAPE...
TMP
...A DEVIL IN PURSUIT?
WHA ?!
SHOONK
HRCK!
WHOA!
AH!
ASAHI-KUN?!
AGH!
SORRY, I'M OKAY! FORGET ME AND JUST GO--
JOLT
?!

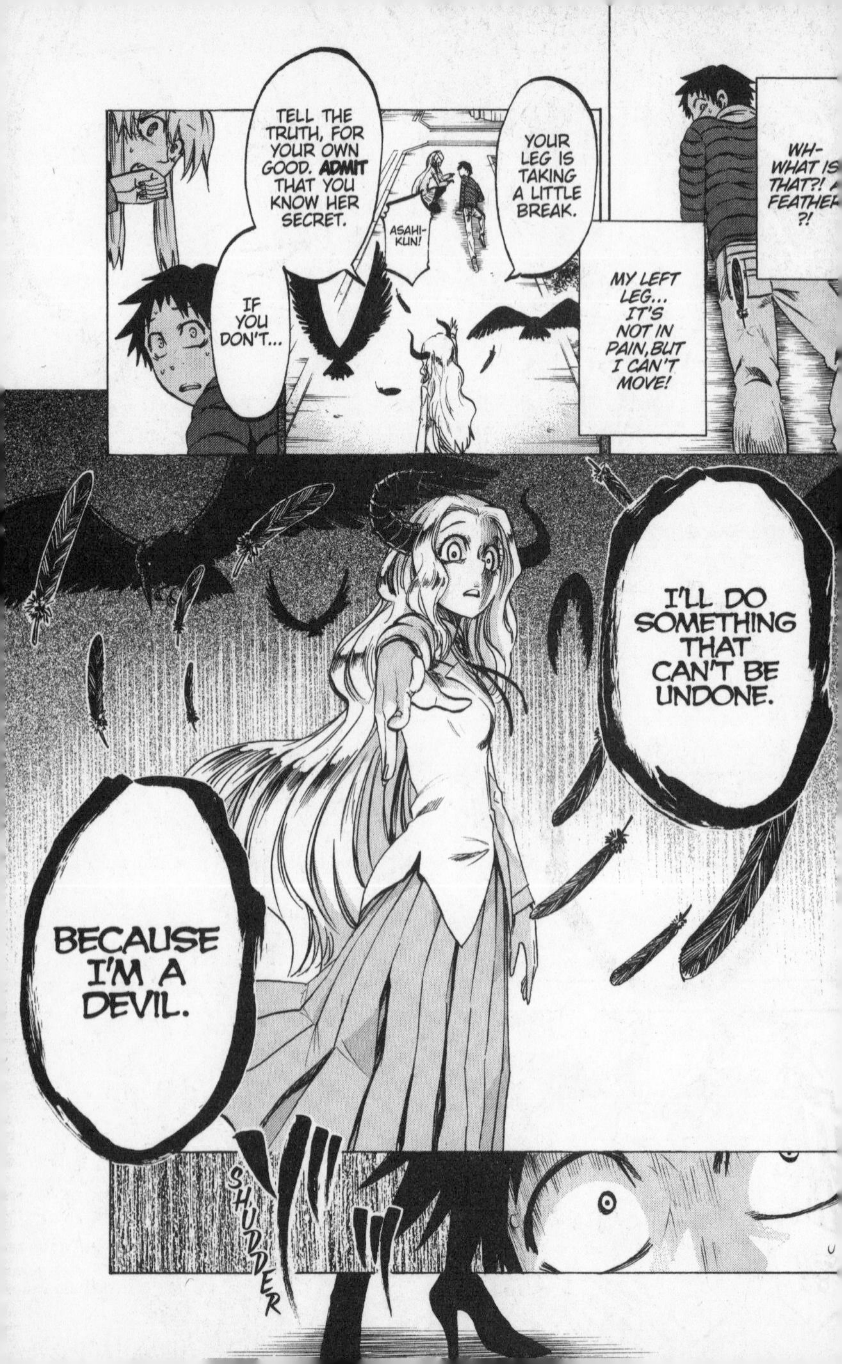

WH- WHAT IS THAT?! A FEATHER?!
MY LEFT LEG... IT'S NOT IN PAIN, BUT I CAN'T MOVE!
YOUR LEG IS TAKING A LITTLE BREAK.
ASAHI-KUN!
TELL THE TRUTH, FOR YOUR OWN GOOD. **ADMIT** THAT YOU KNOW HER SECRET.
IF YOU DON'T...
I'LL DO SOMETHING THAT CAN'T BE UNDONE.
BECAUSE I'M A DEVIL.
SHUDDER

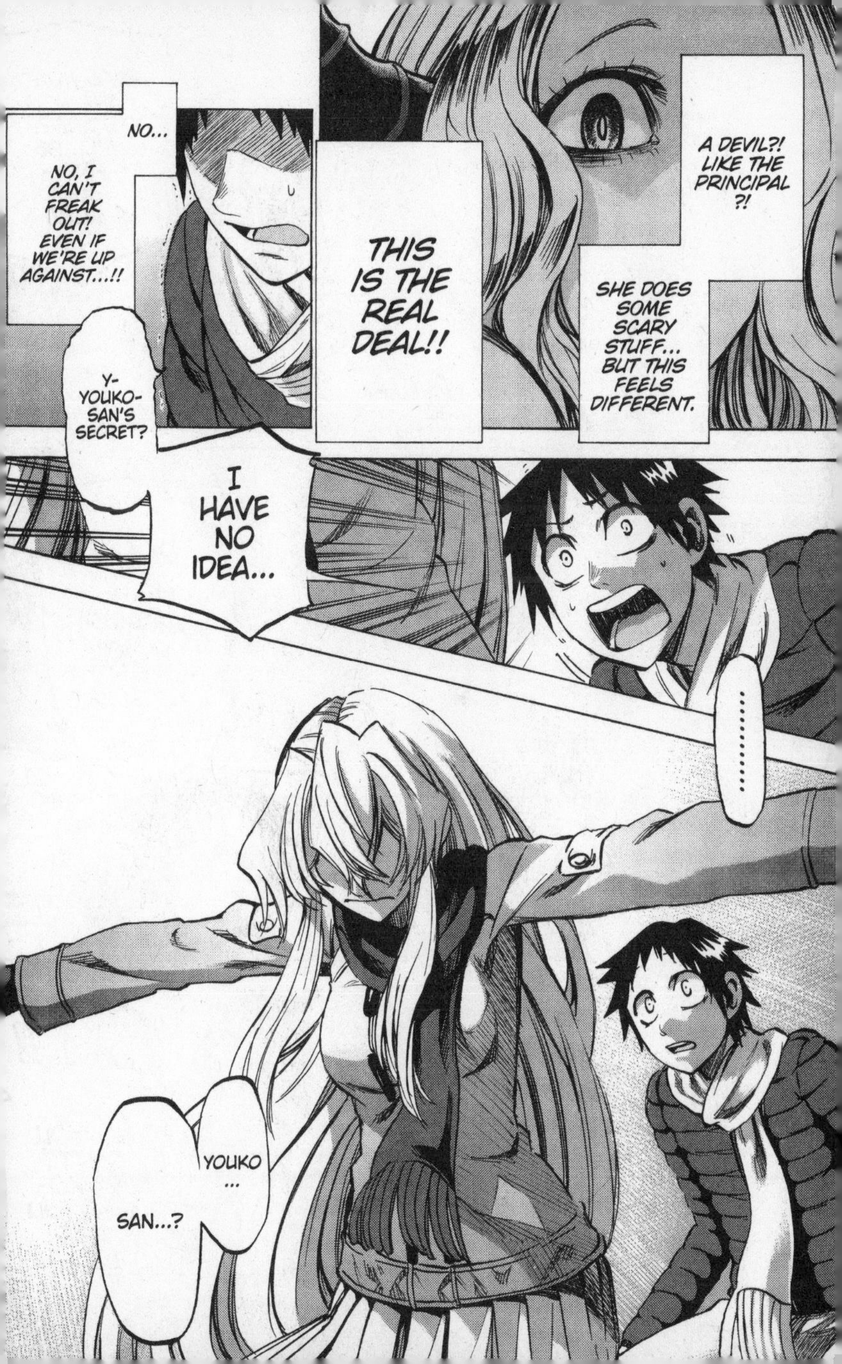

A DEVIL?! LIKE THE PRINCIPAL?!
SHE DOES SOME SCARY STUFF... BUT THIS FEELS DIFFERENT.
THIS IS THE REAL DEAL!!
NO...
NO, I CAN'T FREAK OUT! EVEN IF WE'RE UP AGAINST...!!
Y-YOUKO-SAN'S SECRET?
I HAVE NO IDEA...
......
YOUKO ...
SAN...?

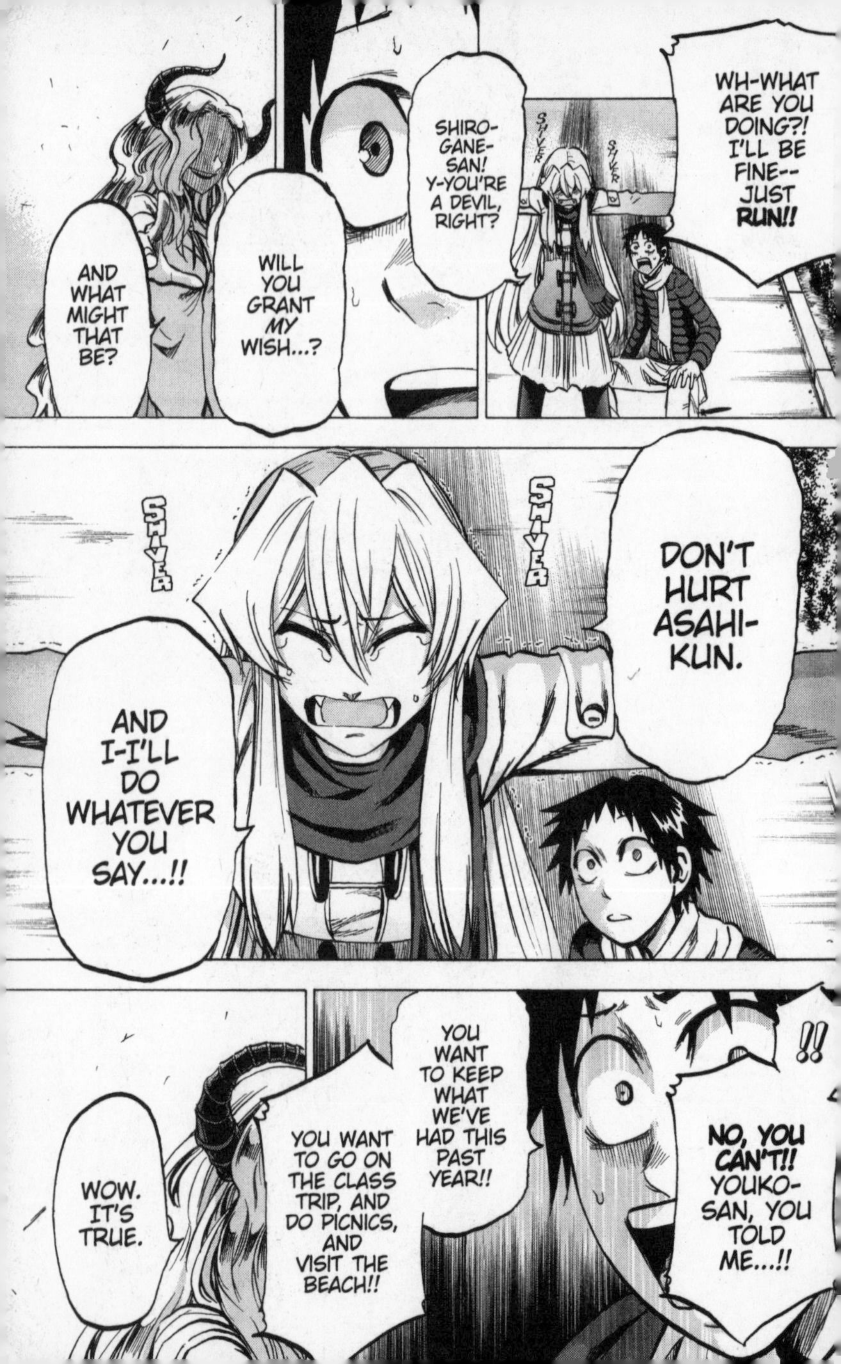
WH-WHAT ARE YOU DOING?! I'LL BE FINE-- JUST RUN!!
SHIVER
SHIVER
SHIROGANE-SAN! Y-YOU'RE A DEVIL, RIGHT?
WILL YOU GRANT MY WISH...?
AND WHAT MIGHT THAT BE?
DON'T HURT ASAHI-KUN.
SHIVER
SHIVER
AND I-I'LL DO WHATEVER YOU SAY...!!
!!
NO, YOU CAN'T!! YOUKO-SAN, YOU TOLD ME...!!
YOU WANT TO KEEP WHAT WE'VE HAD THIS PAST YEAR!!
YOU WANT TO GO ON THE CLASS TRIP, AND DO PICNICS, AND VISIT THE BEACH!!
WOW. IT'S TRUE.

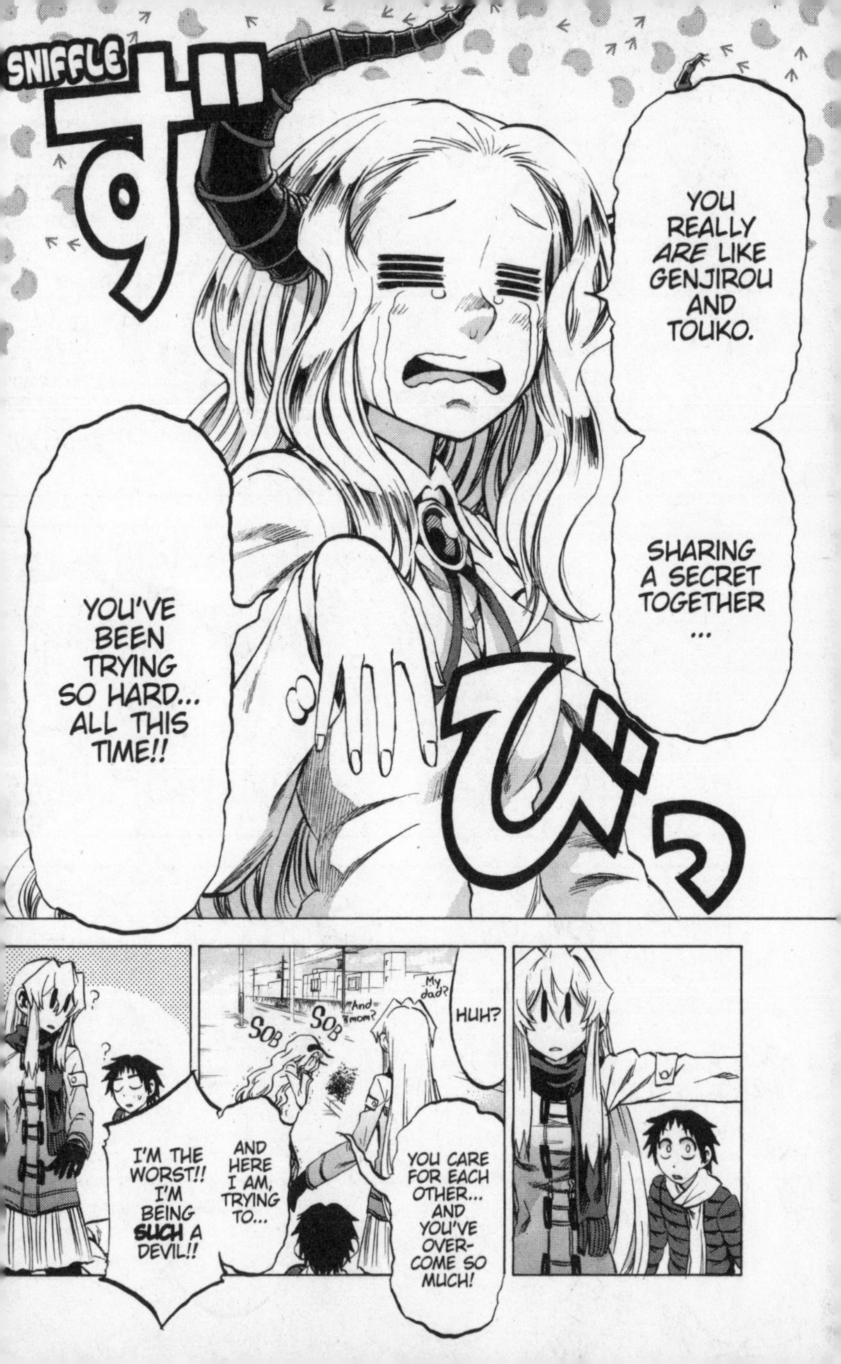
YOU REALLY ARE LIKE GENJIROU AND TOUKO.
SHARING A SECRET TOGETHER...
SNIFFLE
YOU'VE BEEN TRYING SO HARD... ALL THIS TIME!!
HUH?
My dad?
And mom?
SOB
SOB
YOU CARE FOR EACH OTHER... AND YOU'VE OVER-COME SO MUCH!
AND HERE I AM, TRYING TO...
I'M THE WORST!! I'M BEING SUCH A DEVIL!!

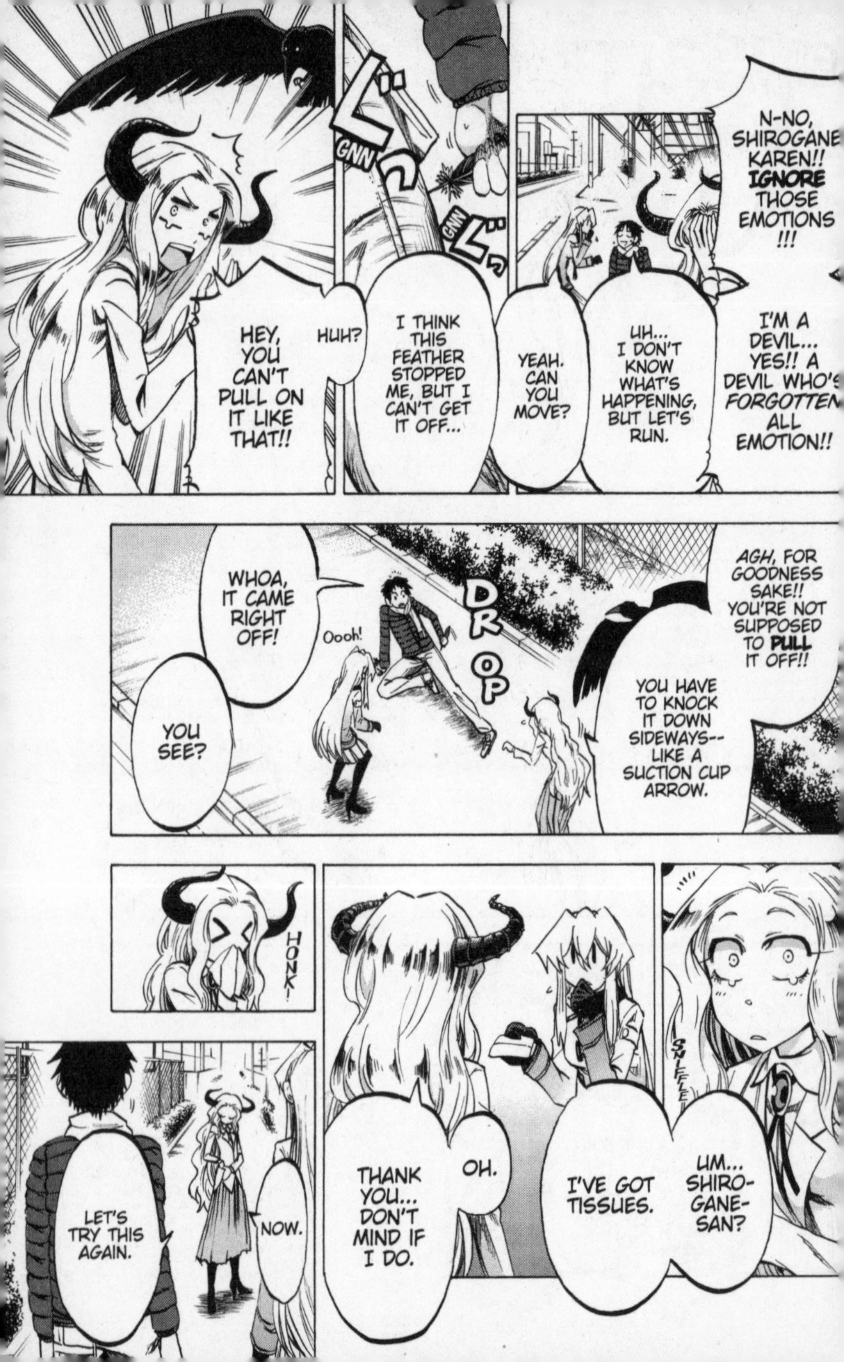
N-NO, SHIROGANE KAREN!! IGNORE THOSE EMOTIONS!!!
I'M A DEVIL... YES!! A DEVIL WHO'S FORGOTTEN ALL EMOTION!!
UH... I DON'T KNOW WHAT'S HAPPENING, BUT LET'S RUN.
YEAH. CAN YOU MOVE?
GNN
GNN
I THINK THIS FEATHER STOPPED ME, BUT I CAN'T GET IT OFF...
HUH?
HEY, YOU CAN'T PULL ON IT LIKE THAT!!
AGH, FOR GOODNESS SAKE!! YOU'RE NOT SUPPOSED TO PULL IT OFF!!
YOU HAVE TO KNOCK IT DOWN SIDEWAYS--LIKE A SUCTION CUP ARROW.
DROP
WHOA, IT CAME RIGHT OFF!
Oooh!
YOU SEE?
UM... SHIRO-GANE-SAN?
I'VE GOT TISSUES.
SNIFFLE
OH.
THANK YOU... DON'T MIND IF I DO.
HONK!
NOW.
LET'S TRY THIS AGAIN.

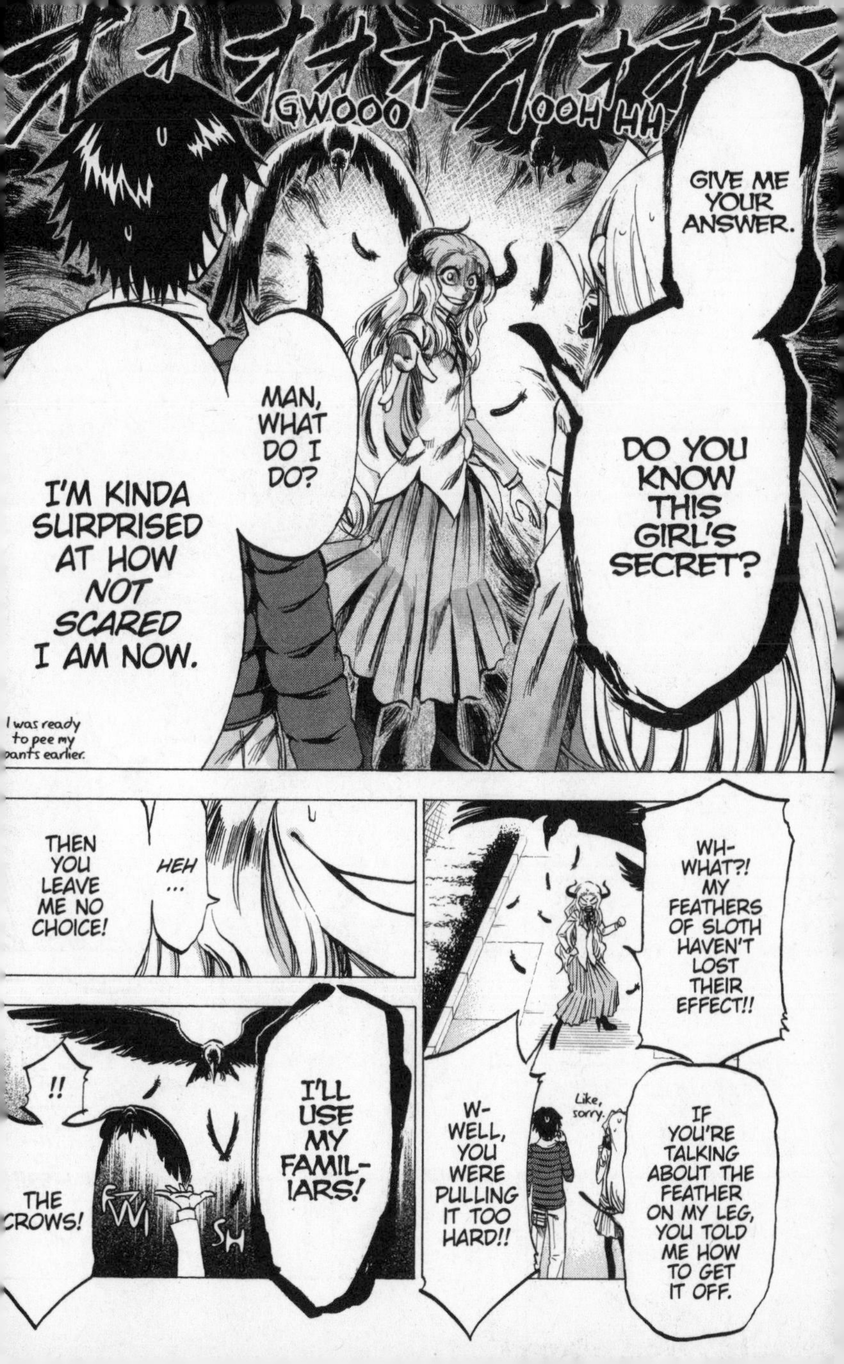
GWOOO OOOH HH
GIVE ME YOUR ANSWER.
DO YOU KNOW THIS GIRL'S SECRET?
MAN, WHAT DO I DO?
I'M KINDA SURPRISED AT HOW NOT SCARED I AM NOW.
I was ready to pee my pants earlier.
WH-WHAT?! MY FEATHERS OF SLOTH HAVEN'T LOST THEIR EFFECT!!
IF YOU'RE TALKING ABOUT THE FEATHER ON MY LEG, YOU TOLD ME HOW TO GET IT OFF.
Like, sorry.
W-WELL, YOU WERE PULLING IT TOO HARD!!
HEH...
THEN YOU LEAVE ME NO CHOICE!
I'LL USE MY FAMILIARS!
!!
THE CROWS!
FWISH

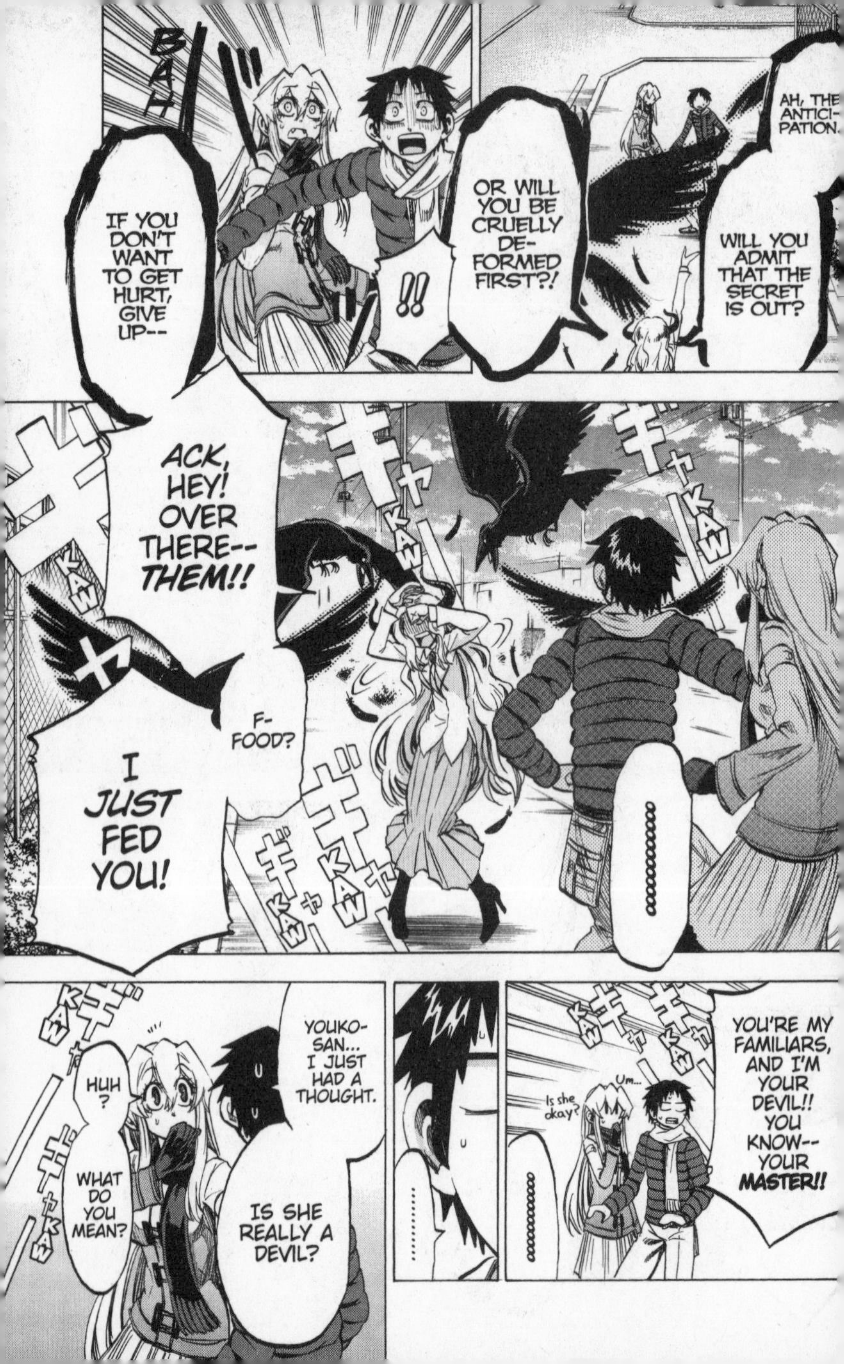
AH, THE ANTICI-PATION.
WILL YOU ADMIT THAT THE SECRET IS OUT?
OR WILL YOU BE CRUELLY DE-FORMED FIRST?!
!!
BAH
IF YOU DON'T WANT TO GET HURT, GIVE UP--
KAW
KAW
......
ACK, HEY! OVER THERE-- THEM!!
KAW
F-FOOD?
KAW
KAW
I JUST FED YOU!
KAW
KAW
YOU'RE MY FAMILIARS, AND I'M YOUR DEVIL!! YOU KNOW-- YOUR MASTER!!
Um...
Is she okay?
......
......
KAW
YOUKO-SAN... I JUST HAD A THOUGHT.
HUH?
IS SHE REALLY A DEVIL?
WHAT DO YOU MEAN?
KAW

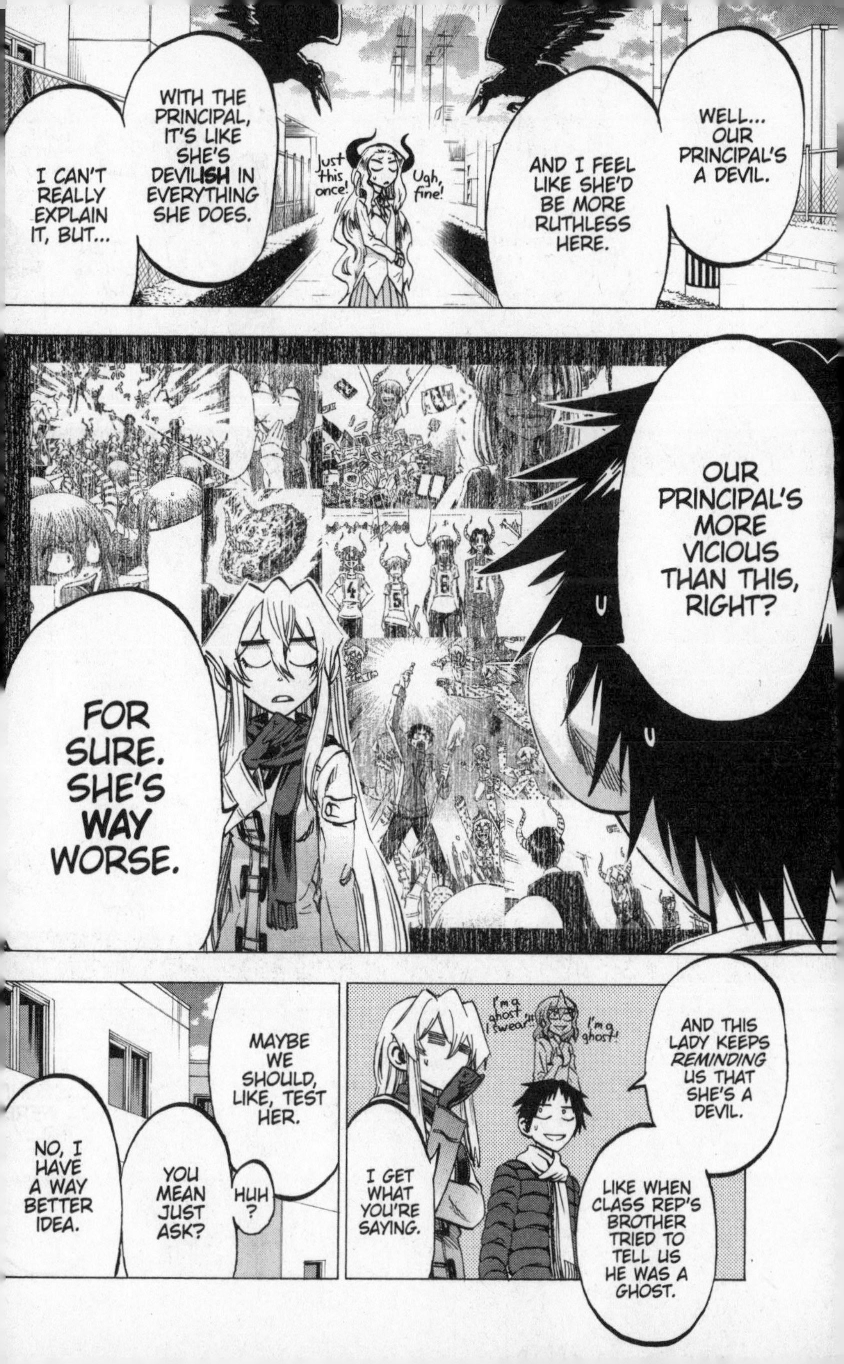

WELL... OUR PRINCIPAL'S A DEVIL.
AND I FEEL LIKE SHE'D BE MORE RUTHLESS HERE.
Ugh, fine!
Just this once!
WITH THE PRINCIPAL, IT'S LIKE SHE'S DEVILISH IN EVERYTHING SHE DOES.
I CAN'T REALLY EXPLAIN IT, BUT...
OUR PRINCIPAL'S MORE VICIOUS THAN THIS, RIGHT?
FOR SURE. SHE'S WAY WORSE.
AND THIS LADY KEEPS REMINDING US THAT SHE'S A DEVIL.
I'm a ghost!
I'm a ghost I swear!!
LIKE WHEN CLASS REP'S BROTHER TRIED TO TELL US HE WAS A GHOST.
I GET WHAT YOU'RE SAYING.
MAYBE WE SHOULD, LIKE, TEST HER.
HUH?
YOU MEAN JUST ASK?
NO, I HAVE A WAY BETTER IDEA.

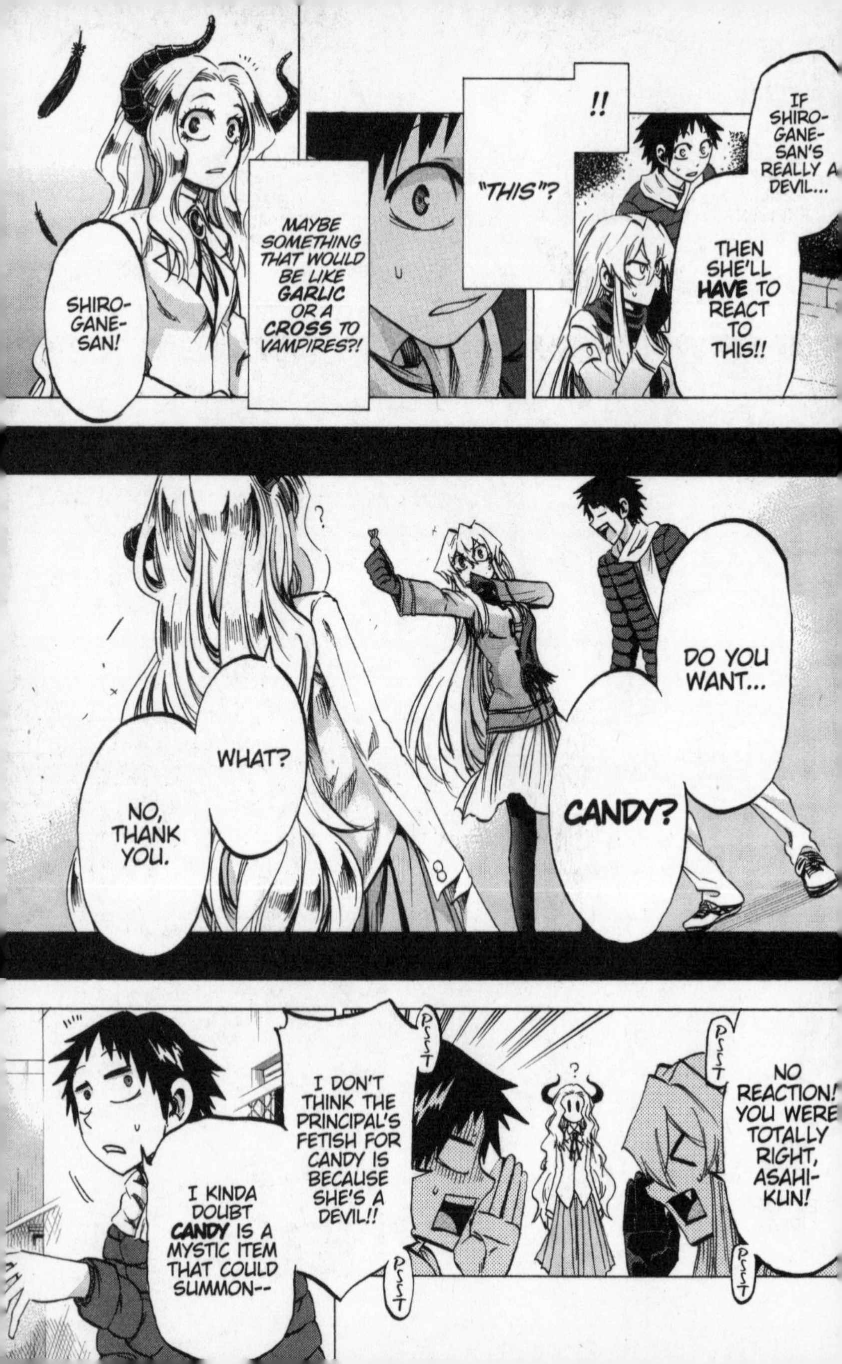
IF SHIRO-GANE-SAN'S REALLY A DEVIL...
THEN SHE'LL HAVE TO REACT TO THIS!!
!!
"THIS"?
MAYBE SOMETHING THAT WOULD BE LIKE GARLIC OR A CROSS TO VAMPIRES?!
SHIRO-GANE-SAN!
DO YOU WANT...
CANDY?
WHAT?
NO, THANK YOU.
PSST
PSST
NO REACTION! YOU WERE TOTALLY RIGHT, ASAHI-KUN!
PSST
PSST
I DON'T THINK THE PRINCIPAL'S FETISH FOR CANDY IS BECAUSE SHE'S A DEVIL!!
I KINDA DOUBT CANDY IS A MYSTIC ITEM THAT COULD SUMMON--

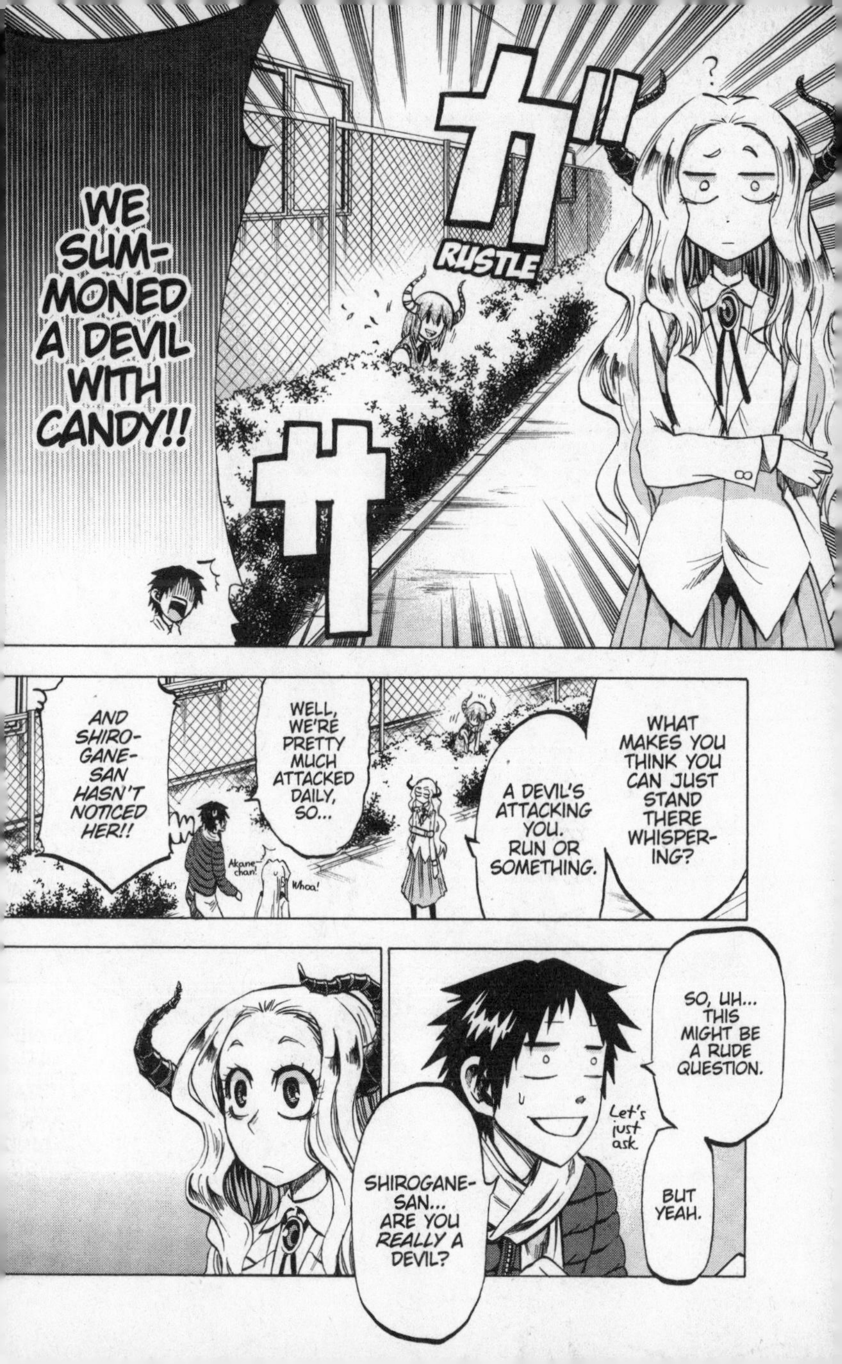
ガ
RUSTLE
サ
WE SUM-MONED A DEVIL WITH CANDY!!
WHAT MAKES YOU THINK YOU CAN JUST STAND THERE WHISPER-ING?
A DEVIL'S ATTACKING YOU. RUN OR SOMETHING.
WELL, WE'RE PRETTY MUCH ATTACKED DAILY, SO...
AND SHIRO-GANE-SAN HASN'T NOTICED HER!!
Akane-chan!
Whoa!
SO, UH... THIS MIGHT BE A RUDE QUESTION.
Let's just ask.
BUT YEAH.
SHIROGANE-SAN... ARE YOU REALLY A DEVIL?

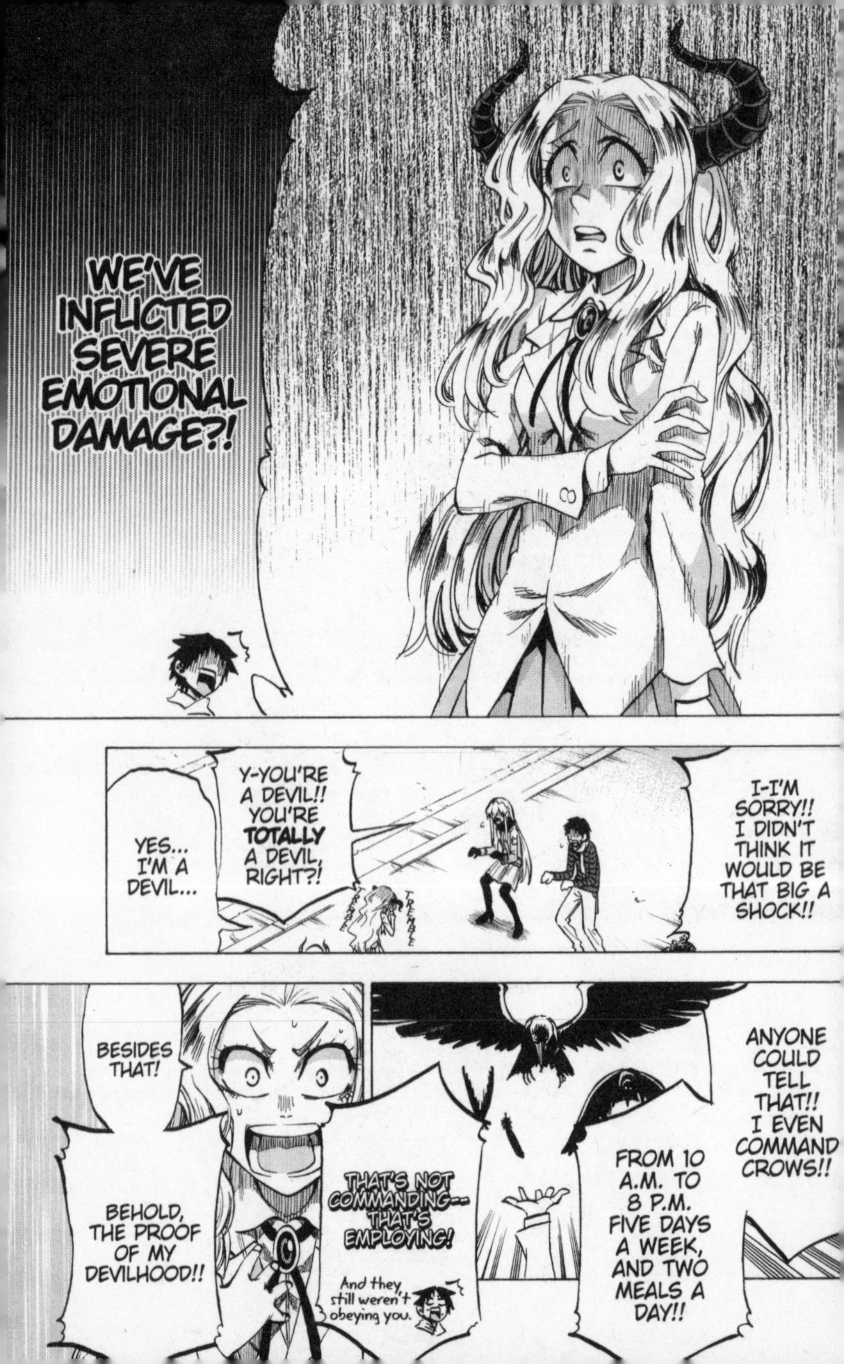
WE'VE INFLICTED SEVERE EMOTIONAL DAMAGE?!
I-I'M SORRY!! I DIDN'T THINK IT WOULD BE THAT BIG A SHOCK!!
Y-YOU'RE A DEVIL!! YOU'RE TOTALLY A DEVIL, RIGHT?!
TREMBLE
TREMBLE
YES... I'M A DEVIL...
ANYONE COULD TELL THAT!! I EVEN COMMAND CROWS!!
FROM 10 A.M. TO 8 P.M. FIVE DAYS A WEEK, AND TWO MEALS A DAY!!
THAT'S NOT COMMANDING-- THAT'S EMPLOYING!
And they still weren't obeying you.
BESIDES THAT!
BEHOLD, THE PROOF OF MY DEVILHOOD!!

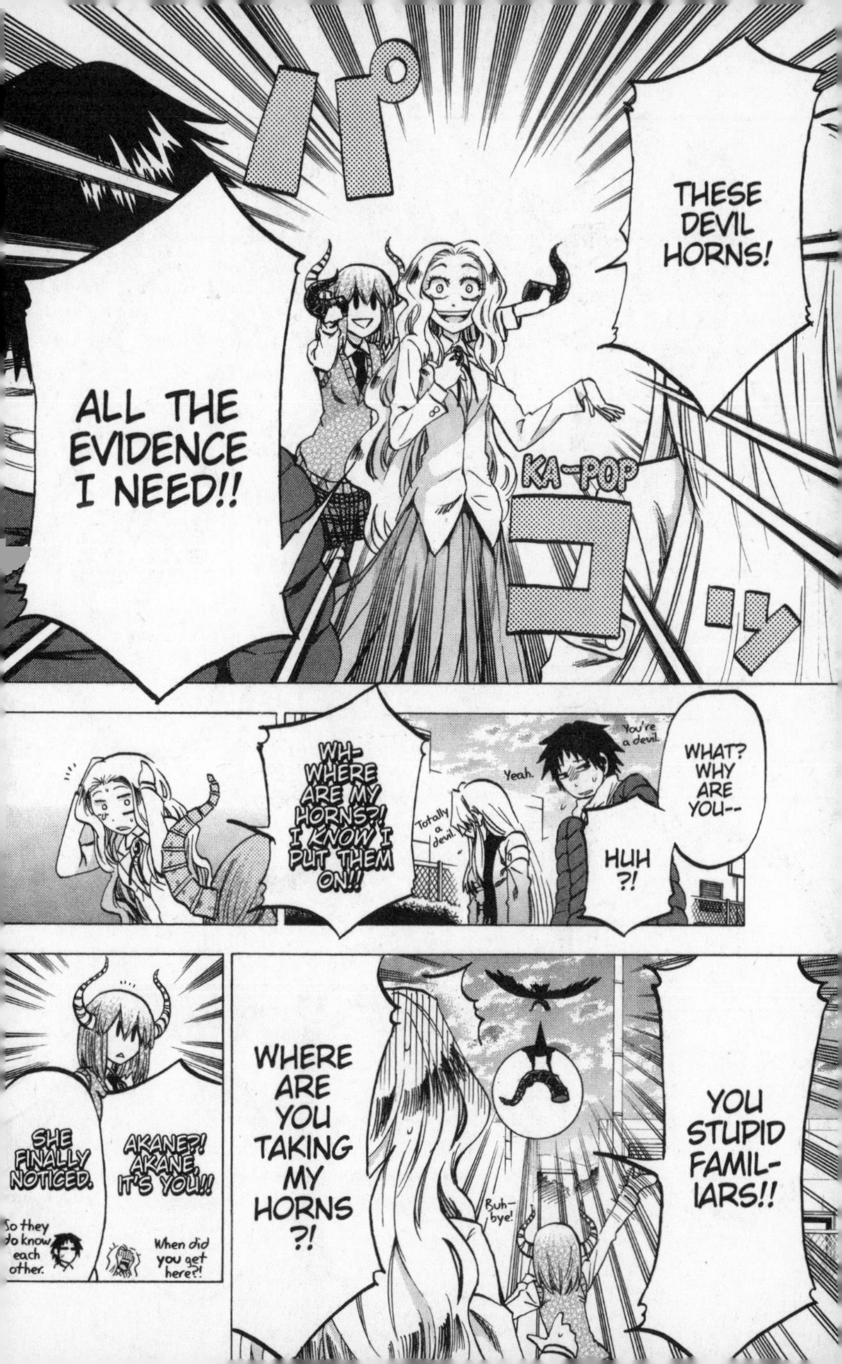
THESE DEVIL HORNS!
ALL THE EVIDENCE I NEED!!
KA-POP
WHAT? WHY ARE YOU--
You're a devil.
HUH ?!
Yeah.
Totally a devil.
WH-WHERE ARE MY HORNS?! I KNOW I PUT THEM ON!!
YOU STUPID FAMIL-IARS!!
Buh-bye!
WHERE ARE YOU TAKING MY HORNS ?!
AKANE?! AKANE, IT'S YOU!!
When did you get here?!
SHE FINALLY NOTICED.
So they do know each other.

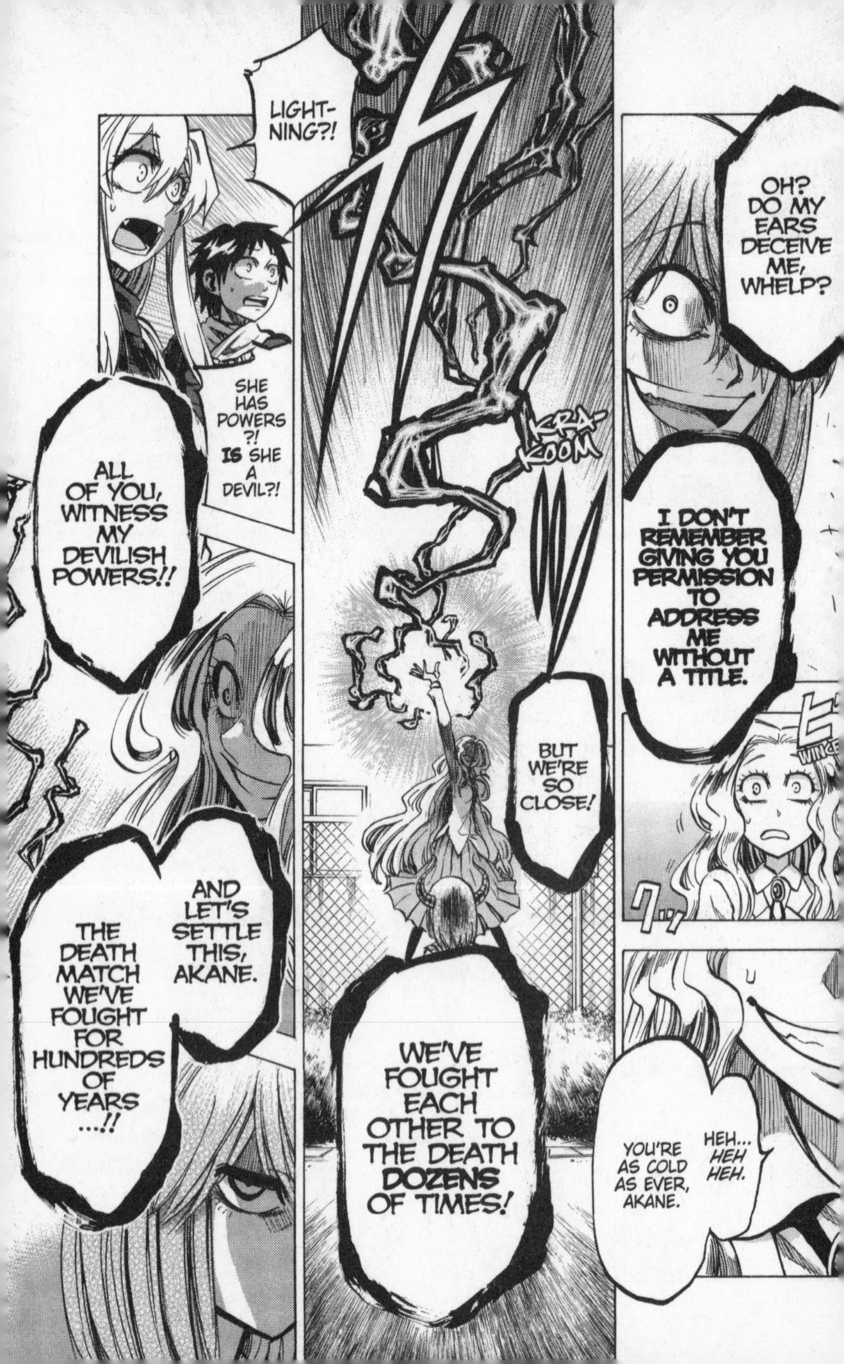
OH? DO MY EARS DECEIVE ME, WHELP?
I DON'T REMEMBER GIVING YOU PERMISSION TO ADDRESS ME WITHOUT A TITLE.
HEH... HEH HEH.
YOU'RE AS COLD AS EVER, AKANE.
KRA-KOOM
BUT WE'RE SO CLOSE!
WE'VE FOUGHT EACH OTHER TO THE DEATH DOZENS OF TIMES!
LIGHT-NING?!
SHE HAS POWERS?! IS SHE A DEVIL?!
ALL OF YOU, WITNESS MY DEVILISH POWERS!!
AND LET'S SETTLE THIS, AKANE.
THE DEATH MATCH WE'VE FOUGHT FOR HUNDREDS OF YEARS ...!!

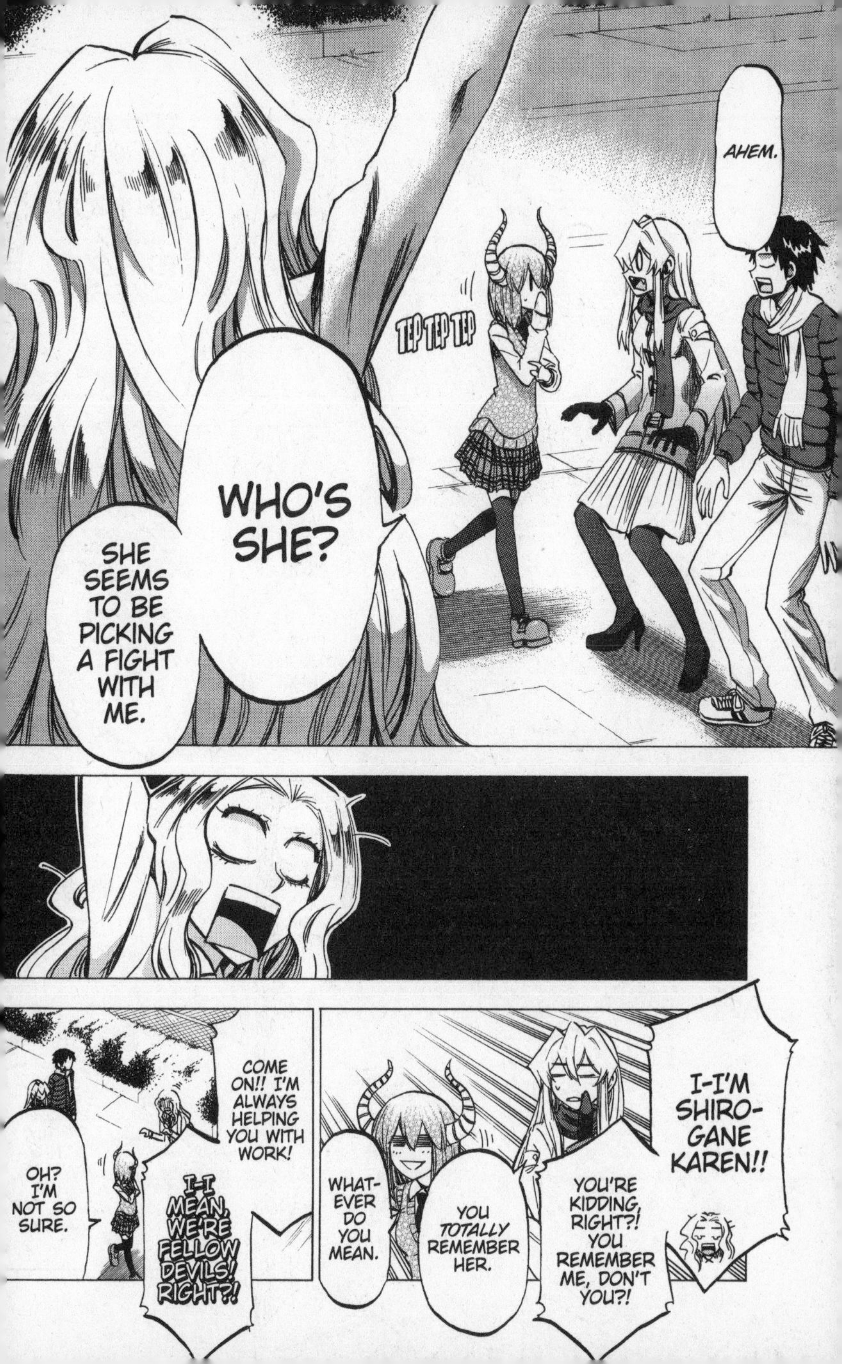
AHEM.
TEP TEP TEP
WHO'S SHE?
SHE SEEMS TO BE PICKING A FIGHT WITH ME.
I-I'M SHIROGANE KAREN!!
YOU'RE KIDDING, RIGHT?! YOU REMEMBER ME, DON'T YOU?!
YOU TOTALLY REMEMBER HER.
WHATEVER DO YOU MEAN.
COME ON!! I'M ALWAYS HELPING YOU WITH WORK!
I-I MEAN, WE'RE FELLOW DEVILS! RIGHT?!
OH? I'M NOT SO SURE.

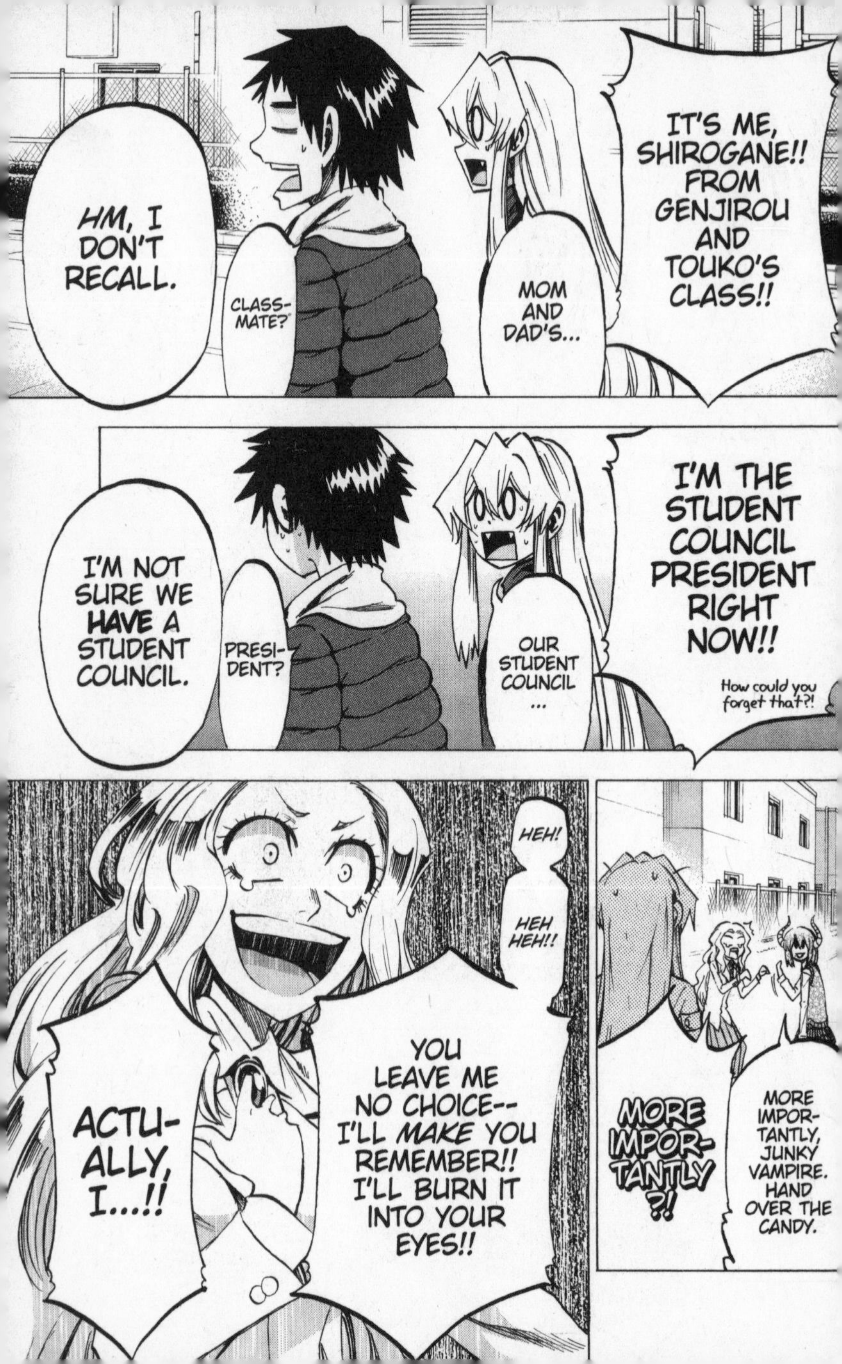

IT'S ME, SHIROGANE!! FROM GENJIROU AND TOUKO'S CLASS!!
MOM AND DAD'S...
CLASS-MATE?
HM, I DON'T RECALL.
I'M THE STUDENT COUNCIL PRESIDENT RIGHT NOW!!
How could you forget that?!
OUR STUDENT COUNCIL ...
PRESI-DENT?
I'M NOT SURE WE HAVE A STUDENT COUNCIL.
MORE IMPOR-TANTLY, JUNKY VAMPIRE. HAND OVER THE CANDY.
MORE IMPOR-TANTLY ?!
HEH!
HEH HEH!!
YOU LEAVE ME NO CHOICE-- I'LL MAKE YOU REMEMBER!! I'LL BURN IT INTO YOUR EYES!!
ACTU-ALLY, I...!!

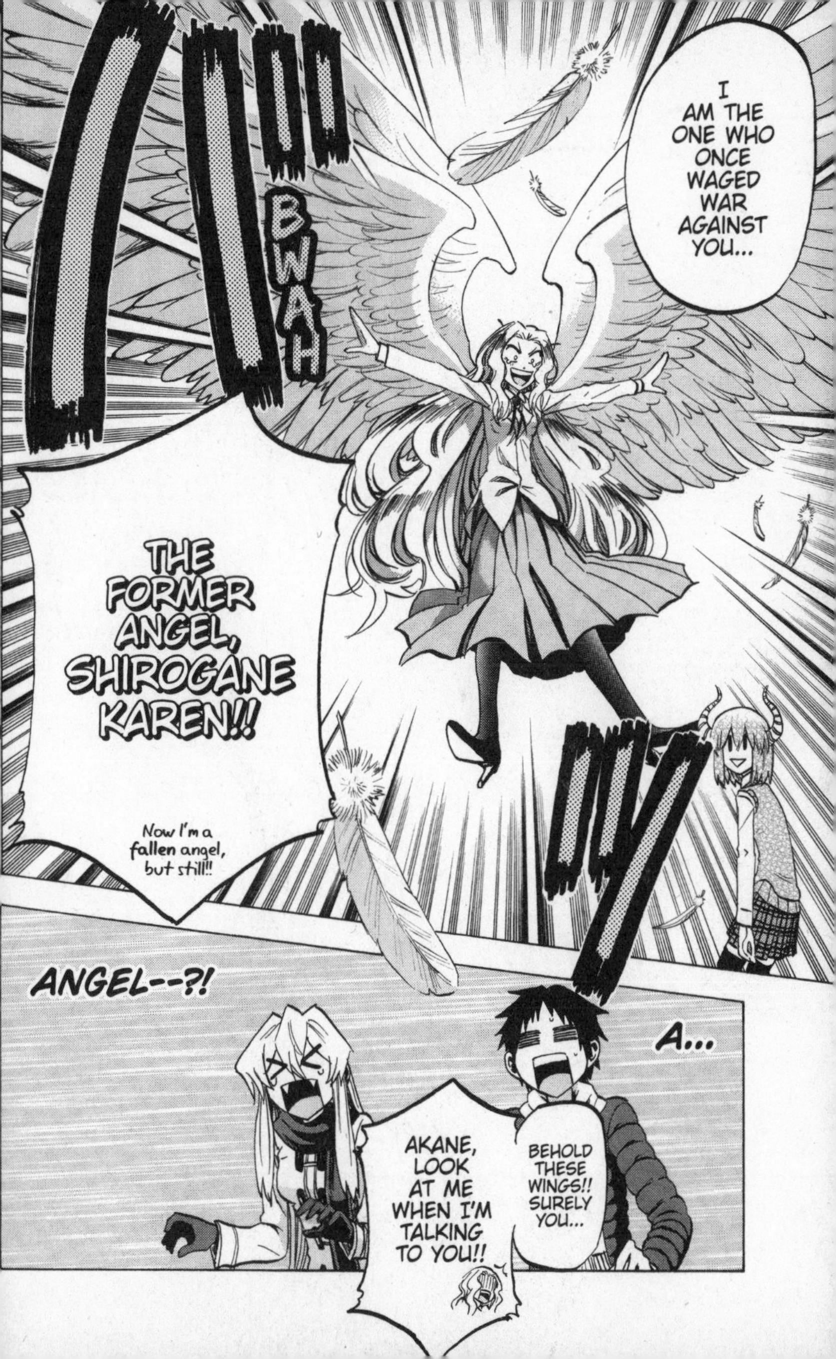
I AM THE ONE WHO ONCE WAGED WAR AGAINST YOU...
BWAH
THE FORMER ANGEL, SHIROGANE KAREN!!
Now I'm a fallen angel, but still!!
A...
ANGEL--?!
BEHOLD THESE WINGS!! SURELY YOU...
AKANE, LOOK AT ME WHEN I'M TALKING TO YOU!!

Chapter 61:
"Let's Talk About Old Times!"

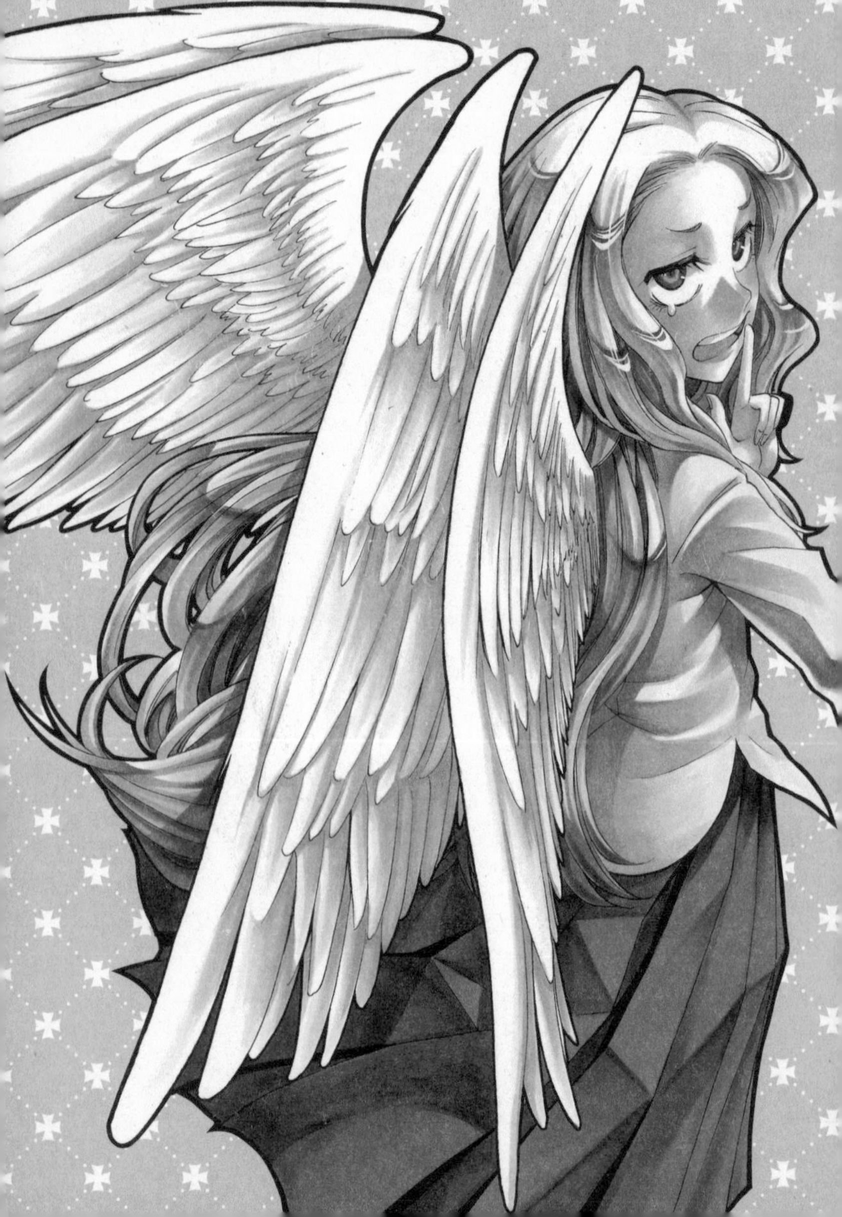

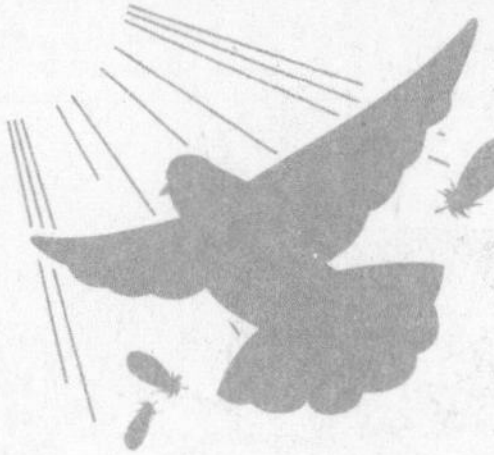

TOP SECRET

My Monster Secret 7

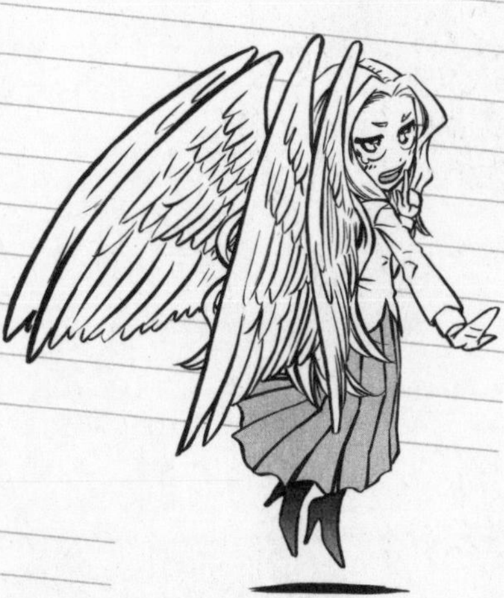

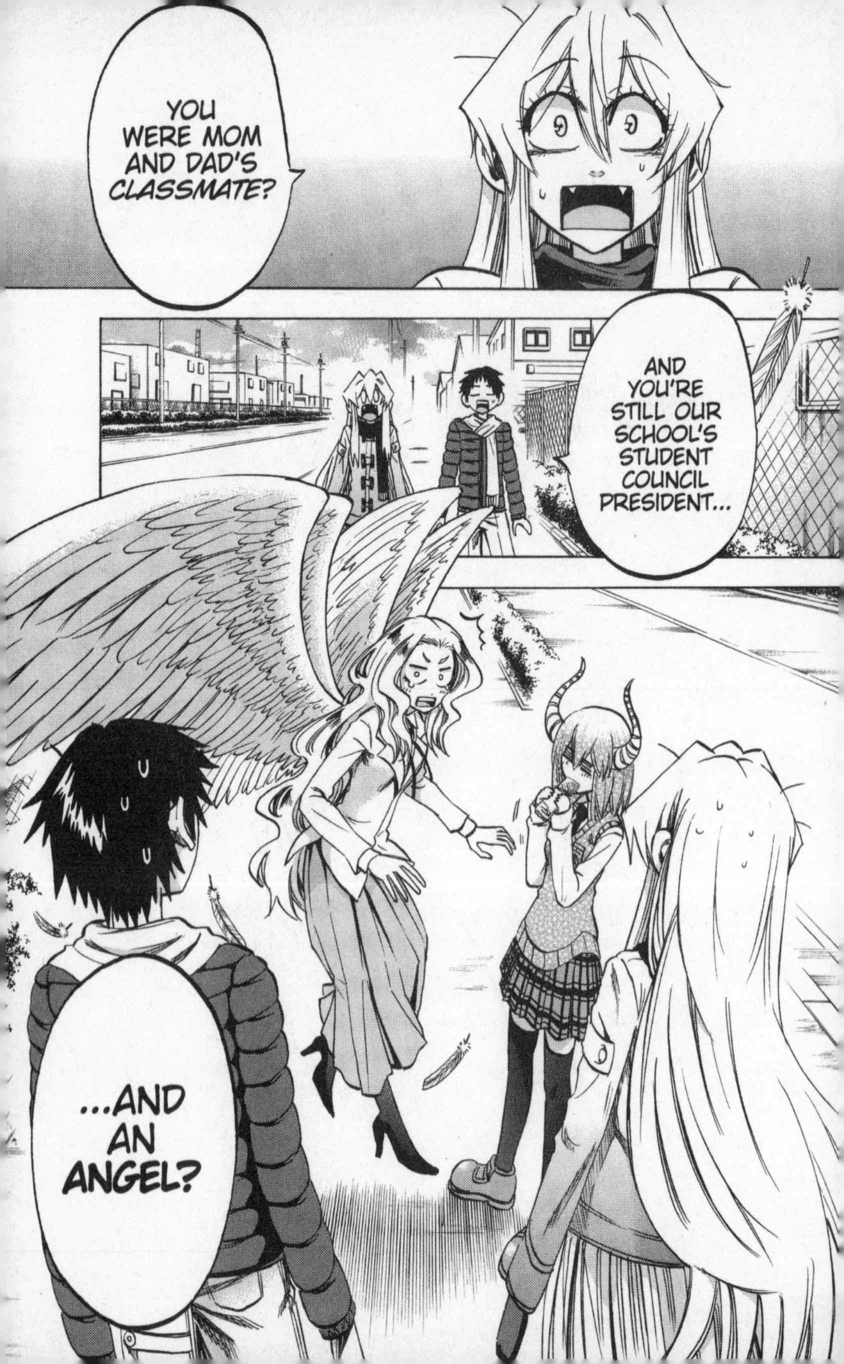
YOU WERE MOM AND DAD'S CLASSMATE?
AND YOU'RE STILL OUR SCHOOL'S STUDENT COUNCIL PRESIDENT...
...AND AN ANGEL?

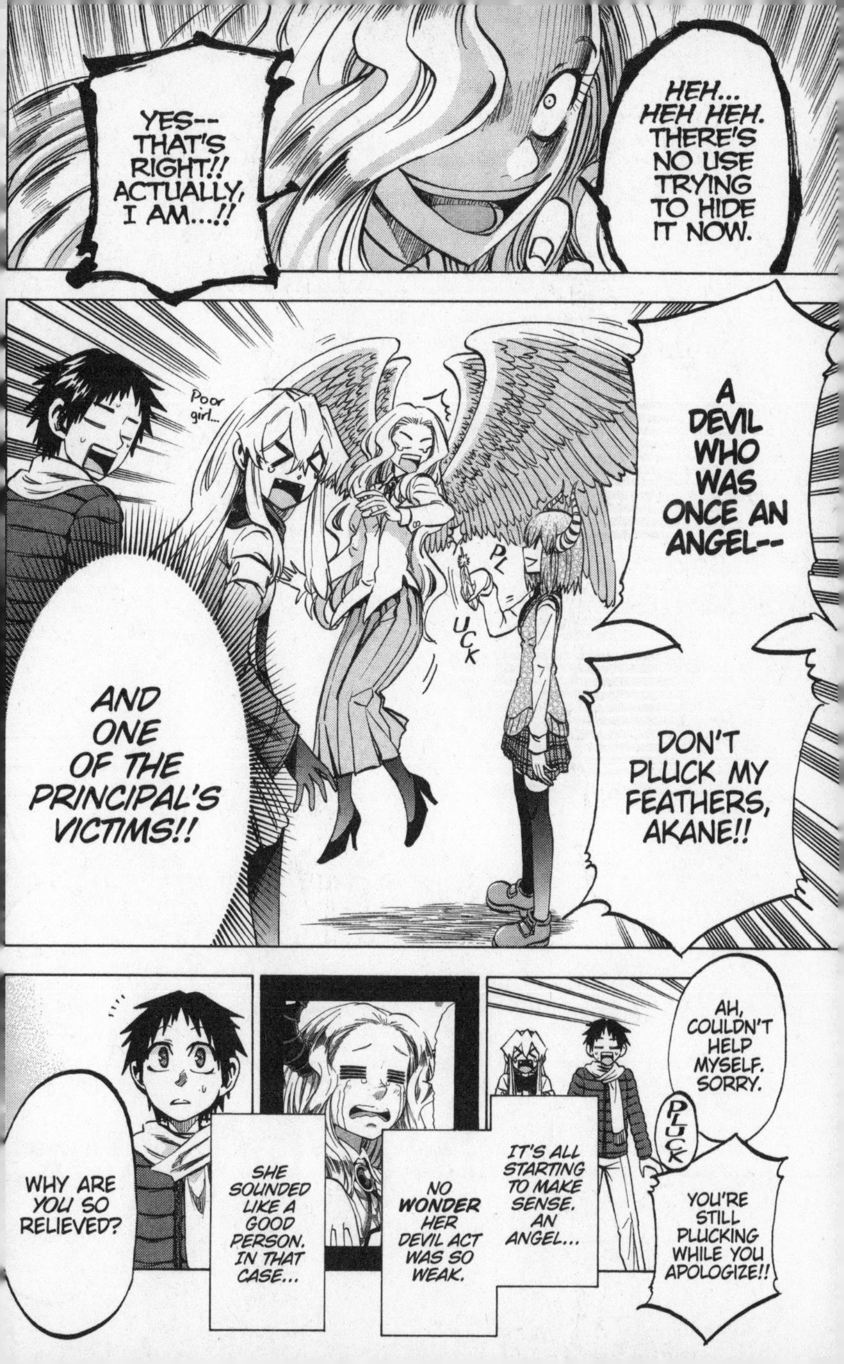
HEH... HEH HEH. THERE'S NO USE TRYING TO HIDE IT NOW.
YES-- THAT'S RIGHT!! ACTUALLY, I AM...!!
A DEVIL WHO WAS ONCE AN ANGEL--
Poor girl...
PLUCK
DON'T PLUCK MY FEATHERS, AKANE!!
AND ONE OF THE PRINCIPAL'S VICTIMS!!
AH, COULDN'T HELP MYSELF. SORRY.
PLUCK
YOU'RE STILL PLUCKING WHILE YOU APOLOGIZE!!
IT'S ALL STARTING TO MAKE SENSE. AN ANGEL...
NO WONDER HER DEVIL ACT WAS SO WEAK.
SHE SOUNDED LIKE A GOOD PERSON. IN THAT CASE...
WHY ARE YOU SO RELIEVED?

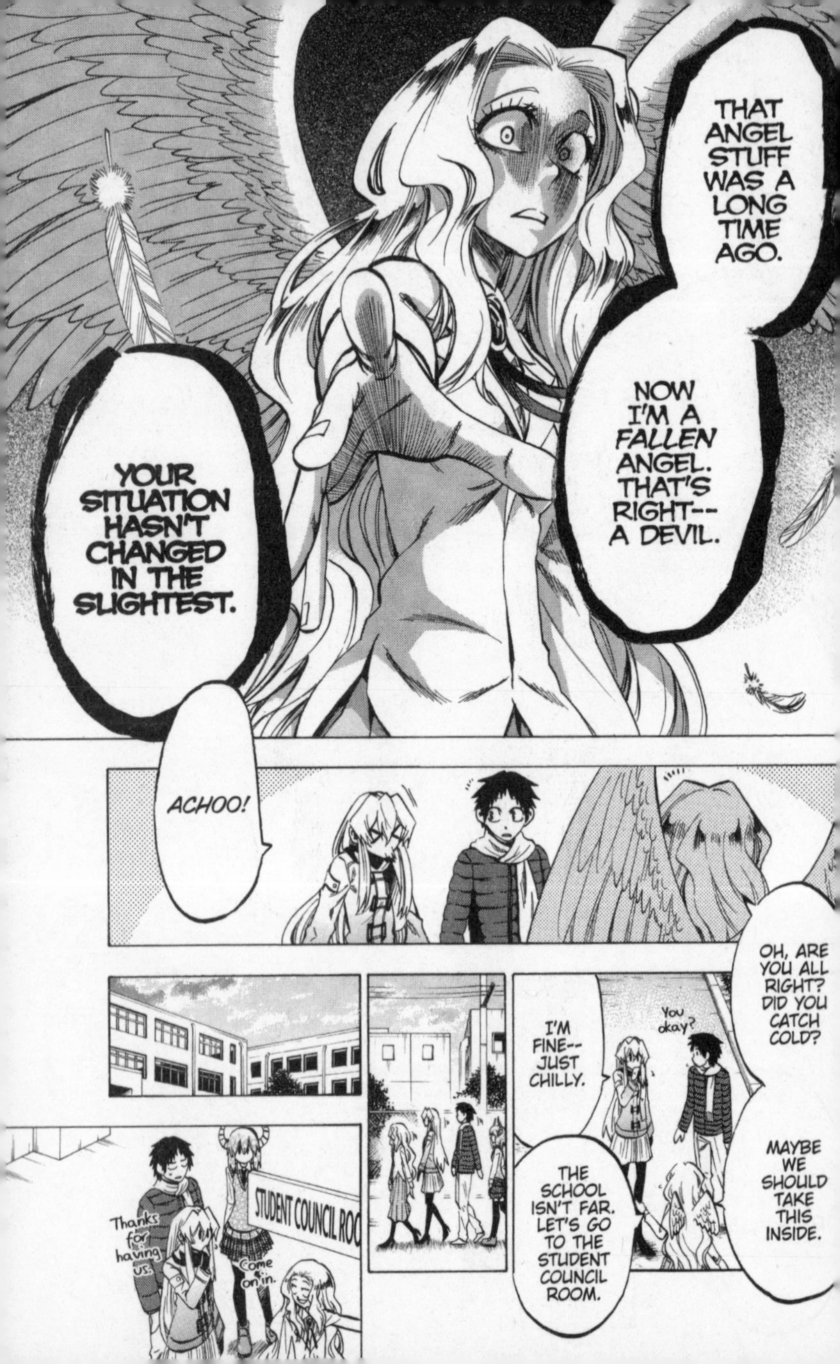
THAT ANGEL STUFF WAS A LONG TIME AGO.
NOW I'M A FALLEN ANGEL. THAT'S RIGHT-- A DEVIL.
YOUR SITUATION HASN'T CHANGED IN THE SLIGHTEST.
ACHOO!
OH, ARE YOU ALL RIGHT? DID YOU CATCH COLD?
You okay?
I'M FINE-- JUST CHILLY.
MAYBE WE SHOULD TAKE THIS INSIDE.
THE SCHOOL ISN'T FAR. LET'S GO TO THE STUDENT COUNCIL ROOM.
STUDENT COUNCIL ROO
Come on in.
Thanks for having us.

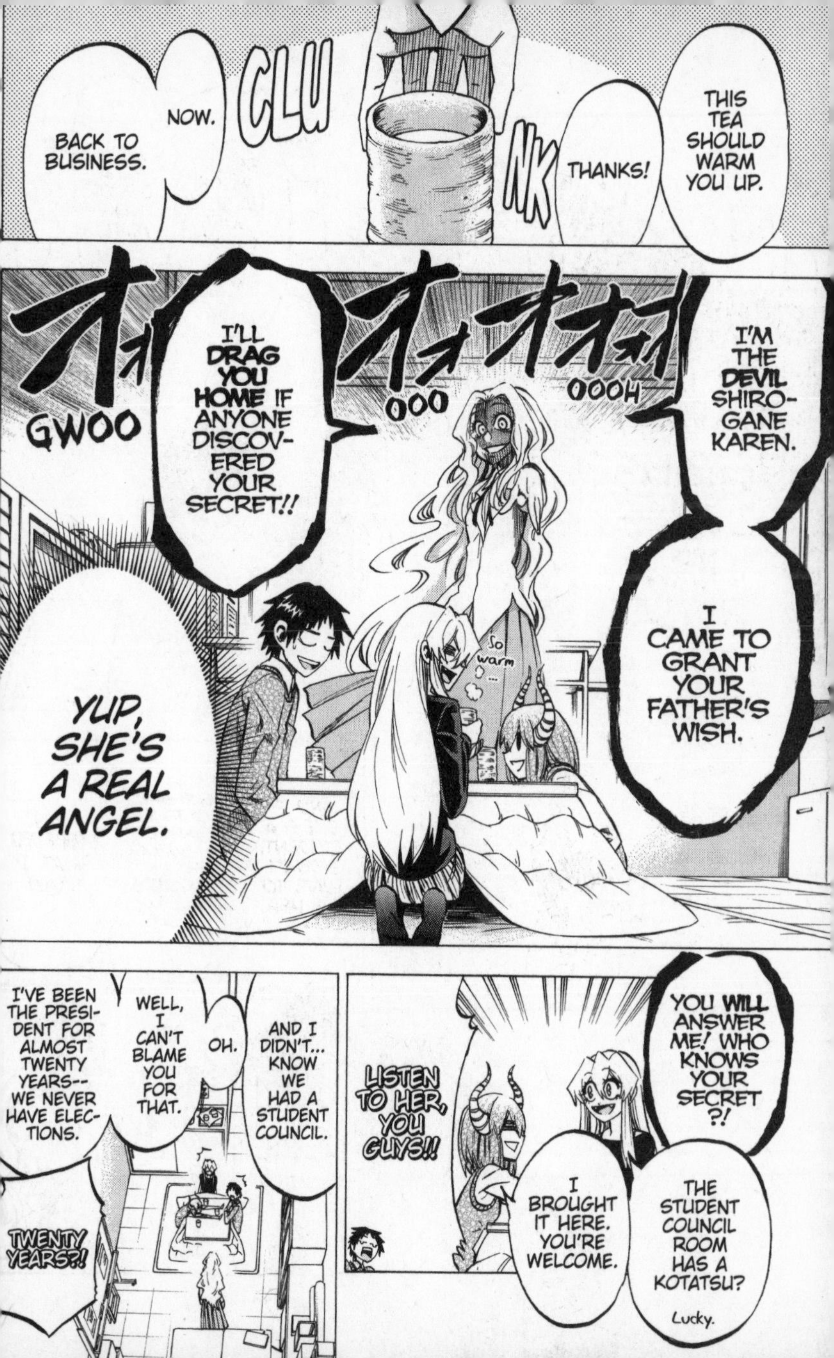
THIS TEA SHOULD WARM YOU UP.
THANKS!
CLUNK
NOW.
BACK TO BUSINESS.
I'M THE DEVIL SHIROGANE KAREN.
I CAME TO GRANT YOUR FATHER'S WISH.
I'LL DRAG YOU HOME IF ANYONE DISCOVERED YOUR SECRET!!
オォオォオオ
GWOO OOO OOOH
So warm...
YUP, SHE'S A REAL ANGEL.
YOU WILL ANSWER ME! WHO KNOWS YOUR SECRET?!
THE STUDENT COUNCIL ROOM HAS A KOTATSU?
Lucky.
I BROUGHT IT HERE. YOU'RE WELCOME.
LISTEN TO HER, YOU GUYS!!
AND I DIDN'T... KNOW WE HAD A STUDENT COUNCIL.
OH.
WELL, I CAN'T BLAME YOU FOR THAT.
I'VE BEEN THE PRESIDENT FOR ALMOST TWENTY YEARS-- WE NEVER HAVE ELECTIONS.
TWENTY YEARS?!

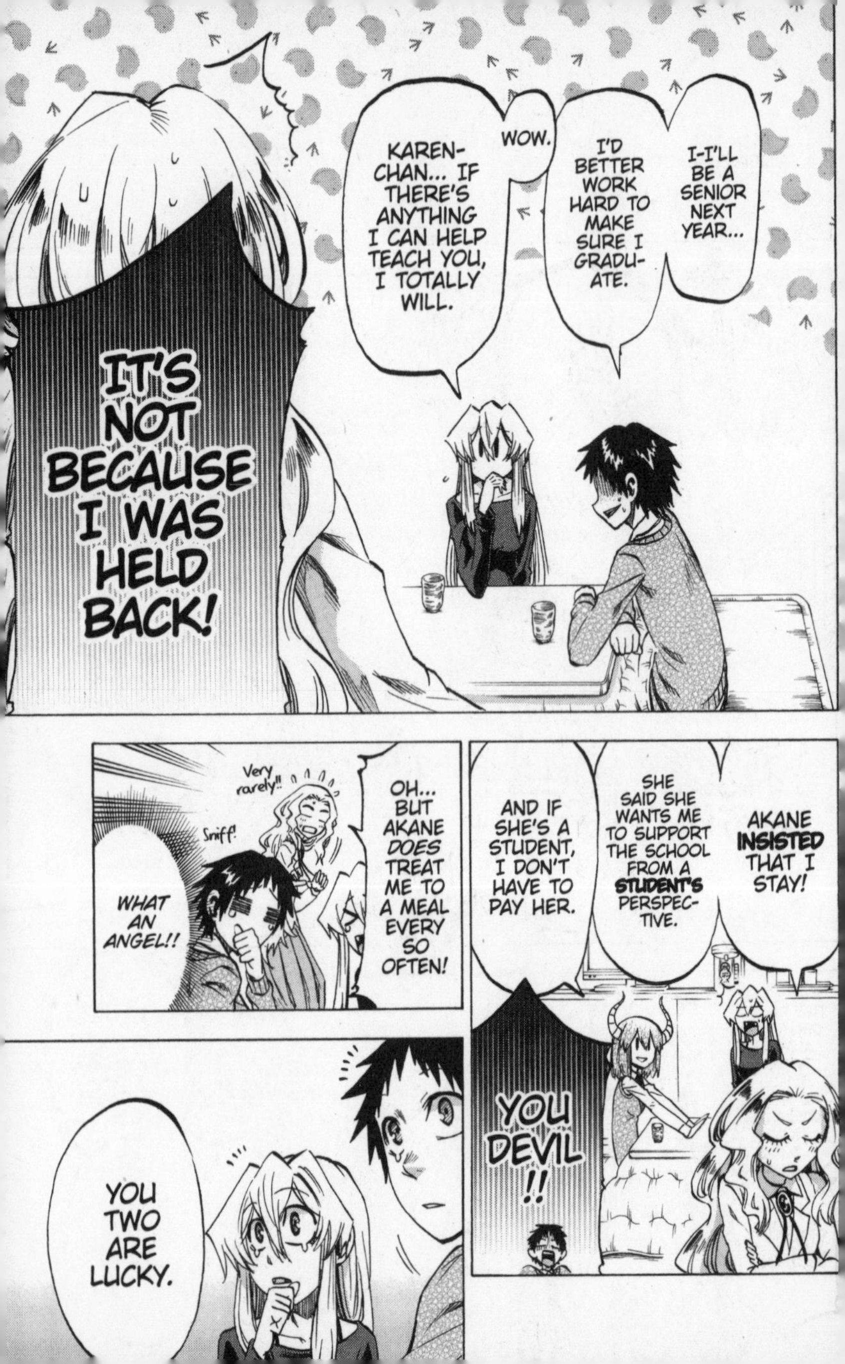
I-I'LL BE A SENIOR NEXT YEAR...
I'D BETTER WORK HARD TO MAKE SURE I GRADUATE.
WOW.
KAREN-CHAN... IF THERE'S ANYTHING I CAN HELP TEACH YOU, I TOTALLY WILL.
IT'S NOT BECAUSE I WAS HELD BACK!
AKANE **INSISTED** THAT I STAY!
SHE SAID SHE WANTS ME TO SUPPORT THE SCHOOL FROM A **STUDENT'S** PERSPECTIVE.
AND IF SHE'S A STUDENT, I DON'T HAVE TO PAY HER.
YOU DEVIL!!
OH... BUT AKANE *DOES* TREAT ME TO A MEAL EVERY SO OFTEN!
Very rarely!!
Sniff!
WHAT AN ANGEL!!
YOU TWO ARE LUCKY.

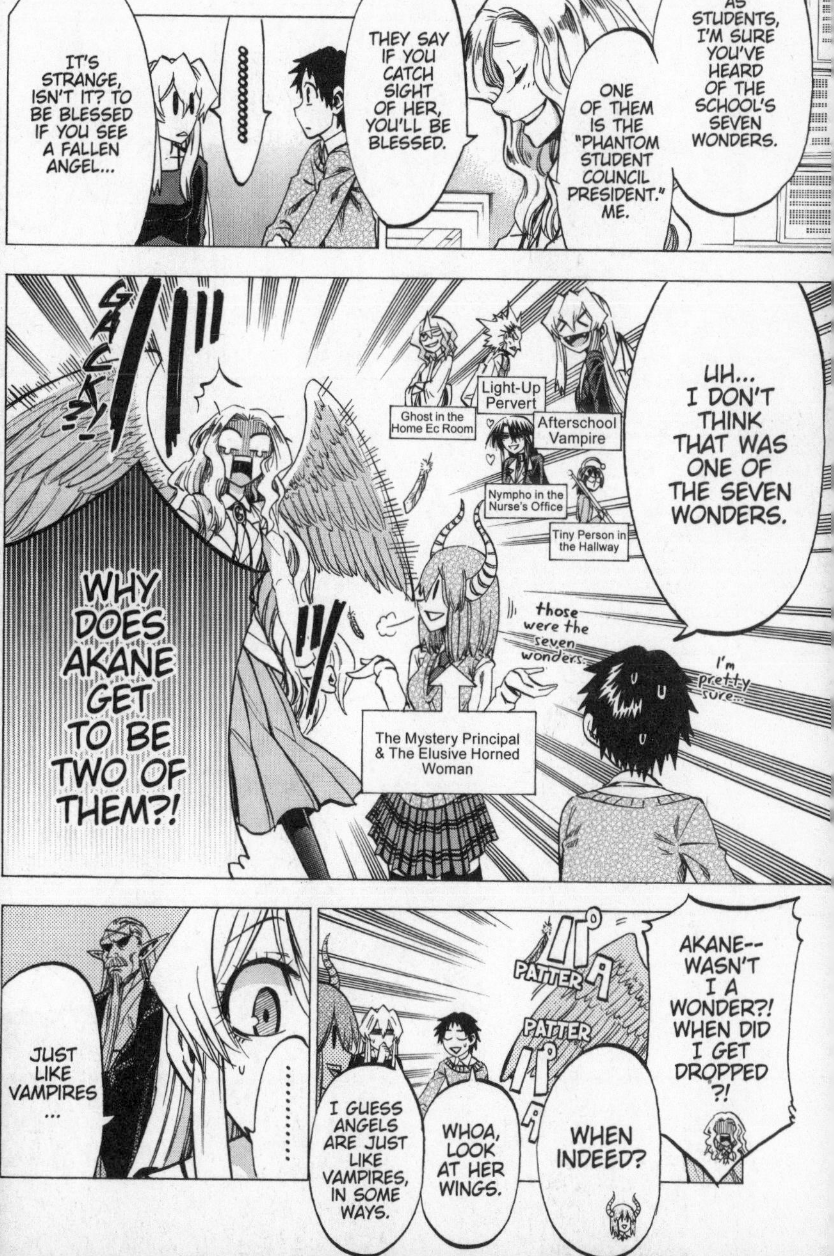

AS STUDENTS, I'M SURE YOU'VE HEARD OF THE SCHOOL'S SEVEN WONDERS.
ONE OF THEM IS THE "PHANTOM STUDENT COUNCIL PRESIDENT." ME.
THEY SAY IF YOU CATCH SIGHT OF HER, YOU'LL BE BLESSED.
....
IT'S STRANGE, ISN'T IT? TO BE BLESSED IF YOU SEE A FALLEN ANGEL...
UH... I DON'T THINK THAT WAS ONE OF THE SEVEN WONDERS.
Light-Up Pervert
Afterschool Vampire
Ghost in the Home Ec Room
Nympho in the Nurse's Office
Tiny Person in the Hallway
those were the seven wonders.
I'm pretty sure...
The Mystery Principal & The Elusive Horned Woman
GACK?!
WHY DOES AKANE GET TO BE TWO OF THEM?!
AKANE-- WASN'T I A WONDER?! WHEN DID I GET DROPPED?!
WHEN INDEED?
PATTER
PATTER
WHOA, LOOK AT HER WINGS.
I GUESS ANGELS ARE JUST LIKE VAMPIRES, IN SOME WAYS.
......
JUST LIKE VAMPIRES ...

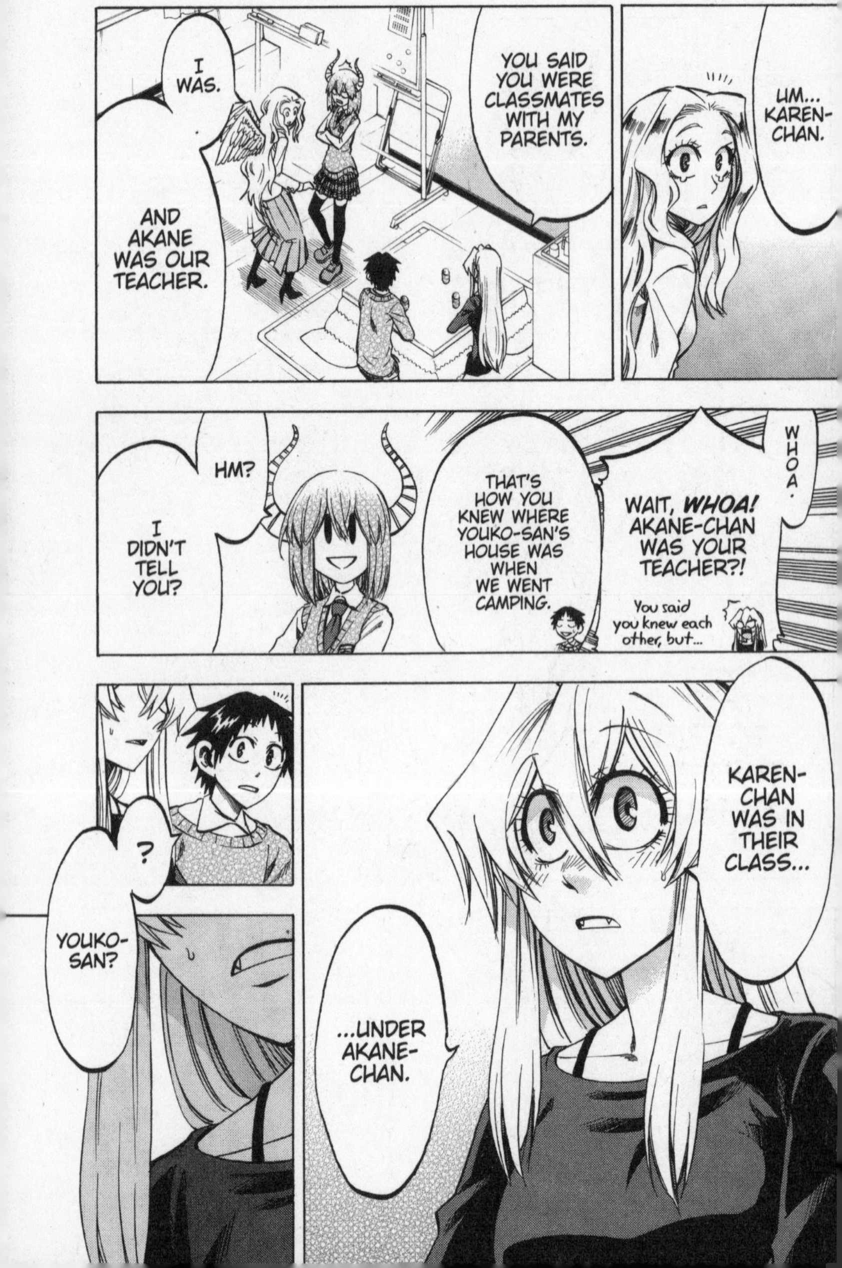
UM... KAREN-CHAN.
YOU SAID YOU WERE CLASSMATES WITH MY PARENTS.
I WAS.
AND AKANE WAS OUR TEACHER.
WHOA.
WAIT, WHOA! AKANE-CHAN WAS YOUR TEACHER?!
THAT'S HOW YOU KNEW WHERE YOUKO-SAN'S HOUSE WAS WHEN WE WENT CAMPING.
You said you knew each other, but...
HM?
I DIDN'T TELL YOU?
KAREN-CHAN WAS IN THEIR CLASS...
...UNDER AKANE-CHAN.
?
YOUKO-SAN?

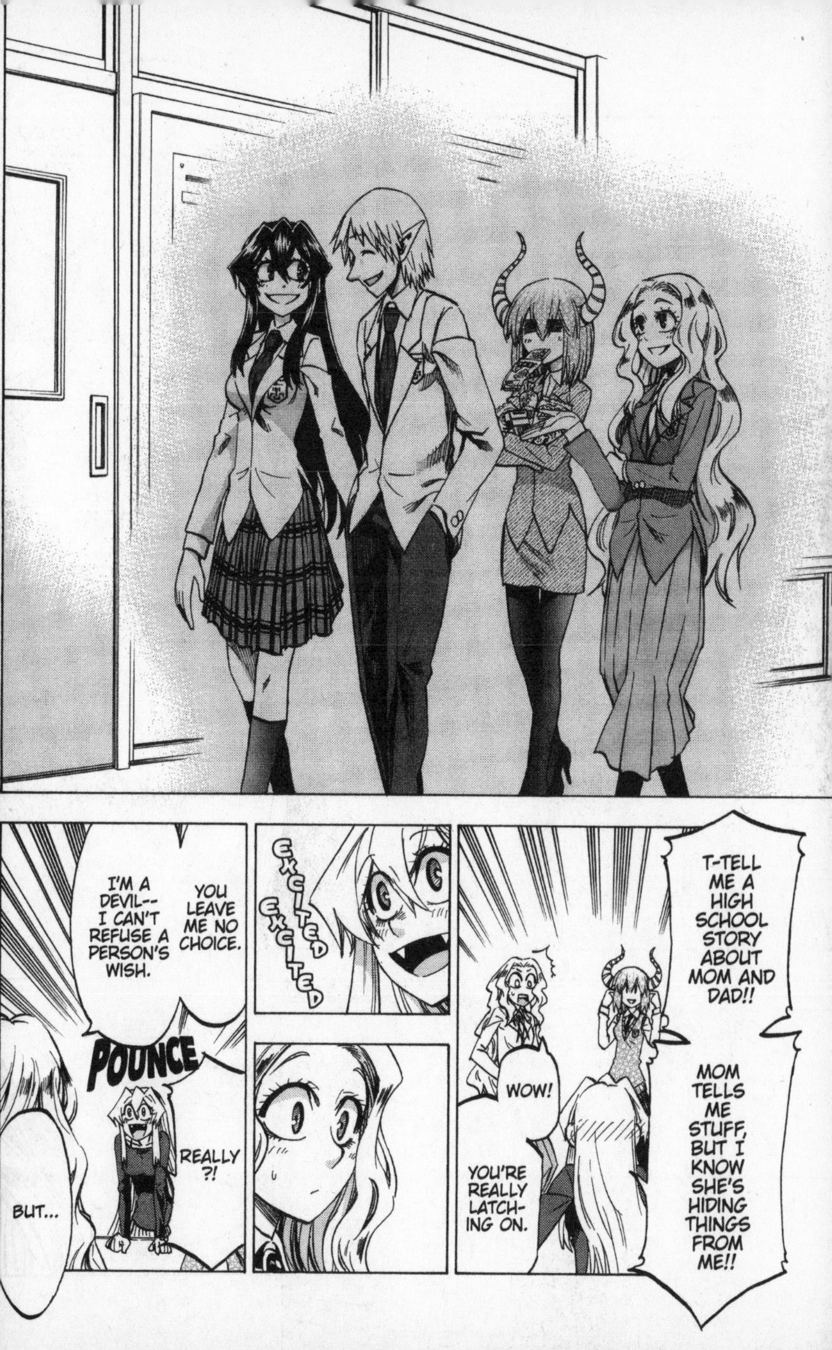
T-TELL ME A HIGH SCHOOL STORY ABOUT MOM AND DAD!!
MOM TELLS ME STUFF, BUT I KNOW SHE'S HIDING THINGS FROM ME!!
WOW!
YOU'RE REALLY LATCH-ING ON.
EXCITED EXCITED
YOU LEAVE ME NO CHOICE.
I'M A DEVIL-- I CAN'T REFUSE A PERSON'S WISH.
POUNCE
REALLY?!
BUT...

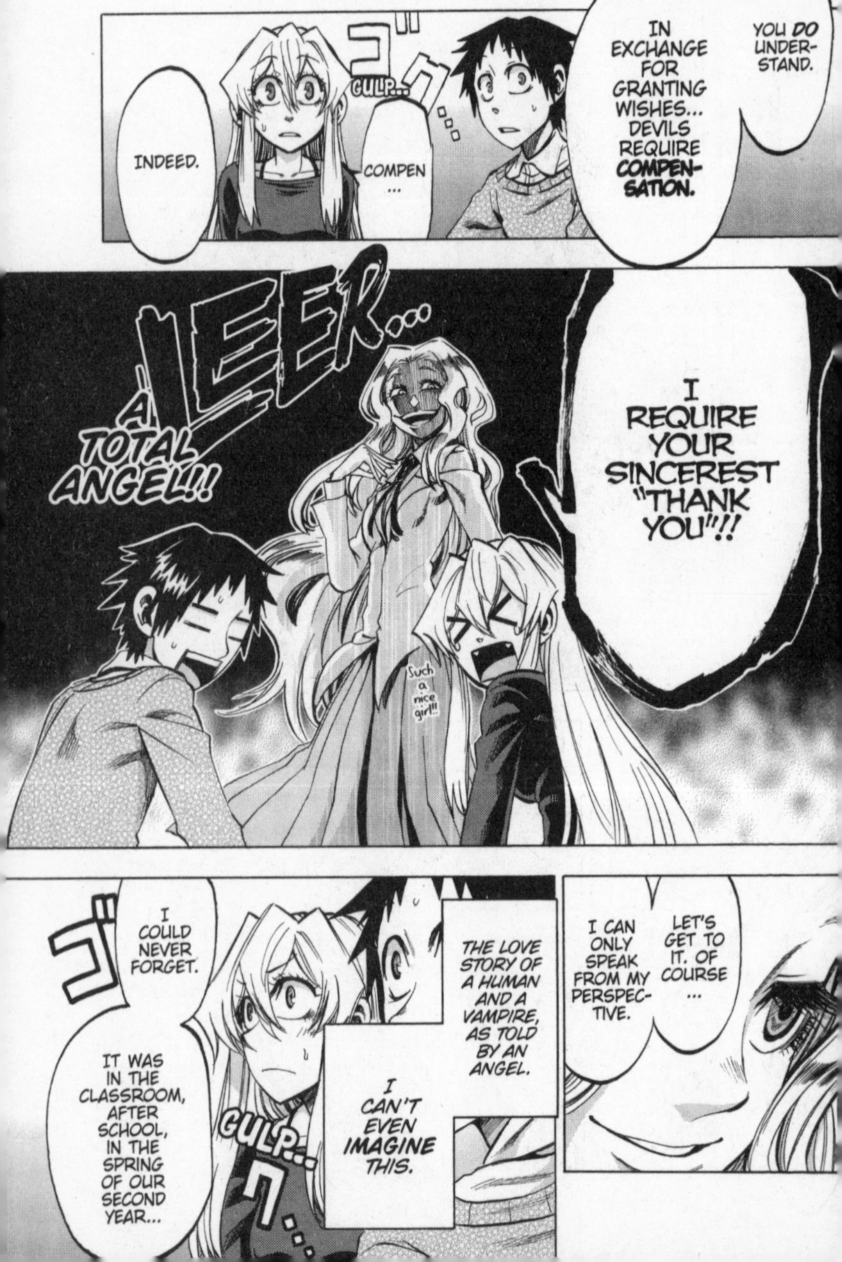

YOU **DO** UNDERSTAND.
IN EXCHANGE FOR GRANTING WISHES... DEVILS REQUIRE **COMPENSATION.**
GULP...
COMPEN ...
INDEED.
I REQUIRE YOUR SINCEREST "THANK YOU"!!
LEER...
A TOTAL ANGEL!!
Such a nice girl!!
LET'S GET TO IT. OF COURSE ...
I CAN ONLY SPEAK FROM MY PERSPECTIVE.
THE LOVE STORY OF A HUMAN AND A VAMPIRE, AS TOLD BY AN ANGEL.
I COULD NEVER FORGET.
I CAN'T EVEN IMAGINE THIS.
IT WAS IN THE CLASSROOM, AFTER SCHOOL, IN THE SPRING OF OUR SECOND YEAR...
GULP...

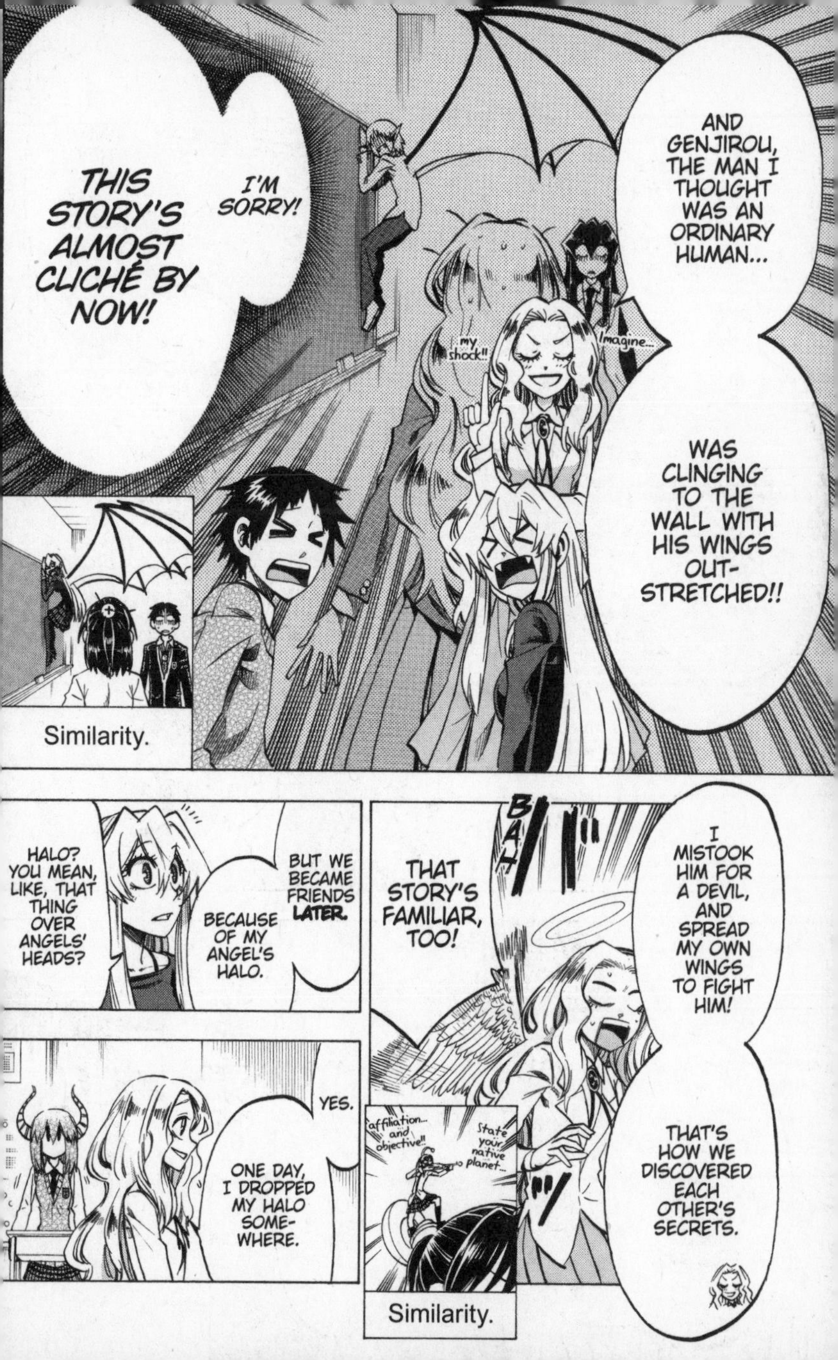
AND GENJIROU, THE MAN I THOUGHT WAS AN ORDINARY HUMAN...
Imagine...
my shock!!
WAS CLINGING TO THE WALL WITH HIS WINGS OUT-STRETCHED!!
I'M SORRY!
THIS STORY'S ALMOST CLICHÉ BY NOW!
Similarity.
I MISTOOK HIM FOR A DEVIL, AND SPREAD MY OWN WINGS TO FIGHT HIM!
BAH
THAT STORY'S FAMILIAR, TOO!
THAT'S HOW WE DISCOVERED EACH OTHER'S SECRETS.
State your native planet...
affiliation... and objective!!
Similarity.
BUT WE BECAME FRIENDS LATER.
BECAUSE OF MY ANGEL'S HALO.
HALO? YOU MEAN, LIKE, THAT THING OVER ANGELS' HEADS?
YES.
ONE DAY, I DROPPED MY HALO SOMEWHERE.

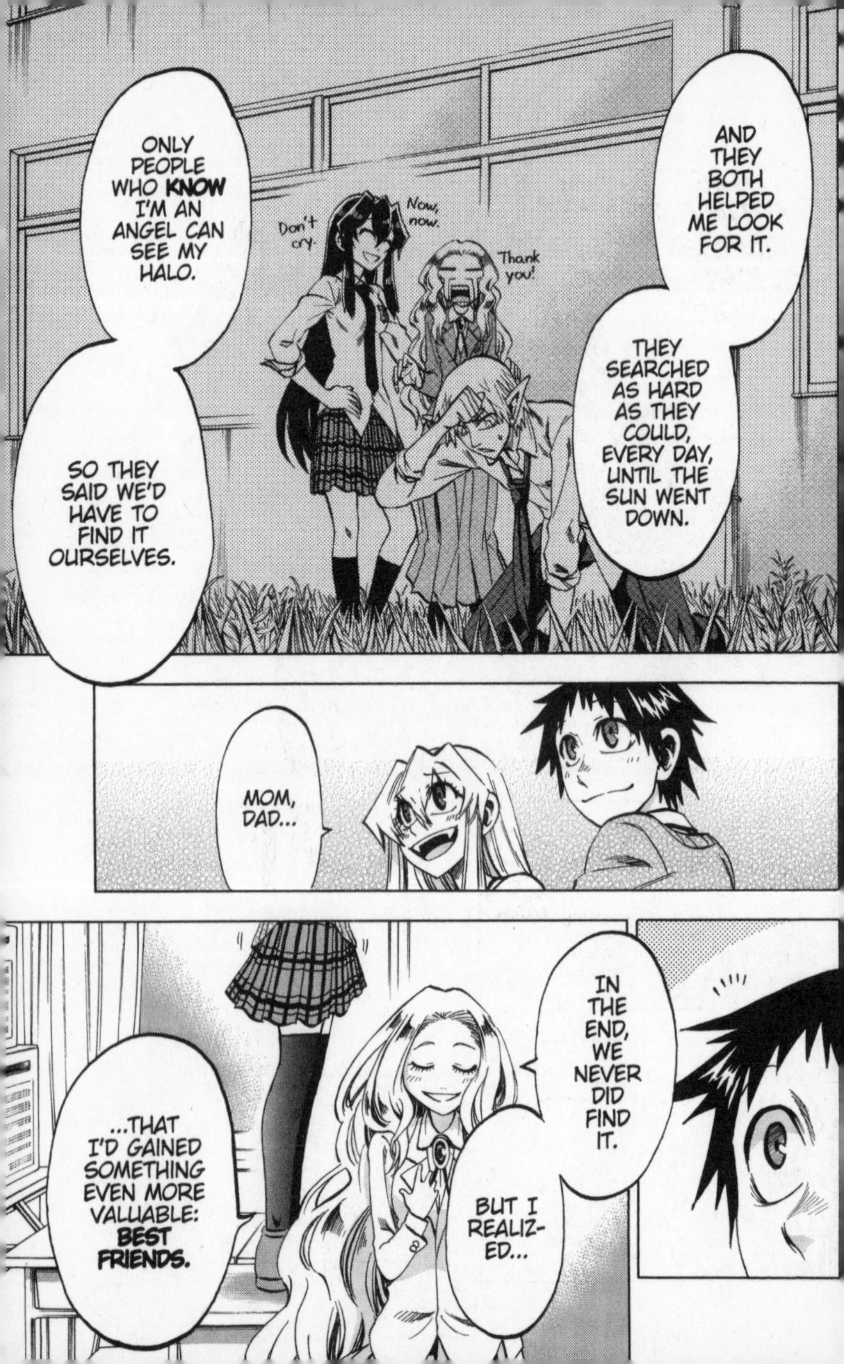
AND THEY BOTH HELPED ME LOOK FOR IT.
THEY SEARCHED AS HARD AS THEY COULD, EVERY DAY, UNTIL THE SUN WENT DOWN.
Thank you!
Now, now.
Don't cry.
ONLY PEOPLE WHO **KNOW** I'M AN ANGEL CAN SEE MY HALO.
SO THEY SAID WE'D HAVE TO FIND IT OURSELVES.
MOM, DAD...
IN THE END, WE NEVER DID FIND IT.
BUT I REALIZ-ED...
...THAT I'D GAINED SOMETHING EVEN MORE VALUABLE: **BEST FRIENDS.**

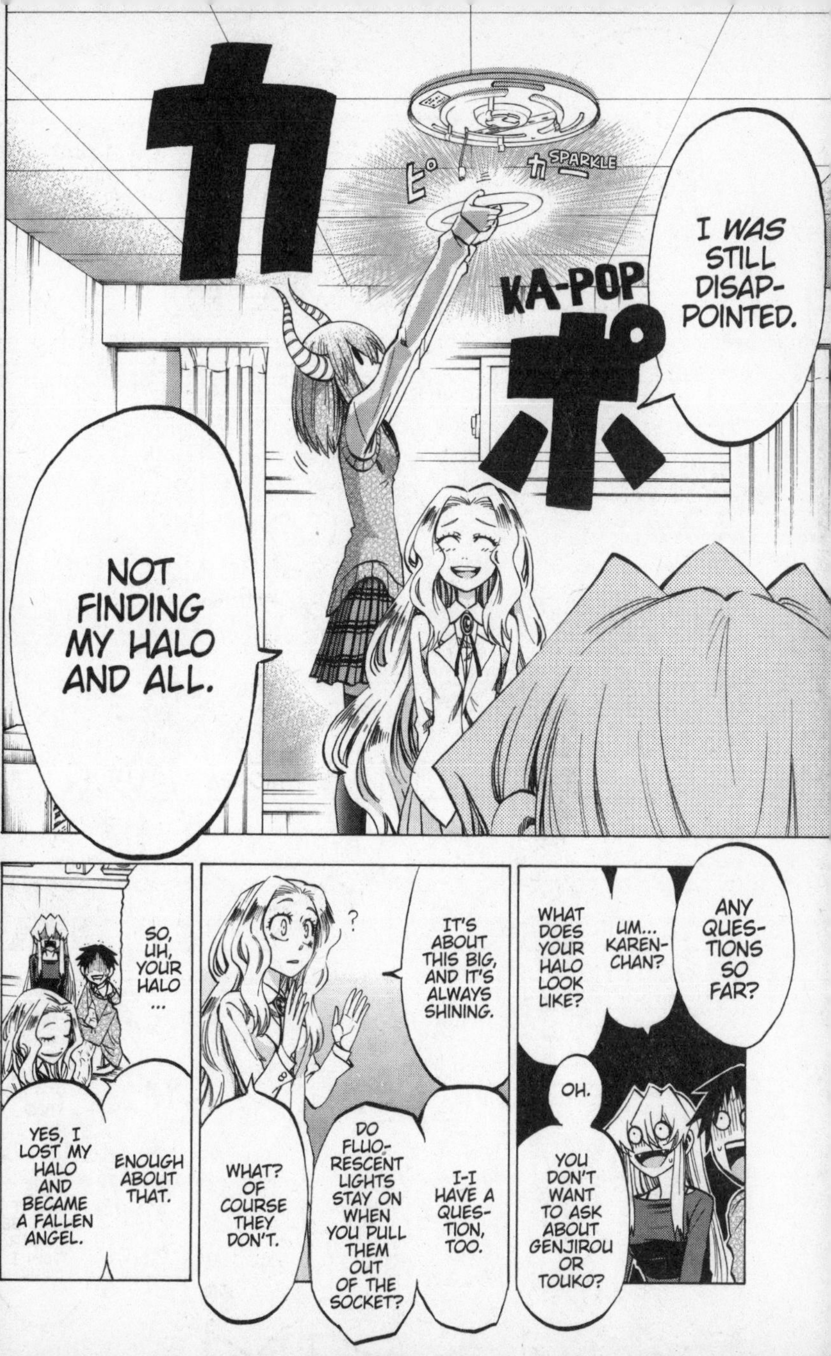
カ
ピ カー
SPARKLE
I WAS STILL DISAP-POINTED.
KA-POP
ポ
NOT FINDING MY HALO AND ALL.
ANY QUES-TIONS SO FAR?
UM... KAREN-CHAN?
WHAT DOES YOUR HALO LOOK LIKE?
OH.
YOU DON'T WANT TO ASK ABOUT GENJIROU OR TOUKO?
IT'S ABOUT THIS BIG, AND IT'S ALWAYS SHINING.
?
I-I HAVE A QUES-TION, TOO.
DO FLUO-RESCENT LIGHTS STAY ON WHEN YOU PULL THEM OUT OF THE SOCKET?
WHAT? OF COURSE THEY DON'T.
SO, UH, YOUR HALO ...
ENOUGH ABOUT THAT.
YES, I LOST MY HALO AND BECAME A FALLEN ANGEL.

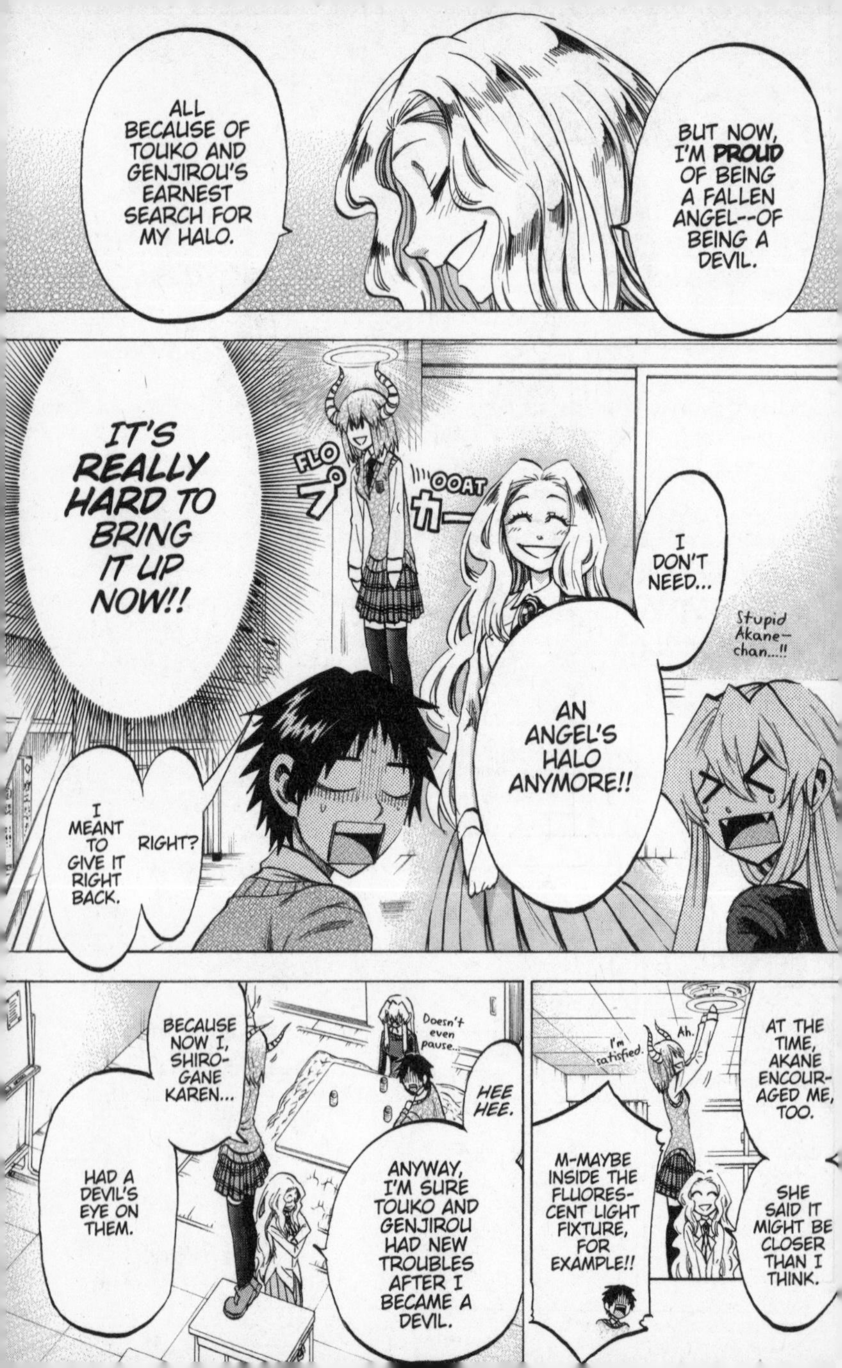
BUT NOW, I'M **PROUD** OF BEING A FALLEN ANGEL--OF BEING A DEVIL.
ALL BECAUSE OF TOUKO AND GENJIROU'S EARNEST SEARCH FOR MY HALO.
I DON'T NEED...
AN ANGEL'S HALO ANYMORE!!
Stupid Akane-chan...!!
OOAT カー
FLO プ
IT'S **REALLY HARD** TO BRING IT UP NOW!!
RIGHT?
I MEANT TO GIVE IT RIGHT BACK.
AT THE TIME, AKANE ENCOURAGED ME, TOO.
Ah.
I'm satisfied.
SHE SAID IT MIGHT BE CLOSER THAN I THINK.
M-MAYBE INSIDE THE FLUORESCENT LIGHT FIXTURE, FOR EXAMPLE!!
HEE HEE.
Doesn't even pause...
ANYWAY, I'M SURE TOUKO AND GENJIROU HAD NEW TROUBLES AFTER I BECAME A DEVIL.
BECAUSE NOW I, SHIROGANE KAREN...
HAD A DEVIL'S EYE ON THEM.

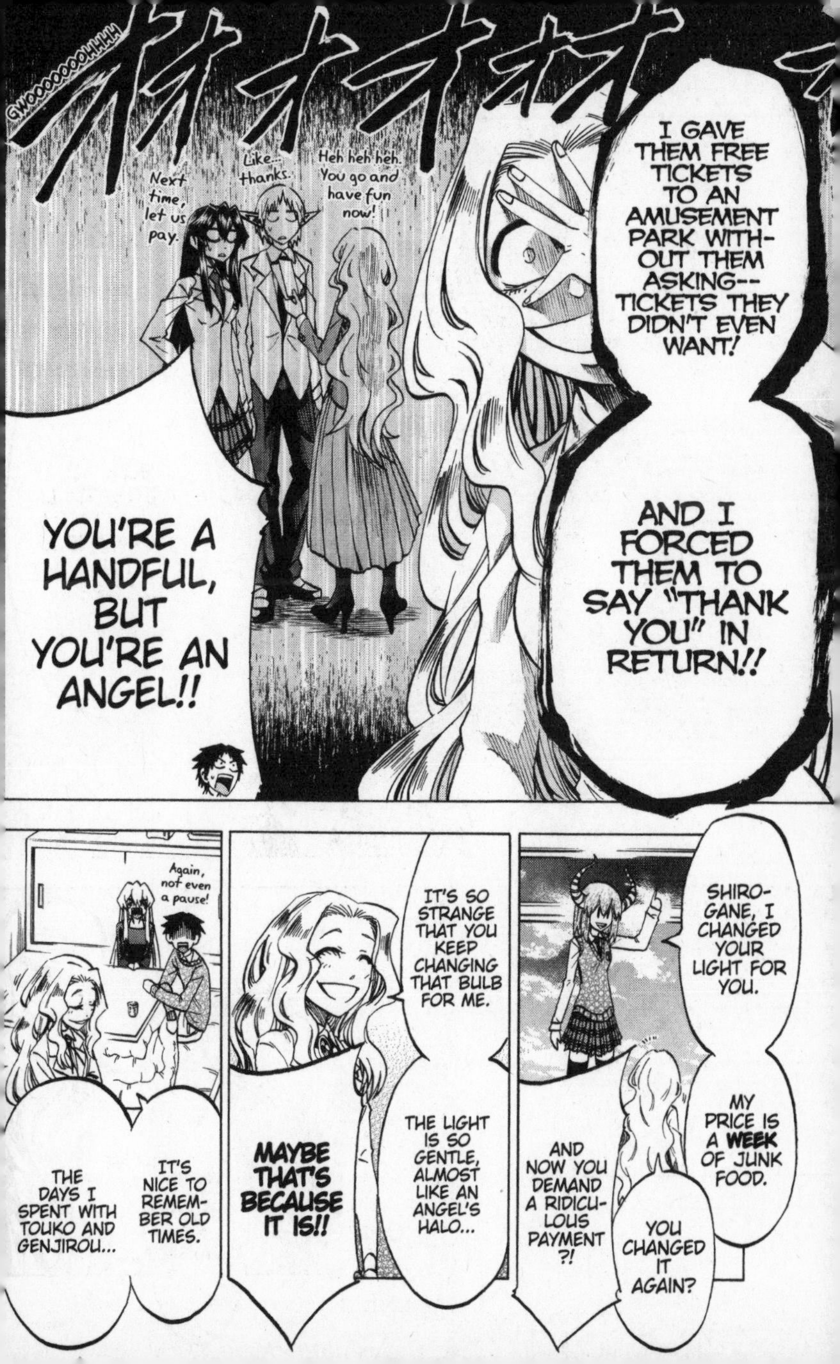
GWOOOOOOOHHHH
I GAVE THEM FREE TICKETS TO AN AMUSEMENT PARK WITH-OUT THEM ASKING-- TICKETS THEY DIDN'T EVEN WANT!
AND I FORCED THEM TO SAY "THANK YOU" IN RETURN!!
Heh heh heh. You go and have fun now!
Like... thanks.
Next time, let us pay.
YOU'RE A HANDFUL, BUT YOU'RE AN ANGEL!!
SHIRO-GANE, I CHANGED YOUR LIGHT FOR YOU.
MY PRICE IS A WEEK OF JUNK FOOD.
YOU CHANGED IT AGAIN?
AND NOW YOU DEMAND A RIDICU-LOUS PAYMENT?!
IT'S SO STRANGE THAT YOU KEEP CHANGING THAT BULB FOR ME.
THE LIGHT IS SO GENTLE, ALMOST LIKE AN ANGEL'S HALO...
MAYBE THAT'S BECAUSE IT IS!!
Again, not even a pause!
IT'S NICE TO REMEM-BER OLD TIMES.
THE DAYS I SPENT WITH TOUKO AND GENJIROU...

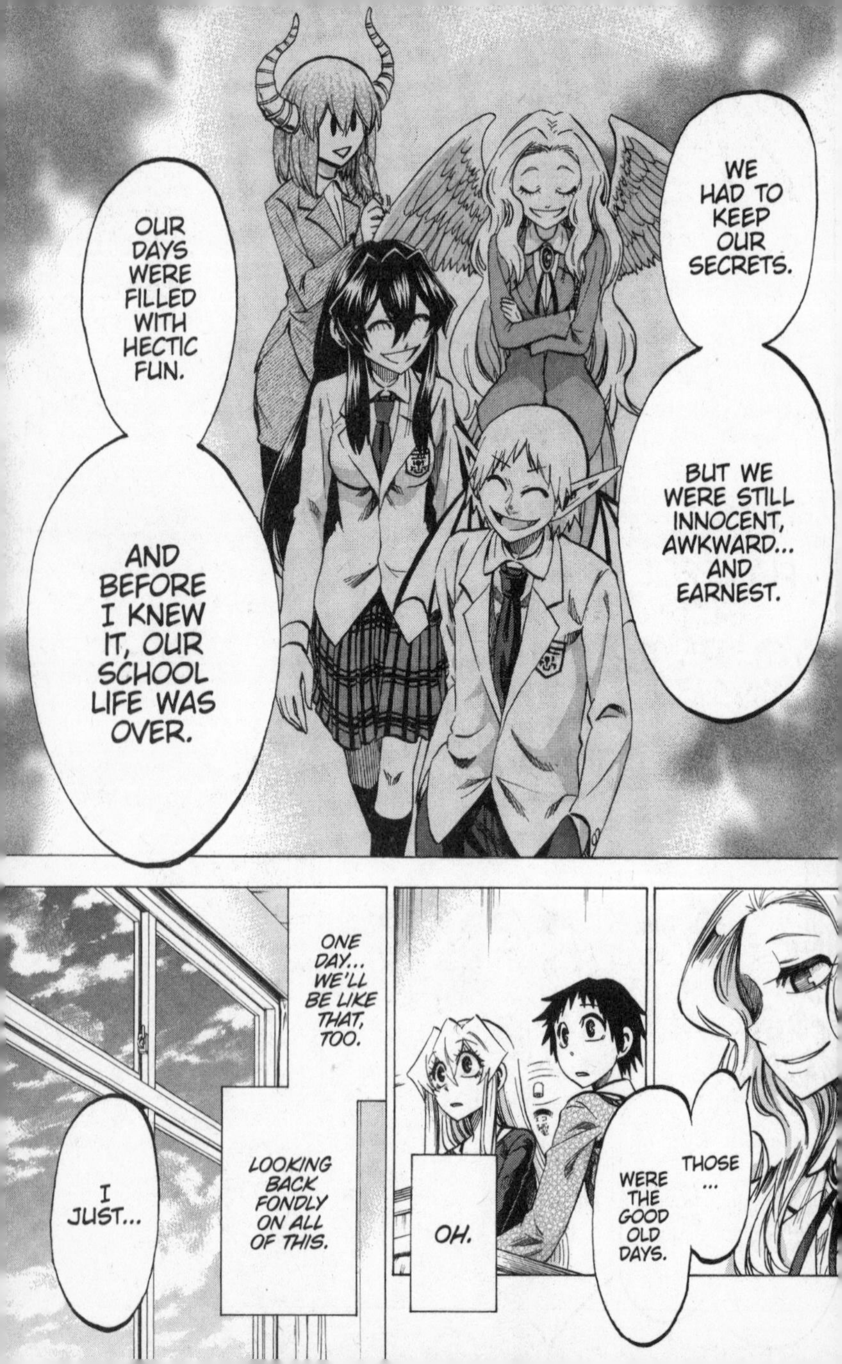
WE HAD TO KEEP OUR SECRETS.
BUT WE WERE STILL INNOCENT, AWKWARD... AND EARNEST.
OUR DAYS WERE FILLED WITH HECTIC FUN.
AND BEFORE I KNEW IT, OUR SCHOOL LIFE WAS OVER.
THOSE...
WERE THE GOOD OLD DAYS.
OH.
ONE DAY... WE'LL BE LIKE THAT, TOO.
LOOKING BACK FONDLY ON ALL OF THIS.
I JUST...

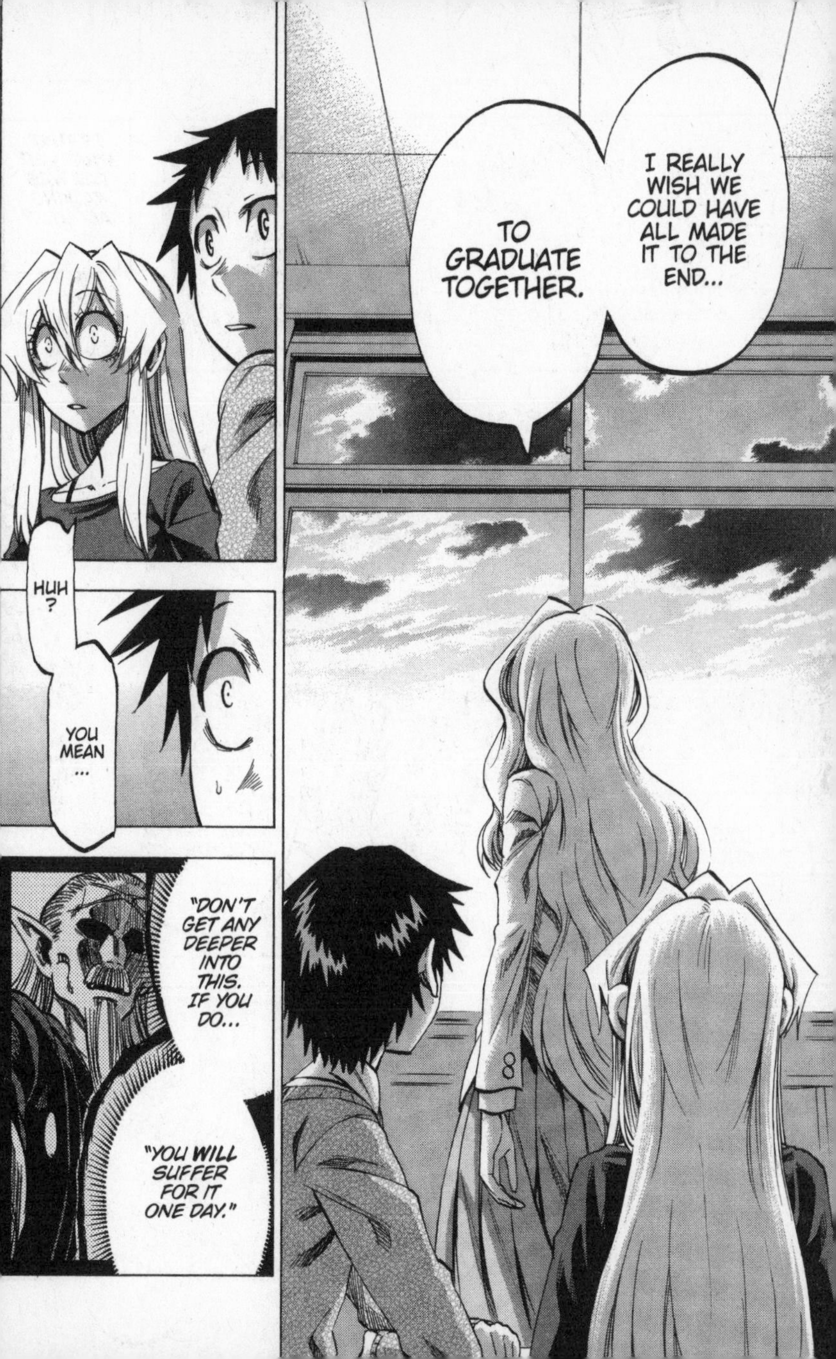
I REALLY WISH WE COULD HAVE ALL MADE IT TO THE END...
TO GRADUATE TOGETHER.
HUH?
YOU MEAN ...
"DON'T GET ANY DEEPER INTO THIS. IF YOU DO...
"YOU WILL SUFFER FOR IT ONE DAY."

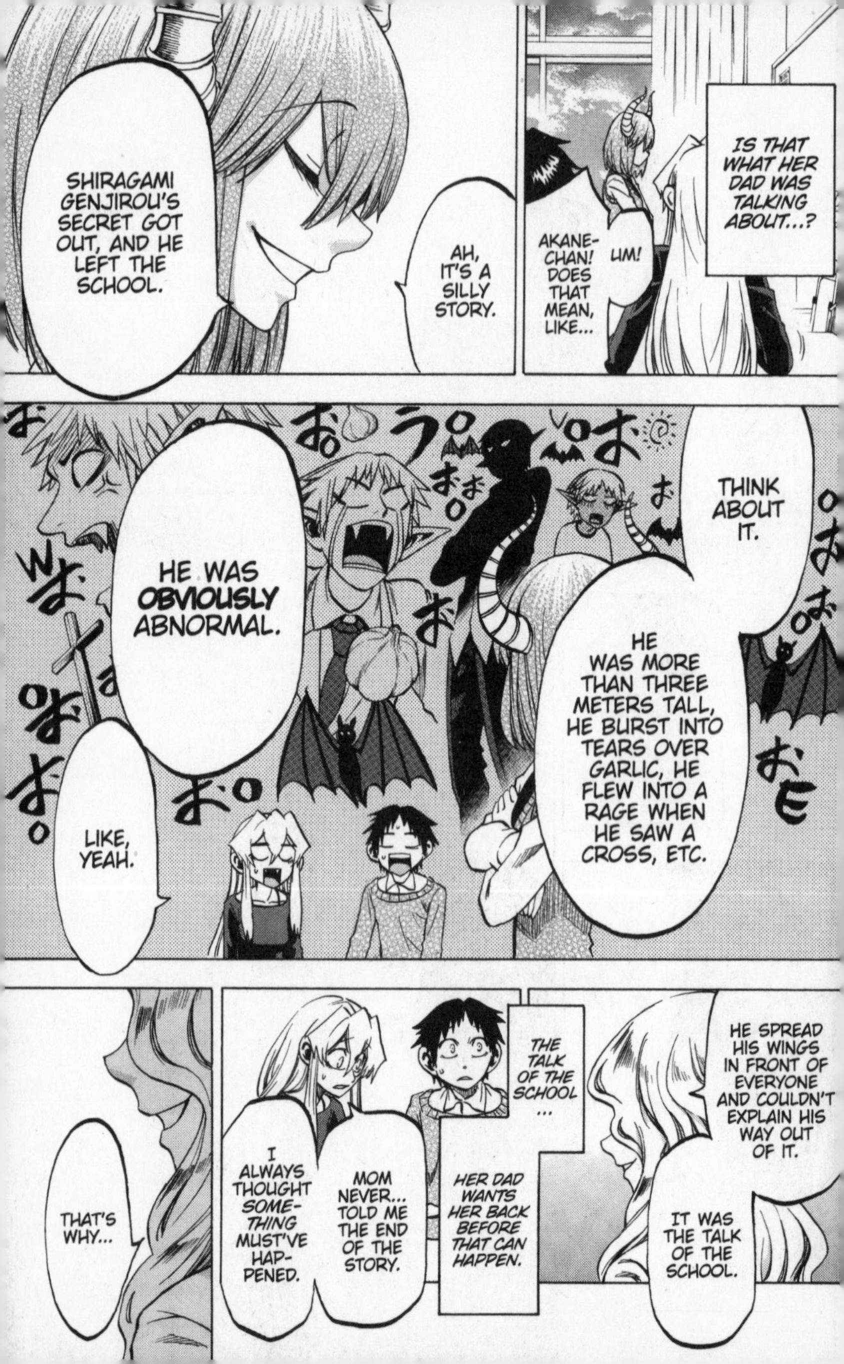
IS THAT WHAT HER DAD WAS TALKING ABOUT...?
UM!
AKANE-CHAN! DOES THAT MEAN, LIKE...
AH, IT'S A SILLY STORY.
SHIRAGAMI GENJIROU'S SECRET GOT OUT, AND HE LEFT THE SCHOOL.
THINK ABOUT IT.
HE WAS MORE THAN THREE METERS TALL, HE BURST INTO TEARS OVER GARLIC, HE FLEW INTO A RAGE WHEN HE SAW A CROSS, ETC.
HE WAS **OBVIOUSLY** ABNORMAL.
LIKE, YEAH.
HE SPREAD HIS WINGS IN FRONT OF EVERYONE AND COULDN'T EXPLAIN HIS WAY OUT OF IT.
IT WAS THE TALK OF THE SCHOOL.
THE TALK OF THE SCHOOL...
HER DAD WANTS HER BACK BEFORE THAT CAN HAPPEN.
MOM NEVER... TOLD ME THE END OF THE STORY.
I ALWAYS THOUGHT SOMETHING MUST'VE HAPPENED.
THAT'S WHY...

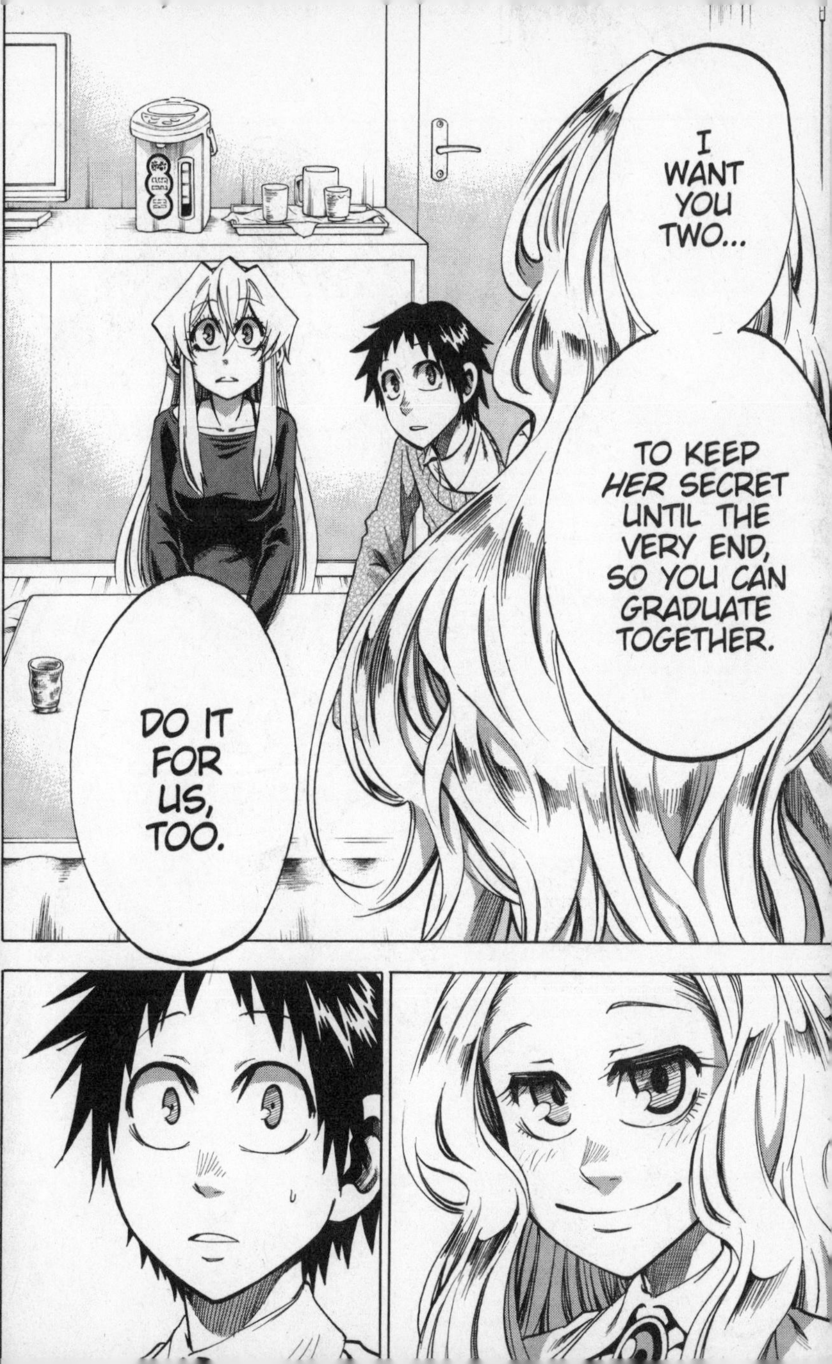
I WANT YOU TWO...
TO KEEP *HER* SECRET UNTIL THE VERY END, SO YOU CAN GRADUATE TOGETHER.
DO IT FOR US, TOO.

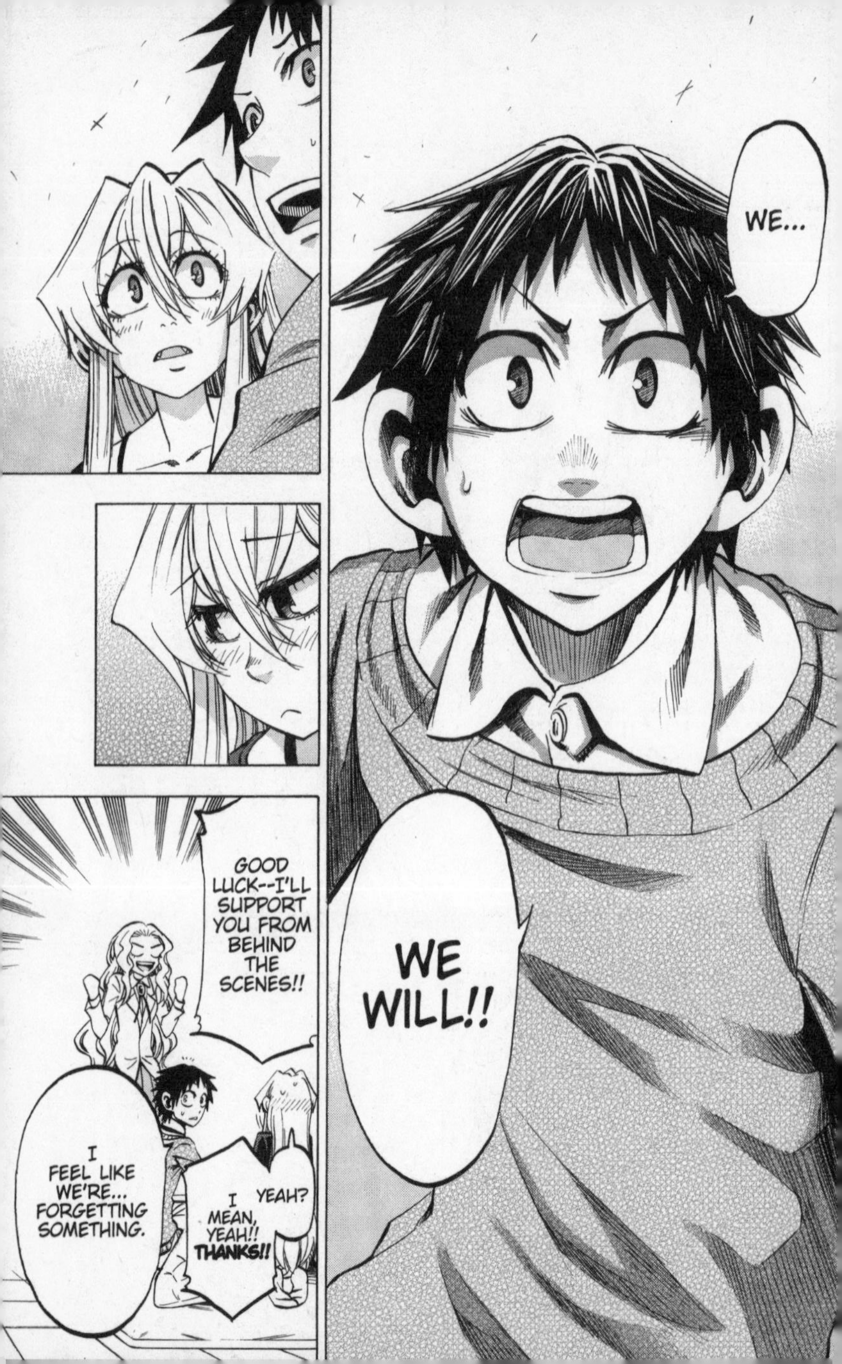
WE...
WE WILL!!
GOOD LUCK--I'LL SUPPORT YOU FROM BEHIND THE SCENES!!
YEAH?
I MEAN, YEAH!! THANKS!!
I FEEL LIKE WE'RE... FORGETTING SOMETHING.

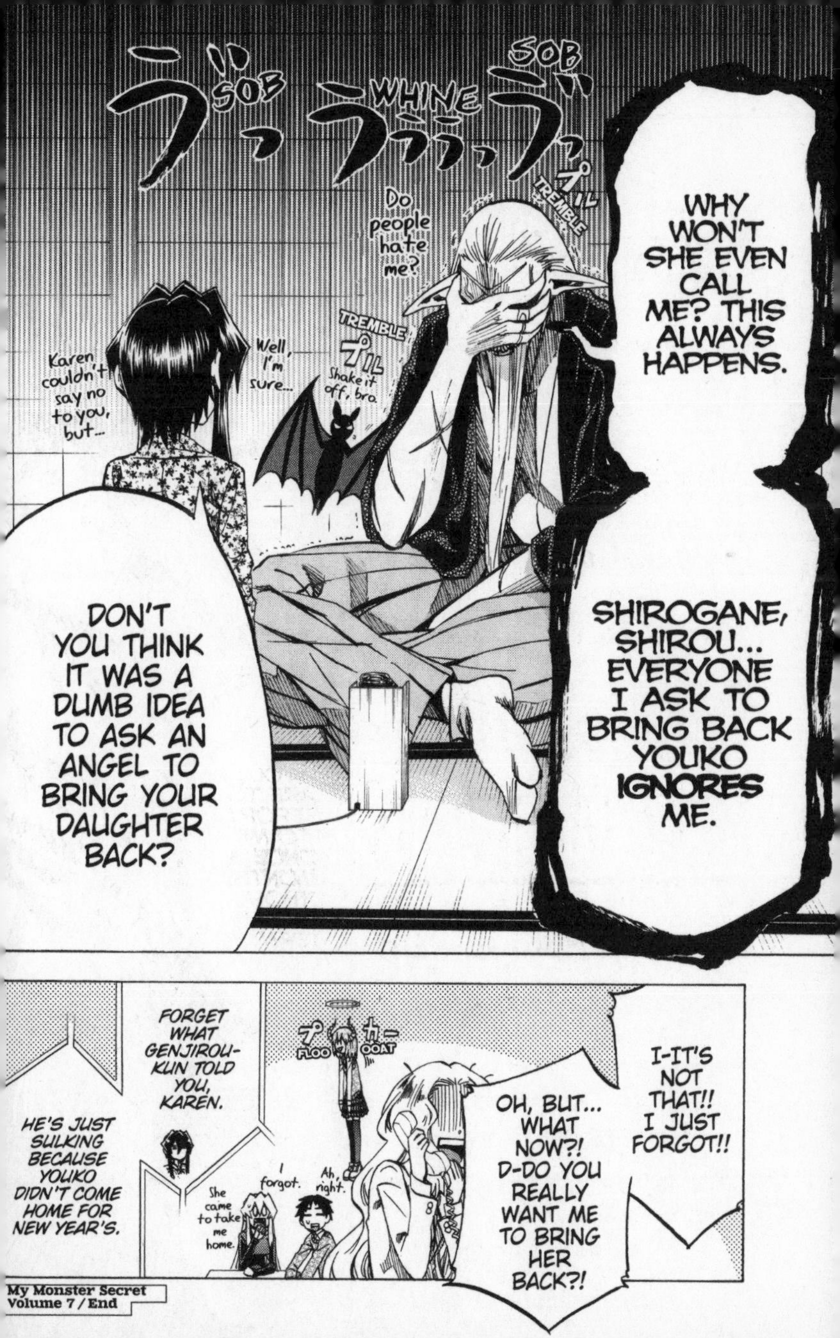
SOB
WHINE
SOB
WHY WON'T SHE EVEN CALL ME? THIS ALWAYS HAPPENS.
TREMBLE
Do people hate me?
TREMBLE
Shake it off, bro.
Well, I'm sure...
Karen couldn't say no to you, but...
SHIROGANE, SHIROU... EVERYONE I ASK TO BRING BACK YOUKO IGNORES ME.
DON'T YOU THINK IT WAS A DUMB IDEA TO ASK AN ANGEL TO BRING YOUR DAUGHTER BACK?
I-IT'S NOT THAT!! I JUST FORGOT!!
OH, BUT... WHAT NOW?! D-DO YOU REALLY WANT ME TO BRING HER BACK?!
FLOO
OOAT
FORGET WHAT GENJIROU-KUN TOLD YOU, KAREN.
Ah, right.
I forgot.
She came to take me home.
HE'S JUST SULKING BECAUSE YOUKO DIDN'T COME HOME FOR NEW YEAR'S.

My Monster Secret
Volume 7 / End

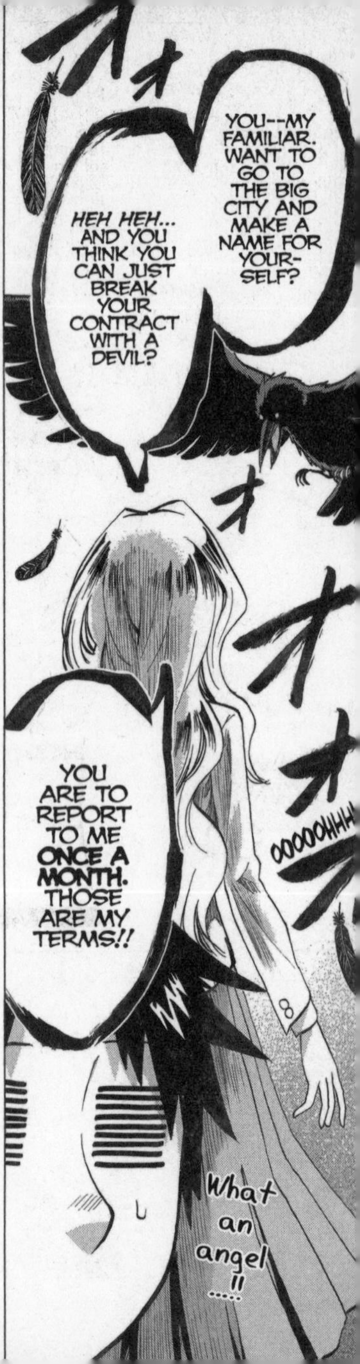
YOU--MY FAMILIAR. WANT TO GO TO THE BIG CITY AND MAKE A NAME FOR YOUR-SELF?
HEH HEH... AND YOU THINK YOU CAN JUST BREAK YOUR CONTRACT WITH A DEVIL?
OOOOOHHH
YOU ARE TO REPORT TO ME **ONCE A MONTH.** THOSE ARE MY TERMS!!
What an angel!!.....

STAFF

- Garage Okada-san
- Shuumeigiku-san
- Seijun Suzuki-san
- Kouki Nakashima-san
- Haruki Mana
- Hiroki Minemura-san

(in syllabary order)

SPECIAL THANKS

- Editor: Mukawa-san, Otsuka-san

I give my thanks to those of you holding this book right now and everyone who let me and this work be a part of their lives.

Eiji Masuda

I am... 7

Snowball Fight

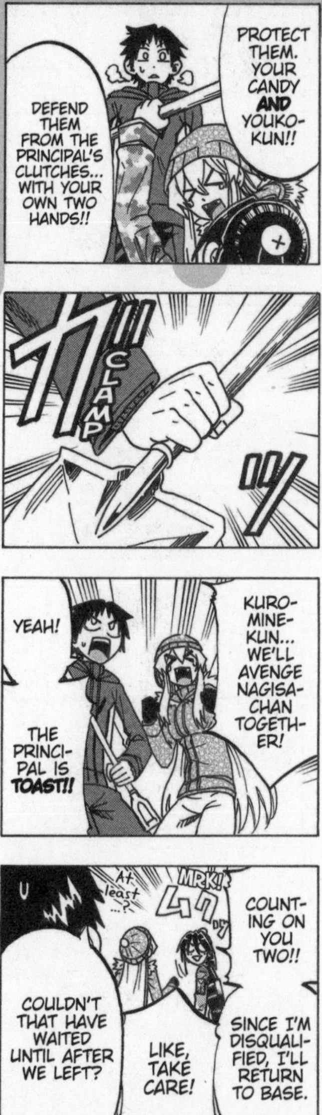
PROTECT THEM. YOUR CANDY **AND** YOUKO-KUN!!
DEFEND THEM FROM THE PRINCIPAL'S CLUTCHES... WITH YOUR OWN TWO HANDS!!
CLAMP
KURO-MINE-KUN... WE'LL AVENGE NAGISA-CHAN TOGETHER!
YEAH!
THE PRINCIPAL IS **TOAST!!**
COUNTING ON YOU TWO!!
MRK!
At least...?
SINCE I'M DISQUALIFIED, I'LL RETURN TO BASE.
LIKE, TAKE CARE!
COULDN'T THAT HAVE WAITED UNTIL AFTER WE LEFT?

Visiting the Sick

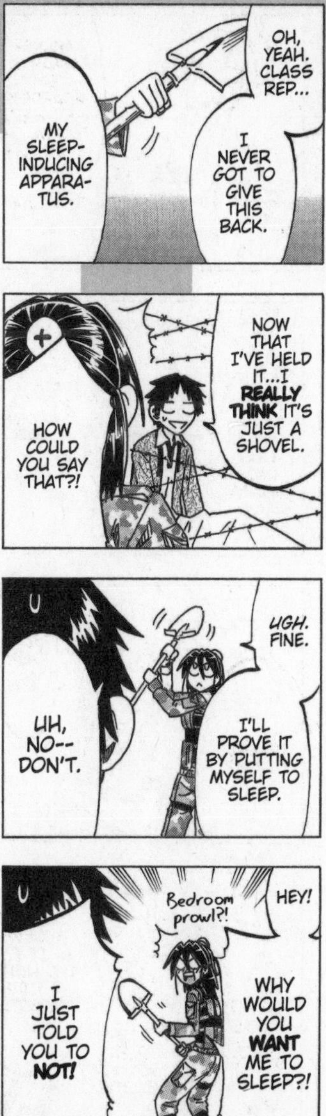
OH, YEAH. CLASS REP...
I NEVER GOT TO GIVE THIS BACK.
MY SLEEP-INDUCING APPARATUS.
NOW THAT I'VE HELD IT...I **REALLY THINK** IT'S JUST A SHOVEL.
HOW COULD YOU SAY THAT?!
UGH. FINE.
I'LL PROVE IT BY PUTTING MYSELF TO SLEEP.
UH, NO--DON'T.
HEY!
Bedroom prowl?!
WHY WOULD YOU **WANT** ME TO SLEEP?!
I JUST TOLD YOU TO **NOT!**

I am 7

Tales of the Past: Part ①

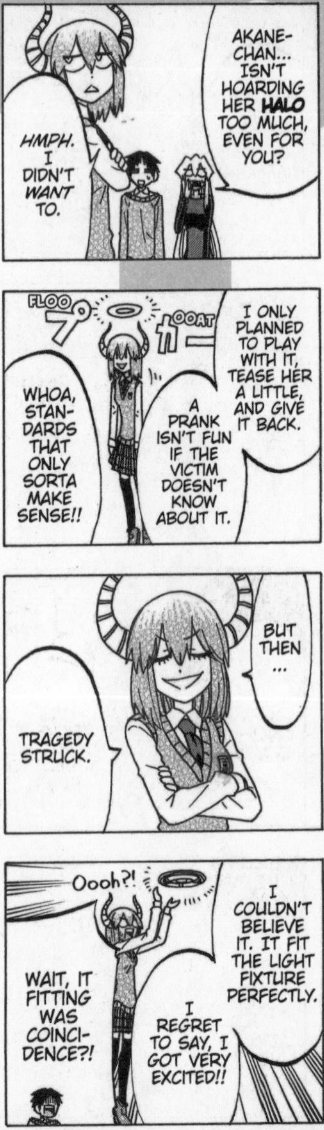
AKANE-CHAN... ISN'T HOARDING HER **HALO** TOO MUCH, EVEN FOR YOU?
HMPH. I DIDN'T *WANT* TO.
FLOO
OOAT
I ONLY PLANNED TO PLAY WITH IT, TEASE HER A LITTLE, AND GIVE IT BACK.
A PRANK ISN'T FUN IF THE VICTIM DOESN'T KNOW ABOUT IT.
WHOA, STANDARDS THAT ONLY SORTA MAKE SENSE!!
BUT THEN...
TRAGEDY STRUCK.
Oooh?!
I COULDN'T BELIEVE IT. IT FIT THE LIGHT FIXTURE PERFECTLY.
I REGRET TO SAY, I GOT VERY EXCITED!!
WAIT, IT FITTING WAS COINCIDENCE?!

Tales of the Past: Part ②

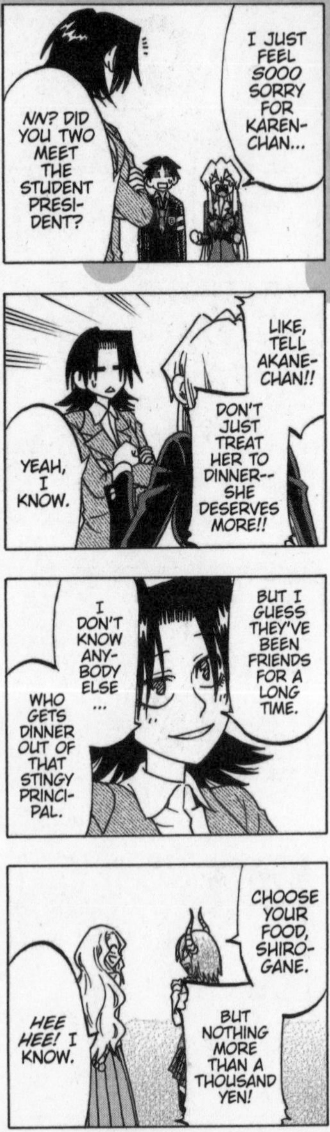
I JUST FEEL *SOOO* SORRY FOR KAREN-CHAN...
NN? DID YOU TWO MEET THE STUDENT PRESIDENT?
LIKE, TELL AKANE-CHAN!!
DON'T JUST TREAT HER TO DINNER--SHE DESERVES MORE!!
YEAH, I KNOW.
BUT I GUESS THEY'VE BEEN FRIENDS FOR A LONG TIME.
I DON'T KNOW ANYBODY ELSE...
WHO GETS DINNER OUT OF THAT STINGY PRINCIPAL.
CHOOSE YOUR FOOD, SHIROGANE.
BUT NOTHING MORE THAN A THOUSAND YEN!
HEE HEE! I KNOW.

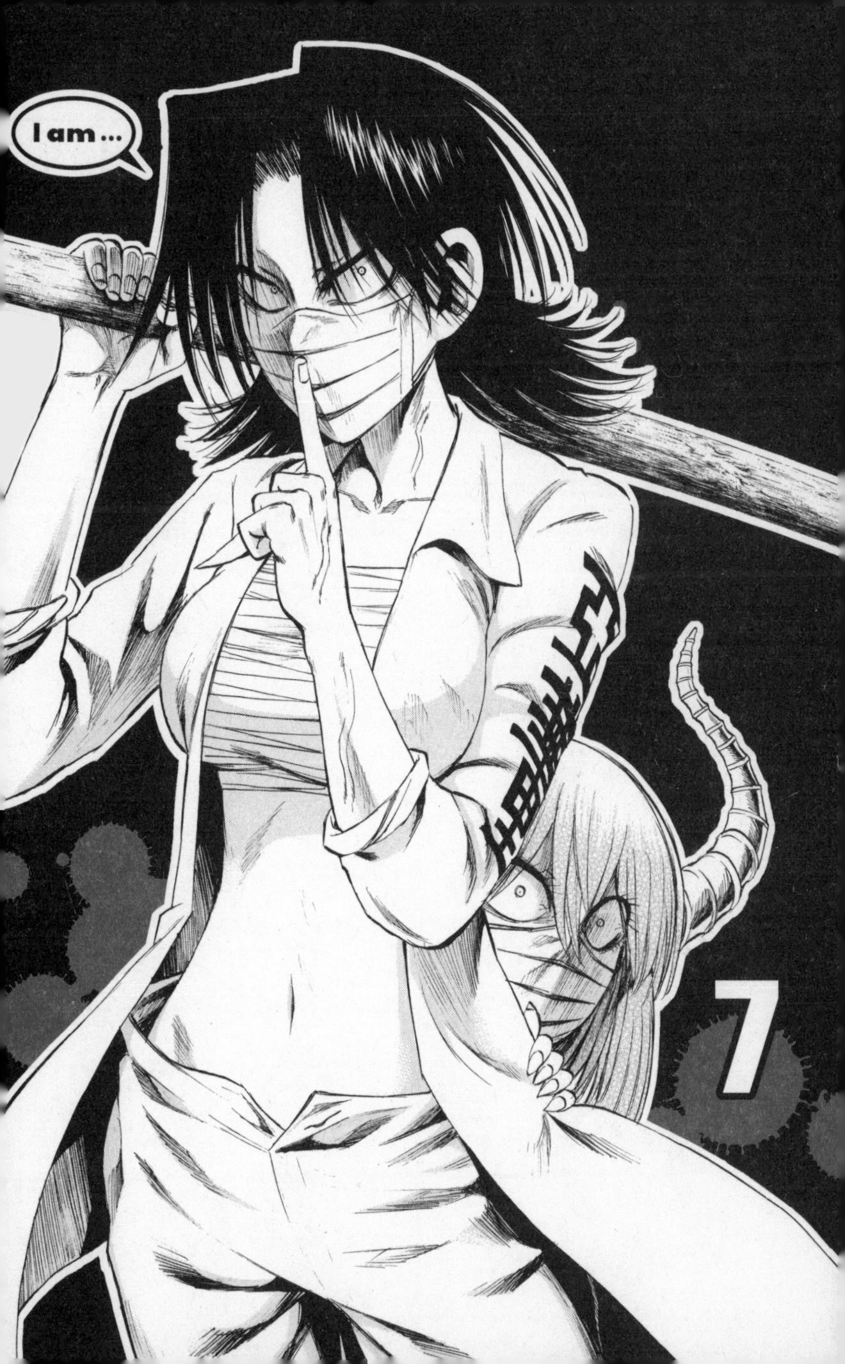
I am ...
7

I am... a Former Bad girl

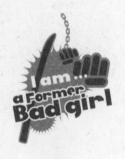

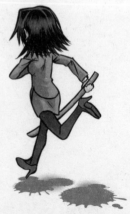

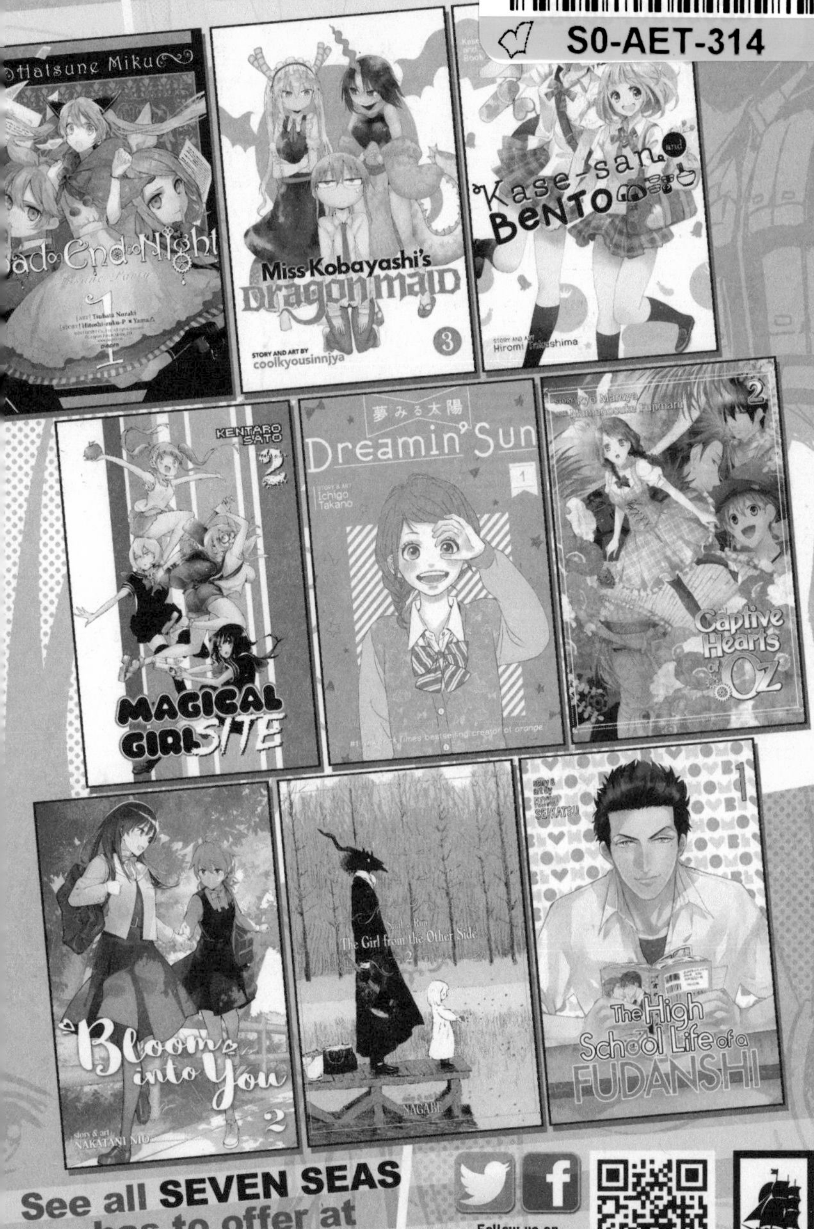
Hatsune Miku
Bad End Night
1
Miss Kobayashi's Dragon Maid
STORY AND ART BY coolkyousinnjya
3
Kase-san and Bento
STORY AND ART Hiromi Takashima
KENTARO SATO
2
MAGICAL GIRL SITE
夢みる太陽
Dreamin' Sun
1
STORY & ART Ichigo Takano
2
Captive Hearts of Oz
Bloom into You
2
story & art NAKATANI NIO
The Girl from the Other Side
2
NAGABE
1
The High School Life of a FUDANSHI